London Gateway

Iron Age and Roman salt making in the Thames Estuary

Excavation at Stanford Wharf Nature Reserve, Essex

London Gateway

Iron Age and Roman salt making in the Thames Estuary

Excavation at Stanford Wharf Nature Reserve, Essex

by Edward Biddulph, Stuart Foreman, Elizabeth Stafford,
Dan Stansbie *and* Rebecca Nicholson

with contributions to this volume and the digital specialist reports by
Enid Allison, Hugo Anderson-Whymark, Katrina Anker, Francesco Berna, Paul Booth,
Lisa Brown, Nigel Cameron, Chris Carey, Dana Challinor, John Cotter, John Crowther,
Denise Druce, Damian Goodburn, Kath Hunter, Lynne Keys, Alice Lyons, Richard Macphail,
Quita Mould, David Mullin, Sylvia M Peglar, Cynthia Poole, Ian Scott, Ruth Shaffrey,
Lena Strid, Helen Webb *and* John E Whittaker

Illustration and design by
Julia Collins, Magdalena Wachnik, Leo Heatley, Elizabeth Stafford *and* Sophie Lamb

Oxford Archaeology Monograph No. 18
2012

The publication of this volume has been generously funded by DP World

Published by Oxford Archaeology as part of the Oxford Archaeology Monograph series

Designed by Oxford Archaeology Graphics Office

Edited by Paul Booth

Figures 1.1, 1.2, 1.9 and 1.10 reproduced from the Ordnance Survey on behalf
of the controller of Her Majesty's Stationery Office © Crown Copyright.
Licence No. AL 1000005569

1996/11A-DMC. Figures 1.4, 1.5 and 3.8 are derived from digital data at 1:50,000 scale,
provided under licence by British Geological Survey.© NERC

Figures 2.27, 5.20 Symbols courtesy of the Integration and Application Network
(ian.umces.edu/symbols/), University of Maryland Center for Environmental Science.

Figures 1.1, 1.6, 1.7, 1.8, 1.9, 1.10 contain Ordnance Survey data
© Crown copyright and database right 2011

Front cover: A representation of a late Roman saltern at
Stanford Wharf Nature Reserve. Drawing by Mark Gridley

ISBN 978-0-904220-71-1

This book is part of a series of monographs which can be bought from all good bookshops
and internet bookshops. For more information, visit www.oxfordarchaeology.com

Typeset by Production Line, Oxford
Printed in Great Britain by Berforts Information Press, Eynsham, Oxfordshire

Contents

Chapter 1: Introduction to Stanford Wharf Nature Reserve
by Edward Biddulph, Stuart Foreman, Elizabeth Stafford, Katrina Anker and Chris Carey

Chapter 2: Landscape evolution from the late Glacial to the post-medieval period
by Elizabeth Stafford and Rebecca Nicholson

Chapter 3: Prehistoric exploitation of the landscape
by Edward Biddulph, Dan Stansbie, Hugo Anderson-Whymark, Lisa Brown and David Mullin

Chapter 4: The Red Hills of Stanford Wharf – salt production in the middle Iron Age
by Dan Stansbie and Edward Biddulph

Chapter 5: Early Roman salt production, burial and wooden structures
by Dan Stansbie, Edward Biddulph and Damian Goodburn

Chapter 6: The salt industry expands – the later Roman period
by Edward Biddulph and Dan Stansbie

Chapter 7: Transformation of the post-Roman marshland
by Edward Biddulph, Dan Stansbie and Damian Goodburn

Chapter 8: Worth its salt – concluding comments
by Edward Biddulph and Stuart Foreman

List of Figures

List of Tables

Contents of Digital Volume

Summary

Stanford Wharf Nature Reserve, Essex, was created to provide a wetland habitat for wading birds and other wildlife at the DP World London Gateway port development. DP World London Gateway funded a series of field investigations at Stanford Wharf Nature Reserve to ensure that archaeological remains were preserved or investigated before the site was flooded. This publication presents the findings of the fieldwork, providing a narrative of the site from the late Glacial period to modern times, and integrating the results of artefactual, environmental and scientific analyses. The full specialist reports, along with other supporting data, form the digital component of the project report and are available to download from Oxford Archaeology's digital library.

The site lies to the south of Stanford-le-Hope, on the north-east bank of Mucking Creek in the lower Thames estuary, approximately 25 miles downstream of the City of London. The investigation recorded a sedimentary sequence commencing in the late Glacial period (from *c* 15,000 years BP), when sea-levels in the region were much reduced, Britain was still joined to the continent, and the Thames was a freshwater river, a tributary of the River Rhine. At the beginning of the Holocene the area at the main port site was largely dry ground, with a varied relief. Sandy land surfaces exposed at Stanford Wharf provided opportunities for human activity; flint tools dating to the Mesolithic and earlier Neolithic period included scrapers and blades. During the mid Holocene, sea-level rise resulted in inundation of the former dry land surface, and a palaeochannel that cut east-west across the length of the site was either incised or reactivated. The channel was surrounded by extensive tidal mudflats backed by salt marsh. Initially it was prone to strong tidal influences and surges, although this influence diminished over time, probably owing to silting. Estuarine environments prevailed at Stanford Wharf into the succeeding periods with the deposition of alluvium across the southern part of the site, and in general the site was characterised by a landscape of salt marsh and tidal creeks until the 17th century, when the land was reclaimed.

The first period of intensive activity at the site dated to the middle Iron Age (*c* 400-100 BC). The evidence was concentrated in the north-western corner of the site and largely comprised red hills, mounds consisting of the debris of long-term salt production, characteristic of the Essex coast. Features including ditches, gullies, pits, and hearths were associated with the red hills. Pottery and scientific dating identifies the Stanford Wharf red hills as among the earliest examples in Essex; such sites have generally been dated to the late Iron Age and early Roman period. Chemical, micromorphological and other scientific analyses revealed that the mounds consisted of fuel ash derived from burnt salt marsh plants and sediment. The plants (with adhering marsh sediment) had been burnt to fuel hearths, above which brine was evaporated to crystallise salt. A by-product of the fuel burning was a salt-rich ash, which was probably mixed with seawater and filtered to create a particularly concentrated brine. The residue from this process was then dumped and used to form occupation or working surfaces. A considerable quantity of briquetage, a coarse ceramic used in salt making, was recovered.

After a break in occupation in the late Iron Age, activity resumed during the early Roman period (*c* AD 43-120). Salt making was located at the eastern rather than the western end of the site. Evidence associated with this activity comprised irregularly-shaped ditches and storage pits, postholes and other cut features, as well as a range of briquetage vessels and furniture. As in the middle Iron Age, salt marsh plants had been used for fuel and, presumably, to create brine, although the formation of a dark soil, rather than a red hill, suggests that little marsh sediment was burnt along with the plants. A notable feature at the western end of the site, unparalleled in Roman Britain, was a 13-metre long, U-shaped timber structure built on the edge of the palaeochannel, a tidal feature. This has been interpreted as a boathouse, and suggests that Stanford Wharf served as a base for trade or fishing.

There was another gap in the sequence of activity during the 2nd century AD, but in the 3rd century, a trapezoidal enclosure was established at the western end of the site. Ash deposited in the ditches and internal pits suggest that the enclosure saw salt production, but the most notable aspect of it was a pit, originally dug to extract brickearth and used subsequently as a cess-pit. Waterlogged conditions within the pit had preserved a wide range of organic material. A saltern south of the enclosure and defined by a hearth, settling tanks, and two horseshoe-shaped ditches designed to trap seawater, provided more certain evidence of salt production in the earlier 3rd century. By *c* AD 250, the site had been reorganised with the layout of new ditches and enclosures. The remains of a timber drain and a deposit of thousands of tiny fish bones were found in one ditch. The abundance and composition of the fish bone assemblage suggest that it represents evidence of fish sauce production. A circular structure was erected in the corner of the now abandoned trapezoidal enclosure. This probably had a clay mass external wall revetted by stakes and wattle. A hearth and a three-celled tank found inside identify the structure as a saltern. Other three-celled tanks were recorded in a saltern at the eastern end of the site. Ash derived from burning salt marsh plants was recovered from theses features, suggesting that the process of salt making was similar to that used in the middle Iron Age. The recovery of seed heads of rush, plantain and thrift at various stages of maturity suggests that salt marsh plants were harvested throughout the growing season. Live plants were now cut above ground level, which sustained growth, but also avoided marsh sediment, thus preventing red hills from forming. Three more salterns were set up within an enclosure at the west end of the site. One of these was equipped with a tile-built hearth. Chemical analysis showed high concentrations of lead on the floor of the saltern, suggesting the use of lead vessels for brine evaporation. Wood charcoal was recovered from another saltern situated within a circular building. The lead traces and charcoal represent a significant change in technology and fuel, although some briquetage vessels and furniture continued to be used throughout the late Roman period. A circular building to the south, dating to the late 3rd century AD, was dominated by four substantial chalk rubble post-bases, which formed a 4.5m wide square. Interpretation of the structure is not certain. What must have been massive timber posts may have provided internal roof support for a structure with a mass clay outer wall.

Coins and pottery indicate that the site was occupied into the second half of the 4th century. Following the Roman period, two isolated (and not *in situ*) oak piles were recorded and radiocarbon dated to the middle Saxon period (*c* AD 650-850). By the late 11th century, the coastal marshes of Essex became increasingly important for sheep pasture and other economic activities. Ditches and gullies in the northernmost area of the eastern end of the site on the higher ground of the gravel terrace are likely to mark out arable fields or areas of grazing for livestock. Exploitation of the marsh to the south appears to have been more limited, and a timber group marks a causeway through the marshland. In the 15th and 16th centuries, the Stanford marshlands belonged to Cabborns Manor, later known as Manor Farm. A relatively costly Beauvais sgraffito ware dish dating to this period was found in one of the ditches at Stanford Wharf. A sheepfold dating to the 17th century or later, and seen on an early Ordnance Survey map, was uncovered. In more recent times, Stanford Wharf was the site of Stanford-le-Hope Oil QF (diversionary fire) bomb decoy. Concrete and brick remains in the eastern end of the site are likely to be from some of these installations.

Foreword

It is often said that geography is one of the main reasons for the success of London as a city. Proximity to the open sea, via a fast flowing, tidal river such as the Thames was always going to be an attractive proposition for people looking to trade. From the early Roman founders of *Londinium* to their modern day equivalents, the UK capital has an ancient history of trade, movement of goods and people.

The area on which we are developing the new port of London Gateway is one of significant natural and archaeological interest. Developing such a vast, modern port facility in such a sensitive location has brought numerous challenges. As an organisation, we are acutely aware that we have environmental responsibilities and we take them extremely seriously.

We are committed to safeguarding habitats as well as to ensuring that the histories of communities living in the Thames Estuary are respected and remembered. Archaeological excavation ahead of the formation of the new Stanford Wharf Nature Reserve has revealed some fascinating archaeological discoveries which have transformed our understanding of the production of one of the most valuable commodities in the Roman world – salt. Clearly the area was as active and important to trade and economy in Roman times, as it is today.

Simon Moore
DP World London Gateway CEO

A primary concern of the London Gateway team is the protection and maintenance of the environment. The creation of the new nature reserve at Stanford Wharf, a project which has involved painstaking work both from ecologists and archaeologists, has been an important milestone in the development of London Gateway. It provides a wetland habitat suitable for a variety of wildlife, particularly wading birds, and a refuge for the thousands of reptiles which have been re-located from the main port development site.

The Reserve was created from farmland to the west of the port site. Before it could be developed and a new sea wall put in place to allow it to be flooded, we carried out an extensive programme of archaeological work to excavate and record the remains identified during earlier survey work. The site was relatively undisturbed by previous development and remains were well-preserved. As a result the team from Oxford Archaeology was able to gain a remarkably detailed picture of the history of salt production on the site and the uses to which the marshlands were put in the Roman and later periods. Many small-scale excavations have taken place on salt-making sites, but the need to reduce ground

level over 30 hectares at Stanford Wharf meant that this archaeological investigation was on an unprecedented scale for a site of this kind in the UK.

London Gateway is proud to be in a position, through the publication of this volume, to make a significant contribution to the knowledge and understanding of Roman industry and trade. The success of the project has been due to the integrated approach which was adopted for the work; archaeologists, environmental specialists, engineers, developers and regulators have all worked effectively together with enthusiasm and commitment.

The archaeological discoveries will be made available to a wider public both through the deposition of the finds and site archive with Thurrock Museum at Grays, Essex, and through the newly opened Thurrock Thameside Visitor Centre at the Stanford Wharf site itself. It is intended that the Centre will form a focal point for local residents and visitors, enhancing their enjoyment of the Reserve and their awareness of its rich environment and heritage.

Marcus Pearson BSc
DP World London Gateway Environmental Manager

Acknowledgements

The archaeological investigations at Stanford Wharf Nature Reserve and subsequent post-excavation work and publication were generously funded by DP World London Gateway. Special thanks are owed to Marcus Pearson, Environmental manager for DP World London Gateway, for his support throughout. Oxford Archaeology is indebted to Gill Andrews, DP World London Gateway's consultant archaeologist, for efficiently and sensitively monitoring the fieldwork and post-excavation work. Oxford Archaeology would also like to thank Richard Havis (Essex County Council Historic Environment Branch), Deborah Priddy (English Heritage Inspector of Ancient Monuments, East of England Region) and Rachael Ballantyne (English Heritage, Regional Science Advisor), who have provided much valuable advice and guidance during the project. Much practical assistance was provided by Cullen, Grummitt and Roe (supervisory team), Carillion plc (principal contractor), Lancaster Earthmoving (earthworks contractor), and Thomson Ecology (ecological contractor).

The fieldwork was directed by Katrina Anker and Chris Carey, and the monograph authors are enormously indebted to them for their advice and support throughout the post-excavation work. Chris Carey is additionally thanked for liaising with palaeoenvironmental specialists in the early stages of the post-excavation work and preparing sub-samples for study. Fieldwork supervisors were Neil Lambert, Rebecca Peacock and Rowan McAlley. The fieldwork was managed by Stuart Foreman, who also managed the post-excavation project with Edward Biddulph. Environmental management was provided by Rebecca Nicholson, and finds management was provided by Leigh Allen. Further support was given by Magdalena Wachnik and Sarah Lucas (graphics management), Elizabeth Stafford (geoarchaeological management), Matt Bradley (geomatics management), Louise Loe (burials management), and Nicola Scott (archives management). Project support, oversight and monitoring was undertaken by Dan Poore (OA Head of Fieldwork), Anne Dodd (Head of Post-Excavation), Bob Williams (Chief Operations Officer) and David Jennings (Chief Executive Officer). The GIS map on which the site figures were based was prepared by Leo Heatley and Roberta Marziani. Leo Heatley was also responsible for generating the distribution plots used in the monograph. Final and additional monograph figures were prepared by Julia Collins. Liz Stafford prepared most of the figures in Chapter 2, and Figure 5.20 in Chapter 5. The reconstruction drawing of a late Roman saltern (Figure 6.58) was by Mark Gridley. Finds were drawn or photographed by Magdalena Wachnik and Sophie Lamb. The monograph was edited by Paul Booth. The digital volume was edited by Edward Biddulph.

The boat depicted in Figure 5.20 is based on a computer-generated model of the Barland's Farm boat by Selina Ali, University of Wales Trinity Saint David. Figure 5.21 is derived from a figure of the Barland's Farm boat by Owain Roberts, and the authors are grateful to Nigel Nayling for agreeing to its use. The plan of a saltern from Middleton, Norfolk, shown in Figure 6.67 is based on figure 47 published in Crowson 2001. The plan of the Westerton tower shown in Figure 6.57 is reproduced by kind permission of Professor W S Hanson. The plan of features from Lymington, Hampshire, shown on Figure 7.13, is reproduced with permission of Andrew Powell of Wessex Archaeology. The sketch of Cabborns Manor (Figure 7.12) was taken from *Unknown Essex* by Donald Maxwell (1925, The Bodley Head).

The authors wish to thank Tom Lane (Archaeological Project Services), who visited the site to provide the benefit of his long experience of investigating salterns in the Fenlands. Kath Hunter thanks Julia Meen, Sharon Cook and Laura Strafford for their sterling work sorting and extracting the plant material. She is also grateful to Kate Griffiths, Wendy Carruthers, Mans Schepers, Bas Van Geel, J P Pals, Dr Janice Kinory, Dr Rachel Ballantyne, Beatrice Hopkinson and Stephen Rippon for their help with identifications and references, and thanks Lena Strid for proof reading and Rebecca Nicholson for redrafting and editing the plant macrofossils report.

Richard Macphail, John Crowther and Francesco Berna would like to thank Kath Hunter for kindly suggesting a 'sea rush' identification for charred plant remains seen in thin section, and thank Kevin Reeves (UCL Institute of Archaeology) for facilitating EDS and Microprobe studies.

The authors of the monograph are especially grateful to Professor Stephen Rippon, Professor of Landscape Archaeology at the University of Exeter, for reading and commenting on the text. Any errors, however, remain the responsibility of the authors alone.

Oxford Archaeology would like to thank the following staff for their significant contribution to the project during and after fieldwork:

Oxford Archaeology
Rebecca Allen, Natalie Anderson, Paul-Samual Armour, Ben Attfield, Simon Birnie, Thomas Black, Harriet

Bloore, Andrew Booth, Abigail Brown, Will Clarke, Ian Cook, Sharon Cook, Geraldine Crann, Peter Crann, Gareth Dickinson, Gary Evans, Peter Gane, Andrew Ginns, Michael Green, Michael Harris, Chiz Harward, Christof Heistermann, Karen Hole, Peter James, Dave Jamieson, Philip Jefferies, Gary Jones, Fiona Keith-Lucas, Marie Kelleher, Mike Kershaw, Anne Kilgour, David Lang, Alex Latham, Steve Laurie-Lynch, Mark Littlewood, Peter Lovett, Wajdan Majeed, Robin Maggs, Roberta Marziani, Ben McAndrew, Alex McAuley, Janice Mcleish, Hefin Meara, Patrick Moan, Stephen Morgan, Sam Oates, Victoria Osborn, Chris Pickard, Dawn Powell, Kay Proctor, Susan Rawlings, Dave Roberts, Ruth Rolfe, Frances Scott, Gareth Shane, Rachel Scales, Philip Stastney, Gemma Stewart, Helen Stocks-Morgan, Laura Strafford, Ashley Strutt, Mark Sycamore, Dan Sykes, Gerry Thacker, Jacob Warrender, Dan Watkeys, Ciara Williams, Mornington Woodall, Kate Woodley, and Mark Woodley.

Pre-Construct Archaeology

Tristan Adfield, Sarah Barrowman, Mike Bazley, Joe Brookes, Matt Edmonds, Phil Frickers, Matt Gould, Matt Harrison, Jim Heathcote, Richard Humphrey, Will Johnson, Paw Jorgensen, John Payne, Alexander Pullen, Guy Seddon, and Aidan Turner.

Chapter 1

Introduction to Stanford Wharf Nature Reserve

by Edward Biddulph, Stuart Foreman, Elizabeth Stafford, Katrina Anker and Chris Carey

INTRODUCTION

The Thames Estuary has been a gateway of cultural change since stone-age tool-makers settled on the floodplains. The estuary has seen dramatic events, such as the Roman Conquest, but has also been a means of developing economic prosperity and social understanding through trade and communication. The redevelopment of port facilities at the former Shellhaven oil refinery at Stanford-le-Hope on the Essex coast provided an important opportunity to investigate some 6000 years of human history, built up layer by layer in the soil.

Stanford Wharf Nature Reserve (NGR TQ 6990 8110), a 44-hectare site bordered by Stanford-le-Hope industrial area to the north, Mucking Creek to the west, and the River Thames to the south (Fig. 1.1), was investigated as part of the London Gateway Port development, which combines the UK's newest deep-sea container port with Europe's largest logistics park. The nature reserve was created from farmland to the west of the main port development to provide a wetland habitat for wading birds and other wildlife, as well as green space for residents and visitors to enjoy. This ambitious project involved reducing the ground level across the whole area, creating a new sea wall, and breaching the existing sea wall to allow the site to be flooded by the tidal waters of the Thames Estuary.

The archaeological fieldwork undertaken in 2009 as a result of the development generated a large amount of data. Some 4000 context record sheets, each accompanied by scale drawings and photographs, described a wide range of features encountered. Some 14,500 sherds of pottery, 7000 fragments of briquetage, 550 worked flints, and 600 fragments of metal were collected, among other finds. Almost 300 samples containing the remains of seeds, plants and charcoal were taken, while 70 monolith cores through the sedimentary sequence were logged. These not only took slices of the stratigraphic layers, but captured pollen, microfauna and diatoms that provide a signature of environmental change. This monograph describes the results and presents an overall understanding of this nationally significant site.

PROJECT BACKGROUND

The major port and park development of London Gateway received planning permission from HM Government on 30th May 2007. The applications were in the form of an outline planning application (OPA) for the park and a harbour empowerment order (HEO) for the port. Archaeological planning conditions attached to the consents required adherence to the London Gateway Archaeological Mitigation Framework (AMF). Stanford Wharf Nature Reserve, formerly known as Compensation Site A, was developed by DP World London Gateway to satisfy planning conditions attached to development of the port. It is located to the west of the main development, in an area of former marshland, which documentary evidence suggests was reclaimed in the early 17th century. The creation of the new mudflat was accomplished by reducing the level of the site by *c* 0.5m and breaching the existing sea wall to allow tidal inundation. Limited areas of deeper excavation, up to *c* 1m in depth, were required in the southern part of the site, and a new sea wall was constructed along the northern edge of the site.

DP World London Gateway funded a series of field investigations at Stanford Wharf Nature Reserve to ensure that archaeological remains were preserved or investigated before the site was flooded. A desk-based assessment, gradiometer survey and trial trenching (OA 2009a) were all undertaken prior to the detailed investigation, and a site-specific archaeological project design was produced to guide the mitigation work (OA 2009b). The mitigation programme involved detailed excavation of the most significant archaeological remains identified in Areas A and B, controlled archaeological stripping throughout the northern part of the site (Areas C and D), and monitoring during construction in the remainder (Areas E-K). An archaeological team was also present during breaching of the existing sea wall (Area L) to record possible evidence for earlier phases of sea defence (Fig. 1.2).

The AMF, site-specific project designs and archaeological fieldwork were approved by Essex County Council (ECC) Historic Environment Branch and English Heritage, which provided archaeological advice to the local planning authorities. Site areas were released in stages to allow construction of the sea wall to proceed behind the archaeological excavation, the spoil from newly excavated areas being used as embankment fill. Each area was subject to a formal handover procedure requiring the approval of ECC (Richard Havis), DP World London Gateway's Archaeological Liaison Officer (Gill Andrews) and DP World London Gateway's Environmental Manager (Marcus Pearson).

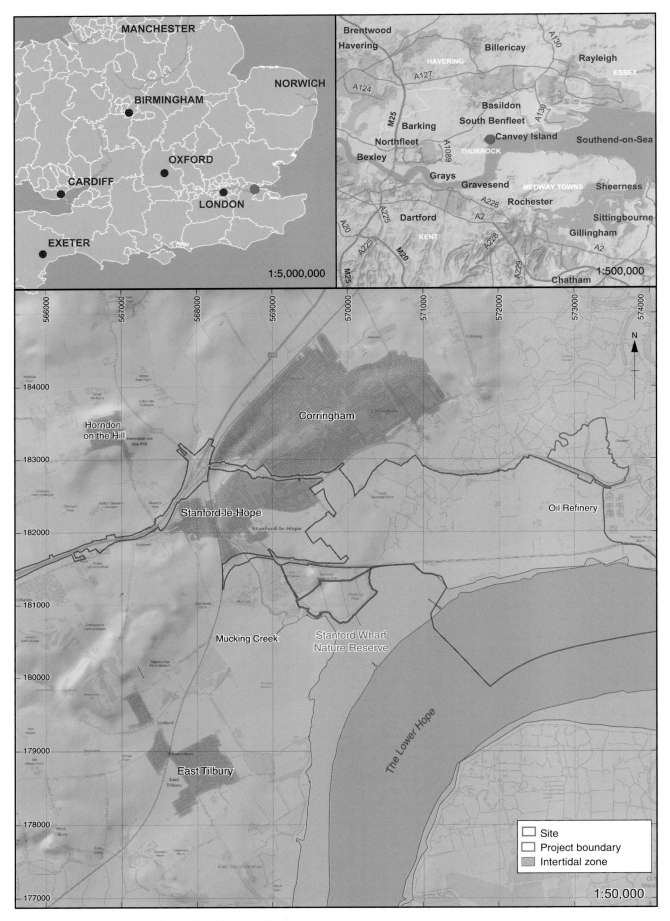

Figure 1.1 Location of Stanford Wharf Nature Reserve

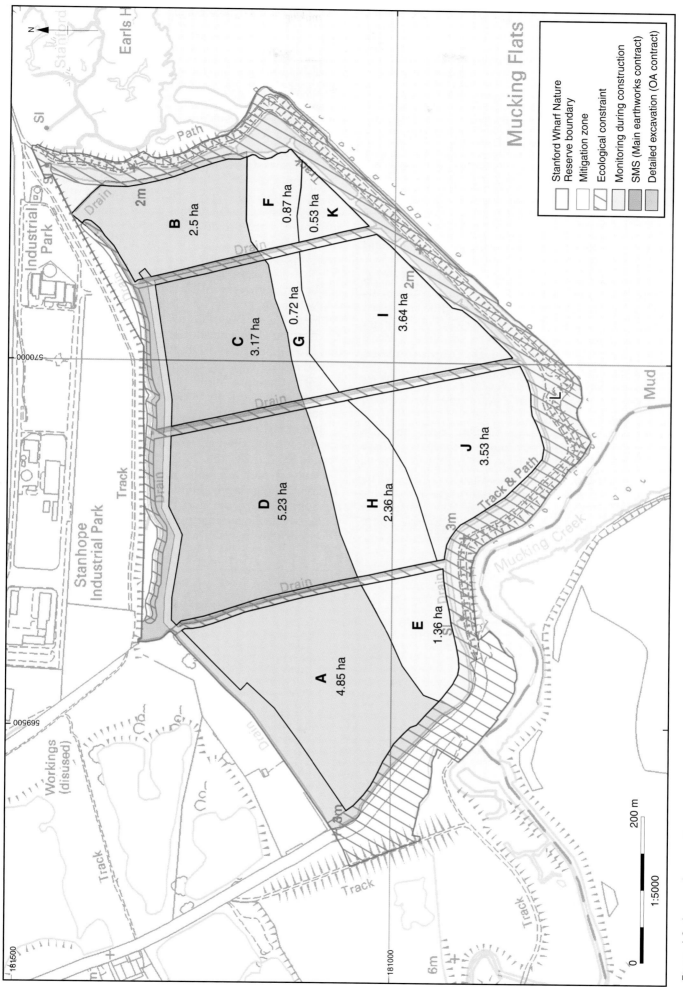

Figure 1.2 Areas of excavation

GEOMORPHOLOGICAL CONTEXT

The regional context

The London Gateway development is located in the Lower Thames Estuary (Fig. 1.1), approximately 25 miles downstream of the City of London. To the east the estuary opens onto the North Sea. Today the estuary is characterised as "tide-dominated" (*sensu* Dalrymple *et al.* 1992) in which major sandbars occur within the outer estuary area, a marine-dominated zone, and tidal meanders in an inner mixed energy zone (Fig. 1.3; Bates and Stafford forthcoming; Bates and Whittaker 2004).

The River Thames lies within a basin known as the London Basin that is bounded to the north by the Chalk escarpment forming the Chiltern Hills and to the south by the Chalk of the North Downs. Younger Eocene sediments occur within a synclinal feature between the Chilterns and the North Downs (Sumbler 1996). This structure defines the distribution of the local basement geology of the site area which is dominated by the Lambeth Group and the London Clay Formation (Fig. 1.4).

The recent geomorphologic development of the area and the establishment of the modern topography have resulted from major drainage pattern modifications during the Quaternary, and in particular events during the last 500,000 years (Gibbard 1994). The Pleistocene deposits of the Lower Thames have been extensively studied (Gibbard 1994; Bridgland 1994; 1995; Bridgland *et al.* 1995); deposition began during the

Anglian glaciation (*c* 500,000 BP) and continued intermittently throughout the Pleistocene. Sediments deposited in cold climate braided stream systems exist as wedges of sand and gravel on the valley sides, subsequently eroded by fluvial incision during periods of lowered sea level to create terraces. Despite extensive research on the Pleistocene deposits, however, considerable controversy exists regarding the age of some of the older sequences and their correlation with the global oxygen isotope stratigraphy (Gibbard 1994; Bridgland 1994). Pleistocene sand and gravel bodies lie to the north-west of the London Gateway development area on the higher ground, as well as beneath the site in certain areas (Fig. 1.5).

The most recent episodes of gravel aggradation in the Lower Thames, responsible for the deposition of the valley bottom gravels (or Shepperton Member, *sensu* Gibbard 1994; 1999) form the template onto which much of the Holocene alluvial and estuarine sedimentation is overlaid (Bates 1998; Bates and Whittaker 2004). This template typically declines in elevation from west to east; therefore older sand and gravel deposits, exposed to the west, are buried beneath the floodplain in an eastwards direction.

In contrast to the relatively well known sequences of Pleistocene age the nature of the Holocene sediments deposited during the last 12,000 years is poorly understood and has only, with few exceptions, been described superficially. Holocene sediments within the development area are part of a continuum forming a wedge thickening downstream from less than 2m at Tower Bridge to reach a maximum thickness of 35m

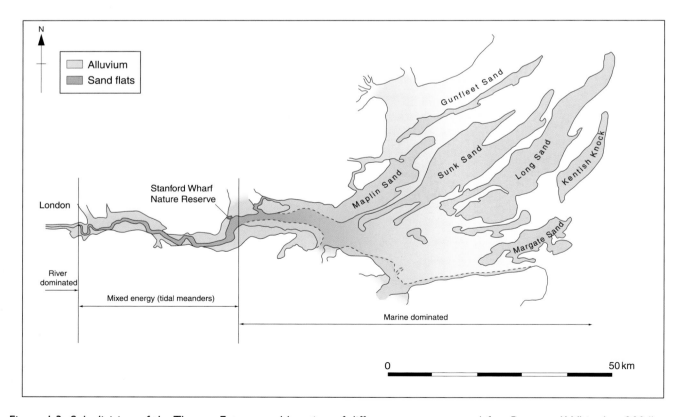

Figure 1.3 Sub-division of the Thames Estuary and location of different estuary zones (after Bates and Whittaker 2004)

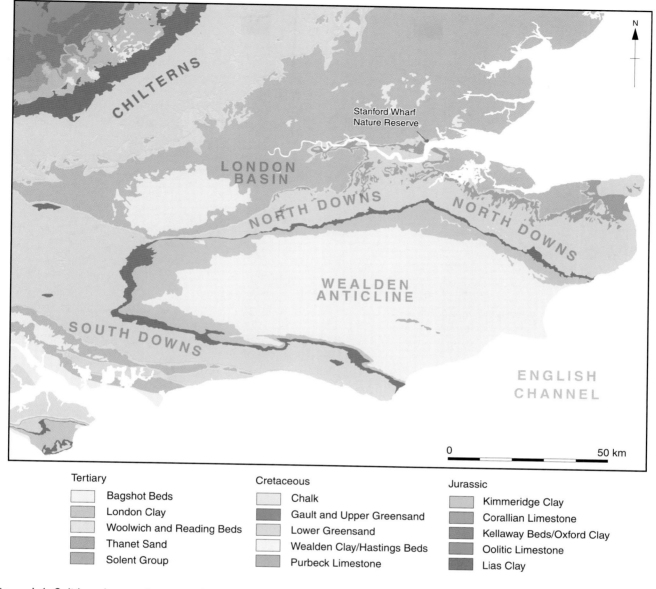

Figure 1.4 Solid geology and topography of south-east England

east of the study area at Canvey Island (Marsland 1986). The Holocene sediments of the Lower Thames Estuary consist of complex intercalated sequences deposited in a variety of environments representing variously: freshwater alder carr, fen, reedswamp, intertidal salt marsh and mudflats. The sediments have been grouped by Gibbard (1999) into the Tilbury Member and are dominated by peats and clay-silts in the inner estuary, with marine sands recorded near the Isle of Grain and Yantlet Channel and Sea Reach south of Canvey Island.

The basis for subdivision of these deposits was established by Devoy during the 1970s (Devoy 1977; 1979; 1980; 1982). His 'Thames-Tilbury' model used borehole stratigraphies integrated with biostratigraphic studies to infer successive phases of marine transgressions (typified by clay-silt deposition) and regressions (typified by peat formation). Devoy's work has resulted in a view of sediment accumulation being controlled

within the area by a combination of factors dominated by sea-level change and tectonic depression of southern England. However, more recent work (eg Bates 1999; Bates and Barham 1995; Bates and Stafford forthcoming; Haggart 1995; Sidell *et al.* 2000; Sidell *et al.* 2002; Sidell and Wilkinson 2004) has highlighted several problems suggesting that the model cannot always be easily applied in terms of lithology or age/altitude analysis, particularly at the scale of a single archaeological site. This is in part a reflection of the complex nature of floodplain environments where sequence accumulation may be influenced by very local factors such as proximity to the terrace edge, the presence of tributaries, islands or 'eyots' and areas of impeded drainage.

More recently a simplified (tripartite) regional model for floodplain development was presented by Long *et al.* (2000). A similar cultural landscape model set out by Bates and Whittaker (2004) examined the likely impact

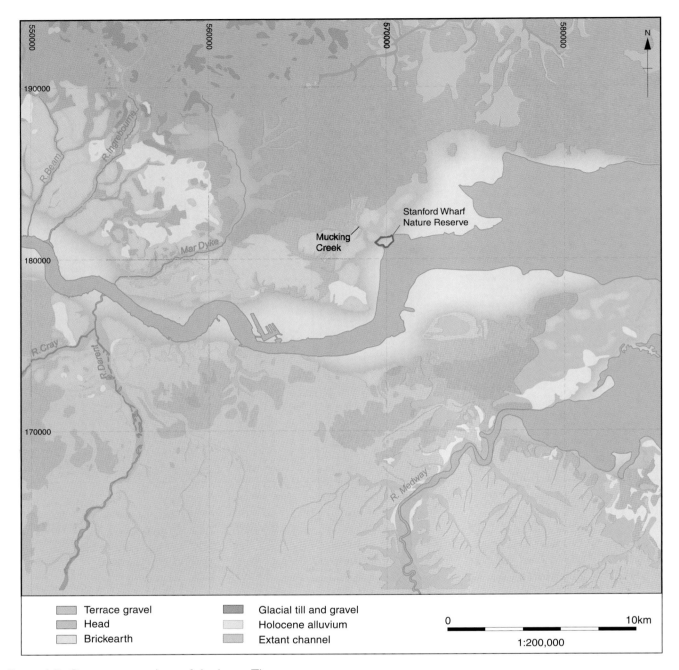

Figure 1.5 Quaternary geology of the lower Thames

of these changes on human activity and provides a useful framework for archaeological investigation. In addition, over the last two decades a number of detailed site-specific investigations have been undertaken, many in association with developer-funded archaeological work, that are beginning to address the complex range of factors responsible for sequence accumulation. These include the Jubilee Line Extension (Sidell *et al.* 2000), High Speed 1 (Bates and Stafford forthcoming) and various sites in Southwark (Sidell *et al.* 2002). It should be noted, however, that much of this recent work has been focussed upstream within the more sheltered part of the inner estuary. The London Gateway development is located closer to the marine dominated zone, thereby offering valuable new comparative data.

Geoarchaeological investigations at London Gateway

The London Gateway port, along with its associated access routes and ecological compensation sites, crosses a series of landscape zones, ranging from the higher Pleistocene terrace deposits, through the lower-lying floodplain and (reclaimed) inter-tidal zone to the main Thames channel beyond. These zones have widely varying archaeological potential. A key objective of the investigations at London Gateway was to develop a clear understanding of the chronological development of the deposit sequences within these zones, and how changes in sea level affected land forms and human land-use since the end of the last cold stage (the Devensian, up to *c* 13ka BP).

An extensive programme of geoarchaeological investigation carried out during the lifetime of the project at the main port site, immediately to the east of Stanford Wharf Nature Reserve, has provided a robust model for landscape evolution of the former low-lying floodplain zone dating back to the beginning of the Holocene (Bates *et al.* 2012). The deposit model for the port site integrated data from boreholes, large scale geophysical survey (electrical resistivity), palaeoenvironmental studies and radiocarbon dating to map deeply buried topographic features associated with the early Holocene topographic template (ie the surface of the East Tilbury Marshes and Shepperton Gravels) as well as examining spatial and temporal diversity during accumulation of the overlying Holocene alluvial deposits. To summarize: during the earlier part of the Holocene (*c* 9-8ka BP) the landscape now occupied by the port was largely dry ground and wooded with a varied relief. Freshwater deposition of organic sediments was occurring in lower lying areas which included a localised basin that may have formed an open body of water such as a small lake. From *c* 8ka BP the basin was beginning to be influenced by brackish water incursion. During the succeeding periods the area was gradually inundated owing to rising river levels, resulting in the deposition of a complex sequence of intercalated organic and minerogenic sediments. Dry ground areas were reduced first to a series of interconnected ridges and then islands, as tidal mudflats, creeks and saltmarshes dominated the landscape. High energy conditions associated with strong tidal regimes were present to the east, typified by the deposition of laminated clays, silts and sand. By *c* 5-4ka BP all former dry ground had disappeared from the port site, buried beneath extensive deposits of intertidal sediment, in some places reaching up to 15m in thickness. These deposits continued to form until the area was reclaimed for agricultural use in the 19th century.

Taking into account the early inundation of the port site; archaeological potential in terms of permanent occupation was considered relatively low. The site of Stanford Wharf Nature Reserve, however, lies to the west of the main port development, adjacent to the current course of Mucking Creek. Preliminary geoarchaeological assessment demonstrated that the Holocene alluvial sequences here, averaging *c* 1.5m in depth, were much shallower than at the port site and predominantly minerogenic in nature (clays and silts). The surface of the Pleistocene deposits lay at much higher elevations, straddling the interface between the higher terrace deposits (ie the Taplow/Mucking Gravels) and the former intertidal zone (Carey *et al.* 2009). As a consequence it was considered that this area would have remained relatively dry land until the mid to late Holocene. A series of resistivity survey and gouge auger transects also revealed the presence of a large palaeochannel bisecting the site east-west. The channel probably had its origins in the Pleistocene but appears to have remained active throughout the Holocene, providing a focus for human activity at the terrace edge. The existence of this activity was confirmed during

subsequent evaluation trenching and open area excavation which revealed extensive evidence of occupation stratified within the alluvial sequence. Although the majority of the archaeological evidence within the alluvium dated to the Roman period and was associated with salt production and other activities, evidence of prehistoric activity in the form of flint scatters was also recovered at the base of the sequence, associated with a possible buried land surface. The area of Roman occupation appears to have been focused north of the east-west palaeochannel extending onto the higher ground of the terrace and was particularly concentrated in the vicinity of Mucking Creek in the western part of the site (Area A); an additional area of dense activity was located in the far eastern part of the site (Area B).

ARCHAEOLOGICAL BACKGROUND

Stanford Wharf in regional context

The excellent archaeological potential of Stanford Wharf Nature Reserve was recognised on the basis of previous discoveries and pre-excavation investigations. A desk-based assessment noted a number of sites and findspots within Stanford Wharf Nature Reserve and the immediate area, including two groups of Roman pottery finds from the foreshore. Further pottery was recovered from the foreshore during walkover surveys in 2002 and 2009. A Roman well is recorded on the county Historic Environment Record within Area A, although the circumstances of discovery and precise location are unknown. Stanford Wharf sits on the western edge of the distribution of red hills, the remains of low mounds of red earth characteristic of salt making along the Essex coast during the Iron Age and early Roman period (Fawn *et al.* 1990), and was known to contain evidence of salt production before the site was made available for large-scale excavation (Fig. 1.6). The remains of a red hill were recorded at the mouth of Mucking Creek (ibid., 65) and have since been destroyed, probably by the plough. Another red hill has been recorded at Corringham, and a further four are known at East Tilbury (ibid.). Salt manufacture is also suspected near Grays (Barford 1988a, 98). Otherwise, the distribution of this distinctive type of feature is concentrated at Canvey Island, along the River Crouch, in the Blackwater Estuary, and around Mersea Island and the River Colne (Fig. 1.6; Rippon 2000, 61, fig. 22). The coast in the north-eastern part of Essex, near Little Oakley and Dovercourt, has also provided evidence for salt production (Barford 2002a).

Extensive salt production is also attested on the opposite side of the Thames on the North Kent marshes in the Medway estuary, the Isle of Sheppey and the Hoo peninsula. Much of the salt-making evidence is attributed to the 1st and 2nd centuries AD (Rippon 2000, 62). No salterns of later Iron Age date have been recorded on the North Kent marshes, although an exceptionally large assemblage of early/middle Iron Age briquetage was found in excavations immediately south of Gravesend, with the salt-making activity likely to have been carried out a short distance north of the site (Morris 2012). The North Kent marshes in the Roman period were also the site of a major pottery industry (Monaghan 1987), and it is probable that the two, seasonal, industries, were associated, not least by way of shared resources, such as clay, fuel, and labour, but also through wider ownership or economic control (Rippon 2000, 60-2). It is likely, too, that ceramic vessels were used for the transportation of salt or generally in the salt-making process. There is another correlation between salt and pottery production, at least geographically, around Poole Harbour in Dorset, and, significantly for Stanford Wharf Nature Reserve, in south Essex.

Stanford Wharf Nature Reserve is set within an extensive zone of Iron Age and Roman settlement distributed across the Thameside region and the hinterland of Roman London that took advantage of both the floodplain and the higher ground of the gravel terraces (Figs 1.7 and 1.8). A number of archaeological sites lie immediately west of Stanford Wharf within the Borough of Thurrock (Fig. 1.8), which contains a rich landscape of enclosures and settlement evidence dating to the later Iron Age and Roman period (Priddy and Buckley 1987). Mucking, the site of prehistoric, Roman and Anglo-Saxon settlements and cemeteries (eg Clark 1993; Hamerow 1993; Hirst and Clark 2009), is situated on the edge of the gravel terrace some 2km west of Stanford Wharf. At the time of excavation, between

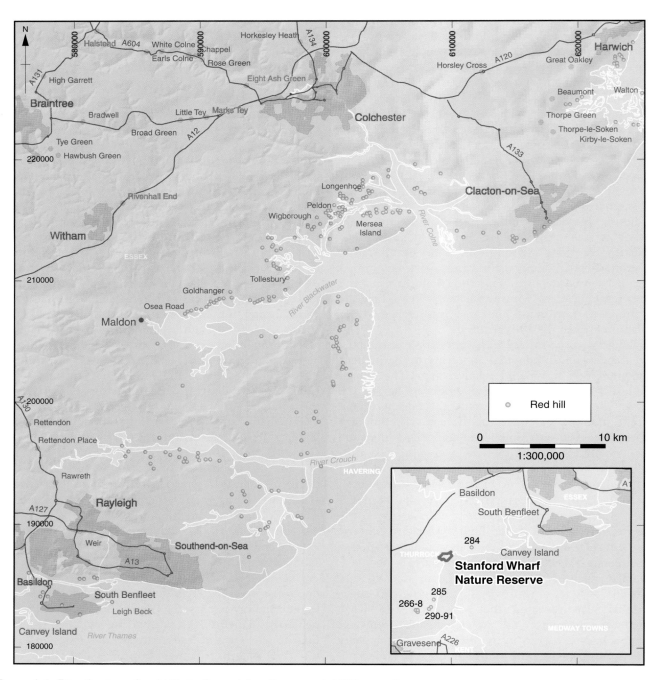

Figure 1.6 Distribution of red hills in Essex (after Fawn *et al.* 1990, map 1)

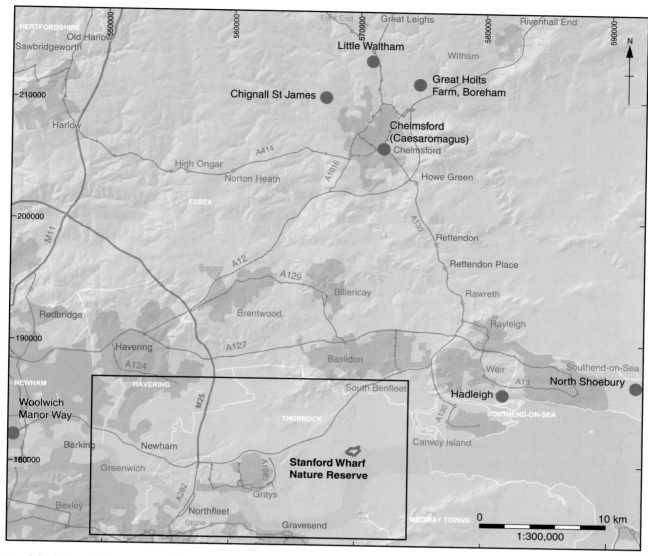

Figure 1.7 Selected Iron Age and Roman-period sites in Central Essex and the Thames Estuary

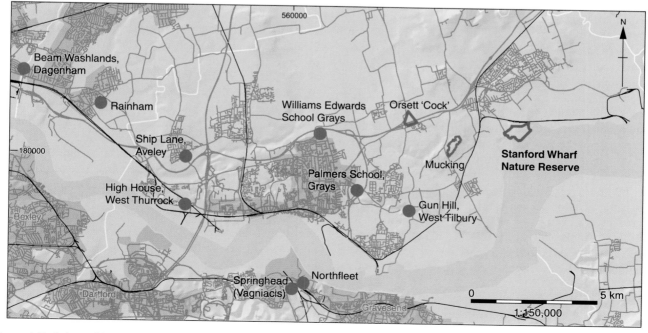

Figure 1.8 Selected Iron Age and Roman-period sites in the vicinity of Stanford Wharf Nature Reserve

1965 and 1978, Mucking was the largest open-area excavation in Europe (Evans and Lucy 2008). A late Iron Age triple-ditched rectangular enclosure and a Roman settlement were established at Orsett 'Cock' (Carter 1998). There was also a Roman occupation site at the Williams Edwards School, Grays (Lavender 1998, 19), while excavation at the Palmers School site at Grays uncovered evidence for pottery production dated to the late 2nd-early 3rd century (Rodwell 1983). At Gun Hill, West Tilbury, the late Iron Age and Roman settlement, occupying a sharply-defined gravel spur north of the Tilbury marshes, comprised an enclosure, field system, structures and kilns (Drury and Rodwell 1973, 48). Further west, a settlement at Ship Lane, Aveley, included large enclosures and structures dating to the 1st and early 2nd century AD, 2nd to 4th century gullies, and a small late Roman enclosure containing a well and hearth (Foreman and Maynard 2002, 123-135), and a prehistoric settlement and early Roman inhumation burials were uncovered at High House, West Thurrock (Andrews 2009). Beyond Thurrock, late Iron Age and Roman occupation was located on a gravel terrace spur jutting into the Thames floodplain at Rainham (Fig. 1.8; Costello 1997, 93). Nearby at Dagenham, excavation uncovered late Iron Age or early Roman enclosure ditches, pits and postholes, and a concentration of hearth or oven bases, which may relate to pottery production, and two pottery kilns, which were operational during the second quarter of the 2nd century and were used to fire sandy grey wares (Biddulph *et al.* 2010). A largely late Roman settlement was recorded at Woolwich Manor Way in East Ham (Fig. 1.7; Stafford *et al.* 2012). Notable inland sites include an Iron Age settlement at Little Waltham (Drury 1978), Roman villas at Chignall St James (Clarke 1998) and Great Holts Farm, Boreham (Germany 2003), and the Roman town of *Caesaromagus*, modern Chelmsford (Wickenden 1992). Sites east of Stanford Wharf include North Shoebury, near Southend, where evidence for middle Iron Age settlement, late Iron Age burials, and Roman-period field systems has been uncovered (Wymer and Brown 1995), and Hadleigh, east of Canvey Island, where a rectangular ditched enclosure of suspected Roman date is known from aerial photography (Hull 1963b, 135). Stanford Wharf is situated *c* 70km south-west of the urban centre at Colchester, and *c* 40km east of the provincial capital at London. On clear days, the inhabitants of Stanford Wharf will have been able to look out over the Thames and see the Kentish side of the river, which contained an equally rich landscape of Roman-period settlement and activity. There was, for example, a villa at Northfleet and a 'small town' at Springhead (Andrews *et al.* 2011), and smaller farming settlements, some originating in the Iron Age, were located near the north Kent coast (eg Simmonds *et al.* 2011; Allen *et al.* 2012).

In January 2009, a gradiometer survey was conducted by South-West Archaeology over all available areas of the site, totalling approximately 38 hectares (OA 2009b). This showed numerous complex magnetic anomalies, although many were suspected to be inter-tidal features (Fig. 1.9). These anomalies were assessed using a combination of geotechnical data, archaeological hand-coring and electrical resistivity survey transects. A topographic survey using LiDAR, a remote sensing technique employing laser pulses to map the ground surface, was also conducted. This also detected the course of the palaeochannel (Fig. 1.10). A series of targeted trenches (Fig. 1.9) was excavated across the whole area in February 2009, demonstrating the presence of complex, stratified archaeological and alluvial sediment sequences. The archaeological remains were concentrated mainly along the western boundary of the site, beside Mucking Creek, with a secondary focus along the eastern boundary of the site, beside another, unnamed, creek. The presence of briquetage, red hill deposits and pottery indicated that these were most likely saltern sites of Iron Age and/or Roman date. The archaeological features and deposits appeared to be concentrated in areas where the gravel terrace rises to the surface in the northern half of Stanford Wharf Nature Reserve, but were sparsely distributed or absent in the southern half where the alluvial deposits are deeper.

In addition to Roman salterns Stanford Wharf Nature Reserve has documentary evidence for post-medieval sea defences, land reclamation and agricultural improvement. In the late 16th and 17th centuries there was a widespread drive by landlords to reclaim areas of Essex marshland from the sea, the usual motivation being to create valuable pasturage for sheep and cattle. The site was not included in the late 19th and 20th century industrial development that occurred at Shellhaven, but formed part of an agricultural buffer zone lying between the historic settlements (eg Stanford-le-Hope and Mucking) on the gravel terrace, and Shellhaven to the east. The marshland character of the area was gradually eroded between the early 17th century and the mid-20th century, as a result of post-medieval reclamation, and subsequent efforts to drain the land for agriculture. Drainage was intensified in the later 20th century with the introduction of mechanised methods (which seems to have had a detrimental affect on the preservation of organic archaeological remains materials in the upper part of the sequence). Nineteenth-century maps of the site show sinuous field boundaries, following the line of natural creeks, but these were replaced in the 20th century with straight boundaries, associated with the mechanical installation of land-drains. The gradiometer survey (Fig. 1.9) shows evidence of land drainage across the central and southern parts of the site. Until the purchase of Stanford Wharf Nature Reserve by DP World in December 2008, the land was actively farmed and was under arable crop. Some areas of historic marshland landscape survive in the vicinity, notably in the remaining portion of Stanford-le-Hope marshes to the east.

During the Second World War, one of a series of 'Oil QF' bomb decoys was built in Stanford-le-Hope marshes, as far as possible from inhabited properties, in

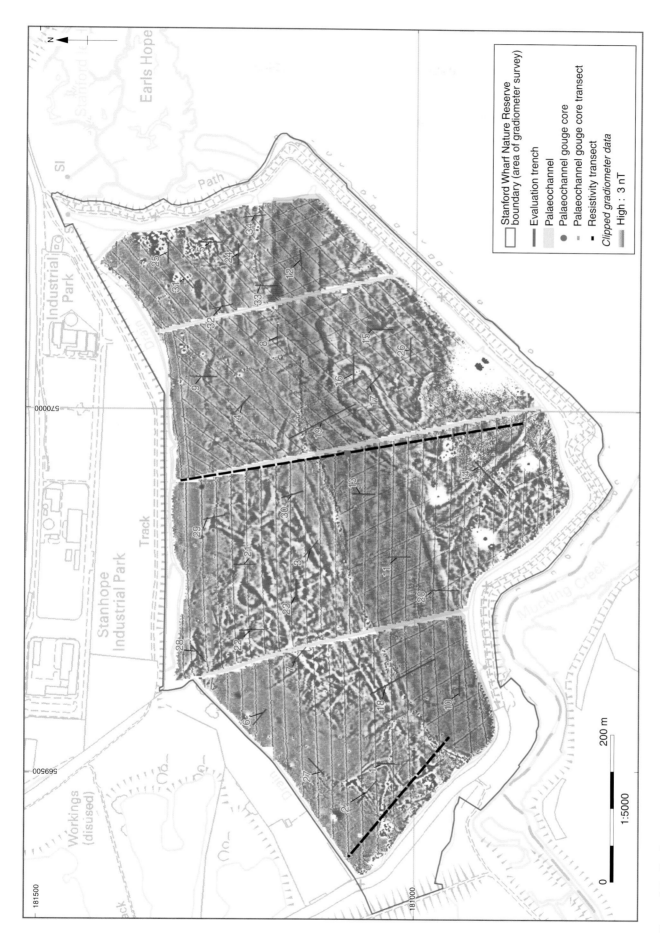

Figure 1.9 Gradiometer survey results, with evaluation trenches also shown

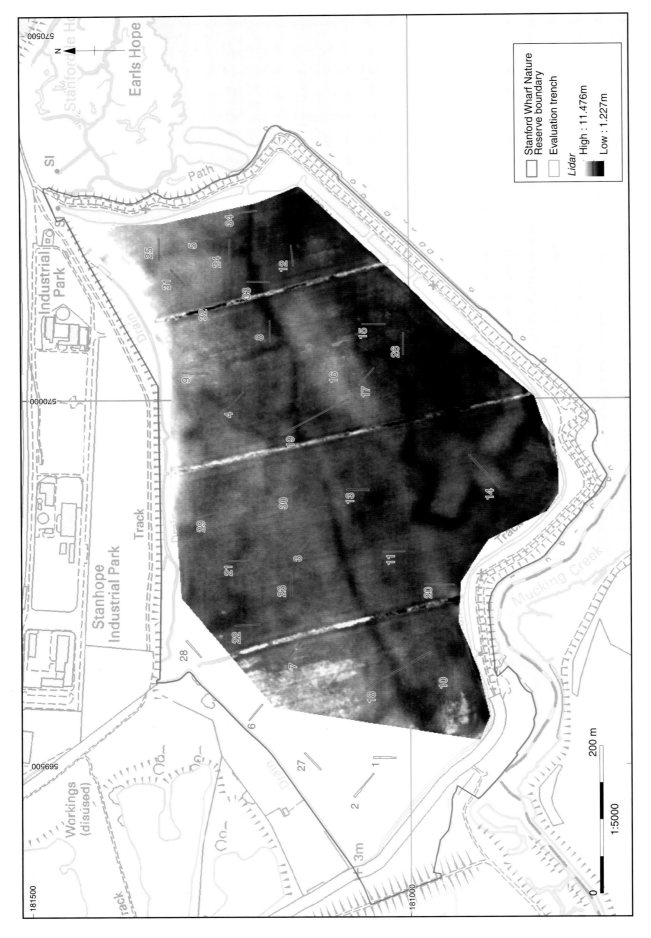

Figure 1.10 LiDAR topographic image

an attempt to divert German bombers away from the Thameshaven oil refinery by simulating bomb-damaged burning oil tanks (Essex Historic Environment Record). In the mid-1970s the southern corner of the site (the same location as the reported bomb decoy control room) was used as a testing site for the Thames Flood Defence Project (S Corbet, pers. comm.). Remains of the testing facility were exposed during the evaluation and watching brief in Area J, and during the breaching of the sea wall in July 2010.

Salt production in Britain and beyond

There are several ways by which the Iron Age and Romano-British salters could have extracted salt from the creeks and channels that brought seawater from the Thames Estuary, although we cannot be certain whether one or a combination of methods were used. Probably the simplest method was to trap the seawater in ponds or channels during tidal inundation, then to transfer it to hearths. The brine boiled and evaporated, allowing salt crystals to form (Fig. 1.11). This method – the so-called *open pan* method – was practised in Roman Britain, including, it appears, at red hill sites in Essex. The remains of hearth walls and floors, as well as fragments of briquetage fire-bars, have been recorded at Leigh Beck, Canvey Island, Peldon, West Mersea, and Goldhanger, east of Maldon (Fig. 1.6; Fawn *et al.* 1990, 21, 70). These sites appear to belong to the earlier Roman period. Pottery from Goldhanger was consistent with a mid to late 1st century AD date (Jefferies and Barford 1990b, 75), and a grog-and-shell-tempered butt-beaker or barrel-shaped jar dating to the 1st century AD was collected from one of the tanks at Peldon (ibid., 74). However, pottery dating to the 3rd and 4th century was recorded at red hill sites at Goldhanger and Wigborough on the Blackwater estuary, and at Langenhoe on Mersea Island (Sealey 1995, 71, 76), and pottery dated to *c* AD 200 or later is known at Leigh Beck (Jefferies and Barford 1990b, 76). The pottery cannot be associated with the red hills, but does hint at later Roman salt making; Barford (2000, 278) suspects a less archaeologically visible process.

Good evidence for the open pan method has been recorded further afield at the late Roman saltern at Blackborough End, Middleton in Norfolk. Two horseshoe-shaped ditches captured water carried by feeder ditches from the tidal flood zone of the Nar Valley (Crowson 2001, 239-40; fig. 47). The water was transferred to a settling tank in the area enclosed by the ditches, allowing the tidal mud and other impurities to settle at the bottom of the tank and, in hot weather, an amount of water evaporation from the action of the sun and wind. The brine, now more concentrated, was then placed into briquetage vessels in an oven and heated to boil off the water and permit crystallisation. In its second phase, Middleton's saltern shifted slightly northwards. There was no enclosure, but water was brought to a pond via a feeder ditch. From there it was transferred to a three-celled settling tank, before being moved to the oven and heated (ibid., 243-4, fig. 54). The

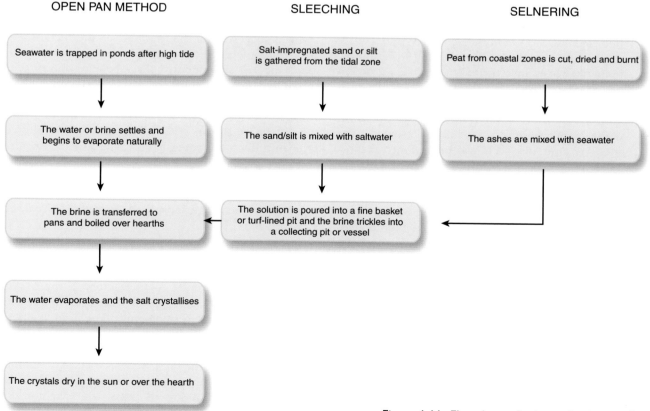

Figure 1.11 Flowchart of salt production methods

open pan method was not confined to coastal salt works, being employed at inland brine springs in the West Midlands and north-west England. At the late Iron Age and Roman salt production site at Droitwich, Worcestershire, brine extracted from wells and natural springs was settled in wood-lined pits and possibly, in the late Roman period, wooden barrels, before being boiled in briquetage vessels on top of hearths (Woodiwiss 1992), while at brine spring sites in Cheshire, the open pan method is attested by the use of hearths and evaporation vessels, including lead pans (Reid and Williams 2008, 14-24; Penney and Shotter 1996, 360-3). The open pan method is also used in traditional production methods in Africa, for example at Uvinza, Tanzania, where natural brine is concentrated and then boiled (Sutton and Roberts 1968, 61-2).

In dry and tropical climates, salt may be obtained by *solar evaporation*, negating the need for artificial heat. In such conditions, for example along the Atlantic or Mediterranean coast of France, in Gujarat or Pondicherry in India, and around the Dead Sea, seawater or brine is channelled into large (usually) square and shallow ponds. The brine evaporates in the heat of the sun, leaving deposits of crystalline salt, which are then raked and harvested.

The salt-rich sand or silts on inter-tidal zones can also be exploited. In a method known as *sleeching*, sand from the shore is collected, placed into specially-designed pits or tanks and filtered. Brine is drawn out and, using the conventional open pan process, boiled to evaporate the water and allow crystallisation. There is little evidence of use of the method in Iron Age or Roman Britain, but it was practised during the Iron Age in Brittany and other parts of northern France (Daire *et al.* 1994, 98-9). In Britain, sleeching is best known in the medieval period, and is attested on the Cumbrian coast (Walsh 1991), Dorset and other coastal locations (Keen 1988a and b). One site that has been investigated in detail is located at Wainfleet St Mary (McAvoy 1994), situated between Skegness and Boston in Lincolnshire. Sand was collected from the shore of the Wash and transported in carts to the higher ground (the 'toftland') behind the tidal zone. The sand, or sleech, was poured into shallow rectangular pits, whose slightly sloping bases were covered in layers of peat and turf. As the pits were filled with seawater, the sand was trapped in the organic filter and the brine trickled from the bottom of the pit into deeper reservoirs or sumps. The brine was then boiled. The waste products – the sand and peat left in the filtration units – were dumped in mounds, which remain visible in the coastal landscape. Forms of sleeching have emerged in different parts of the world. For example, in Tanzania, salt-impregnated sand collected from the edges of Surughai and other swamps is mixed with water and filtered to create a brine, which is then boiled in pans and vessels (Mbogoro and Mwakipesile 2010, 21). At Kibiro, in Uganda, loose soil is spread over salt-rich sediments on the edge of Lake Albert in specially prepared areas known as salt gardens. The level of salinity in the soil increases through capillary action. The

soil is collected, placed in pans and mixed with water. The pans, which are raised above the ground, are perforated, and the brine trickles through the holes into ceramic pots or other containers placed underneath. The brine is boiled over fires in steel pans set up in covered buildings until salt crystals form (Connah *et al.* 1990, 31-5).

A method of salt extraction which may have more relevance to Stanford Wharf is *selnering*. In the Wadden Sea region of the Netherlands, where the method is attested from the 13th century onwards (although it may have been introduced earlier, in the Iron Age or Roman period), peat which formed in the marshy tidal zone was cut, leaving a grid-like pattern across the marshland (Tys 2006, fig. 5). The peat was dried, then burnt, and the ashes were mixed with seawater to create a brine, which was filtered and boiled (ibid., 26). A similar method, by which eel grass (*Zostera*) growing in seawater is collected and burnt, resulting in salty ash ready for filtering, is also attested in the Netherlands, as well as Denmark (D Cranstone, pers. comm.). At Kolhorn, in the Netherlands, pits containing enormous quantities of ash derived from eel grass and dated by pottery to the 11th and 12th centuries were interpreted as evidence for salt making based on eel grass (van Geel and Borger 2005). In Japan, 8th-century literature records a method whereby concentrated brine was obtained from seaweed (Kondo 1975, 61). In the Manga region of Niger, one recently practised traditional method involves digging a pit to bring up underground brine. Vegetation is soaked in the pit, and then dried and burnt. The ashes are wrapped in bark and shaped into bricks, which are transported some distance away from the brine extraction sites to salthouses, where the ashes are mixed with water and boiled (Gouletquer 1975, 47-51). The use of both foreshore sediment and plants is suggested for the Iron Age salt production site at La Challonnière, on the western coast of France. Salters raked the soil and gathered the vegetation, burnt them, mixed the ashes and burnt soil with seawater, then filtered the solution to produce brine, which was evaporated over hearths (Dartevelle *et al.* 1998, 45-6). The use of plants is not known in British salt making, although a silty clay layer in a ditch enclosing late Bronze Age or early Iron Age salt-production hearths and gullies at Billingborough, Lincolnshire, was tentatively interpreted as a deposit that derived from the burning of marine grasses or wood which had absorbed seawater (Cleal and Chowne 2001, 14).

In the modern industrialised world evaporated salt is produced in factories under carefully-controlled conditions, but the principles of extraction have changed little from Roman times. At the factory of the Maldon Salt Company, salt water is syphoned from the river Blackwater into large settling tanks. The brine is filtered to remove river sediments, then transferred to steel pans. The water is boiled to remove impurities, then slowly evaporated to form the salt crystals. Once any remaining water is drained, the crystals are transferred to the drying hopper, resulting in pure salt (Maldon Salt Company, nd).

There is clearly a wide variation in salt extraction methods across time and cultural and geographical zones. What is interesting about the archaeological remains at Stanford Wharf is that there is also variation, and it need not be assumed that salt production throughout the periods of activity represented was identical and unchanging. These remains must be examined in view of the known different production methods to ascertain which was responsible for the archaeological signatures uncovered at the site.

FIELDWORK MITIGATION

On the basis of the evaluation results the site was divided into archaeological areas, which were subdivisions of the geoarchaeological zones, Areas A to L (Fig. 1.2). The boundaries running east-west were defined on the basis of the geoarchaeological zones, although these were not precisely defined in all areas, and were reviewed and refined in the course of extensive soil stripping. The boundaries running north-south followed modern field boundaries. Areas A to L had different archaeological potentials, and therefore required different approaches to mitigation.

Three main approaches were proposed:

- Detailed excavation (Areas A and B)
- Strip, map and sample excavation (Areas C and D)
- Monitoring during construction (Areas E to K)

- Targeted monitoring during construction (Area L and the sea wall breach)

Large-scale open area excavation work was focused predominantly at the edge of the gravel terrace in the northern half of Stanford Wharf Nature Reserve. The most intensive investigations were concentrated in the vicinity of Mucking Creek, in Area A, although detailed excavation was also undertaken in Area B (Figs 1.12 and 1.13). The total area identified for detailed excavation was 7.35ha. A further 8.4ha was subject to strip, map and sample excavation, and 13ha was subject to 'monitoring during construction'. Examination of existing boundaries and drainage ditches throughout the site, including the existing sea wall, was constrained by ecological factors, since these were suitable newt habitats. Excavation plans initially excluded these areas, but this was reviewed in light of archaeological results from topsoil stripping in Areas A to K. The existing field boundaries were subject to strip, map and sample excavation once ecological mitigation was complete. The planned breach in the existing sea wall (Fig. 1.14) was subject to monitoring during construction to record the structure and any evidence for the date of the original reclamation. The remainder of the sea wall was left *in situ*.

Detailed method statements and an overall research framework for the excavation work were provided in the London Gateway Archaeological Mitigation Framework (2003, updated 2008). In addition, geoarchaeological and palaeoenvironmental studies were undertaken

Figure 1.12 Aerial photograph of Area A (copyright Essex County Council Historic Environment Team)

alongside excavation work as a contribution to the site-wide palaeoenvironmental study, and to answer archaeological questions at a local scale. Methods statements and the research framework for palaeoenvironmental sampling and analysis were described in a site-wide palaeoenvironmental project design (2008).

RESEARCH OBJECTIVES

The development of the London Gateway Archaeological Mitigation Framework involved close reference to the archaeological regional research frameworks for the Greater Thames Estuary (Williams and Brown 1999) and south-east England (Glazebrook 1997; Brown and Glazebrook 2000). The archaeological programme for Stanford Wharf Nature Reserve explicitly sought to address the objectives of these frameworks, particularly that of the Greater Thames Estuary.

Research aims based on these frameworks were drawn up on completion of the fieldwork programme in October 2009 and presented in the post-excavation scoping report (OA 2009c). They represented a revision of aims presented in the Stanford Wharf Nature Reserve project design (OA 2009b), including aims and objectives that emerged in the course of the excavation. Consequently, the revised and updated aims informed the process of post-excavation assessment.

Figure 1.13 Aerial photograph of Area B (copyright Essex County Council Historic Environment Team)

Figure 1.14 Viewing the breach of the sea wall (photograph courtesy of Nick Strugnell)

The stratigraphic, artefactual and palaeoenviron-mental assessments resulted in a robust baseline dataset. An overarching objective of the analysis was to build on the baseline study to provide a detailed description of the stratigraphic sequence, chronology, the finds, sediments and palaeoenvironmental evidence. Much of the analysis focused on the following themes:

- Geomorphology, hydrology and vegetation reconstruction
- The pre-Roman alluvial sequence
- Site chronology
- Salt-making methods and processes
- The character and formation of the red hills, and the reworked red hill material
- Economic activity
- Site organisation and domestic occupation
- Selection of fuel for brine evaporation
- Artefacts from salt-related features
- The transition from briquetage to lead salt vessels
- The function of the multi-ditched enclosures
- The appearance of the Roman-period structures
- The date and form of the sea defences

REPORT STRUCTURE

This monograph presents a narrative and discussion of the archaeology and palaeoenvironment of Stanford Wharf Nature Reserve from the late Glacial period to modern times. Overall, the monograph takes an integrated approach, bringing in key findings of the stratigraphic, artefactual and environmental analyses to build a picture of site use and development. Chapter 2 focuses on the landscape evolution of the site and places the archaeological sequence in its environmental context. The chapter describes the site's geomorpholog-ical zones and broadly outlines the stratigraphy and key sedimentary units. It describes the alluvial sequence that shaped the site and reviews the evidence for environmental change and human impact on the environment, concluding with an overall integrated landscape history.

Chapter 3 presents the limited evidence for early prehistoric activity, focusing on pottery and flint tools to provide a picture of landscape exploitation. The evidence is also placed in its regional context. The regionally important red hills and other evidence for salt production in the middle Iron Age are described in Chapter 4. Key artefactual and environmental evidence is provided to enhance our understanding of the formation and use of the red hills, and the discussion addresses questions of salt working, organisation and seasonality.

Chapter 5 describes the internationally significant boathouse, a very rare Roman survival in northern Europe. Other early Roman features presented in the

chapter include a cremation burial and evidence for salt production. The chapter concludes with a discussion that places these features into wider context. Chapter 6, which forms the largest part of the monograph, is devoted to the late Roman period. Evidence for industrial-scale salt production is described, and the discussion focuses on the process of production, and the use of associated features and structures. The chapter concludes with a consideration of how the salt works were organised and who owned them. A description of the post-Roman activity is offered in Chapter 7. Aspects discussed include medieval field systems, post-medieval reclamation, and Second World War bomb decoys. The monograph concludes with an overview and afterword (Chapter 8).

Findings from specialists' environmental and artefact reports on which conclusions and interpretations are drawn have been integrated into the monograph text. The full reports, along with supporting data and illustra-tions, are available to download free from Oxford Archaeology's digital library, http://library.thehuman-journey.net/909. Where the reports have been referenced in the monograph, the authors of the reports are identi-

Table 1.1: Chronology of the archaeological periods referenced in this volume

Broad period	Detailed period	Date range
Post-Roman		
	Second World War	1939-1945
	Modern	AD 1800-Present
	Post-medieval	AD 1500-1799
	Medieval	AD 1066-1499
	Late Saxon	AD 850-1066
	Middle Saxon	AD 650-850
	Early Saxon	AD 410-650
Roman		
	Late Roman (phase LR2)	AD 250-410
	Later Roman (phase LR1)	AD 200-410
	Middle Roman	AD 120-250
	Early Roman	AD 43-120
Late prehistoric		
	Late Iron Age	100 BC-AD 43
	Middle Iron Age	400-100 BC
	Early Iron Age	700-400 BC
Early prehistoric		
	Late Bronze Age	1100-700 BC
	Middle Bronze Age	1500-1100 BC
	Early Bronze Age	2400-1500 BC
	Later Neolithic	3000-2400 BC
	Earlier Neolithic	4000-3000 BC
	Mesolithic	8500-4000 BC
	Early Post-Glacial	10000-8500 BC
Palaeolithic		
	Late Glacial (Late Upper Palaeolithic)	15,000-10,000 BP
	Upper Palaeolithic	30,000-10,000 BP
	Middle Palaeolithic	150,000-30,000 BP
	Lower Palaeolithic	500,000-150,000 BP

fied (for example, Biddulph and Stansbie, specialist report 2), and readers are invited to consult the digital volume for detailed information. In cases where a feature or aspect of the site is identified largely by the environmental or artefactual evidence, such as the probable early Roman boathouse or the late Roman cess-pit 1249, larger extracts from the specialist reports have been included. The extracts are given as stand-alone sections and are attributed to the report author. Readers are still invited to consult the digital report for further information.

The phasing scheme and chronological terms used in the monograph are given in Table 1.1.

THE ARCHIVE

The complete project archive has been prepared in accordance with current professional practice (Walker 1990; Brown 2007; IfA nd). The archive, including the finds, will be deposited with Thurrock Museum in accordance with their guidelines (site code: COMPA09).

Chapter 2

Landscape evolution from the late Glacial to the post-medieval period

by Elizabeth Stafford and Rebecca Nicholson

INTRODUCTION

This chapter will primarily discuss the results of the geoarchaeological and palaeoenvironmental analysis from Stanford Wharf Nature Reserve, although evidence from the main London Gateway port site to the east and the wider region will be referenced where appropriate. The focus is on the natural environment, how the landscape evolved, the factors driving change, and the rate at which this occurred, as well as the influence this may have had on the nature of activities carried out at the site. The geomorphological background outlined in Chapter 1 provides the general context and the contribution of the site to current regional models will be reviewed at the end of the chapter. The following sections integrate data from both field investigations and a wide range of specialist laboratory analyses, the detailed reports of which may be found in the digital archive.

STRATEGIES AND METHODS

Geoarchaeological desk-based and field investigations

At the inception of the project it was recognized that the estuary location of the site, with the potential for significant depths of Holocene sediments, required a focused geoarchaeological approach. This was particularly important during the early stages of investigation when a range of techniques was integrated into the evaluation strategy in order to predict more accurately the location of areas of higher archaeological potential. Traditional desk-based assessment included the use of geological (Figs 1.4 and 1.5) and historical maps (eg Figs 7.14 and 7.15) as well as geotechnical data, LiDAR (Fig. 1.10) and aerial imagery (Figs 1.12 and 1.13), which were incorporated into a project GIS. This was followed by an initial programme of purposive gradiometer (Fig. 1.9) and electrical resistivity survey, ground truthed by hand augering (Figs 2.1 and 2.2; Carey and Dean 2009), While the gradiometer survey was intended to map cultural features lying at shallow depths (*c* 1.0m) across the site, the electrical resistivity survey, comprising two roughly north-south transects (Transects 1 and 2), was designed to characterize broadly the more deeply buried sub-surface stratigraphy. In particular the survey aimed to trace the interface between Pleistocene gravels and the overlying Holocene alluvium and to map the profile of a large east-west palaeochannel indicated on the LiDAR and aerial imagery. The combined results of the desk-based assessment, geophysical surveys and augering allowed for the development of a preliminary deposit model. Four broad geomorphological zones were identified across the site, each with differing archaeological potential, providing a basis for targeted evaluation trenching and later open area excavation (Areas A-D, Fig. 2.2; see also Chapter 1 and *Geomorphological zones* below).

Throughout the field investigations a dual approach to the recording of the sediment sequences was adopted. A standard archaeological recording system was used in addition to detailed geoarchaeological recording of the key alluvial units or 'facies' which were assigned a unique set of numbers (prefixed by the letter G, see *Summary of stratigraphic architecture* below). The recording strategy was supervised by the project geoarchaeologist (Dr Chris Carey, then at OA) and in order to integrate the archaeological and geoarchaeological records, the 'G' numbers were noted on context records and matrices where relevant. This is an appropriate response to complex stratigraphies containing both anthropogenic signatures and natural processes in alluvial environments. Adoption of a context-only recording strategy was considered inappropriate because of four key weaknesses commonly encountered in archaeological recording strategies:

1) the lack of separation of pre-depositional, depositional and post-depositional attributes during context recording

2) a lack of clear criteria by which man-made stratigraphies can be separated from natural stratigraphies

3) limited recording of sedimentological structures on site at a within-context and between-context scale

4) limited separation of descriptive and interpretative terminologies

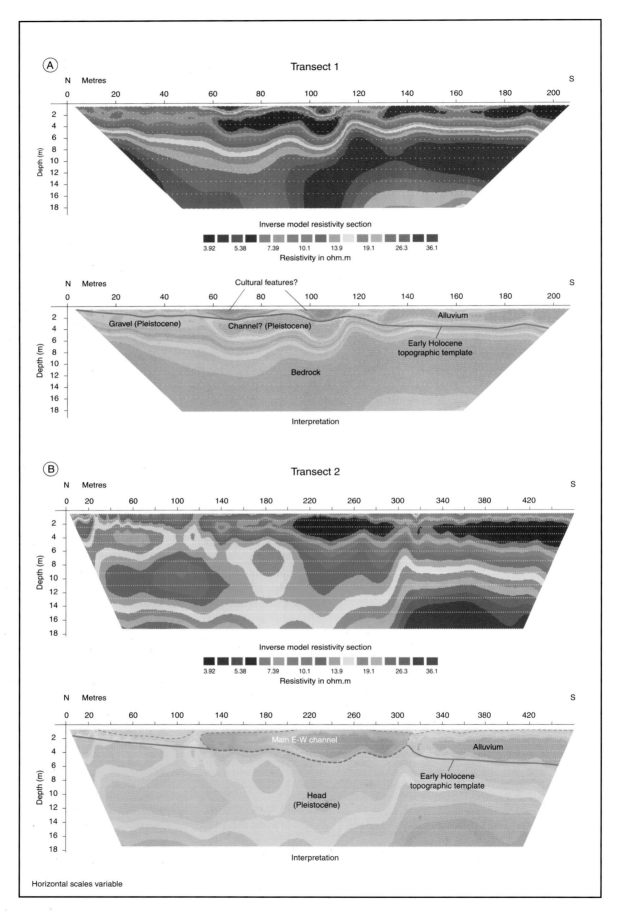

Figure 2.1 Resistivity profiles

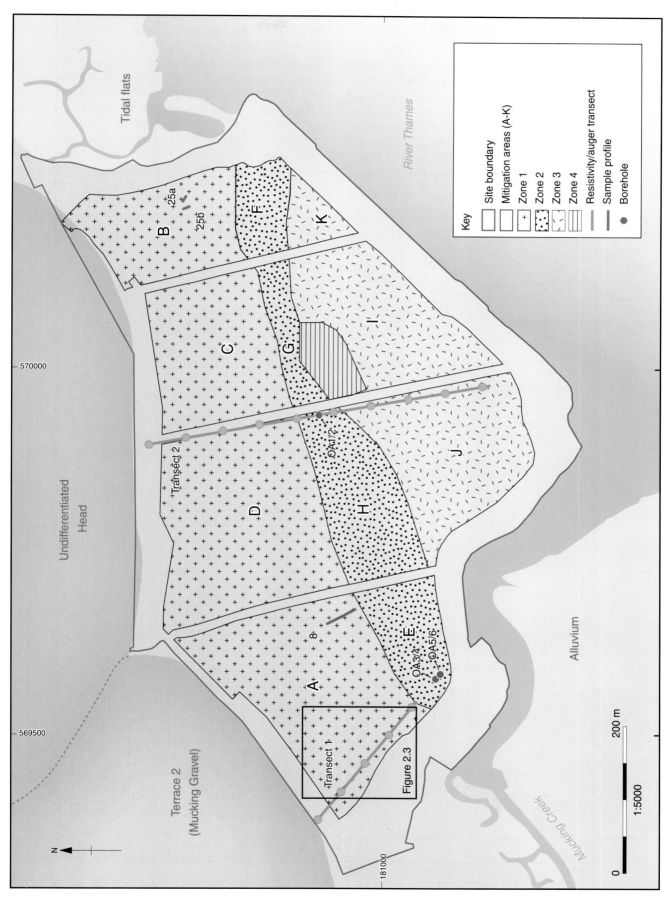

Figure 2.2 General plan of geology (BGS), geomorphological zones, areas of investigation and key sample profiles

Sampling strategies

During the excavation stages systematic sampling across vertical and lateral sequences was undertaken at a number of locations across the site. The strategy was devised to sample a wide area including alluvial sediment sequences positioned away from the main areas of activity, not just areas of interest or 'problem' deposits. Key issues for sampling included the evolution of the coastal landscape and vegetation from the early prehistoric to Romano-British periods, the utilisation of the coastal resource and the sources and types of fuels used in the salt extraction process in the Iron Age and Roman periods.

Undisturbed monolith samples from 38 profiles were recovered for sediment analysis (micromorphology and chemistry) and the recovery of microfossils (eg ostracods, foraminifera, diatoms and pollen). These were taken through the red hill deposits, industrial features such as tanks and hearths, floors, ditches, pits and the palaeosols and alluvial deposits representing all major sediment units across the site. Certain features such as the ditches associated with saltern 9501 were sampled in multiple interventions to allow for spatial analysis of the sediments if deemed appropriate after assessment. Bulk samples of 10-40 litres were also recovered for macroscopic remains (eg plant remains, insects and fauna). Table 2.1 summarises the total numbers of samples recovered from each of the

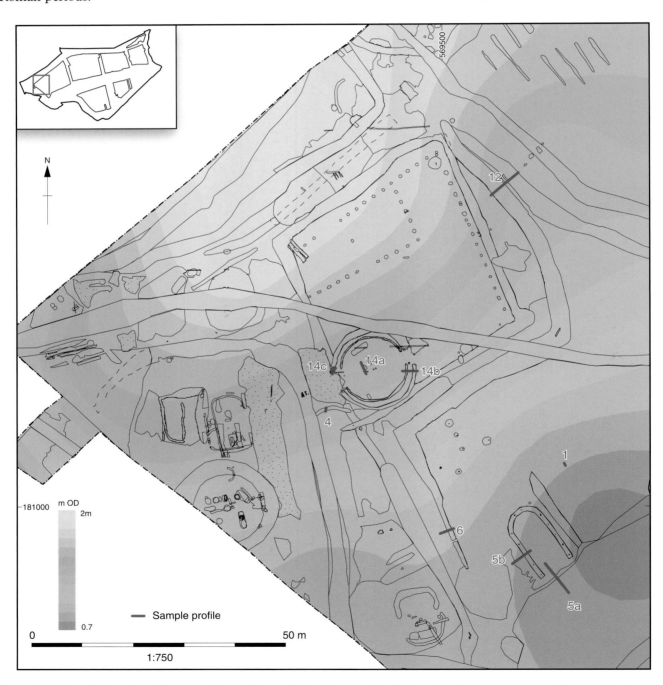

Figure 2.3 Area A, location of key sample profiles and elevation model of the early Holocene topographic template in relation to recorded archaeological features

Table 2.1: Quantification of samples by area

Area	No. monoliths	No. bulk samples	Totals
A	100	288	388
B	21	38	59
C	5	4	9
D	5	17	22
Totals	131	347	478

excavation areas. Where deposits appeared to have potential for the recovery of anaerobically preserved material, 20 litre bulk samples were taken primarily for the recovery of waterlogged plant remains and insects, with additional sediment collected if charred remains, shell or bone were also present. Samples from red hill and other dry deposits were 40 litres in volume wherever possible, although the thickness of deposits within excavated features and test pits dictated smaller sample size in a number of cases. Outside the excavation areas, undisturbed sediment cores from six boreholes (OA1-OA6) through the fills of the main east-west palaeochannel were also retrieved.

Post-excavation laboratory analysis

A range of materials was examined during the assessment stages from a representative series of deposits. This provided preliminary information on preservation levels, environments of deposition, and changes in hydrology, local and regional vegetation patterns. The results and recommendations from the individual specialist assessments were incorporated into the post-excavation project design and were considered in terms of the site-wide research objectives. From the original 38 sample profiles 10 were chosen for further laboratory analysis with reference to the alluvial sequences (Figs 2.2 and 2.3; Table 2.2), the majority deriving from the intensive excavations carried out in Area A. The post-excavation analysis was coordinated by Dr Chris Carey.

Scientific dating

Radiocarbon dating
A series of samples was submitted for radiocarbon dating from key lithostratigraphic units, the number limited by

Table 2.2: Summary of analysed alluvial sequences

Profile	Area	Sequence description	C14 dating	OSL dating	Chem-istry	Micro-morphology	Diatoms	Pollen	Ostracods and forams
1	A	Roman occupation soils and prehistoric palaeosol (G4) separated by alluvial deposit (G5b), above the early Holocene sand (G3)	•	•	•	•		•	•
4	A	Prehistoric palaeosol (G4) above the early Holocene sand (G3)	•						
5	A	Alluvial sequence (G5a/b/c) with prehistoric peat deposit (G39)		•				•	
6	A	Roman occupation deposits separated by alluvium		•	•			•	
8	A	Alluvial sequence (G5a/b/c) with prehistoric peat deposit (G39)	•	•	•	•	•	•	•
12	A	Outer Roman enclosure ditches				•	•	•	•
14	A	Roman roundhouse outer ditch and underlying alluvium (G5b)		•	•	•	•	•	•
25	B	Salt making debris and alluvium		•	•	•	•	•	
OA3	E	East-west palaeochannel fills	•	•			•	•	•
OA5	E	East-west palaeochannel fills	•						

Table 2.3: Summary of key sediment units

Unit	Description	'G' no.	Archaeological period
Pleistocene			
Terrace Gravel	Sandy gravel	-	Middle to Upper Palaeolithic
Head	Orangey brown silty clay	G18	
Brickearth	Light greyish yellow silty clay with a trace of sand	G42	
Sand	Yellowish grey silty sand	G3	Late Palaeolithic to Early postglacial
Early Holocene topographic template			
Palaeosol	Grey to brown sandy silt, locally clayey	G4	Mesolithic to Bronze Age
Holocene alluvial stack			
Lower alluvium	Bluish grey silty clay	G5(a)	Mesolithic to late Bronze Age
Organic alluvium	Black to dark brown peaty clay	G39	Late Bronze Age
Middle alluvium	Bluish grey silty clay	G5(b)	Late Bronze Age and Iron Age
Upper alluvium	Bluish grey silty clay grading to orangey brown	G5(c)	Roman and post-Roman

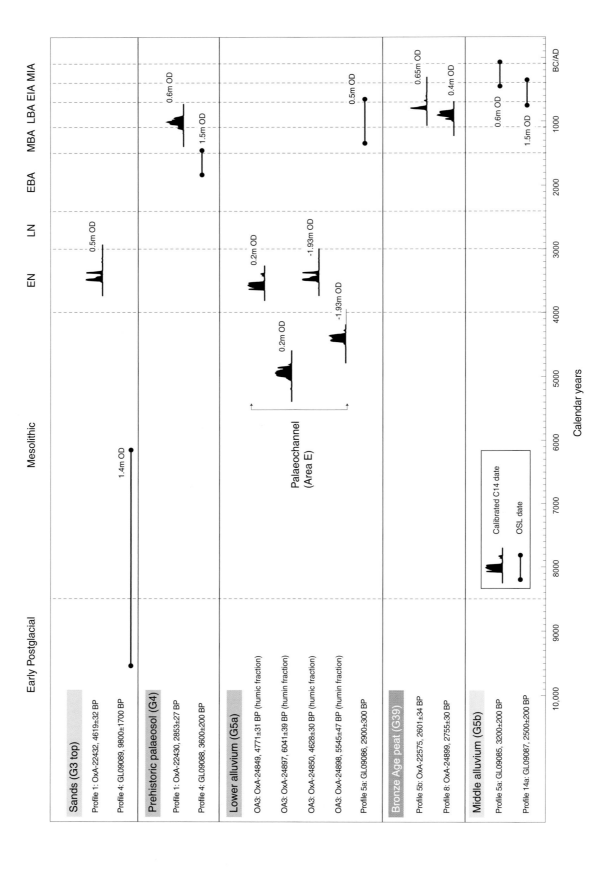

Figure 2.4 Summary of the scientific dating results from soils and alluvial sediments

Table 2.4: Radiocarbon dating of key sediment units

No.	Area	Sample profile	'G' no.	Sample no.	Context no.	Material	Lab code	δ13C (‰)	C14 Age BP	Calibrated date (2σ, OxCal v.4.17)	Period
2	A	1	G3 (top)	1073	1145	Charcoal	OxA-22432	-24.8	4619 ± 32	3520-3340BC (95.4%)	EN
4	A	1	G4	1052	1077	Twigs (indet.)	OxA-22430	-24.9	2853 ± 27	1120-920BC (95.4%)	LBA
6	E	OA3	G5a	3.68m bgl	-	humin	OxA-24897	-25.91	6041 ± 39	5050-4830BC (94.5%)	LMeso-EN
7	E	OA3	G5a	3.68m bgl	-	humic	OxA-24849	-26.21	4771 ± 31	3650-3510BC (92.4%) 3410-3380BC (3.0%)	EN
8	E	OA3	G5a	1.55m bgl	-	humin	OxA-24898	-25.95	5545 ± 47	4490-4320BC (94.5%)	LMeso-EN
9	E	OA3	G5a	1.55m bgl	-	humic	OxA-24850	-25.8	4628 ± 30	3520-3350BC (95.5%)	EN
11	A	5b	G39	1268	5845	Waterlogged seeds	OxA-22575	-26.3	2601 ± 34	840-750BC (89.1%) 690-660BC (4.9%)	LBA-EIA
12	A	8	G39	1125	1915	Mixed seeds	OxA-24899	-26.67	2755 ± 30	620-590BC (1.3%) 980-820BC (95.4%)	LBA

Table 2.5: OSL dating of key sediment units

No.	Area	Sample profile	'G' no.	Sample no.	Context no.	Lab code	Age (years) BP	Date range	Period
1	E	OA5	-	-	4-4.3m bgl	GL09091	329,000 ± 36,000	Pleistocene	Palaeolithic
3	A	4	G3 (top)	1389	6195	GL09089	9800 ± 1700	9490-6090BC	EPG-Meso
5	A	4	G4	1388	6196	GL09088	3600 ± 200	1790-1390BC	EMBA
10	A	5a	G5 (a) /G22	1386	5982	GL09086	2900 ± 300	1190-590BC	LBA-EIA
13	A	5a	G5 (b)	1385	5980	GL09085	2200 ± 200	390-10BC	MLIA
14	A	14a	G5 (b)	1387	6001	GL09087	2500 ± 200	690-290BC	EMIA

availability of suitable material. Where possible, short-lived macrofossils from secure contexts were selected (Table 2.4). These included 12 samples of waterlogged wood, charred and waterlogged seeds together with two paired sediment dates (humic and humin fraction) from borehole OABH3, where plant macrofossils were not present in sufficient quantities to date. During the post-excavation assessment, four of these samples were submitted to the Scottish Universities Environmental Research Centre (lab. code SUERC (GU)) in East Kilbride, Scotland for Accelerator Mass Spectrometry (AMS) dating. The remaining eight samples, which relate to the Holocene sediment sequences, were dated by Oxford Radiocarbon Accelerator Unit (ORAU) (lab. code OxA). The radiocarbon results are quoted in accordance with the international standard known as the Trondheim convention (Stuiver and Kra 1986). They are conventional radiocarbon ages (Stuiver and Polach 1977). All dates from samples submitted from this project have been calibrated using datasets published by Reimer et al. (2004) and the computer program OxCal (v4.17) (Bronk Ramsey 1995; 1998; 2001) (Table 2.4), with the end points rounded outwards in the form recommended by Mook (1986). In the text the calibrated age estimates are quoted, with the radiocarbon years in parentheses. The calibrated date ranges cited in the text are those for 95.4% (2σ) confidence.

As discussed by Howard et al. (2009) the variability that can result from analysing different parts of the carbon fraction (humic and humin) and different types of remains (plant macrofossils) from sediments taken from fluvial environments (lacustrine, bogs and mires) is well known, but there is still some debate regarding which is the most significant. Results obtained by Howard et al. (ibid.) from organic sequences taken from organic rich sediments deposited by freshwater channels, suggested that in general the humin and humic acid fraction dating results were statistically consistent. The sediments from borehole OA3 were alluvial in origin, with a significant brackish component and no identifiable plant remains. These are therefore particularly difficult deposits to date with any degree of certainty, and this should be borne in mind. The decision to date both the acid insoluble/alkali soluble (humic acid) and alkali/acid insoluble (humin) fractions of the samples was taken to provide some indication of the degree of uncertainty. In the case of these paired sediment samples, the results

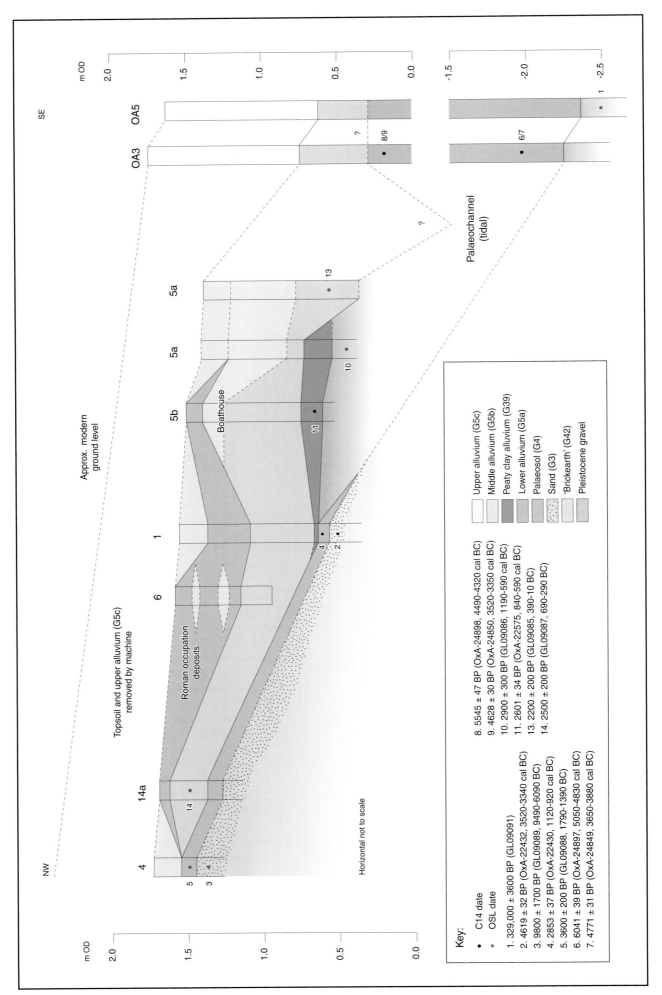

Figure 2.5 Stratigraphic correlation of key sample sequences (NW-SE) across Area A

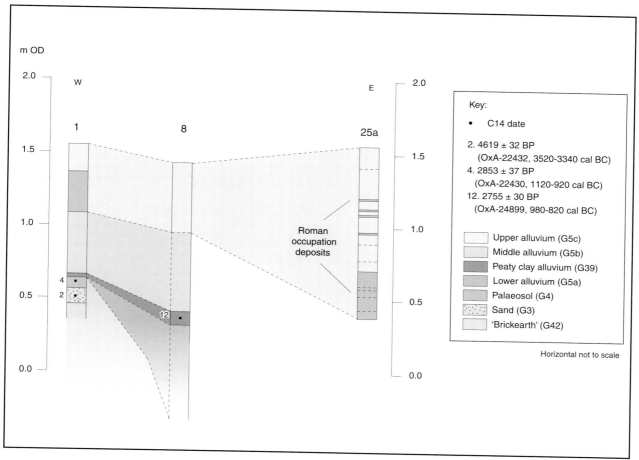

Figure 2.6 Stratigraphic correlation of key sample profiles (W-E) across Areas A and B

from the humic and humin fractions differed by some 1000 years, but both series of dates were at least in the correct stratigraphic order. In both cases the humin fraction gave the older (late Mesolithic to early Neolithic) date while the humic fraction, representing the more mobile fraction and therefore potentially the less reliable in this type of deposit, dated to the middle Neolithic in both cases (Table 2.4; Fig. 2.4).

Optically stimulated luminescence dating
Seven samples from the sediments were collected for optically stimulated luminescence dating (OSL) and processed by Dr Philip Toms at the University of Gloucester. These were retrieved where it was thought unlikely that deposits could be securely dated by artefact or radiocarbon dating. Five conventional sediment samples (GL09085-GL09089) – those located within matrix-supported units composed predominantly of sand and silt – were collected within opaque plastic tubing (150 x 45mm) forced into section faces. Each tube was wrapped in cellophane and parcel tape in order to preserve moisture content and integrity until ready for laboratory preparation. A further two conventional sediment samples, one hosted within a monolith (GL09090) and one from borehole core OABH5 (GL09091), were later submitted to the laboratory. The ages reported are years before the date of reporting (2010) and the errors are based on analytical

uncertainty and quoted at 1σ (Table 2.5). Full details can be found in the digital archive.

GEOMORPHOLOGICAL ZONES

The preliminary geoarchaeological assessment of the site produced clear definition of the depth and spatial distribution of the Holocene sediment sequence (Carey and Dean 2009). The various data sets showed a large degree of correlation in the results from the different surveys, and in identifying major geomorphic features across the site. On this basis the site was divided into four distinct geomorphic zones (Fig. 2.2) summarised below.

Zone 1
This zone (Areas A-D) is dominated by Pleistocene terrace deposits to the north-west (Terrace 2; Taplow/Mucking Gravel) and to the east of these by undifferentiated Head deposits. The surface of these deposits lies at relatively high elevations, but slopes gently from north to south. The depth of the overlying Holocene alluvium is between *c* 1-2m, deepening southward. This zone is located at the edge of the floodplain and the higher terrace which outcrops to the north and for much of the Holocene has lain above the area of marine influence. The whole of Zone 1 was considered to have high potential for the preservation of

archaeological remains. This was reflected in the gradiometer plots which suggested the presence of well-defined archaeological features throughout, and confirmed during the later evaluation trenching.

Zone 2

This zone (Areas E-H) is defined by the presence of a large palaeochannel aligned WSW to ENE. The resistivity survey clearly defined this palaeochannel (Transect 2), with the gradiometer survey showing it to traverse the whole of the site. The depth of the palaeochannel was shown to reach up to *c* 5-6m, with the fills dominated by fine-grained silty clay sediments preserved in waterlogged conditions.

Zone 3

Zone 3 (Areas I-K) incorporated the swathe of ground south of the palaeochannel (Zone 2). Here the resistivity survey demonstrated that the surface of the Pleistocene deposits lies at much lower elevations and is overlain by significant thickness (*c* 6-7m) of Holocene intertidal sediments The gradiometer survey identified little in the way of structural archaeology in this zone, except some remains liable to be associated with the Second World War activity and with inter-tidal creeks.

Zone 4

This zone was identified as an area of raised topography located within Zone 2, and was interpreted as a localised island standing marginally proud of the surrounding floodplain. This area was tentatively defined as having high potential to contain geoarchaeological resources.

SEDIMENTARY SEQUENCES AND ENVIRONMENTS OF DEPOSITION

Summary of stratigraphic architecture

During the evaluation stages 28 sediment units (G1-G28) were initially recorded. Further exposure of the alluvial sequences during the detailed excavations

reduced these to nine key groups (Table 2.3). Age estimates for each unit have been achieved through a combination of archaeological stratigraphy and scientific dating (Tables 2.4 and 2.5; Fig. 2.4). Figures 2.5 and 2.6 illustrate correlation of key sample profiles across the site area. As the construction impact of the scheme generally comprised *c* 0.5m ground reduction across the site, exposure of more deeply buried horizons was limited to a smaller number of discrete interventions.

Pre-Holocene deposits and basement topography

Pleistocene terrace deposits (Terrace 2, Mucking Gravel Formation), formed during MIS (marine isotope stage) 8 to MIS 6 (300,000-130,000 BP), currently outcrop above the (reclaimed) floodplain, to the north-west of the site, at a height of *c* 5m OD (Fig. 2.2). These deposits, dominated by sand and gravel units, are typically associated with high-energy rapid sedimentation in braided channels during Pleistocene cold climate episodes. However, fine–grained fossiliferous interglacial deposits (MIS 7) are known to occur within this formation, recognised at sites at Aveley, Ilford, West Thurrock, Crayford and Northfleet (see Bridgland 1994). The resistivity survey (Transect 1, Fig. 2.1a) demonstrated that in the north-western part of the site (Area A) the surface of the Pleistocene gravels lies at a depth of *c* 1-2m, becoming more deeply buried southwards at *c* 4m below ground level. An OSL sample of the top of a sand and gravel unit at the base of borehole OA5 at 4.0-4.3m depth (-2.39m to -2.69m OD, Area E) produced a date of 329,000 ± 36ka BP (GL09091) which is broadly consistent with the Lower Mucking Gravel (MIS 8; Fig. 2.5). Overlying the gravels in the western part of the site a fine-grained 'brickearth' type deposit was noted (G42). The age of formation of this deposit is unclear and it may represent either an inter-glacial deposit (MIS stages 7 or 5) or a silt deposit formed in the Devensian (MIS 2). 'Brickearth' is a polygenetic term, representing a number of deposits that are difficult to date based on visual inspection.

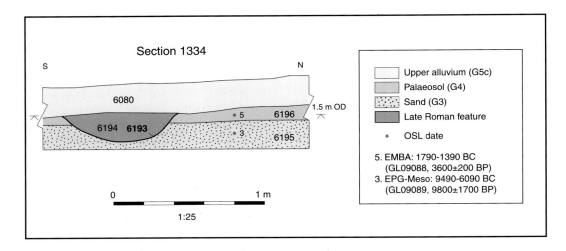

Figure 2.7 Sample profile 4

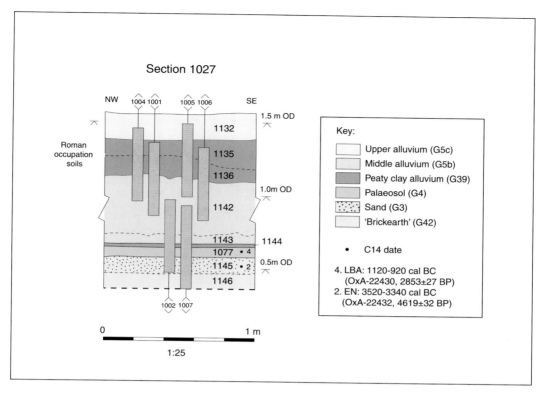

Figure 2.8 Sample profile I

Superficially similar deposits derive from a number of Pleistocene stages. The sediment stratigraphy as exposed during excavation gave no further indication of its date. There is some indication that this deposit was being actively quarried during the Roman period: it is likely that the large quantities of briquetage salt-making vessels and equipment recovered were made on site using locally extracted Brickearth.

In the central and western parts of the site the Pleistocene stratigraphy is dominated by Head deposits, which outcrop at the surface immediately to the north of the site (Fig. 2.2). This is illustrated in resistivity Transect 2 (Fig. 2.1b) in which Head deposits lie at depths of *c* 1-5m below the surface north-south.

A major palaeochannel (Zone 2, Areas E-H), identified during the preliminary geoarchaeological assessment, dissects the site on a broadly WSW-ENE orientation. The channel measured a maximum of *c* 120m in width and 5-6m in depth. Although the predominantly minerogenic silty clay fills produced Holocene radiocarbon dates, it is possible that the channel has its origins in the Pleistocene.

The early Holocene sands and prehistoric palaeosol (G3 and G4)

Above the brickearth lay a light grey to yellow silty sand deposit, with localised clay pockets (G3). The upper surface appeared weathered, described as a 'dirty' grey to brown sandy silt, and was interpreted in the field as the remnants of a prehistoric palaeosol or landsurface (G4). This sequence of deposits was largely exposed in

the northern part of Area A where artefactual material from the upper 0.1m of the silty sand palaeosol comprised quantities of Neolithic and Bronze Age worked flint (see Chapter 3)

Figure 2.9 Photograph of sand (G3) overlain by palaeosol (G4) in sample profile I

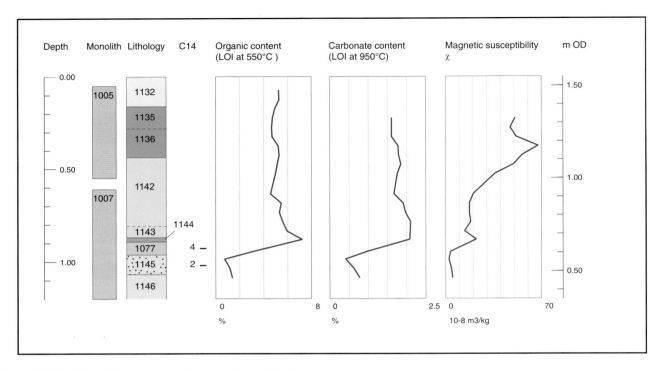

Figure 2.10 Bulk sediment properties, sample profile 1

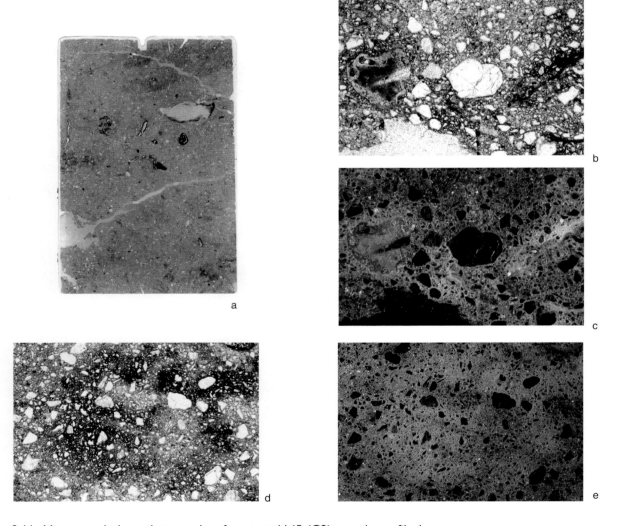

Figure 2.11 Micromorphology photographs of context 1145 (G3), sample profile 1

Unfortunately an OSL date on the sediment from the upper part of the silty sand (G3) in sample profile 4 (Fig. 2.7) produced a very wide range of 9800 ± 1700 BP (GL09089, 9550-6150 BC). A radiocarbon determination on charcoal from sample profile 1 (Fig. 2.8) produced an even later date of 4619 ± 32 BP (OxA-22432, 3520-3340 cal. BC). Given the fact that the samples were taken where the sand was relatively thin the sediment is likely to have been much affected by bioturbation and soil forming processes. Dates from the overlying horizon (G4) suggest that the landsurface was extant, prior to major alluvial inundation, up until the latter part of the Bronze Age. An OSL date from sample profile 4 produced a date of 3600 ± 200 BP (GL09088, 1850-1450 BC) and a radiocarbon date of 2853 ± 27 (OxA-22430, 1120-920 cal. BC) was returned from sample location 1.

Palaeoenvironmental assessment indicated that microfossils were poorly preserved in both G3 and G4. In sample profile 1 bulk sediment analysis of the silty sand (G3; context 1145, Fig. 2.10) demonstrated that it was almost entirely minerogenic (LOI: 0.74–1.38%) with a very low carbonate content (0.41–0.77%). The exceptionally low X values suggest either that this part of the sequence has been significantly affected by a loss of iron through gleying, or, more likely, is derived from a different (less iron-rich) parent material than deposits further up the sample profile (Macphail et al., specialist report 24).

Thin section analysis (Macphail et al., specialist report 24) revealed unit G3 (context 1145) to be a moderately poorly sorted fine sandy silt loam, with a few small flint gravel clasts (Fig. 2.11). Two burned flint grains (rubefied, max 650µm) and rare wood charcoal (max 1.5mm) were also present. The sediment was generally iron-depleted and characterised by many textural intercalations associated with matrix void infills and thin pale clay void coatings. Relict iron-stained, once-humic broad burrows occurred in the matrix. Occasional iron-stained root traces (and void hypocoatings) and other burrows also occurred. The deposit is probably the remnants of a lower topsoil of a Holocene palaeosol with occupation traces. In the main, the soil lost structure when it was slaked by later inundation, hence the textural intercalations and associated pedofeatures, and current massive structure (cf The Stumble

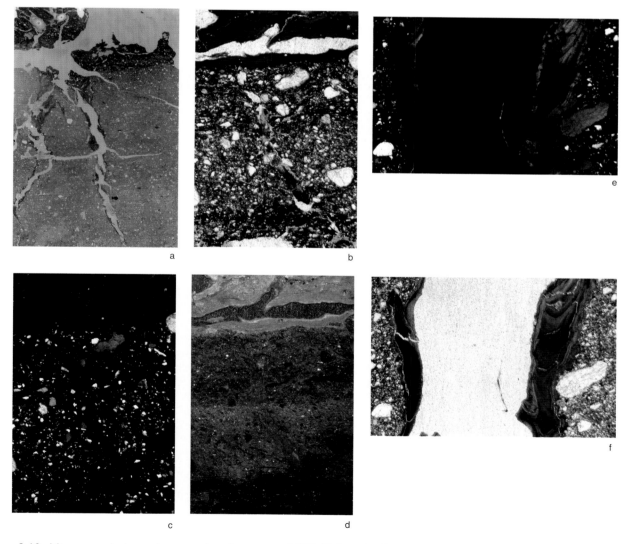

Figure 2.12 Micromorphology photographs of contexts 1077 (G4) to 1143 (G5b), sample profile 1

and other River Crouch and Blackwater sites in Essex: Macphail 1994; 2009; Macphail *et al.* 2008; 2010; Wilkinson and Murphy 1995; Wilkinson *et al.* 2012).

Unit G4 overlying (context 1077) was a partially slaked and partially intact occupation topsoil (Ah). It is the remnants of the palaeosol, with locally slaked topsoil forming a massive soil with muddy pans (slurries). Later (alluvial) clay inwash is recorded. There were large areas both of 1) very fine charcoal-rich weakly humic fine sandy silt loam and patches of poorly humic soil (burrow mixed), and 2) homogeneous fine sandy silt loam as massive non-porous soil with sloping matrix pans as part of the intercalatory fabric (Fig. 2.12). Rare flint gravel and wood charcoal (max. 1.5mm) occur in the former (1). Vertical fissures were characterised by microlaminated coatings of brown clays and dusty clay, rich in very fine charred and detrital organic matter.

The alluvial sequence (G5a-c and G39)

Lower alluvium (G5a, early prehistoric)

The first of several homogeneous alluvial blocks, given the general number of G5 (minerogenic alluvium) formed the main fill of the Zone 2 palaeochannel (Area E, OA3 and OA5), extending northwards into the southern part of Area A (Fig. 2.5). The alluvium generally comprised a bluish grey silty clay with a trace of sand. Four radiocarbon dates on humic and humin fractions of the sediment in borehole OA3, towards the base of the palaeochannel at -1.93m OD, and the top of the sampled sequence at 0.2m OD have proved difficult to interpret (see *Scientific dating* above), but date deposition from the late Mesolithic to early Bronze Age (Fig. 2.4; Table 2.4). In sample profile 5a in the southern part of Area A an OSL date for the top of the G5a produced a late Bronze Age-early Iron Age date of 2900 ±300 BP (GL09086; 1250-650 BC).

Bulk sediment analysis was carried out on samples taken at 0.05m intervals through the alluvial deposits in borehole OA3 (Fig. 2.13; Macphail *et al.*, specialist report 24). In appearance the sediment appeared fairly uniform in character: grey, highly minerogenic and fine-textured, with only rare traces of possible charcoal in two of the samples. The analytical data for these sequences appear to confirm these observations, with none of the properties measured displaying particularly wide variability (organic carbon, 5.12–8.38%; carbonate, 4.19–6.51%; and X, 11.9–26.2 x 10^8 m^3 kg^1). The samples with the higher LOI values are the ones most likely to be associated with hiatuses in sediment accumulation. Carbonates were present throughout the sequence, with the high values all occurring towards the bottom. One somewhat higher X value (26.2 x 10^8 m^3 kg^1) at the top of OA3 could possibly be indicative of a period of hiatus and exposure as the sediments accumulated, especially as it coincides with a relatively high organic carbon. Otherwise, the X data display very little variability and would appear to provide little evidence of any changes in environmental conditions during sedimentary accretion.

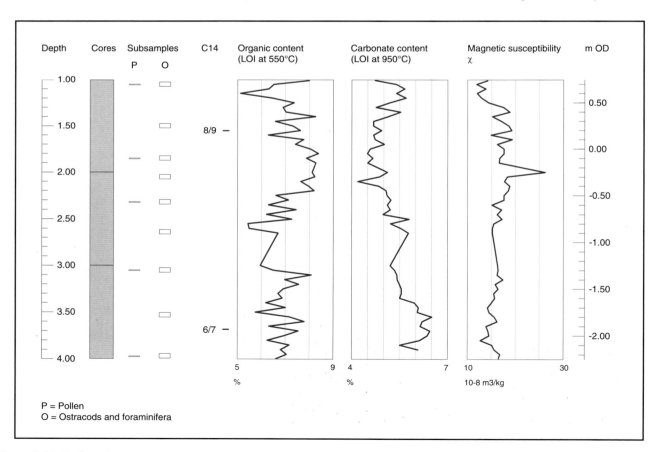

Figure 2.13 Bulk sediment properties, borehole OA3

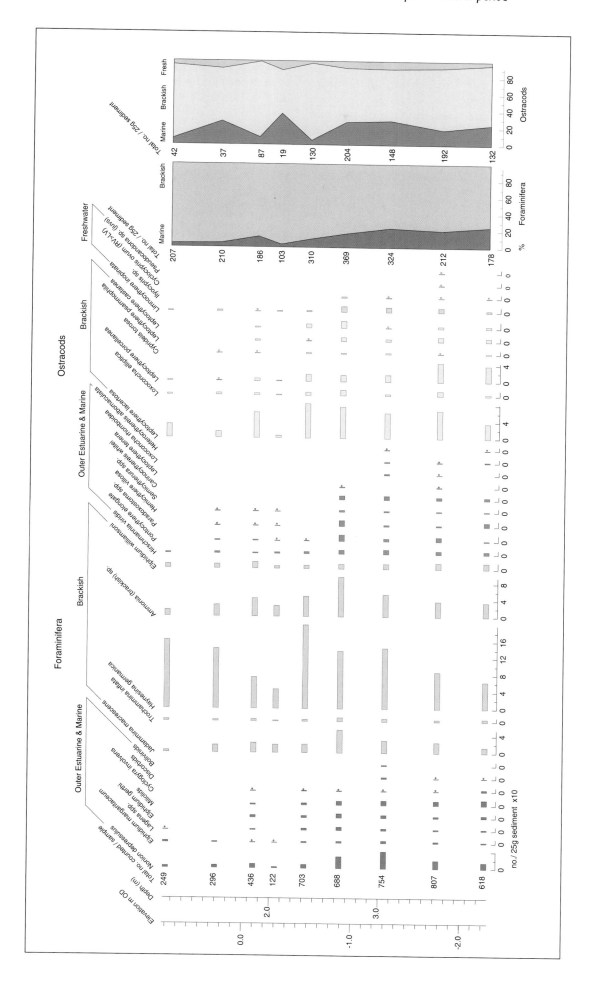

Figure 2.14 Ostracods and foraminifera from borehole OA3

Nine samples were analysed from borehole OA3 for ostracods and foraminifera (Fig. 2.14; Whittaker, specialist report 22). Two species of mid-high salt marsh foraminifera occur throughout; *Jadammina macrescens* was the commonest, with *Trochammina inflata* in lower abundance. Foraminifera of low-mid salt marsh and tidal flats comprised three species; *Haynesina germanica* was the commonest, increasing in numbers upwards. The brackish species of *Ammonia* varied whereas *Elphidium williamsoni* was the least common. Of the ostracods indicative of brackish mudflats, two species of *Leptocythere* dominate the assemblage, *L lacertosa* and *L porcellanea* being the commonest, the former particularly so. This evidence, in association with the other species found, indicates that tidal mudflats prevailed throughout in the proximity of the channel, rather than giving any indication of the formation of a protected creek, as the would-be key species of the latter, *Cyprideis torosa*, was always extremely rare. The sequence for OA3 provides the best evidence at Stanford Wharf of marine influence during the earlier prehistoric period. All the samples contain foraminifera and ostracods that are essentially marine or can penetrate outer estuaries. Most are quite small and probably have been washed in, in suspension with the spring tides or by tidal surges (eg the foraminifer *Nonion depressulus* which can appear in quite large numbers). Many of the benthonic ostracods (eg *Pontocythere elongata* and *Hemicythere villosa*) are also only represented by small juveniles and

again appear to be washed in. Others within this component are phytal species which are associated with marine algae (eg the ostracod *Paradoxostoma*), or cling to seaweeds and sea-grasses (eg the miliolids). It would be generally true to say that this marine component is strongest in the lower part of the borehole, diminishing especially near the top. This may give an indication that the channel was more prominent initially and perhaps more prone to tidal surges. Over time, it gradually silted up, with the dominance of the adjacent mudflats becoming more apparent. The freshwater component of the palaeochannel was surprisingly low throughout and the channel does not represent the course of even a small river. Only a few species of non-marine ostracods are found, the only one of any significance being *Limnocythere inopinata,* which usually inhabits coastal ditches, and therefore may have been washed out by an overtopping Spring tide. In conclusion, the palaeochannel was surrounded by extensive tidal mudflats backed by salt marsh. Initially, it was prone to strong tidal influences and surges bringing in the outer estuarine/marine component. One such catastrophic event may have formed the channel in the first place. This influence diminished over time, probably as a result of silting. Any freshwater component was always at a minimum.

The pollen assemblages from borehole OA3 were very similar throughout (see *Vegetation* below) suggesting the presence of mixed deciduous woodland on the higher drier ground with areas of grassland/

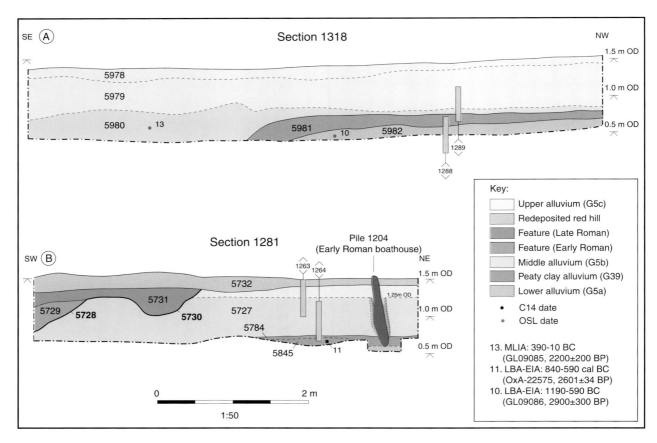

Figure 2.15 Sample profile 5

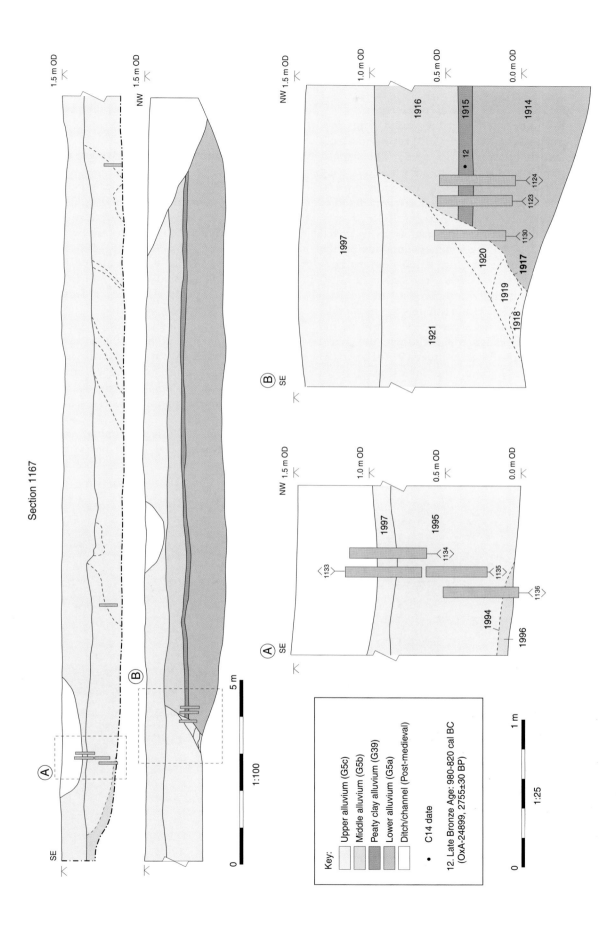

Figure 2.16 Sample profile 8

pasture and heathland. There was little evidence in the pollen assemblages for salt marsh in the local area in the lower levels, but there was increasing evidence for salt marsh encroaching in the upper levels with the goosefoot family (Chenopodiaceae) and sea plantain (*Plantago maritima*).

Peaty clay alluvium (G39, late Bronze Age)

Post-dating this minerogenic wedge was a thin dark brown to black peaty clay deposit (G39) recorded across the southern extent of Area A (Fig. 2.5). The deposit was dated in sample profile 5b (Fig. 2.15) to 2601 ± 34 BP (OxA-22575, 840-590 cal. BC). A broadly equivalent deposit in sample profile 8 (Fig. 2.16) was dated to 2755 ± 30 BP (OxA-24899, 980-820 cal. BC).

In places this deposit appeared significantly mixed and eroded (Fig. 2.17). Bulk sediment analysis on the deposit in sample profile 5a (Fig. 2.18) demonstrates peaks in organic content (11.9%), carbonate (2.62%) and X (16.3 x 10^8 m^3 kg^1) compared to the alluvial deposits above and below. Unfortunately no ostracods, foraminifera or diatoms were recorded in any of the sample sequences investigated. Although the plant remains from sample profile 8 (context 1915; Fig. 2.16) indicate a freshwater habitat, the insect assemblage suggests that salt marsh also existed close by (see *Vegetation* below).

In sample profile 1 (Fig. 2.8) the deposit was very thin and directly overlay the palaeosol (G4). Here thin section analysis revealed the deposit to be a brown, moderately humic loamy clay, a muddy mixture of clayey alluvium

and slaked topsoil. The pollen assemblage suggested that deciduous woodland was present on the higher drier ground with perhaps some fringing freshwater alder and willow carr. Open grassland areas, however, were present and pollen of the goosefoot family together with thrift and/or sea lavender (*Armeria/Limonium*) and sea plantain (*Plantago maritima*), similar to the evidence from sample profile 8, suggests that some lower salt marsh was present in the area (see *Vegetation* below).

Middle alluvium (G5b, late Bronze Age and Iron Age)

The alluvium (G5b) above the peaty clay was deposited across the topographic gradient (Fig. 2.5). OSL dating suggests that deposition occurred during the Iron Age. In sample profile 5a (Fig. 2.15) context 5980 was dated to 2200 ± 200 BP (GL09085, 450-50 BC) and in sample profile 14a (Fig. 2.19) context 6001 was dated to 2500 ± 200 BP (GL09087, 750-350 BC). At the latter location the alluvium also seals a feature containing middle Iron Age pottery (6013).

Bulk sediment analysis on sample profile 1 (Figs. 2.8 and 2.10) demonstrated higher X values than the lower alluvium analysed in borehole OA3 (max. 49.6 x 10^8 m^3 kg^1), which could possibly be indicative of low levels of enhancement likely to be associated with natural ripening/pedogenic processes (Macphail *et al.*, specialist report 24).

Thin section analysis (Macphail *et al.*, specialist report 24) revealed the lower part of G5b (context 1143) to consist initially of very charcoal-rich silty to

Figure 2.17 Photograph of peaty clay (G39) in sample profile 5a

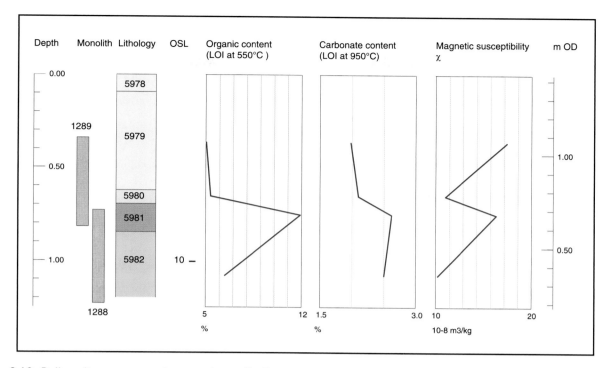

Figure 2.18 Bulk sediment properties, sample profile 5a

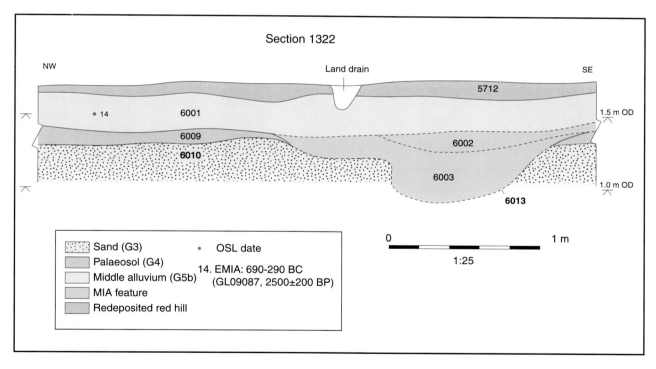

Figure 2.19 Sample profile 14a

fine sandy laminae (Fig. 2.12) which included fine root channels and 'brown clay' which was also found as thick void coatings in fissures down-profile (perhaps evidence of periodic drying). This is followed by deposition of humic clay laminae which included clasts of humic and charcoal-rich fine sediment ('rip up' clasts). The overlying deposit, context 1142, was composed of broad burrow mixed dark brownish silty clay sediment, with relict laminae, and anthropogenic deposits. The latter were dominated by fused siliceous material rich in

phytoliths, and charred and rubefied monocotyledonous plant fragments (Fig. 2.20), in addition to very abundant charcoal, white nodules of melted siliceous material/'straw' and briquetage fragments. This context represents a major spread of probable salt-making fuel ash waste onto alluvium, with biota coarsely mixing this into the sediment.

Context 1142 contained a poorly preserved mixed assemblage of marine, brackish and freshwater diatom species (Cameron, specialist report 26). It is notable

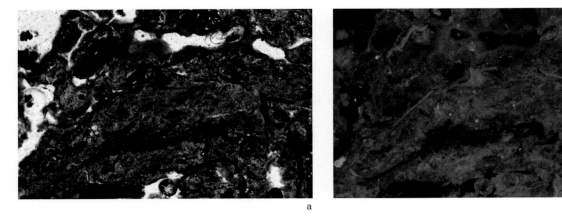

a   b

Figure 2.20 Micromorphology photographs of context 1143 (G5b), sample profile 1

that aerophilous diatoms were present, such as the freshwater *Pinnularia major* and *Hantzschia amphioxys*, along with the halophile *Navicula mutica*. Aerophilous diatom species are tolerant of desiccation and are able to grow in habitats that are subject to drying out for prolonged periods (Johansen 1999). They may originate from within the water body, for example on the bank or bottom of a water body that has occasionally dried out. Alternatively, they may be introduced with eroded material including soil (Lund 1945; 1946). A better preserved diatom assemblage (Cameron, specialist report 21) was analysed from context 1916 in sample profile 8 (Fig. 2.21). Marine and brackish water diatoms were present; however, the aerophilous halophile *Navicula cincta* comprised almost 70% of the assemblage, again indicating a high shore habitat subject to long periods of drying out.

Upper alluvium (G5c, Roman and later)

The upper alluvium (G5c) dates to the period of Roman occupation and later (Fig. 2.5). It is largely defined as the body of sediment sealing Roman occupation deposits but also includes discrete silting units within Roman features and alluvium intercalated thinly between occupation horizons.

Sample profile 6 in Area A included a complex series of Roman occupations horizons intercalated with naturally deposited alluvium (Fig. 2.22). Thin section analysis (Macphail *et al.,* specialist report 24) revealed that the occupation deposits were largely composed of briquetage debris and fused phytolith-rich fuel ash waste. These deposits formed exterior space trampled and mesofauna-worked accumulating spreads. They are interdigitated with marine alluvium showing that they were still located in the intertidal zone. Foraminifera were

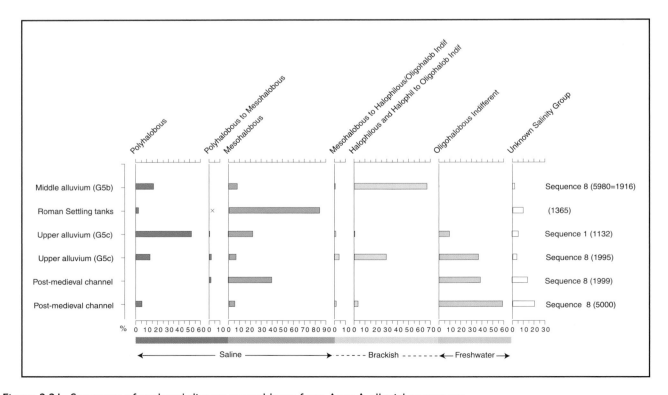

Figure 2.21 Summary of analysed diatom assemblages from Area A alluvial sequences

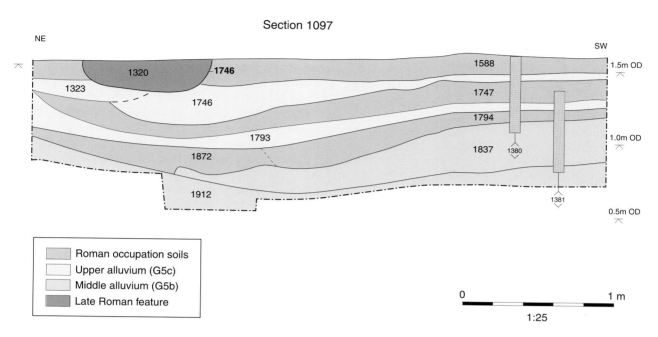

Figure 2.22 Sample profile 6

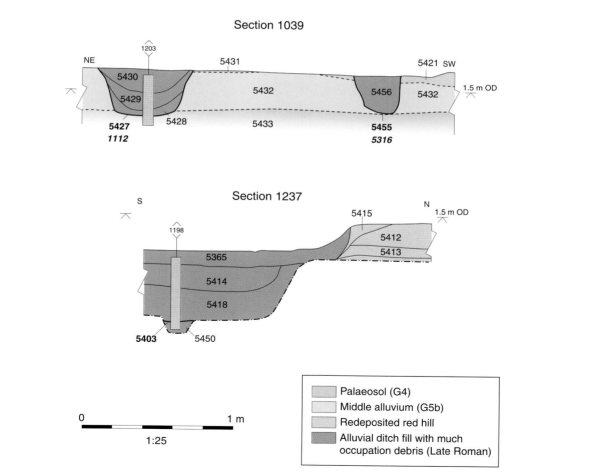

Figure 2.23 Sample profiles 14b and 14c

only found in the alluvium (context 1837) immediately below the occupation deposits (Whittaker, specialist report 26). Here there were two agglutinating species present (*Trochammina inflata* and *Jadammina macrescens*), both being epifaunal and infaunal down to 0.6m; they are herbivores and detrivores, living exclusively on mid-high salt marsh (Murray 2006). Diatoms, although poorly preserved in this sample profile, do provide some information (Cameron, specialist report 26). Generally assemblages from the alluvial deposits comprised a mixture of brackish water, marine, halophilous and freshwater diatoms. In context 1793, for example, the marine planktonic diatoms *Paralia sulcata* and *Actinoptychus undulatus* were present with the brackish water planktonic species *Cyclotella striata*. Benthic mesohalobous diatoms included *Diploneis interrupta* and *Navicula navicularis*. Freshwater non-plankton com-

prised *Frustulia vulgaris*, the aerophiles *Hantzschia amphioxys* and *Navicula mutica* (also halophilous) and chrysophyte stomatocysts. In alluvial context 1746 the diatoms represent brackish water habitats with benthic taxa such as *Nitzschia navicularis*, *Scoliopleura tumida* and *Diploneis interrupta*, and the brackish water planktonic diatom *Cyclotella striata*. The pollen assemblages (Peglar, specialist report 23) provide evidence for local salt marsh throughout the profile, with pollen of the goosefoot family dominating in an open environment.

Thin section analysis of the fills of the outer ditch of saltern 9501 in Area A (Fig. 2.23, sample profiles 14b and 14c), dated to the late Roman period, demonstrated that the feature was cut into estuarine clay (G4b). The fills of the ditch were water lain; a basal layer included laminated byre waste, indicating animal management, and debris of burned hearth and kitchen (eg fish bone)

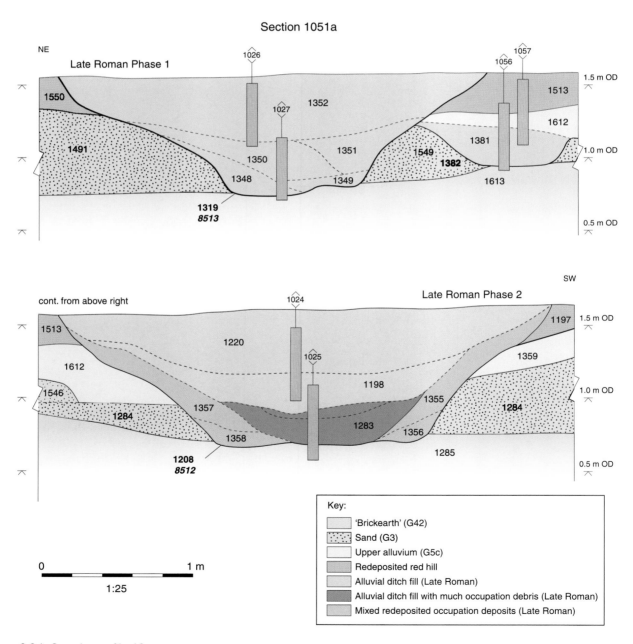

Figure 2.24 Sample profile 12

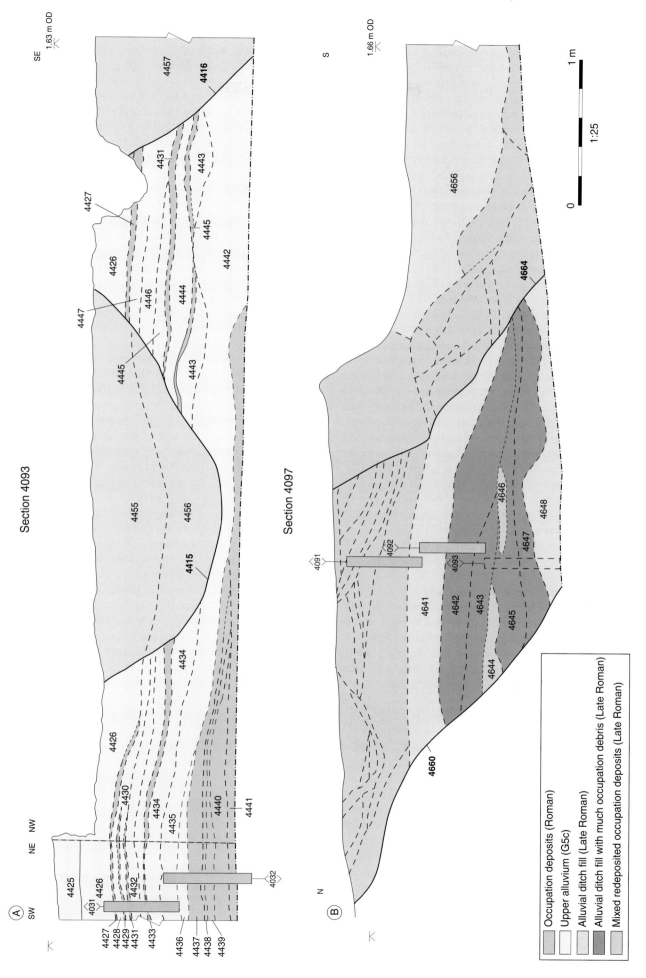

Figure 2.25 Sample profiles 25a and 25b

origin. Here, and in the inner ditch, where natural alluviation predominates, human cess and coprolitic waste again indicate domestic occupation. The fills contained brackish salt marsh agglutinating foraminifera, and brackish water diatoms, although it is not clear whether these are *in situ* or introduced from occupation activities (Cameron, specialist report 21; Whittaker, specialist report 22). Pollen from the basal ditch fill 5418 included significant amounts of pollen from wheat (*Triticum* sp.), probably reflecting the deposition of cereal waste into the feature. While pollen from cereals and wild grasses can be very similar, in this case the grains are much larger than any wild grass pollen (Andersen 1979). Quite high values for salt marsh taxa are evidence of the existence of some local salt marsh (Peglar, specialist report 23).

The late Roman trackway ditch 8513 in Area A contained alluvial deposits (sample profile 12, Fig. 2.24). Samples from the earliest fill (1381) and alluvial deposit 1612, along with the lower fills of the late Roman phase 2 ditch 8512 (contexts 1283 and 1198) produced good faunas of agglutinating foraminifera indicative of mid-high salt marsh. Fill 1198 also contained a calcareous foraminifer (*Haynesina germanica*) indicative of low-mid salt marsh and tidal mud (Whittaker, specialist report 22). Foraminifera were absent from the upper ditch fills (contexts 1352 and 1220). Diatoms were poorly preserved in this sample sequence but do indicate estuarine conditions, with perhaps a greater input of open water and coastal planktonic species in context 1198 (Cameron, specialist report 21). The pollen assemblages again indicated the presence of salt marsh quite close by (Peglar, specialist report 23).

Similar deposits were recorded to the east in Area B dated to the Roman period. Sample profiles 25a and 25b recorded a complex sequence of occupation deposits with intercalated alluvium, cut by the main late Roman channel, 8536/8540 (Fig. 2.25). In the lower fills of intervention 4660 (contexts 4647 and 4648), across the southern part of the channel, foraminifera and ostracod evidence attest to a brackish mid-high salt marsh interspersed with or fronted by tidal mudflat, giving way to tidal mudflat alone in context 4645.

The final sequence from the upper alluvium derives from sample profile 8, cut by a post-medieval ditch or channel (Fig. 2.16a). Alluvial contexts 1996 and 1995 contained abundant foraminifera and ostracods, indicative of tidal mudflats and creeks, backed by salt marsh. Context 1997 was rich in brackish foraminifera. The fauna contained many specimens of *Trochammina inflata* and *Jadammina macrescens*, both species being herbivores and detrivores, typical of mid-high salt marsh. They are also joined by two other agglutinating foraminifera species – *Tiphotrocha comprimata* and *Miliammina fusca* – again detrivores. The occurrence of two calcareous foraminifera (*Haynesina germanica* and a brackish species of *Ammonia*), in association, attests to the presence either of mudflats fronting the salt marsh or creeks within the salt marsh (Whittaker, specialist report 22). The diatoms from context 1997 were also consistent with a fully tidal estuarine environment. In contrast the fills of the post-medieval ditch or channel, for which percentage diatom analysis was carried out, indicated high shore marginal habitats subject to relatively infrequent estuarine flooding. The latter sedimentary environment appears to have been affected by drying out of the habitat resulting in the preferential preservation of robust diatoms and the occurrence of aerophilous taxa (Fig. 2.21; Cameron specialist report 21).

VEGETATION

Evidence from pollen and plant macrofossils has been used to examine changes in the vegetational environment resulting from environmental change and human factors. While the waterlogged plant macrofossils provide evidence for the vegetation at the sampling location, pollen can provide an indication not only of the local vegetation growing on the saltmarsh, but also of vegetation growing on the nearby dry land and further away in the catchment area of the site, although distinguishing between the last two sources of pollen can be difficult. Charred macrofossils have provided evidence for the human use of local and more distant resources.

When interpreting the pollen assemblages, a range of taphonomic factors have to be considered, including the amount of pollen produced by different kinds of plants and the variable potential of pollen grains from different plants to disperse. In addition, some types of pollen grains have tougher walls and so survive better than others, a factor also true for seeds. Although the model is complex and subject to many factors, generally pollen from lime (*Tilia*), elm (*Ulmus*), beech (*Fagus*) and ash (*Fraximus*) is likely to be found fairly close to the point of production, while pollen from pine (*Pinus*), hazel (*Corylus*) and birch (*Betula*) is likely to be more widely dispersed. Alder produces relatively large amounts of pollen compared with other trees (Moore and Webb 1978, 109-111). As discussed by Peglar (specialist report 23), interpreting pollen assemblages from alluvial deposits is particularly problematic, since the pollen and spores in these aquatic sediments may have originated from inwash into the river Thames from anywhere within its catchment area, or from the sea. This may result, in particular, in the over-representation of coniferous pollen (including pine and spruce) which have airsacs allowing the pollen to float. Some reworking of sediments, with their associated pollen, may also have occurred.

Early prehistoric

Woodland and heathland

Pollen preservation was very poor in early prehistoric palaeosol G3 (context 1145, Fig. 2.8) and the lower part of overlying unit G4 (context 1077). A radiocarbon sample from 1077 gave a very late middle-late Bronze Age date for material from within this part of the

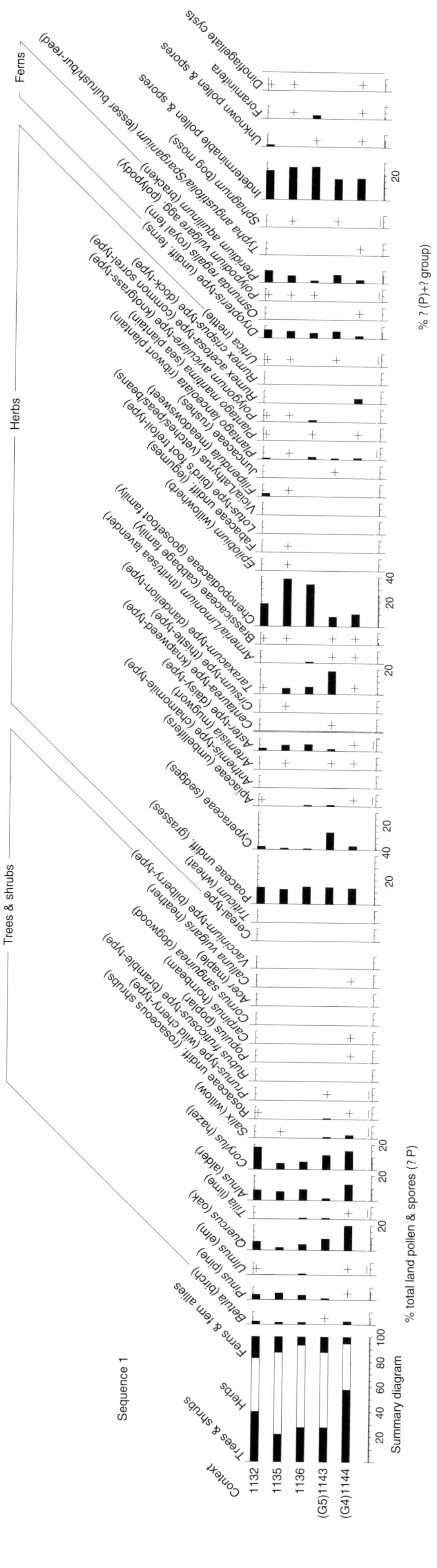

Figure 2.26 Pollen assemblages from sample profile 1

palaeosol (see above), but the presence of both Neolithic and Bronze Age worked flint illustrates the mixed nature of material within this layer (see above and Chapter 3).

Based on the radiocarbon dates (see above) the earliest pollen sequence from the site came from Mesolithic-Neolithic alluvial deposits (G5a) within borehole OA3, the fills of the main east-west palaeochannel (Fig. 2.5). Five samples were analysed, from depths of 3.97m, 3.05m, 2.32m, 1.85m and 1.05m (see Fig. 2.13). Bearing in mind the caveats above, the pollen evidence allows some suggestions to be made as to the local and more regional vegetation types present when the sediments were laid down.

Similar pollen assemblages occur in all five samples from OA3, dominated by tree and shrub pollen including oak, hazel, alder, elm and lime with birch and pine also present. Since elm and lime produce little pollen compared with oak and hazel, even though the values here are relatively low they are still high enough to indicate that these taxa were a significant component of the deciduous woodland growing on drier land probably in the vicinity of the site at the time (Peglar, specialist report 23). Elm pollen values dropped dramatically all over northern Europe at about 5000 BP, probably as a result of disease aided by human interference in the woodland (Peglar 1993). At the adjacent port site a radiocarbon date of 5104 ± 53 BP (Wk-19953; 3990-3770 cal. BC at 94.1%) was obtained from a horizon some 40mm below the point where lime effectively disappeared from the pollen record (Bates *et al.* 2003), and so from a purely palynological point of view the sequence from OA3 is probably older than this. Heathland seems also to have been present locally; small amounts of heather (*Calluna vulgaris*) pollen are present throughout the sampled sequence (Fig. 2.26; Peglar, specialist report 23).

Tidal flats, salt marsh and grassland

Microfossils from the alluvial unit G5a sampled in borehole OA3 provide evidence for tidal mudflats prevailing within and in the vicinity of the large channel. Following the development of tidal mudflat, long-rooted salt tolerant plants such as glasswort or samphire (*Salicornia* sp.) and eel grass (*Zoster marina*) and cordgrass (*Spartina* sp.) would have begun to colonise, gradually followed by plants such as sea aster, sea lavender and sea plantain as the surface stabilised and soil fertility improved (Fig. 2.27). Samples from OA3 included pollen from many herbs including grasses and taxa which may be associated with grassland/pasture located some distance away, but there is little evidence in the pollen from the lower samples for the presence of salt marsh, although evidence from the foraminifera and ostracods indicates clear marine influence in the channel (see above). There is, however, increasing evidence for salt marsh encroaching in the upper two samples (1.85m and 1.05m below ground level) with pollen from the goosefoot family (Chenopodiaceae) increasing and sea plantain (*Plantago maritima*) also present.

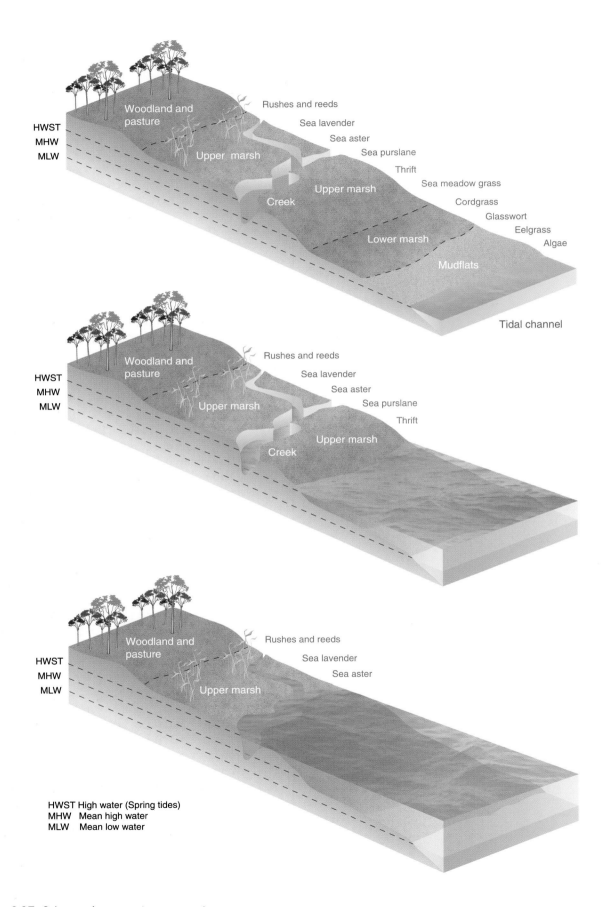

Figure 2.27 Salt marsh vegetation succession

Arable agriculture?

It is notable that although pollen grains from some wild grasses found in wetland locations are morphologically very similar to those from cereals (Behre 2007), in borehole OA3 two pollen grains from the sample taken at 2.32m depth have been identified as of wheat type (*Triticum* sp.*)* and are much larger than any wild grass pollen (Andersen 1979; Peglar, specialist report 26).This is, tentatively, the earliest evidence for any cereal agriculture at or close to the site, although of course the material in the alluvial sediments may have come from a relatively wide catchment area. The earliest deposits from the site to provide any preserved plant macrofossils are those from the early Holocene silty sand (G3). While pollen from this deposit was assessed as 'uncountable' (Peglar, specialist report 26) and plant remains were not well preserved either, a few charred cereal remains were recovered from contexts 1672 and 1909 but may be intrusive from the layer above (Hunter, specialist report 19). A radiocarbon date from charcoal on the silty sand (G3) gave an early Neolithic date of 3520-3340 cal. BC (4619 ± 32 BP: OxA-22432), but this date represents only one event for a surface which is likely to have been exposed and utilised for a considerable length of time (see above).

Later prehistoric

Generally in the Lower Thames, the Bronze Age is characterised by deforestation on higher ground, together with a significant expansion of wetlands (see for example Stafford *et al.* 2012). It is likely that beyond the salt marsh, freshwater and brackish pools and patches of cleared grassland existed alongside alder and fen carr, with deciduous woodland persisting on the drier land of the terrace edge.

Most of the evidence for vegetation during the later prehistoric period comes from pollen and plant remains recovered from sediment unit G39, a thin peaty, organic clay located across the southern part of Site A and dated to the late Bronze Age. In places this deposit appeared significantly mixed and eroded (see above) and this has to be borne in mind when considering the microfossil and macrofossil assemblages. Some parts of the peat were clearly leached: an attempt to date organic sediment from context 1144 failed due to insufficient carbon (ORADS ref. P27309).

Woodland

As reported by Peglar (specialist report 23), pollen from later Bronze Age context 1144 (G39) in sample profile 1 is dominated by tree and shrub pollen (nearly 60% of total pollen (TP)), particularly oak and hazel, with birch, pine, elm and lime, consistent with the presence of woodland along a dryland terrace edge (Fig. 2.26). Other trees and shrubs represented include alder and willow, trees of wet soils such as are found today along river banks and in fens and marshes. This assemblage therefore generally suggests that there was mixed

deciduous woodland growing on drier soils nearby at this time, perhaps with some fringing alder and willow carr. The very low elm value here suggests that the sediments are of post elm-decline age, and the scarcity of lime pollen, which is very robust and easily identified even when corroded (Peglar 2008) is also consistent with a post-lime decline date (that is, after the mid/late Bronze Age).

Alluvial deposit 1143 (G5b, Fig. 2.8) overlying 1144 included relatively low levels of oak, hazel and alder pollen, suggesting a depletion in local woodland consistent with the expansion of brackish conditions below the terrace edge (Fig. 2.26, Peglar, specialist report 23). The charcoal evidence, although limited, also suggests that woodland dominated by oak, hazel and alder was available on drier land nearby through at least the middle Iron Age to later Roman periods (Druce, specialist report 20), while small amounts of willow, lime and wild cherry-type (*Prunus*) pollen recorded in deposit 1143 likewise indicate the presence of these trees in the later prehistoric period. Yew (*Taxus*) is completely absent from the pollen profiles at the site but a piece of yew (probably driftwood) was found in alluvium during the Northern Triangle evaluation (OA 2008) and was radiocarbon dated to the early Bronze Age (OxA-19948, 3713 ± 36 BP). Elsewhere in the Lower Thames yew woodland colonised the peatland in the later Neolithic and early Bronze Age, forming a plant community that has no known modern analogue in the UK (see below).

Wetland expansion

Pollen from silty clay 1144 (G39) included taxa indicative of grassland or waste ground such as common sorrel-type (*Rumex acetosa*-type), daisy-type (*Aster*-type), umbellifers (Apiaceae), ribwort plantain (*Plantago lanceolata*) and dandelion-type (*Taraxacum*-type). That lower and higher salt marsh was present nearby is suggested by pollen from the goosefoot family which includes that of glasswort (*Salicornia*) and oraches (*Atriplex*) species (spp.), together with odd grains of thrift and/or sea lavender (*Armeria/Limonium*) and sea plantain (*Plantago maritima*), as well as a few, probably reworked, remains of dinoflagellate cysts and foraminifera (Peglar, specialist report 23).

In sample profile 8 the immature leached organic clay context 1915 (G39, Fig. 2.16) has been directly radiocarbon dated to the late Bronze Age at 980-820 cal. BC (OxA-24899, 2755 ± 30 BP). Plant remains within this horizon included partially humified monocotyledonous leaf and stem fragments together with a few seeds from weeds of wet places, including water crowfoots (*Ranunculus* subgen *Batrachium*), watermint (*Mentha aquatica*), sedges (Cyperaceae) and common spike rush (*Eleocharis palustris*), all of which indicate a freshwater rather than salt marsh habitat at this location (Hunter, specialist report 19). Insects within context 1915 have been fully reported by Allison (specialist report 18) and, in contrast to the macrofossils, were generally indicative of deposition in a salt marsh environment, with *Bembidion assimile*, which lives among dense vegetation and reeds in wetland and salt marsh, particularly abundant. Also identified were *Ochthebius marinus* and *O ?viridis*, both of which are found in salt marsh with shallow brackish pools, as well as *Bembidion minimum* or *normannum* and *Pogonus chalceus*, both found in salt marsh and under tidal litter (Luff 2007, 97, 103). Other beetles indicative of salt marsh include *Dyschirius salinus* which lives on clay or fine silt/sand banks in coastal locations and *Bembidion varium* which is found on bare ground near water, most frequently in salt marshes in south-east England (Luff 1998, 77). There were also, however, hints of transitional habitats to marsh or fen with possibly fresher water, for example with the occurrence of *Ochthebius dilatatus* which in Britain tends to occur in muddy, fresh or brackish, mainly stagnant water. *Cyphon* also indicated shallow standing water with abundant waterside vegetation or litter, and fen-like conditions were also suggested by two other water beetles, *Coelostoma orbiculare* and *Cymbiodyta marginellus*. Another common beetle, *Pterostichus vernalis*, prefers damp or shaded lowland habitats, especially grassland with litter (Luff 1998, 93; 2007, 115). The dung beetle group made up 4% of the terrestrial assemblage (21% of the decomposer group), suggesting that if there were animals grazing drier parts of the marsh or grassland they were present in fairly low densities or at some distance from the point of sampling (Allison, specialist report 18).

Waterlogged seeds from context 5845 in sample profile 5 (G39, Fig. 2.15b) have also been dated to the late Bronze Age/early Iron Age at 840-750 cal. BC (89.1%) (OxA-22575, 2601 ± 34 BP). Dried out, previously waterlogged remains from this peaty deposit located at the base of the Roman sequence included common seeds from club-rush (*Bolboschoenus* sp./ *Schoenoplectus* spp.) and a seed of celery leaved crowfoot (*Ranunculus scleratus*) (W Smith, specialist report 26), the former typical of alluvial soils in both brackish and freshwater habitats and the latter found on damp, nutrient-rich mud, including grazed salt marshes with shallow fresh water. Again, these are very likely to represent plants actually growing at this location. Pollen from an equivalent context (5981, Fig. 2.15a) was well preserved and dominated by herbs. Grass (Poaceae) accounted for 38% of the assemblage and this, together with many other pollen types from plants associated with grassland and pasture, indicates the presence of open, probably grazed, areas nearby, while high values for sedges (Cyperaceae) suggest an expansion of wetland, with lesser bulrush/bur-reed (*Typha angustifolia/ Sparganium*) also present, indicating areas of standing water. Tree and shrub pollen was very sparse, and this may indicate widespread woodland clearance by this time, although it should be noted that an expansion of coastal wetland could account for the decrease in arboreal pollen, something argued for some early-middle Bronze Age sites along the Thames Estuary (Waller and Grant 2012). There is, however, very little evidence in

this pollen assemblage of salt marsh occurring locally, or of any marine influence, although generally the Lower Thames at this period is characterised by sea level rise and the expansion of brackish conditions (Bates and Whittaker 2004). Two grains of cereal-type pollen were also found in context 5981 but as this type also includes several wild grasses (Andersen 1979) the evidence cannot be used to infer that cereal cultivation was taking place nearby. Above G39, alluvial deposit 1143 (G5b, Fig. 2.8), dated by OSL to the later prehistoric period,

a

|— 2 mm —| b

Figure 2.28 A. Sea thrift *(Armeria maritima)* (photo: Ballookey Klugeypop), B. Seeds of thrift recovered from archaeological deposits at Stanford Wharf

also produced a pollen assemblage dominated by plants characteristic of grassland, possibly pasture, together with plants characteristic of marshes and fen; pollen from sedges and rushes almost certainly derives from plants growing close by, on the alluvium (Fig. 2.26). Sea levels were rising at this time, and this part of the site would probably have been inundated periodically, forming a landscape of grassland, brackish mudflats and wetter zones colonised by sedges and rushes where freshwater from the terrace ran into the estuary. The plant macrofossils from this horizon include a significant number of charred seeds from rush, sea lavender (*Limonium* sp.) and sea plantain, as well as a few sedge (*Carex* spp.) nutlets, suggesting the burning of vegetation collected from the saltmarsh (Hunter, specialist report 19).

Salt making
Assemblages dating to the middle Iron Age came from deposits associated with salt making, mainly in the north-western corner of Area A. Consequently pollen was poorly preserved or absent and plant macrofossils comprised charred remains only, with leaf/stem and seed heads from salt marsh plants identified in earlier deposits present, including rushes, sea plantain and thrift. These suggest the harvesting and burning of local salt marsh vegetation to fuel the salt-making process (Hunter, specialist report 19) (Fig. 2.28). That cereals, particularly spelt wheat but also emmer wheat, barley and oats, were being grown in the vicinity of the site is suggested by the consistent but relatively low-level presence of cereal grain and chaff across the site in the Iron Age and the Roman phases, although these may represent straw and other cereal waste imported for fodder, bedding, thatch and possibly fuel.

Roman

During the Iron Age and Roman periods the saltmarsh was occupied and utilised, but the archaeological evidence suggests a hiatus in activity between the middle Iron Age and early Roman periods.

Woodland and heathland
Evidence from charcoal and pollen suggests that the composition of the nearby woodland had changed little between the later prehistoric and late Roman times, with deciduous woodland dominated by oak, hazel and alder with occasional sloe/blackthorn and/or wild cherry, willow/poplar, birch, field maple and ash. Given that the site straddles the interface between the intertidal zone and the higher river terrace deposits, it is possible that areas of both carr and dry woodland existed fairly close by (Druce, specialist report 20). Pollen evidence from the late Roman outer ditch of saltern 9501 in Area A (Fig. 2.23; sample profile 14b) appears to show an increase in deciduous and scrub woodland towards the top of the profile at the expense of arable, which may reflect the gradual abandonment of fields and regrowth of scrubby woodland (Peglar, specialist report 23). This contrasts with earlier Roman evidence from sample profile 6, which shows a gradual decrease in woodland trees and shrubs through time with increasing grasses and other herbs, particularly those characteristic of grasslands and pastures (ibid.).

The presence of heathland, or the importation of heathland resources, is indicated by the occasional pollen grain of heather (*Calluna vulgaris*) and bilberry-type (*Vaccinium*-type) recorded in late Roman alluvial deposit 1793 towards the base of sample profile 6 at the site (Peglar, specialist report 23) as well as by the presence of broom/gorse (Leguminosae) type charcoal in several late Roman deposits. However, it is worth noting that the species included in this type may grow in a fairly wide range of habitats including open woods, rough ground and grassland, and they are also commonly associated with maritime cliffs and heathland (Druce, specialist report 20).

Development and utilisation of the salt marsh
Salt marsh was clearly present in the vicinity of Area B, as demonstrated by the charred plant remains from fills within early Roman ditch 4844 which include abundant charred remains from salt marsh plants including sea lavender, sea plantain, sea-milkwort (*Glaux maritima*) and rush, including seed capsules from sea rush (*Juncus maritimus*) (Hunter, specialist report 19). The pollen from early Roman alluvial deposit 4210 (G5b) included quite a lot of goosefoot-family pollen, probably from nearby salt marsh, but was dominated by grasses and herbs associated with grassland/pasture, with moderate amounts of pollen from trees of deciduous woodland, with oak, hazel and alder represented, along with pine and birch. As mentioned above, the pine pollen may reflect inputs from outside the local area as a result of flooding. Samples from Area A also provided abundant evidence for local salt marsh. Sample profile 6 included abundant pollen of the goosefoot family (which it should be noted includes plants characteristic of arable fields as well as those characteristic of salt marsh) together with a few grains from sea plantain in context 1747, while the pollen assemblages from Roman anthropogenic soil contexts 1136 and 1135 and overlying alluvium 1132 in sample profile 1 (Fig. 2.8) are dominated by goosefoot family (Chenopodiaceae) which is consistent with an open landscape dominated by salt marsh (Fig. 2.26), although it should be noted that not all sources of the pollen are necessarily local. Other plants recorded include sea aster (*Aster tripolium*), thrift (*Armeria maritima*) and/or sea lavender and daisy-type (Peglar, specialist report 23). While an increase in pine pollen may reflect inputs from outside the local area, possibly signifying the tidal nature of the site at this time with input from the sea, an increase in tree and shrub pollen in the overlying late Roman alluvium 1132, together with a decrease in pollen from salt marsh plants, may indicate a lowering of the sea level and reduced marine influence at this time (Peglar, specialist report 23). Plant macrofossils in 1132 included charred seeds from rush (*Juncus* spp.) and

small-sized wild grasses together with anaerobically preserved seeds of fumitory (*Fumaria* spp.), hemlock (*Conium maculatum*) and possible water crowfoot, suggesting both the presence and the utilisation of local salt marsh (Smith, specialist report 26). Quite high values of salt marsh taxa also occur in the pollen assemblages from the outer ditch of saltern 9501, particularly in context 5414 (sample profile 14c) (Peglar, specialist report 23) and the presence of salt marsh is also reflected in the large numbers of charred seeds found in later Roman deposits such as tank fill 1331, which includes abundant monocotyledonous stem/leaf fragments, probably from a salt marsh plant (Fig. 6.31, section 1050), as well as over a thousand rush seeds, many sea plantain seeds and capsules and a few seeds from sea lavender, lesser sea spurry, sea milkwort and sea arrow grass (Hunter, specialist report 19), plants typical of middle and upper salt marsh.

Arable agriculture and cereals

A few definite pollen grains of wheat (*Triticum* sp.) were identified in Area B contexts 1747 and 1746 (Fig. 2.22), which suggests that wheat was being grown or processed nearby in the earlier Roman period. In Area A, late Roman context 5418, which represents the organic basal fill in the outer ditch of saltern 9501 (Fig. 2.23, sample profile 14c), has nearly 5% wheat pollen, which is a high value for cereal grains which are heavy and do not travel far (Peglar, specialist report 23). It is likely that by the late Roman period wheat was being grown close by and/or was being processed close to the site and at least some of the waste was being dumped or blown into open features, as also demonstrated by exceptionally well preserved charred cereal remains including complete or near complete ears of spelt with straw recovered from late Roman enclosure ditch 9506 (Hunter, specialist report 19). Spelt can be grown on relatively poor and heavy soils but is intolerant of brackish soils, so would not have been cultivated on the saltmarsh. Here the cereal remains occur together with a few arable weeds, particularly stinking chamomile (*Anthemis cotula*), suggesting cultivation on drier and probably clay rich soils. Elsewhere, cereals were found together with charred seeds from salt marsh plants, but may in this case represent dumps of mixed fuel, some of which may come from plants grown on drier land, although barley can tolerate slightly brackish soils. It has been suggested that hulled barley and flax were cultivated on coastal marshes in the northern Netherlands (Rippon 2000, 94).

Human occupation

High values of dandelion-type pollen and other taxa of waste ground and habitation found in later Roman deposits such as context 5418, at the base of the outer ditch of saltern 9501, come from plants of drier ground. This deposit also included high values for cereal pollen, probably a reflection of the dumped byre material described by Macphail *et al.* (above and specialist report 24). The waterlogged fills of a late

Roman quarry pit 1249 included relatively large numbers of henbane and nettle seeds which probably suggest the presence of an area of middening close by, although henbane originated as a shoreline plant that adapted to colonise and move with human settlement (Hunter, chapter 6 and specialist report 19). This feature appears to have been re-used as a cesspit, as demonstrated not only by the presence of seeds of edible fruits, including possible fig, but also by small crushed and digested fish bones (see below and Hunter and Nicholson, chapter 6 and specialist reports 16 and 19). The fills also contain insects consistent with the presence of foul organic matter within the pit, including bean or seed weevils (Bruchinae) which are often associated with deposits that appear to have contained urine and faeces, where it is presumed they were eaten with infested pulses and subsequently voided in faeces (Allison, chapter 6 and specialist report 18). It is therefore likely that the nettles, at least, grew around this feature which would have been rich in phosphate and nitrogen.

Pollen assemblages recorded from a series of alluvial and probably dumped later Roman deposits in Area B (Fig. 2.25, fills of intervention 4660 across channel 8536/8540) are very difficult to interpret owing to their mixed and varied nature, which is perhaps not surprising given the intertidal location and nature of these deposits. The occurrence of three species of agglutinating foraminifera in context 4641 might actually attest to the onset of tidal conditions at this point in the sequence; all are typical of mid-high salt marsh but appear to be *in situ* (Whittaker, specialist report 22). Most of the samples taken from these fills are dominated by herb pollen, particularly grasses and taxa characteristic of both grassland/pasture, arable fields (including cereal types) and waste ground and waysides. Pollen of taxa of deciduous scrub/woodland are consistently low in all but context 4648, the lowest fill examined within the channel.

Exotics

Several plants introduced during the Roman period or imported from elswhere in the Empire were identified. Walnut (*Juglans regia*), represented by a nutshell fragment in the fill of late Roman pit 1249, is generally considered to be a Roman introduction into Western Europe, with pollen records providing evidence of trees rather than simply the importation of nuts. Records of walnut come from several Roman and post-Roman sites in London, including an early Roman record from the Temple of Mithras (Scaife in Sidell *et al.* 2000). Coriander (*Coriandrum sativum*) seeds were found in the same pit fill; the plant is also a Roman introduction and has been found at a number of Roman sites around London. A possible fig seed (*Ficus carica*) from the same pit would, if indeed from this fruit, probably have been imported; fig seeds in archaeobotanical contexts in Britain are all believed to derive from imported dried fruit (Dickson and Dickson 1996). Stone pine (*Pinus pinea*) produces the pine nuts used in Italian dishes

Figure 2.29 A. Stone pine tree *(Pinus pinea)* (photo: Vicky Padgett), Rome   B. A stone pine cone recovered from a late 1st to 2nd century waterhole at Claydon Pike, Gloucestershire

today. A cone bract from this tree was found in fill 5103 of ditch 8551, in a sample comprising almost pure fish bone (see Chapter 6). Similar examples have been found at a number of Roman sites in London and elsewhere in England, with examples often found in association with religious or public sites (Stevens 2011, 103-4), but it is not clear whether trees were planted in Britain by the Romans, since it is possible that cones were imported (ibid.; Fig. 2.29)

Salt making

The utilisation of salt marsh plants as fuel in the salterns is discussed in Chapters 4-6 and by Hunter (specialist report 19). Analysis of charred plant remains has demonstrated that the salterns were fuelled at least in part by leaf/stem material with seed heads from salt marsh plants harvested nearby. The scarcity of rhizome/root fragments suggests that the plants were not lifted up together with turf or peat; but rather cut, to allow regular cropping. The presence of seed heads of rush, plantain and thrift at various stages of maturity may suggest that the material was harvested throughout the growing season. The fact that charcoal-rich samples come largely from the late Roman features suggests that a shift in fuel use may have taken place at the site, as discussed by Druce (specialist report 20). Much of the oak charcoal appears to be from small roundwood and the alder/hazel and broom/gorse (Leguminosae) also generally consisted of small roundwood or 'rods' less than *c* 10mm in diameter or of up to 6 or 7 growth rings. Given that there is a long tradition of harvesting rods on a seven-year cycle (Rackham 2003), it is quite feasible that this material represents local coppicing and collection of small brushwood specifically to provide fuel for the salt-making industry.

Post-Roman

Post-Roman vegetation is indicated only by pollen recovered from sample profile 8 (Fig. 2.16; contexts 1995 and 1997). These assemblages suggest that mixed deciduous woodland, mainly of oak, hazel and alder, was growing in the area at this time with an understorey including ferns (*Dryopteris*-type and polypody (*Polypodium vulgare* agg.)), with open areas of grassland/pasture. It is interesting that there appears to be a higher representation of deciduous woodland than found earlier, perhaps as a result of abandonment and regrowth (Peglar, specialist report 23). Occasional grains of cereals including those of rye (*Secale cereale*) and oats/wheat-type (*Avena/Triticum*-type) are again present; an indication that these cereals were probably grown on drier land nearby. Several of the recorded taxa may be associated weeds of arable fields, including mugwort (*Artemisia*), daisy-type (*Aster*-type), dandelion-type (*Taraxacum*-type), cabbage family (Brassicaceae), knotgrass-type (*Polygonum aviculare*-type) and goosegrass family (Chenopodiaceae). The last includes taxa characteristic of arable fields as well as those characteristic of salt marsh (Peglar, specialist report 23). There is also some evidence of salt marsh, but with characteristic taxa at quite low values suggesting that by this date salt marsh occurred at some distance from the site; by this time the vegetation would have been that of a high shoreline, subject to occasional flooding from the estuary.

AN INTEGRATED LANDSCAPE HISTORY

The evidence presented in the preceding sections has focused on the analysis and correlation of individual sample sequences across Areas A and B. These particular sequences were selected for detailed study because, taken together, they include all the major components of the Holocene alluvial stratigraphy outlined in Table 2.3. The post-excavation work has included detailed study of the sediments through techniques such as micromorphology and soil chemistry as well as examination of the biological remains, providing information on the environments of deposition and associated vegetation. At this point in the narrative it is now appropriate to take a step back from the detail and consider the evidence in terms of landscape evolution, both at the site and the regional scale.

As outlined in Chapter 1, previous studies in the Lower Thames area have resulted in the production of a series of models related to Holocene estuary evolution. One of the more recent models, proposed by Bates and Whittaker (2004), set out a series of broad landscape phases and examined the likely impact of these changes on human activity. This model provides a useful framework in which to examine and compare the evidence at Stanford Wharf, although, as previously noted, both the model and data from many other recent investigations (eg the Jubilee Line Extension, the LVMP, High Speed 1, and the A13) are very much focused on areas upstream closer to London and may not be wholly applicable to the current study area.

Landscapes of the late Glacial

From a topographic perspective the site at Stanford Wharf currently occupies a position traversing the edge of the 2nd Gravel Terrace (the Mucking Formation) and reclaimed marshland overlooking the Thames Estuary. However, towards the end of the last glacial period, the Devensian, the landscape would have been very different. During this period regional research has shown sea levels were much lower, Britain was still joined to the continent and the Thames was a freshwater river, a tributary of the River Rhine (eg Morigi *et al.* 2011, fig. 1.5). This period equates to Stage 1b of the Cultural Landscape Model (CLM) of Bates and Whittaker (2004) where occasional human activity may have occurred associated with channel margins with sporadic finds across the contemporary floodplain surface.

Following the Last Glacial Maximum (LGM, *c* 18,000 years ago) the main Thames channel is likely to have occupied the lower lying ground to the south-west

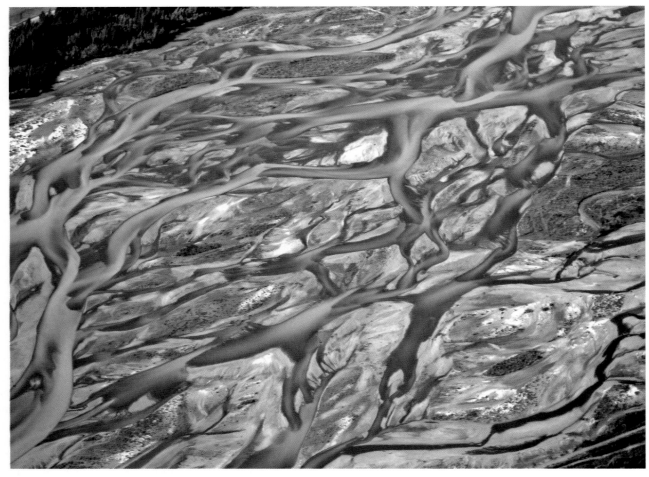

Figure 2.30 A braided river, Christchurch, New Zealand (photo: Geoff Leeming)

of the current site where aggradation of the Shepperton Gravel occurred in high-energy fast flowing braided channels; a network of transient streams with sand and gravel bars (Fig. 2.30). At Stanford Wharf erosion under cold climate periglacial conditions is likely to have occurred across the sparsely vegetated unstable ground of the higher, older, Mucking terrace. This may in part account for the thick deposits of Head and 'Brickearth' and sand recorded in the northern, central and eastern parts of the site. Remnants of younger gravel terraces may lie buried beneath the Holocene floodplain deposits to the south-west beneath the current Thames channel.

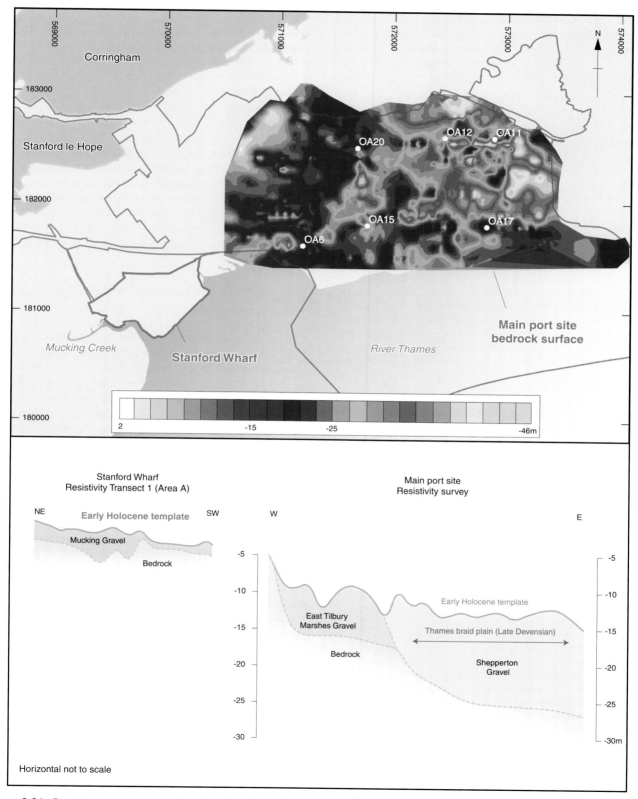

Figure 2.31 Resistivity survey mapping the elevation of the bedrock surface across the London Gateway port site (after Bates et al. 2012) and correlation of the buried gravel terrace deposits with Stanford Wharf

During the deposit modelling work at the main port site to the east (Bates *et al.* 2012; Fig. 2.31) the probable base of East Tilbury Marshes Gravel (MIS 6–MIS 2) was mapped at approximately -15m OD and the base of the Shepperton Gravels (MIS 4–MIS 2) at -25m OD, based on the long profiles provided by Gibbard (1994, figs 37 and 48).

The late Glacial period, from *c* 15,000 BP, is generally characterized by a series of extreme climatic oscillations (Fig. 2.32). Broadly, however, a period of warmer conditions (the Windermere Interstadial, *c* 15,000-13,000 BP), was followed by an intense climatic deterioration when temperatures in the east of England and mainland Europe may have returned to Arctic conditions (the Loch Lomond Stadial, 13,000-11,500 BP). Following this there was then a gradual climatic amelioration approaching the Holocene.

During this period the Thames in the London area appears to have been in transition to an anastomosing form with a reduced rate of sedimentation and fewer active channels (Sidell *et al.* 2000, 14). Organic deposits infilling abandoned channels have occasionally been recorded, for example, at Bermondsey Lake and Silvertown Village (ibid.) where accumulation continued into the early Holocene.

Previous studies have demonstrated that the environment during the warmer interstadial phase was characterised by the spread of alder, birch, willow and hazel woodland with an associated fauna which included lynx, beaver and aurochs (Schreve *et al.* in Morigi *et al.* 2011, 140). The cold periglacial environment of the Loch Lomond Stadial in the Thames Valley sees a return to open and very dry tundra vegetation such as dwarf birch, juniper and other low growing arctic shrubs. 'Sub-arctic meadow' vegetation probably grew in moister areas, with sedges in cut-off channels on the floodplain. Scots pine trees and perhaps birch trees grew in stunted clumps in sheltered localities on the valley sides (ibid., 143). Associated seasonal fauna may have included reindeer, wild horse, wolverine, and steppe pika (ibid., 142).

Early Holocene land surfaces and the freshwater river

According to the model of Bates and Whittaker (2004, CLM Stage 2) the surface of the Pleistocene deposits described above would have defined the topography of the early Holocene landscape, which in turn would have influenced patterns of later sediment accumulation. Following climatic amelioration, but prior to sea level rise attaining near present day levels, the area is likely to have been characterised by relict late-glacial features, but with a stable channel within the old late-glacial main channel. The floodplain of the river adjacent to the main channel would have stabilised with the development of the Holocene vegetation. Local pockets of sediment accumulation are likely to have accrued during this time in channels and hollows on the gravel surface. A key ecotonal area probably existed adjacent to the main Thames channel and tributaries, and higher ground would have provided additional landscape resources within different environments.

At the beginning of the Holocene the area of the main port site was largely dry ground, with a varied relief. Freshwater deposition of organic sediments occurred in lower lying areas which included a localised basin that may have formed an open body of water such as a small lake. Age estimates for the onset of organic sedimentation date from 8290-7980 cal. BC (SUERC-35575, 8985 ± 35) in OA15 at -11.59m OD (Fig. 2.31; Bates *et al.* 2012).

Higher ground would have provided additional landscape resources within different environments. The presence of a weathered horizon and associated archaeological remains at the upper contact of the sandy facies at Stanford Wharf indicates that the sands at these

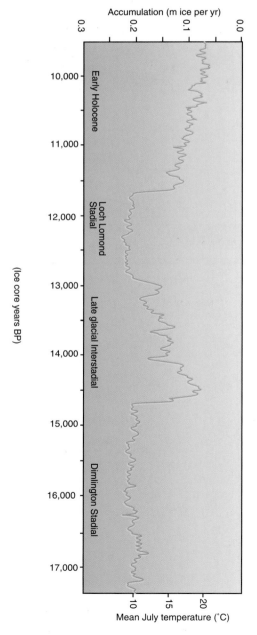

Figure 2.32 Late glacial climatic oscillations

locations were exposed as a land-surface. The landscape associated with this horizon, after climatic amelioration but prior to the onset of sedimentation across the topographic gradient (dated to the late Bronze Age in Area A) was one of relative stability with minimal sediment deposition and little chance of stratigraphic development, preserving artefact assemblages of Mesolithic and Neolithic and Bronze Age date.

Evidence for vegetation in the Lower Thames Valley in the earlier part of the Holocene has been reviewed by Sidell *et al.* (2000) and more recently by Batchelor (2009), and is discussed further in Stafford *et al.* (2012), although sites with good pollen preservation are sparse. Typically an initial phase of birch and pine woodland seems to have been superseded by the mid Holocene with lime, oak, elm, hazel and alder (Scaife in Sidell *et al.* 2000, 111). Lime appears to have been of particular

importance prior to the later prehistoric and may have been growing in damp woodland as well as on the better drained terraces (ibid.).

Mid to late Holocene estuarine incursion

During the mid Holocene, CLM Stage 3 of the Bates and Whittaker (2004) model, sea level rise resulted in inundation of the former dry land surface and began to influence sedimentation and fluvial dynamics within the valley floor area. As the sea level rose, channel stability will have decreased causing the start of flooding of low-lying areas. The floodplain surface is likely to have become unstable as a result of widespread flooding and rapid sedimentation. Minerogenic sedimentation characterises this phase. While sediment accumulation

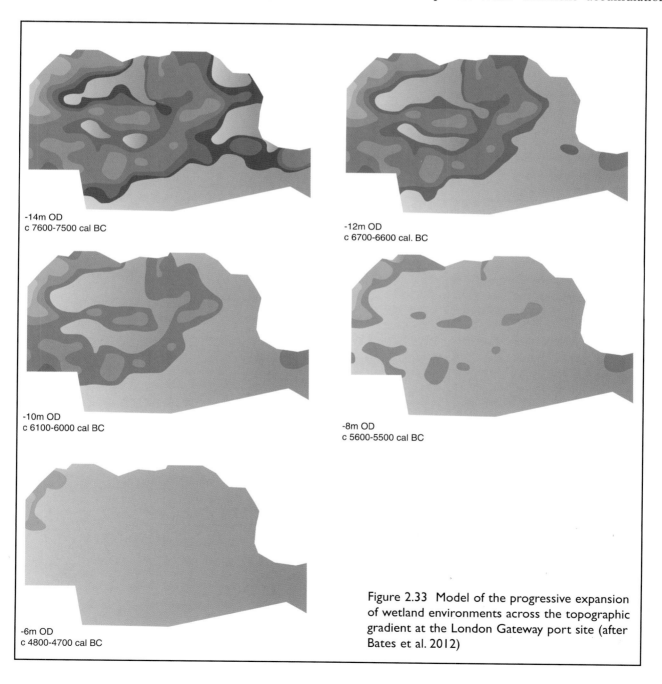

-14m OD
c 7600-7500 cal BC

-12m OD
c 6700-6600 cal. BC

-10m OD
c 6100-6000 cal BC

-8m OD
c 5600-5500 cal BC

-6m OD
c 4800-4700 cal BC

Figure 2.33 Model of the progressive expansion of wetland environments across the topographic gradient at the London Gateway port site (after Bates et al. 2012)

during this stage will have begun under freshwater conditions, it would have been subsequently transformed by the onset of estuarine conditions as marine inundation occurred. During this period the ecotonal zone between wet and dry ground will have migrated inland and risen in datum across the flooding surface. Thus wetland environments began to expand at the expense of the dry ground areas. Temporary landsurfaces may have existed within the flooding area but these are likely to have been ephemeral and of local significance only. Human activity would probably have remained focused on channel marginal situations and areas of the floodplain not inundated. Later still, more extensive inundation would eventually focus activity on the floodplain margins and any remnant islands of sand and gravel within the floodplain (ibid.).

The spread of brackish or marine conditions has been documented at the main port site from around *c* 6500 cal. BC, evident through the analysis of microfossils such as diatoms, ostracods and foraminifera as well as waterlogged plant remains. The area was rapidly inundated, resulting in the deposition of a complex sequence of intercalated organic and minerogenic sediments. Dry ground areas were reduced first to a series of interconnected ridges and then islands as tidal mudflats, creeks and salt marshes dominated the landscape (Fig. 2.33). High energy conditions associated with strong tidal regimes were present to the east, typified by the deposition of laminated clays, silts and sand. By the beginning of the Neolithic almost all former dry ground is likely to have disappeared from the port site, buried beneath extensive deposits of intertidal sediment (Bates *et al.* 2012).

Pollen evidence from the port site discussed in Bates *et al.* 2003 indicates the presence of woodland locally during the mid to late Holocene; this consisted principally of oak with elm and hazel probably on the higher drier areas, and lime and alder on wetter substrates. Microcharcoal identified in the boreholes perhaps suggests some clearance, although whether by humans or lightening strike cannot be confirmed. More recent work at the port site (Bates *et al.* 2012) suggests significant diversity in the floodplain environments at any one time: shifting zones occupied by mudflats, salt marsh with tidal creeks, through to freshwater marsh and fen. Freshwater influence was noted associated with areas of higher ground, particularly along the western inland edge between *c* 6000-3600 cal. BC, associated with short-lived episodes of peat accumulation. In borehole OA20 plant remains included rhizomes of cf *Phragmites australis* (common reed) together with some seeds from plants which today grow in wet, freshwater habitats; lesser

Figure 2.34 Active salt marsh at Mucking Flats, Essex

spearwort (*Ranunculus flammula*) and gipsywort (*Lycopus europaeus*). In borehole OA06, although seeds from salt marsh goosefoot (*Chenopodium* cf *chenopodiodes*) suggest localised areas of brackish mudflats, seeds from plants such as sedges (*Carex* sp) and fennel pondweed (*Potamogeton* cf *pectinatus*) are indicative of wet places, and fat-hen (*Chenopodium album* L.) indicates dry land. A similar environment of wet meadows and marshy land is represented from peat dating to *c* 2900-2500 cal. BC in borehole OA06 (Huckerby in Bates *et al.* 2012).

It is during this period of mid Holocene inundation that the main east-west palaeochannel (Zone E) at Stanford Wharf was either incised or reactivated, based on the date from the humin fraction of the basal minerogenic sediment on borehole OA3 of 5050-4830 cal. BC (OxA-24897, 6041 ± 39 BP). Microfossil evidence indicates that the channel was surrounded by extensive tidal mudflats backed by salt marsh. Initially it was prone to strong tidal influences and surges, although this influence diminished over time probably owing to silting. On the higher, drier ground the pollen from the palaeochannel sequence suggests that deciduous woodland was present with areas of grassland/pasture and heathland. In general, estuarine environments clearly prevailed in the vicinity of Stanford Wharf into the succeeding periods with the deposition of the Lower Alluvium (G5a) across the topographic gradient in the southern part of Area A. This sediment unit has been dated by OSL in sample profile 5a to the Bronze Age at 1190-590 BC (GL09086, 2900 ± 300 BP).

It is worthy of note that the very extensive deposits of mid Holocene peat, which commonly occur up to 3m in thickness in floodplain situations upstream, were not present either at the main port site or at Stanford Wharf,

probably due to the site's position within the estuary. The thick peat deposits upstream, CLM Stage 4 of the Bates and Whittaker (2004) model, mark a major expansion of freshwater alder carr in the inner part of the estuary during the Neolithic and Bronze Age, associated with a reduction in the rate of sea-level rise. This also correlates with the model for estuary contraction at around 4900-1250 cal. BC proposed by Long *et al.* (2000) and with data from nearby Crossness, where the channel was estimated to have contracted from 4700m to 670m in width between 3600 and 2000 BC (Devoy 1979). The sequences also broadly fit within the time range for Devoy's Tilbury III and IV peat (3550-2050 BC and 1450 BC-AD 200 respectively). At Stanford Wharf a short-lived episode resulting in the deposition of a thin clayey peat unit (G39), dated in sample profile 5b to 840-590 cal. BC (OxA-22575, 2601 ± 34) and in sample profile 8 to the late Bronze Age 980-820 cal. BC (OxA-24899, 2755 ± 30 BP), may be associated with this phase, as may a number of thin (<0.50m) peaty units and ephemeral organic clays found intercalated within the minerogenic sediments at the port site (Bates *et al.* 2012).

At Stanford Wharf, following the deposition of the clayey peat, estuarine conditions rapidly returned with the deposition of the Middle Alluvium (G5b) across Area A, dated by OSL in sample profile 5a to 390-10 BC (GL09085, 2200 ± 200 BP) and in sample profile 14a to 690-290 BC (GL09087, 2500 ± 200 BP). Very little environmental change was detected during the deposition of the Upper Alluvium (G5c) during the Roman and later periods and it appears that salt marsh and tidal creek environments prevailed until documentary and cartographic sources show that the land was reclaimed in the 17th century (Rippon 2012).

Chapter 3

Prehistoric exploitation of the landscape

by Edward Biddulph, Dan Stansbie, Hugo Anderson-Whymark, Lisa Brown and David Mullin

FROM THE MESOLITHIC TO THE BRONZE AGE (Figs 3.1-3.4)

Archaeological deposits and features dating before the later Iron Age predominantly survived below the impact level of the ground reduction necessary to create the ecological habitat, and as a result were largely preserved *in situ*. However, sandy deposits exposed along the north edge of Area A contained worked flint flakes and tools, which provide the earliest evidence for human activity at Stanford Wharf Nature Reserve (Fig. 3.1). The majority of the flint artefacts were recovered from a relatively elevated sandy layer, labelled geomorphological unit G3. This unit has been dated to the Mesolithic by an OSL date of 9490-6090 BC (9800 ± 1700 BP; GL09089), and charcoal recovered from the surface of this deposit has been radiocarbon dated to the middle Neolithic (3520-3340 cal. BC at 95.4% confidence; 4619 ± 32 BP: OxA-22432). A series of test pits were dug within the G3 deposit, and the spoil was sieved in spits to examine the distribution of flint (Fig. 3.2). The flints were mainly found scattered on or close to the surface of the sand, within the top 10cm spit, or within the irregular features. Animal bone identified as cattle and large mammal by Lena Strid was recovered from unit G3. Most animal remains were sub-adult or adult, although three calf bones were also found in unit G3. Two samples from contexts 1672 and 1909 within unit G3 contained rare charred cereal remains, including a glume base from a glume wheat identified as emmer (*Triticum dicoccum*) or spelt (*T spelta*) (Hunter, specialist report 19). These remains complement two pollen grains identified as emmer/spelt wheat from borehole OA03 within the palaeochannel at a depth of 2.32m (Peglar, specialist report 23). Various irregular shallow features cutting the top of G3 (such as 1309, 1311 and 1313) were interpreted as tree-throw holes or hollows.

More flintwork was collected from geomorphological unit G4, also in Area A. This was a silty sand deposit which overlay unit G3, and from which an OSL date of 1790-1390 BC (3600 ± 200 BP; GL09088), corresponding to the early-middle Bronze Age, was obtained. The flint was in fresh condition and likely to have been contemporary with the deposit, although the flakes and blades recovered provide only a broad Neolithic or Bronze Age date on technological grounds. Flint-tempered pottery was recovered from context 1454, a sandy layer at the base of a sequence of deposits outside the west entrance of the late Roman saltern 9501. One of the seven sherds recovered belonged to a bowl dated to the early Neolithic, though on the basis of their condition, the sherds are almost certainly residual.

There was a trace of Bronze Age activity in Area B. Pit 4111 was located below the north-west corner of late Roman saltern 6711 (Figs 3.3 and 3.4). It had been cut into naturally-laid gravel (4139) and was sealed by another gravel layer (4102). Part of the pit had been cut by late Roman ditch 4063. The pit was oval in plan, and measured 0.9m long, 0.78m wide and 0.3m deep. The feature contained two silty sand deposits with frequent charcoal and burnt flint. Worked flint and flint-tempered pottery were recovered, the latest pieces of which dated to the later Bronze Age.

Alluvial deposits in areas A, B and D that were laid by marine inundation during the later prehistoric period – an OSL date of 390-10 BC (2200 ± 200 BP; GL09085) indicates that this phase of alluviation continued into the later Iron Age – also contained flint-tempered pottery dated to the late Bronze Age. The material included sherds belonging to a flat base and a flat-topped rim, possibly from a bowl.

THE FINDS

Worked flint (Figs 3.5 and 3.6)

In total, 331 flints were recovered from unit G3 in Area A (in all, 471 flints were recovered from Area A and a further 77 from other parts of the site). A full worked flint report is available in the digital archive (Anderson-Whymark, specialist report 11), and is summarised here. The Area A unit G3 assemblage is dominated by thin, regular flakes, although blades and bladelets form 12.8% of the flake assemblage (Table 3.1). In general, the blades and flakes appear to form part of the same industry, but two exceptionally regular, parallel-sided blades with dorsal blade scars, derive from a blade-orientated industry of Mesolithic date. The proportion of blades in the assemblage is comparable to that in later Neolithic assemblages in south-east England. However, the initiation of blade production through the removal of a crested blade and the rejuvenation of cores through the removal of platform tablets are characteristic of earlier Neolithic reduction techniques. The assemblage, therefore, probably dates to the middle Neolithic, and as

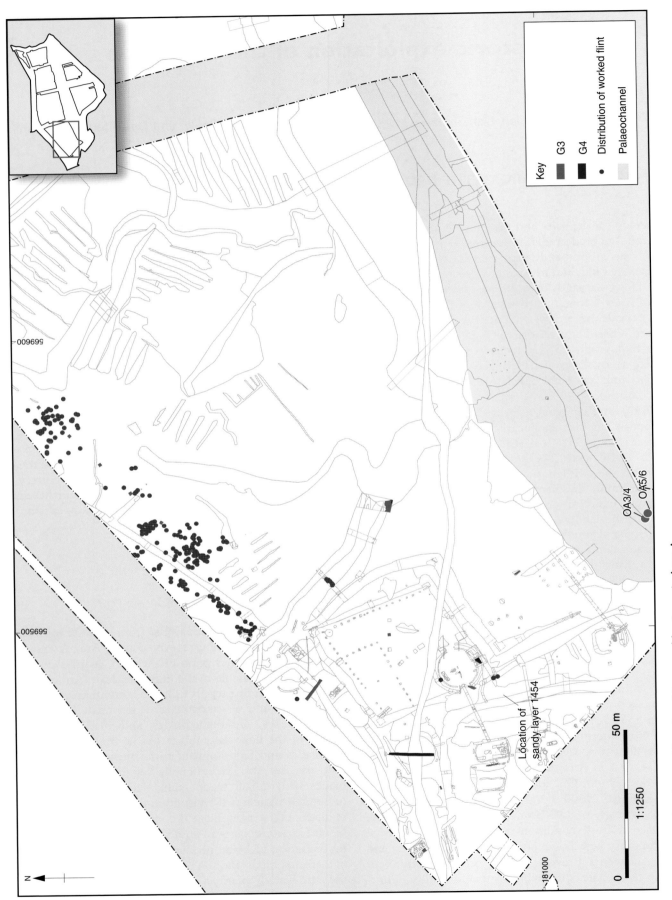

Figure 3.1 Plan of earlier prehistoric evidence and horizons in Area A

Figure 3.2 Test pit through the sandy unit G3

Figure 3.4 Pit 4111

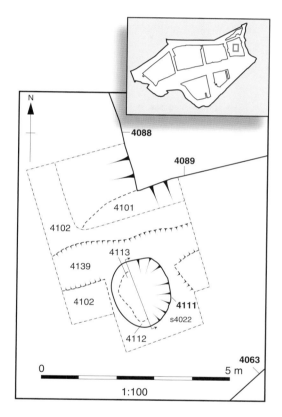

Section 4022

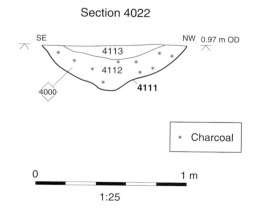

Figure 3.3 Plan of Bronze Age pit 4111, Area B

such it is likely to be contemporary with the radiocarbon date obtained from charcoal recovered from the surface of G3.

The assemblage contained a number of cores, pieces of irregular waste and a small number of cortical flakes, which indicate that some flint knapping was being undertaken at this location. However, no refits were located to demonstrate *in situ* knapping and the distribution of the flints reflects a diffuse scatter. It is, therefore, likely that the scatter accumulated through the use and abandonment of flint tools over a period of time, with only occasional brief knapping episodes. Retouched artefacts are comparatively common, representing 6.4% of flints in the deposit excluding chips, and several unretouched flakes show use-wear visible to the naked eye. The range of retouched tools is comparatively limited with nine scrapers, five serrated flakes (Fig. 3.5, no. 1), four edge-retouched flakes, a backed knife (Fig. 3.5, no. 2) and a crude pick-like tool (Fig. 3.5, no. 3). The scrapers are dominated by broad, thick, flake forms, including a disc scraper on a non-flake blank and horseshoe-shaped types (Fig. 3.5, nos 4-6), but two were manufactured on broad blades (Fig. 3.6, nos 7-8) and another was manufactured on a blade-like flake (Fig. 3.6, no. 9). The scrapers may indicate the preparation of hides, although these tools could also have been used for other tasks, such as wood-working. In contrast, the serrated flakes represent the processing of silica plants into fibres for cordage or textiles (Juel Jensen 1994; Hurcombe 2007). The backed knife is manufactured on a large broad flake and shows only minimal edge retouch on the left hand side. The right hand side and distal end have extensive edge-rounding (Fig. 3.5, no. 2).

Unit G4, a Bronze Age soil horizon overlying unit G3 in Area A, yielded 40 flints, most of which were in fresh condition and are likely to be broadly contemporary with the deposit (Table 3.1). The assemblage is dominated by broad flakes and blades are notably less common than in the unit G3 assemblage; this indicates that the flake debitage may be of a later date than the material in the unit below, although technological attributes allow only a broad Neolithic or Bronze Age date to

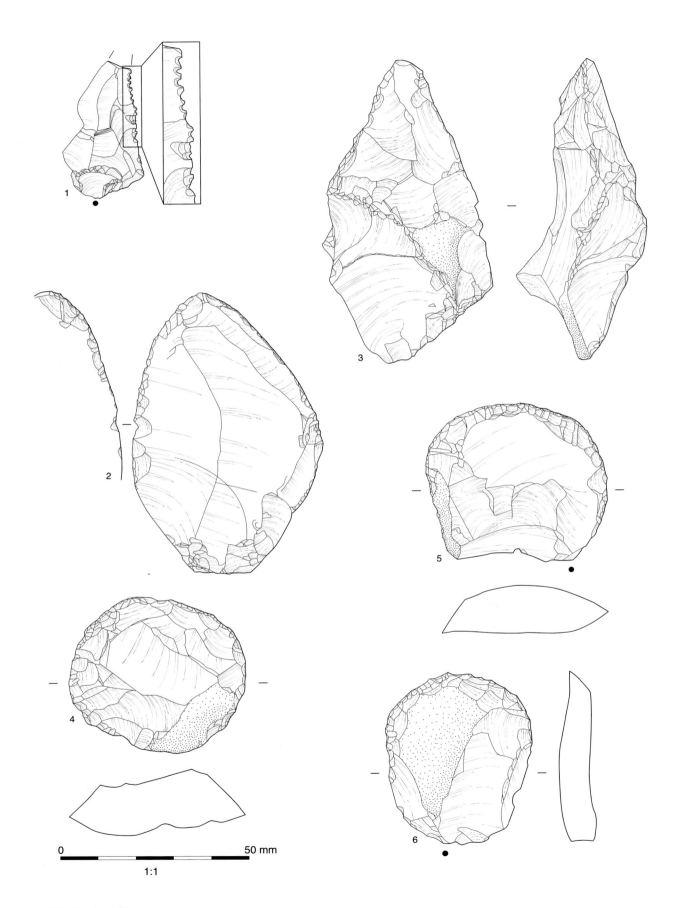

0   50 mm
1:1

Figure 3.5 Worked flint, nos 1-6

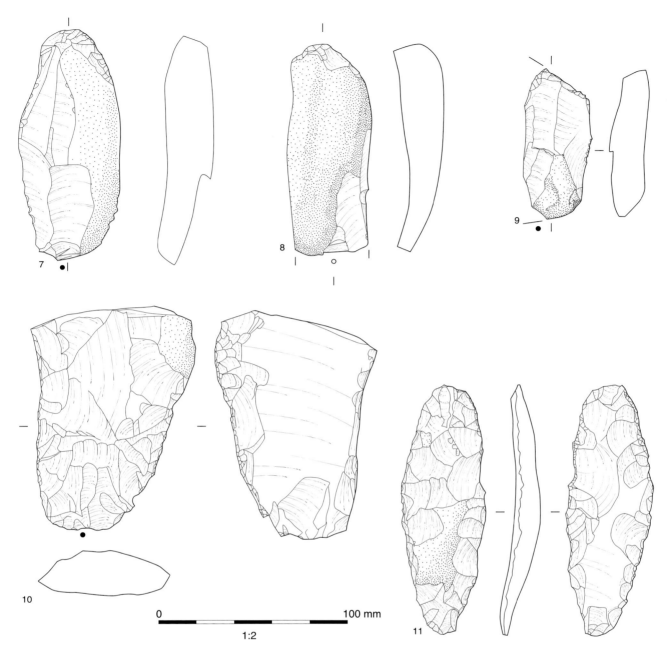

Figure 3.6 Worked flint, nos 7-11

be proposed. A large flake with invasive bifacial working (Fig. 3.6, no. 10) is the only retouched tool, although a flake struck from the blade edge of a Neolithic polished flint axe was also recovered.

Twelve flints in fresh condition were recovered from pit 4111 in Area B, comprising eight flakes, two blades, a chip and a tested nodule. One of the blades is parallel-sided and probably dates from the Mesolithic, but the flakes are of broad proportions and were struck using hard hammer percussion. These flakes probably date from the later Bronze Age and they are broadly contemporary with the pit.

An unstratified artefact, but one of intrinsic interest, is a leaf-shaped knife that has invasive bi-facial flaking from direct percussion. The left hand side has additional secondary slight abrupt retouch on the ventral surface that forms a sharp spur on the side of the knife (Fig. 3.6,

no. 11). The knife probably dates from the early/middle Neolithic and a direct parallel was recovered from the early Neolithic middens in Area 6 at Dorney Lake, Eton (Anderson-Whymark forthcoming).

Pottery (Fig. 3.7)

Seven sherds of flint-tempered pottery were recovered from context 1454. These included a simple, out-turned flat-topped rim, which probably represents fragments of an undecorated bowl of early Neolithic date (Fig. 3.7, no. 1). This material is almost certainly residual within this deposit. A single coarse flint-tempered vessel from alluvial clay 6672 was represented by five sherds from a flat base (Fig. 3.7, no. 3). A total of 21 sherds recovered from alluvial clay 2002 included a simple flat-topped rim,

Table 3.1: The flint assemblage from Area A by artefact type (*Percentages excluding chips and hammerstones)

CATEGORY TYPE	1385/G4	Area A context 1386/G3	Other contexts/residual	Grand Total
Flake	27	210	62	299
Blade	1	18	5	24
Bladelet	1	15	1	17
Blade-like		14	1	15
Irregular waste		17	3	20
Chip		14		14
Sieved chips 10-4 mm	4		7	11
Sieved chips 4-2 mm			4	4
Rejuvenation flake core face/edge		1		1
Rejuvenation flake tablet		1		1
Rejuvenation flake other		1		1
Crested blade		1		1
Flake from ground implement	1			1
Single platform blade core		3		3
Other blade core		1		1
Tested nodule/bashed lump	3	7	3	13
Single platform flake core	1	1	1	3
Multiplatform flake core	1	4	2	7
End scraper		5		5
Side scraper		2		2
End and side scraper		1	2	3
Scraper on a non-flake blank		1	1	2
Serrated blade/flake		5	3	8
Backed knife		1		1
Other knife			1	1
Retouched flake		4	3	7
Misc. retouch	1			1
Pick		1		1
Hammerstone		3	1	4
Grand Total	40	331	100	471
Burnt unworked flint No./Wt. g		38/163g	62/2463g	100/2626g
Burnt worked flints No. (%)★	5 (13.9)	10 (3.2)	1 (1.1)	16 (3.7)
Broken worked flints No.(%)★	12 (33.3)	89 (28.3)	20 (22.7)	121 (27.6)
Retouched flints No. (%)★	1 (2.8)	20 (6.4)	10 (11.4)	31 (7.1)

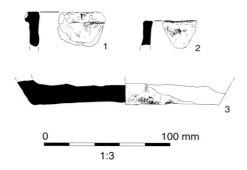

0   100 mm

1:3

Figure 3.7 Earlier prehistoric pottery

possibly from a bowl (Fig. 3.7, no. 2). Its fabric is a fine micaceous sandy clay with very small, sparse white flint. Context 4193 yielded a single body sherd in a glauconitic sandy ware with ill-assorted flint and lumps of powdery iron oxide. This may be of late Bronze Age or slightly earlier date. Context 4112 produced a single small body sherd in flint-tempered fabric. A range of three flint-tempered fabrics was represented by five sherds of pottery from context 4788, again all of them body sherds. Further information on the pottery is available in the digital archive (specialist report 1).

DISCUSSION (Fig. 3.8)

The evidence from Stanford Wharf indicates that the site saw intermittent activity during the Mesolithic, Neolithic and Bronze Age periods. The site joins others that emerged on the lower terraces along the Thames Estuary in the Mesolithic consequent upon the retreat of the ice and subsequent environmental change, which brought new opportunities and resources (Fig. 3.8). At Mucking, groups of pits, some containing Grooved Ware, indicate Neolithic and early Bronze Age occupation, and flint tools spanning the Mesolithic to later Bronze Age have also been recovered (Evans and Lucy 2008). A scatter of Neolithic and early Bronze Age flint artefacts was recovered from the Grays bypass, c 11km south-west of Stanford Wharf (Wilkinson 1988). Neolithic and Bronze Age flint was collected from excavations at West Thurrock on the route of High Speed 1 (Andrews 2009). Pits containing Neolithic or early Bronze Age flint have been found at Ockendon (Biddulph et al. 2012), and a pit dating to the early Bronze Age was uncovered at Rainham (Costello 1997). Flint scatters associated with buried land surfaces dating to the early and late Mesolithic periods were recorded at

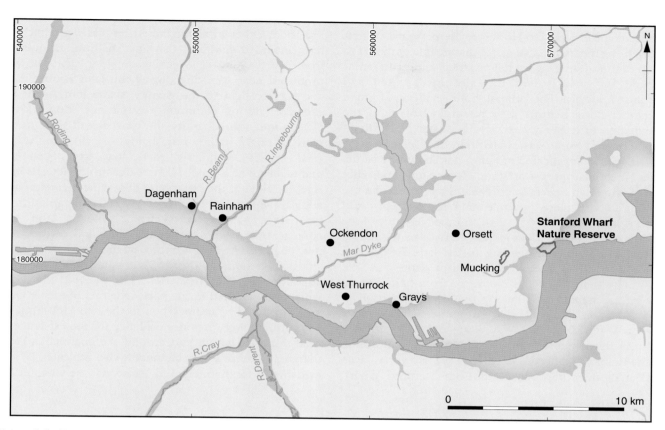

Figure 3.8 Earlier prehistoric sites mentioned in discussion

Beam Washlands, Dagenham on a gravel promontory *c* 1 km to the north of the Thames floodplain. One of the flint scatters produced material belonging to a Late Upper Palaeolithic long blade industry (Champness and Donnelly 2012). Assemblages of Neolithic pottery and worked flint were recovered along the A13 in Tower Hamlets, Newham, Barking and Dagenham (Stafford *et al.* 2012). The excavations also uncovered a fragment of belt slider made from Whitby jet, which attests to long-distance exchange networks. More significantly, several Bronze Age timber stake-built structures and brush-wood trackways with associated wetland edge occupation were recorded.

The lithic assemblage from Stanford Wharf provides sparse evidence for Mesolithic activity in the landscape, although it is possible that Mesolithic horizons are present below the impact level. The evidence for middle Neolithic activity is more compelling, but only a limited proportion of unit G3 was excavated along the northern edge of the site as the majority of the deposit was below the impact level and has been preserved *in situ*. The site therefore potentially contains a Neolithic land surface with extensive *in situ* scatters resulting from various activities; the extent of these scatters is, however, unknown. The limited portion of the unit G3 land surface that was excavated can, therefore, only provide a very limited insight on activities undertaken at this location. The knapping of local flint pebbles certainly represents one activity, but a high proportion of retouched tools indicates that the scatter results from the performance of a variety of other tasks. The

dominance of scrapers and serrated flakes, however, indicates that the working of hides and plant materials were significant activities. The limited assemblages of Bronze Age flint in unit G4 and Pit 4111 are uninformative regarding activities undertaken during this period.

Although the Neolithic pottery is likely to be residual, it is significant since pottery of this date is rare in the immediate area. During excavations at Mucking North Ring (Bond 1988), small amounts of Neolithic bowl were recovered, the majority of the Neolithic assemblage there comprising late Neolithic Grooved Ware. Neolithic flint-tempered bowl fragments were also recovered from the Orsett causewayed enclosure (Hedges and Buckley 1978). The late Bronze Age material from Stanford Wharf fits in well with the assemblage from the North and South Rings at Mucking, where fabrics were dominated by flint inclusions (Barrett and Bond 1988, 25-7). Thin-section analysis on those fabrics suggests that material for the pottery derived from local sources (Bond 1988, 52). The small number of vessels from Stanford Wharf and their fragmentary state mean that comparison with the large assemblage from Mucking is not possible, beyond noting the similarities in fabrics and suggesting that activity on both sites may have been contemporary.

It is difficult to get an idea of the scale of activity at Stanford Wharf; Bronze Age pit 4111 can be identified as a hearth, which provided heat for cooking, preparation of materials for working, and warmth, but other hearths, along with surfaces, working areas, and other features may lie undiscovered in the modern intertidal zone below the level of development impact on the archaeological deposits. However, the presence of flint tools in fresh condition suggests that people gathered to knap flint and process animal products and plants in or around the site. Pottery was also made, used and discarded locally. The animal bone evidence from a Neolithic horizon hints at a pastoral element to the occupation of the gravel terrace. The later Neolithic of southern and south-eastern Britain saw an emerging presence of domesticated animals, dominated by cattle. Late Neolithic evidence at White Horse Stone and other sites along High Speed 1 across Kent has revealed a use of cattle, particularly juvenile animals, for dairy and meat (Garwood 2011, 55, 123), and the Neolithic of the middle and upper Thames is characterised by the retreat of woodland and the opening of the land for grazing (Robinson 2011, 186). We cannot rule out the possibility that the cereals recovered from unit G3 and the palaeochannel also belong to this early period of domestication. After all, charred emmer wheat from a site at Woolwich Manor Way along the A13 provided definitive evidence of early Neolithic cereal cultivation in the vicinity (Stafford *et al.* 2012, 117). However, given the small quantities recovered from Stanford Wharf, both the animal bone and the cereals may represent later intrusion. Other locally gathered resources are likely to have included wildfowl, fish and shellfish. Briquetage from North Ring at Mucking suggests that salt was produced near Mucking during the later Bronze Age, and was brought to the vicinity of the monument for exchange during community gatherings (Bond 1988, 52), although the quantity and character of some of the material might suggest production very close to the site (*ibid.*, 50-51). Similarly, there may have been salt manufacture at Stanford Wharf during the late Bronze Age, the time of the first phase of marine incursion and alluvial deposition over Area A. A small amount of briquetage was recovered from an early Iron Age context, but as with the animal bone and cereals, this may be intrusive. That is not to say that conditions at the site before the later Bronze Age would not have been conducive to salt production. The alluvial unit G5a, which was sampled in the palaeochannel borehole OA3 and was dated by radiocarbon to the late Mesolithic to early Bronze Age, provides evidence for the existence of tidal mudflats within and around the channel. A clear marine influence in the channel is also indicated by the evidence of foraminifera and ostracods (see Chapter 2).

Chapter 4

The Red Hills of Stanford Wharf – salt production in the middle Iron Age

by Dan Stansbie and Edward Biddulph

INTRODUCTION

Middle Iron Age activity was concentrated in the north-western corner of Area A and largely comprised red hills, mounds consisting of the debris of long-term salt making activity on the site (Fig. 4.1). Also present were several ditches, gullies and pits, along with hearths associated directly with the salt making activity itself. Red hills 9504, 6707, 9505 and 6717 formed a relatively tightly clustered linear group, running roughly parallel to the north-western limit of excavation, before turning to the north and running beyond it (Fig. 4.2). A further red hill (6718) lay to the south and was not examined in detail. A deposit of red hill-like soil (8009) lay in Area J. The red hills were sub-circular or sub-rectangular in plan and measured a maximum of 14m SW-NE by 9m NE-SW. Several of the red hills (6707, 6717, and 9504) incorporated salt-production hearths and pits, which had been cut into the fabric of the mounds at various stages in their formation, presumably indicating their use as working platforms. In addition, there were a number of middle Iron Age features which were possibly associated with salt making activity, but which had no definite connection with it, either stratigraphic or otherwise. These included ditches and pits. Ditch 6253 was overlain by red hill 6717 and curvilinear ditch 5300 lay immediately to its north-west. Immediately to the south of the main group of red hills were two short parallel stretches of ditch (6318 and 6321). Sub-circular pits 6010 and 6013 also lay some distance to the south of the main group of red hills and may not have been directly associated with salt-making activity.

AREA A: THE RED HILLS (Figs 4.1 and 4.2)

Red hill 9504 (Figs 4.2-4.5)

Red hill 9504 measured 9.4m east-west by at least 6.9m north-south, although it was cut away by a modern drainage ditch (6708) to the south and extended beyond the limits of excavation to the north. The mound comprised a complex sequence of multiple layers of brownish-red silty clay, with charcoal inclusions, interspersed with dumps of fired clay and other ceramic material, and discrete features, including hearths, pits

and gullies (Figs 4.2-4.5). An OSL date of 250 BC-AD 150 (2000 ± 200 BP; GL09090) was obtained from context 6350, a red hill deposit within 9504. Middle Iron Age pottery was recovered from interventions through the sequence, but later Roman pottery (including a grey ware dropped-flange dish and a mortarium in Colchester buff ware) collected from basal deposits uncovered in one slot through the red hill suggest that the red hill had been subject to significant disturbance and reworking, possibly relating to the creation of working surfaces associated with 3rd and 4th century salt-working and activity in enclosure 9506.

Charred plant remains from environmental samples collected from red hill 9504 were dominated by salt marsh species. Kath Hunter (specialist report 19) identified small quantities of sedge nutlets and sea lavender and sea plantain seeds, but relatively large numbers of rush seeds, some with seed capsules. One sample contained occasional monocotyledonous leaf/stem fragments. Also recorded were three lesser sea spurry seeds, possible glasswort achenes, and a few sedge nutlets. All samples contained a few grass caryopses. Wheat, and spelt in particular, was the dominant cereal, but not in any large quantity. Moderate amounts of cereal chaff were seen, and one sample had a single free threshing rachis fragment. A single oat floret, apparently of a wild type, was present.

Features within red hill 9504

Several discrete features were cut into the north-eastern end of red hill 9504. These included six possible salt production hearths or ovens (5196, 5198, 5475, 5671, 6132 and 6201). Of these only hearth 6201, which was sub-circular, was seen in plan, although all were observed in section and were generally flat based with gently sloping sides. The features were 0.38-1.20m in diameter by 0.07-0.16m in depth. All were filled with a single silty clay deposit, which contained fired clay – probably deriving from the walls or floors of the features – and occasional to moderate amounts of ash or charcoal. Feature 5198 comprised a circular dump of briquetage, fired clay and pottery contained within a flat-based cut with moderately sloping sides. Feature 5475 contained 34 sherds of middle Iron Age pottery weighing 1117g. In addition there were seven pits (5829, 5833, 5837, 5928, 5944, 6125 and 6130), all sub-circular or oval in plan

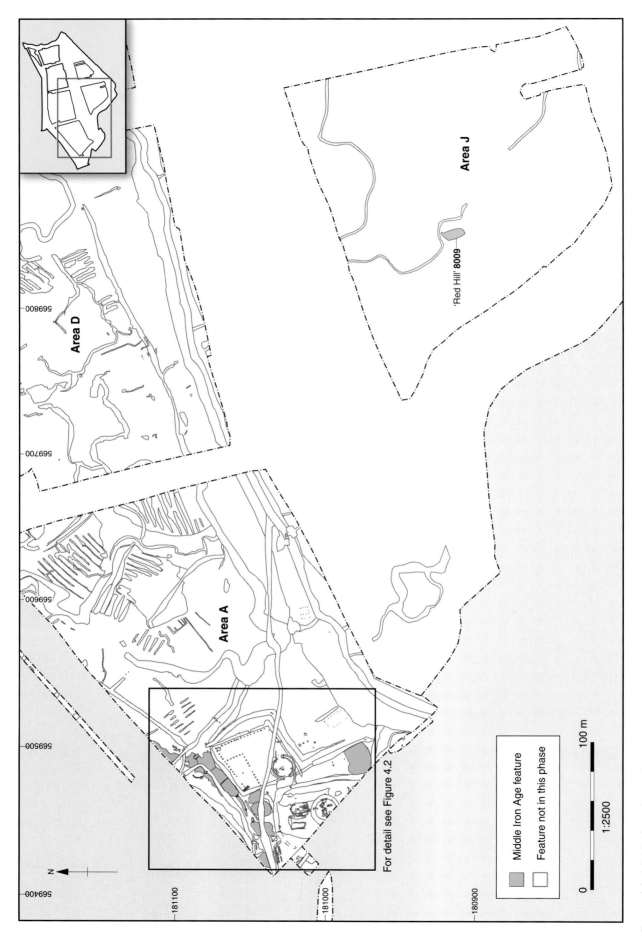

Figure 4.1 Middle Iron Age activity

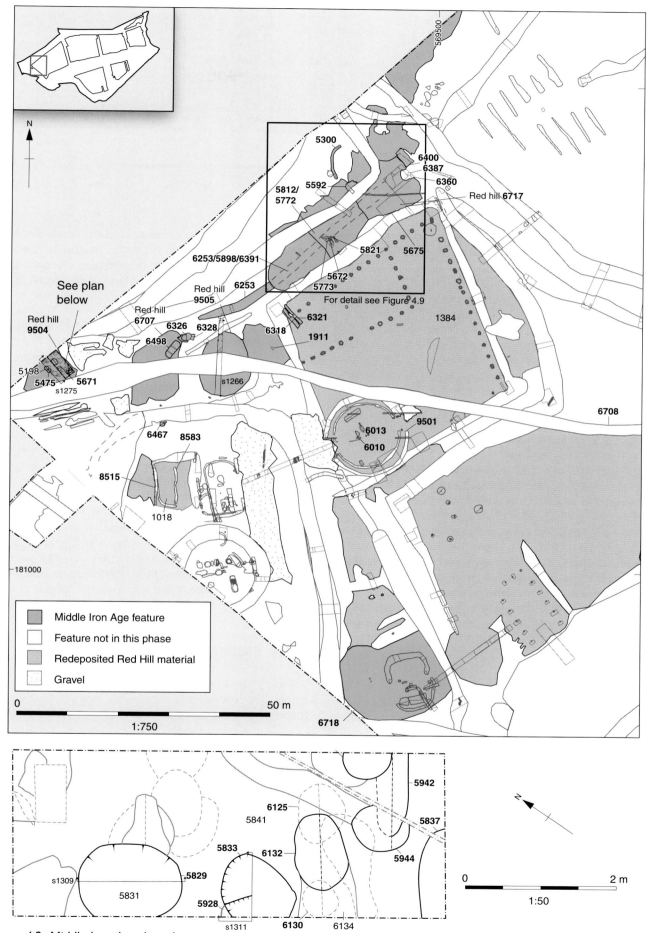

Figure 4.2 Middle Iron Age, Area A

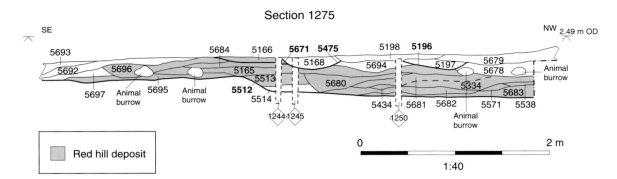

Figure 4.3 Section through red hill 9504 and plan of associated features

Figure 4.4 West facing section (1276) through red hill 9504

(Fig. 4.2 bottom). The pits measured 0.44-1.3m in diameter by 0.14-0.4m in depth. In profile these features were concave or flat-based with gently sloping sides, and the majority contained a single fill. Two pits (5829 and 5833) were lined with clay and contained three and two fills respectively (Figure 4.5). Pit 5944 produced a single, intrusive, sherd of Roman grey ware, while pit 5829 contained a single fragment of indeterminate animal bone. The rounded south-west terminal of a SW-NE-aligned gully (5942; Fig. 4.2 bottom) was located. This was 1.1m long and 0.07m deep and its concave profile contained a single fill.

Red hill 6707 (Figs 4.2 and 4.6)

Red hill 6707 was situated to the east of red hill 9504, and like 9504 was cut by modern drainage ditch 6708

(Fig. 4.2). The mound measured *c* 14m north-south by *c* 9m east-west and up to 0.26m in height. It was very roughly rectangular in plan, comprising a sequence of layers and cut features similar to that encountered in red hill 9504.

Features associated with red hill 6707 (Fig. 4.6)
A number of features had been cut into the red hill (Fig. 4.6). Feature 6498 was cut into the north-eastern corner and may have been a salt production hearth or a brine pit. The feature was sub-rectangular in plan and flat based with steep concave sides (Fig. 4.6). It was aligned NE-SW and measured 3.8m in length by 1.5m in width and 0.22m in depth. Feature 6328, orientated east-west and immediately to the north-east of feature 6498, was also sub-rectangular in plan, but was smaller at 1.3m long, just under 1m wide, and 0.16m deep. In profile, the feature had a flat base and steeply sloping sides. Feature 6328 was cut by oval pit 6326, which measured 2m in length by 0.9m in width and 0.16m in depth and had a flattish base, with steep sides. The fills of pit 6326 produced a single rim sherd of middle Iron Age pottery, along with two fragments of indeterminate animal bone. All three features were filled with deposits of clay or silty clay, with inclusions of burnt clay and briquetage.

Red hill 9505 (Figs 4.2 and 4.7-4.8)

Red hill 9505, to the east of red hill 6707, comprised two contiguous sub-circular mounds, one *c* 13.28m in diameter, and the other at least 7.22m in diameter (Fig. 4.2). The eastern mound was *c* 0.18m in height, and

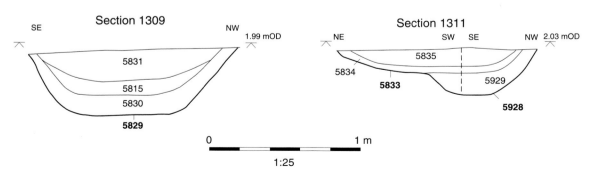

Figure 4.5 Sections through clay-lined pits 5829 and 5833, red hill 9504

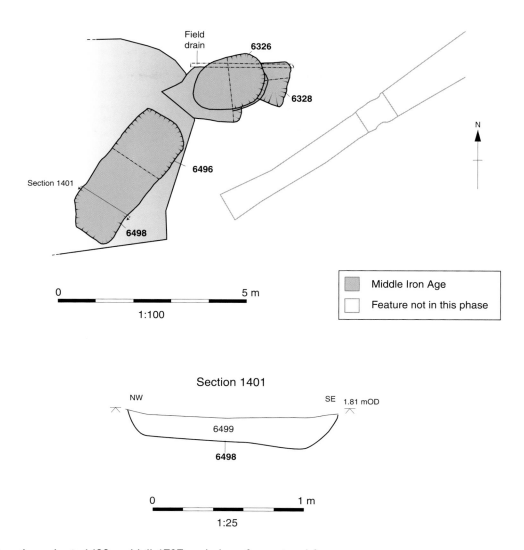

Figure 4.6 Section through pit 6498, red hill 6707, and plan of associated features

comprised a single layer of brownish-red silty clay, with little evidence for internal differentiation, while the western mound was up to 0.3m high with at least four main deposits of burnt material (Figs 4.7-4.8). The western mound produced a single sherd of middle Iron Age pottery. An oval posthole (1911) was cut into the centre of the eastern mound. It had a flat base and steeply sloping sides and measured 0.2m in depth and 0.76m across its widest extent. The single fill of the posthole produced six sherds of middle Iron Age pottery, including a fragment from a jar. Another posthole (5478), to the west, contained only fragments of fired clay. The uppermost recorded layer of red hill 9505, context 5482, contained ten sherds of middle Iron Age pottery.

Red hill 6717 (Figs 4.2 and 4.9-4.11)

Red hill 6717 was situated to the north-east of red hill 9505 (Fig. 4.2). It was linear in plan, aligned SW-NE and measured *c* 42m SW-NE by a maximum of *c* 16m NW-SE, and was probably formed from several contiguous mounds (Fig. 4.9). The mound comprised a sequence of multiple layers of brownish red silty clay

containing dumps of briquetage and charcoal (Figs 4.10 and 4.11). Several industrial features, probably related to salt making activity, were dispersed through the sequence. The red hill, including its associated features, produced a large assemblage of middle Iron Age pottery, comprising 299 sherds, weighing 3389g and incorporating parts of 18 jars and three other vessels. Four sherds of middle Roman pottery were recovered, but these came from an upper layer and were intrusive.

Micromorphological analyses of the sediment sequence through red hill 6717 (Macphail *et al.*, specialist report 24) revealed that the red hill was predominantly made up of burned salt marsh sediment which had been incidentally gathered alongside marine wetland plant fuel. The red hills probably formed rapidly due to the dumping of fuel ash waste, a formation process similar to farm mound accumulations where minerogenic peat was used as a fuel. General fragmentation occurred because the spreads formed ephemeral trampled 'occupation surfaces'; marine clay inwash also occurred at times.

The composition of environmental samples from red hill 6717 (Hunter, specialist report 19) was consistent with the results of the micromorphological analysis. The

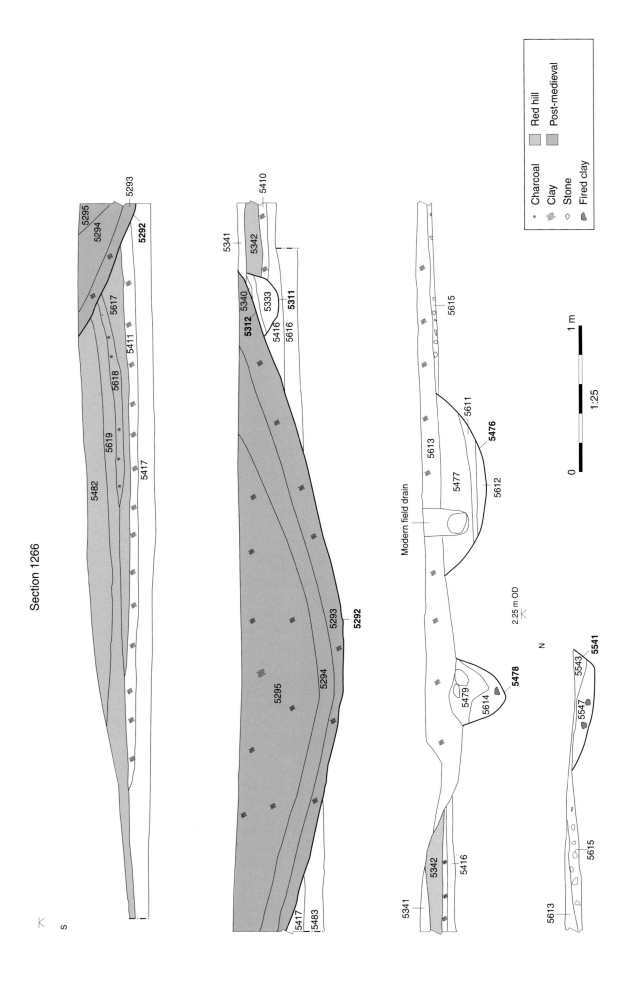

Section 1266

Modern field drain

2.25 m OD

Charcoal   Red hill
Clay   Post-medieval
Stone
Fired clay

0   1:25   1 m

Figure 4.7 Section through red hill 9505

samples contained varying quantities of fuel ash slag and abundant monocotyledonous leaf/stem fragments. Rush seeds were recorded, but no seed capsules were present. Other salt marsh plants included sea plantain, sea lavender, and thrift. Wild seeds included cleavers, stinking chamomile, dock, black bindweed, and scentless mayweed, along with four possible rye grass caryopses. Cereal remains included grains and chaff from glume wheat, in particular spelt, although five possible emmer glume base fragments and four indeterminate barley rachis fragments were identified. Spelt-type spikelets and a single oat floret base were also present. In addition, legume seeds, including a single

Figure 4.8 East facing section (1266) through red hill 9505

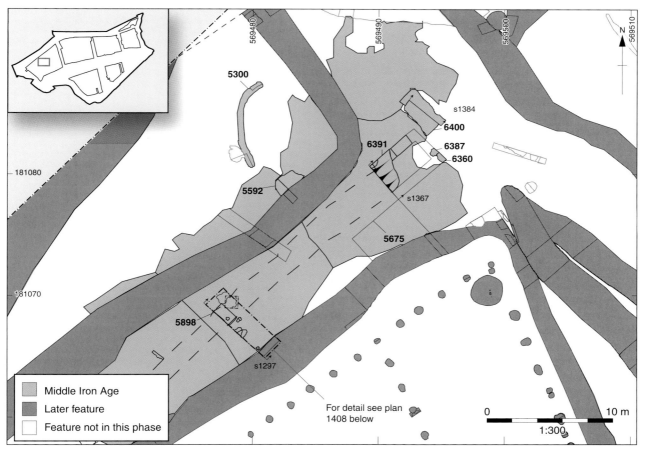

Middle Iron Age

Later feature

Feature not in this phase

For detail see plan 1408 below

0   10 m

1:300

Plan 1408

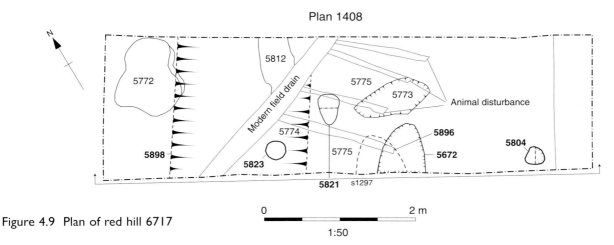

Figure 4.9 Plan of red hill 6717

0   2 m

1:50

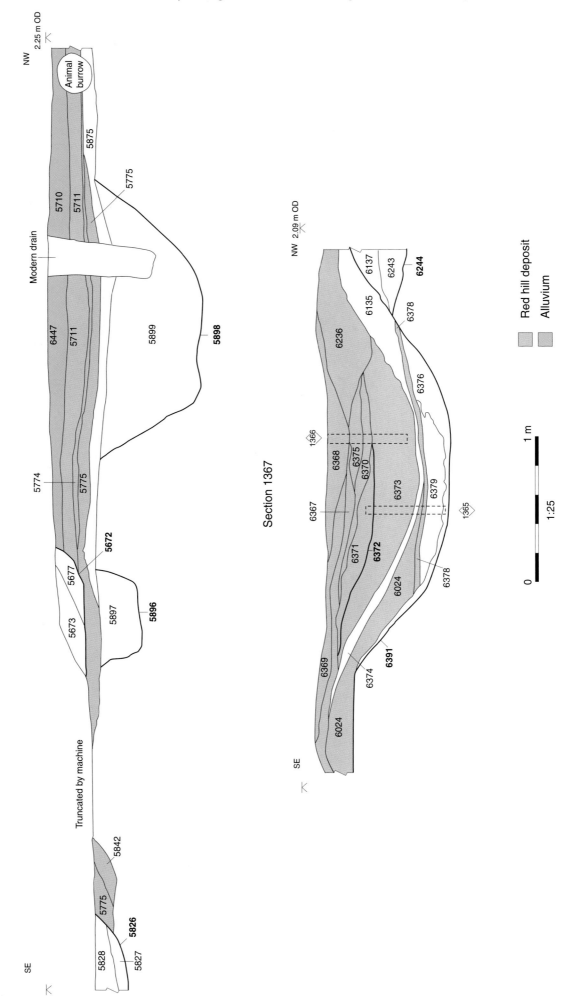

Section 1297

Section 1367

Red hill deposit

Alluvium

0   1:25   1 m

Figure 4.10 Sections through red hill 6717

Figure 4.11 Red hill 6717, looking north-east (sections 1370, 1369 and 1368); ditch 6391 in foreground

garden pea, were recorded, as were a possible hawthorn and selfheal nutlets.

Features within red hill 6717 (Fig. 4.9)
Three irregularly-shaped features interpreted as salt-production hearth bases (5772, 5773, 5812) were situated close together in the west central part of the red hill (Fig. 4.9). All three were revealed as patches of burnt clay, briquetage fragments and the remains of fuel, and in the course of excavating around the features to define their edges, were revealed as slightly raised features up to 0.14m thick, 1.2m long, and 0.9m wide. Feature 5812 contained a single sherd of middle Iron Age pottery. A pit (5672), ovoid in (incomplete) plan with a flat base and steeply sloping sides, was cut into the red hill to the south of structures 5772, 5773 and 5812. The pit measured 0.7m in extant length by 0.2m in depth and contained 12 sherds of middle Iron Age pottery, including part of a jar. Ovoid pit or posthole 5821, which was also cut into the uppermost red hill deposits, lay north-east of pit 5672. The feature measured 0.45m in length by 0.30m in width and was 0.24m deep with vertical sidea and a flat base. It contained two sherds of middle Iron Age pottery.

Pits 5592 and 5675 were isolated features in the eastern part of the red hill. Pit 5592 on the north-western side of the red hill was sub-circular in plan, and in profile was flat based with steeply sloping sides, measuring 2.3m in length by 0.65m in depth. Ten sherds of middle Iron Age pottery, including fragments of two jars, were recovered from it. Pit 5675 was situated on the south-eastern side of the red hill, south-east of pit 5592, and was a small concave-profiled feature 0.45m across and 0.15m deep seen only in section. The remaining features were situated on the north-eastern side of the red hill. Pits 6360 and 6387 were only partly excavated but were both probably roughly oval in plan, but different in profile; 6387, *c* 0.6m across and 0.13m deep had a shallow curving profile and a single fill overlain by red hill deposits, while 6380, with a flattish base and near-vertical sides, measured at least 0.78m across and cut both the red hill deposit and the fill of 6387. This pit had one or two clay fills – it is uncertain if the upper of these was a discrete fill or formed part of a wider deposit overlying the red hill materials. A further, larger pit, 6400, situated on the western edge of red hill 5717, was rectangular in plan, with an uneven base and concave sides; it measured at least 3.8m in length by 1.6m in width and 0.54m in depth (Fig. 4.12). The feature was filled with a series of alluvial deposits (6393-6395), overlain by a more widespread alluvial deposit (6392). It was interpreted during excavation as a natural hollow, but its reasonably regular shape in plan suggests that it had been deliberately dug, and presumably designed to serve a purpose related to salt production.

Red hill 6718 (Fig. 4.2)

Red hill 6718 was situated in the southern part of Area A, immediately to the west of late Roman ditch 8552. It had maximum surviving dimensions of approximately 19.7m NE-SW by 15.3m NW-SE, and was formed of multiple layers of brownish red silty clay. Some 30 sherds of middle Iron Age pottery, including three S-profiled jars, were retrieved from a test pit dug

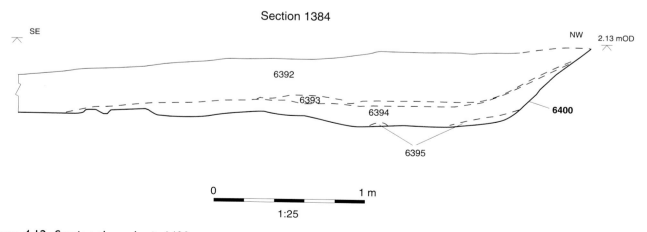

Section 1384

SE

NW 2.13 mOD

6392

6393

6394 **6400**

6395

0   1 m
         1:25

Figure 4.12 Section through pit 6400

through the centre of the mound. The red hill subsequently served as a surface for late Roman saltern 5808. No detailed investigation of it was undertaken.

OTHER MIDDLE IRON AGE FEATURES
(Fig. 4.2)

Apart from the red hills and associated industrial features, a few other middle Iron Age features were recorded. Linear feature 6253/5898/6391 was orientated NE-SW and for most of its known length was overlain by red hill 6717. The feature was at least c 50m long. It was exposed in two interventions through the red hill (Fig. 4.10), and a longer portion of it was uncovered at its western end, where it terminated. The feature had a slightly irregular U-shaped profile, with concave, and sometimes convex sides, and an uneven base. Its depth was reasonably constant at c 0.5m deep (although it was 0.65m deep in section 1297), but its width was more variable, increasing towards the east from c 1.5m to 2.25m. It was filled with up to three clay deposits, although towards its eastern end, where it was covered by red hill 6717, the upper fills of the ditch consisted of red hill deposits. Five fragments of middle Iron Age glauconitic pottery were recovered from its western terminus (6253), and an additional sherd of glauconitic pottery was recovered from the second fill of 6391. The feature's slight irregularity at its west end and its variable width might identify it as a natural channel, rather than deliberately dug ditch, but the evidence is not conclusive, and the latter intereptation seems more likely.

On the north side of red hill 6717 was a short (7.75m) length of curvilinear ditch (5300), 0.65m wide. The feature contained a rim sherd from a middle Iron Age jar weighing 10g. To the south-west of red hill 6717 were two short parallel stretches of ditch, 6318 and 6321. Both were aligned NW-SE and measured c 5m in recorded length by 1.12m and 0.50m in width respectively; their extent to north-west and south-east is unknown. The features were filled with silty clay; ditch 6321 contained three middle Iron Age body sherds weighing 3g. A section through the late Roman saltern 9501 exposed a ditch or pit, 6013 (Fig. 2.19). The feature, which measured c 1.8m wide and 0.6m deep, had been cut into a prehistoric palaeosol (unit G4), and reached the natural sand (unit G3). It was filled with two silty clay deposits and sealed by alluvium, which was in turn overlain by redeposited red hill layer 5712 (equivalent to 1384, see below). The primary fill of the feature contained a fragment from a middle Iron Age jar.

REDEPOSITED RED HILLS (Figs 4.1 and 4.2)

Red hill 8009 was situated in the southern part of the investigated landscape in Area J, which was subject to an archaeological watching brief (Fig. 4.1). The red hill soil was roughly sub-rectangular in plan and comprised a

layer of mid-dark red sandy clay up c 0.15m thick. An area approximately 15m in length by 6m in width was exposed. The deposit produced a relatively substantial assemblage of middle Iron Age pottery totalling 45 sherds, weighing 546g, and including parts of six jars. The deposit sits at a height of between c 1.25m and 1.35m AOD, and is a little higher than the suggested height of the floor surface of the early Roman boathouse (see Chapter 5). This suggests that the deposit, though deriving from a middle Iron Age red hill, represents a redeposited material laid in the Roman, or more likely, the post-Roman period, possibly as a sheep refuge.

A spread of grey-pink silty clay (1018), some 10m east-west by 9m north-south in area and over 0.2m in depth, was recorded close to the western edge of Area A. It overlay alluvium and was cut by gullies from a late Roman shelter or structure (6513, 8515 and 8516). No dating evidence was recovered, though a fragment of flat briquetage was found. The layer is likely to be the remains of another red hill.

A more extensive spread of redeposited material (including context 1384) derived from red hills was recorded across the central and southern parts of Area A. There were particular concentrations within and south of the late Roman enclosure 9506, although the layer was more extensive than shown on plan, being recorded in section underlying the late Roman occupation sequence against the western edge of Area A and below alluvium along the southern edge where a deep sequence of deposition was encountered. The part of the deposit seen within the enclosure contained a chronologically mixed pottery assemblage, which included middle Iron Age, early Roman and late Roman material. The deposit overlay brickearth and is likely to have formed between the middle Iron Age and the later Roman period, attracting material during its formation and use as a working surface. The character of the deposit, a very fine-grained soil, potentially points to a degree of natural deposition by tidal action, with material from the in situ red hills located at the edge of the tidal zone being dragged back towards the sea by the tide (C Carey, pers. comm.). However, the red hill soil was undoubtedly valued as a resource of material with which to create dry occupation surfaces over alluvium and for other purposes; Fawn et al. (1990, 5) note that in more recent times, soil from red hills in Mersea was carted away by farmers to mix into the heavy agricultural soils. The red hills are likely to have been quarried by Stanford Wharf's inhabitants since their abandonment in the middle Iron Age.

THE FINDS

Pottery (Figs 4.13-4.14)
by Edward Biddulph and Dan Stansbie

Over 500 sherds of pottery were recovered from the features dated to the middle Iron Age. A further 550 sherds were found as residual occurrences in later con-

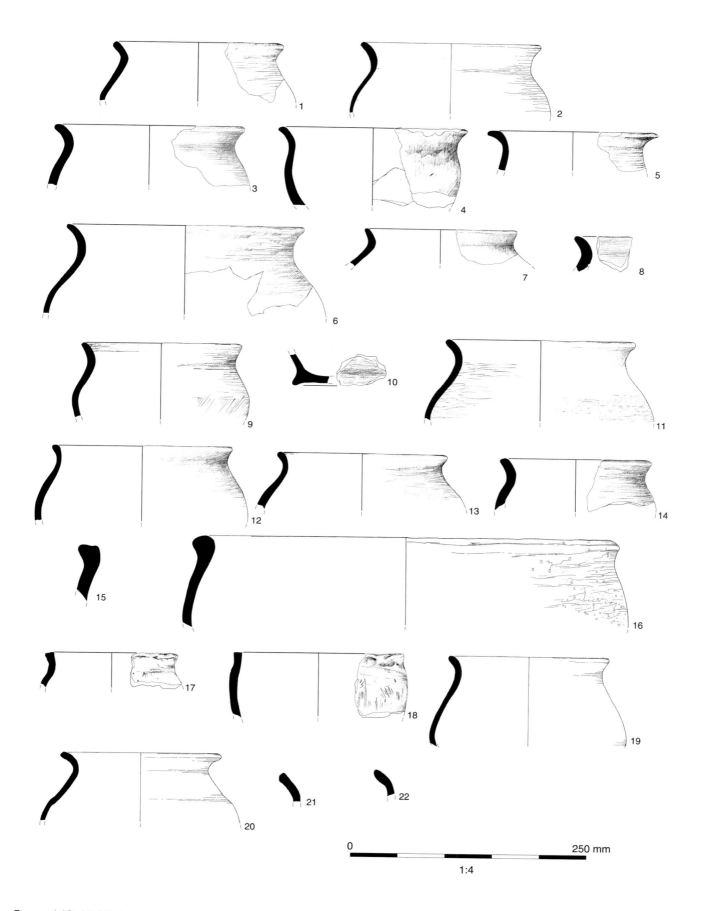

Figure 4.13 Middle Iron Age pottery

0 ——————————————— 50 mm

1:1

Figure 4.14　Body sherd from middle Iron Age pottery vessel with internal residue

Table 4.1: Middle Iron Age pottery from key ceramic groups, c 400-100 BC. Quantification by EVE. * = fabric present, but with no surviving rim. G = Jar

Fabric	G Bead rim	G Everted rim	G Necked	G S-profile	G Unspecified	G Vertical rim	Total	%
ESH	0.03						0.03	1
FLINT	0.47						0.47	15
FLSAND							*	
GLAUC		0.40	0.07	1.58	0.13		2.18	70
GRF							*	
GRS							*	
MICW					0.03		0.03	1
MWSRS							*	
RED							*	
SAND		0.17		0.08	0.07	0.09	0.41	13
SHELL							*	
STOR							*	
Total	0.50	0.57	0.07	1.66	0.20	0.12	3.12	-
%	16	18	2	53	6	4	-	-

texts. The assemblage from contemporaneous features was dominated by glauconitic fabrics (GLAUC), which took a 70% share of the group by EVE (Table 4.1). Glauconitic pottery, with a distinctive fabric tempered with rounded dark grains, was found in quantity at Little Waltham, north of Chelmsford. Petrological examination of fabric samples from that site suggested that the source of the pottery was the same as that for similar Kentish material (Peacock and Williams 1978, 58), whose origin is concentrated in the Medway valley (Pollard 1988, 31). This does not rule out an Essex source for the pottery from Stanford Wharf, and indeed glauconite also occurs as greensand in the local Thanet Sands, which lie west of Stanford-le-Hope. Given this geology, and the dominance of glauconitic pottery at Stanford Wharf, a local, rather than Medway, source is likely. Forms conform to types recorded at Little Waltham – jars with everted rims (and short pedestal bases) (Drury 1978, type 13) (Fig. 4.13, nos 1 and 3), jars with an S-profile (eg ibid., types 11 and 14) (Fig. 4.13, nos 4-14), and jars

with vertical rims (ibid., type 4). Necked jars and bead-rimmed jars were also recorded. Flint-tempered pottery (FLINT) accounted for 15% of the phase assemblage (Fig. 4.13, no. 16). As with the glauconitic pottery, the flint is likely to have been sourced locally; the Bullhead Bed, for instance, which is characterised by rounded flint nodules in clay, lies at the base of the Thanet Sands. Forms were restricted to bead-rimmed jars (as ibid., type 5). Sand-tempered pottery contributed 13% of the phase assemblage. The fabric shared a number of forms with glauconitic pottery, namely S-profile jars and jars with vertical or everted rims (Fig. 4.13, nos 2 and 20-21). Minor quantities of miscellaneous coarse ware (MICW) and shelly fabrics (ESH, SHELL) were recorded. A small amount of intrusive Roman-period pottery was noted. A sherd in a sandy fabric and recovered as a residual occurrence from late Roman gully 6060 had a burnt clay material adhering to its internal surface. This may be the ashy residue of burnt salt marsh plants and sediment (Fig. 4.14).

Briquetage and fired clay (Fig. 4.15)
by Cynthia Poole

A considerable quantity (94kg) of briquetage and fired clay was recovered from contexts assigned to the middle Iron Age (Table 4.2). The majority of the material derives from red hill deposits and comprised briquetage vessels, furniture, structural material and fuel debris. No complete vessels were recovered, and though some joining fragments were found, it was difficult to calculate overall size or definitive shape of the containers. Where possible, each vessels was assigned to one of six categories based on general known forms: V1 (cylindrical vessels or moulds), V2 (flared vessels), V3 (rounded bowl-shaped vessels), V4 (troughs), V5 (trays), V6 (cone), while less specific codes – V7 (flat sherds), V8 (curved sherds), and V9 (indeterminate) – were also used. A range of portable furniture, such as pedestals and firebars, was also identified. Some of these had a very clear-cut form, and were clearly prefabricated and possibly fired prior to use, while others were more variable in shape and character, being made on the spot as and when required and fired as a result of use.

Of the vessels, types V5 and V6 were not found on the site. The red hills contained vessels of type V1 (Fig. 4.15, nos 6, 9 and 13), V3 (Fig. 4.15, no. 14) and V4 (Fig. 4.15, no. 12), and furniture included cylindrical pedestals (type PD3/PD16; Fig. 4.15, no. 19), tapered firebars (type FB4; Fig. 4.15, no. 27), and triangular pedestals (type PD19; Fig. 4.15, nos 24 and 25). The latter is the only form that occurred exclusively in middle Iron Age deposits. There were fewer recognisable forms from redeposited red hill layers, though vessel forms included types V1, V2 (flared vessel) and V4, and furniture included a cylindrical pedestal and rectangular sectioned firebar. A bellows guard was found in pit 6361. It took the form of a curving tubular object with a diameter of c 120mm (100mm internally) and a surviving length of 62mm. The walls were 15-18 and 28mm thick. All pieces have a rough moulded surface with greenish grey salt vitrified surface. The general characteristics would be consistent with a tubular bellows guard. A similar example was found at Danebury, Hampshire (Poole 1984, 407, fig. 7.49 and 7.71) in middle Iron Age levels and another at Springhead in a mid-Roman pit (Poole 2011, 322). Fabrics were dominated by those of sandy clay or brickearth, with a few organic, grass-tempered vessels also present.

AREA B

Some traces of reddened material were observed in Area B, particularly along the eastern baulk of the excavation. This suggests that another red hill extends beyond the investigated area.

DISCUSSION

Chronology

The red hills are dated to the middle Iron Age by an OSL date and abundant pottery. The pottery assemblage comprised 465 sherds, weighing over 6200g, and was distributed throughout the layers of burnt clay and silt which made up the red hills, with a particularly large concentration in red hill 6717, but was also found in the salt-making hearths, ditches and pits (Table 4.3). It was dominated by glauconite-tempered fabrics, which probably derived from local deposits of greensand to the west of the site, and a broadly middle Iron Age date (400 BC-100 BC) for the S-profile, vertical rimmed jars and everted rim jars recorded is based on parallels from Little Waltham (see Biddulph and Stansbie above). It has not been possible to refine the dating of the red hills or the fluctuating intensity of the activity on the basis of

Table 4.2: Briquetage – summary (based of number of records) of diagnostic vessel forms and furniture by phase.

Forms	Fabrics	Iron Age	Early Roman	Middle Roman	Late Roman
V1 mould	Gp B (sandy)	17	0	1	4
V2 mould	Gp B (sandy)	2	0	0	1
V3 bowl	GpA (vegetal)	2	1	0	3
	Gp B (sandy)	6	0	0	5
V4 trough	GpA (vegetal)	0	5	0	27
	Gp B (sandy)	10	0	0	6
Briquetage vessels (all)	GpA (vegetal)	19	40	3	208
	Gp B (sandy)	75	6	9	197
Pedestal PD3/PD16	GpA (vegetal)	2	0	0	2
	Gp B (sandy)	11	0	1	0
Pedestal PD18	GpA (vegetal)	0	0	0	16
Pedestal PD19	Gp B (sandy)	8	0	0	2
Firebar FB6/FB4a	GpA (vegetal)	1	1	0	4
	Gp B (sandy)	0	0	0	1
Plates	GpA (vegetal)	0	0	0	6
	Gp B (sandy)	0	0	0	2
Wedge W1b	GpA (vegetal)	0	4	0	5
	Gp B (sandy)	0	0	0	1

Briquetage vessels

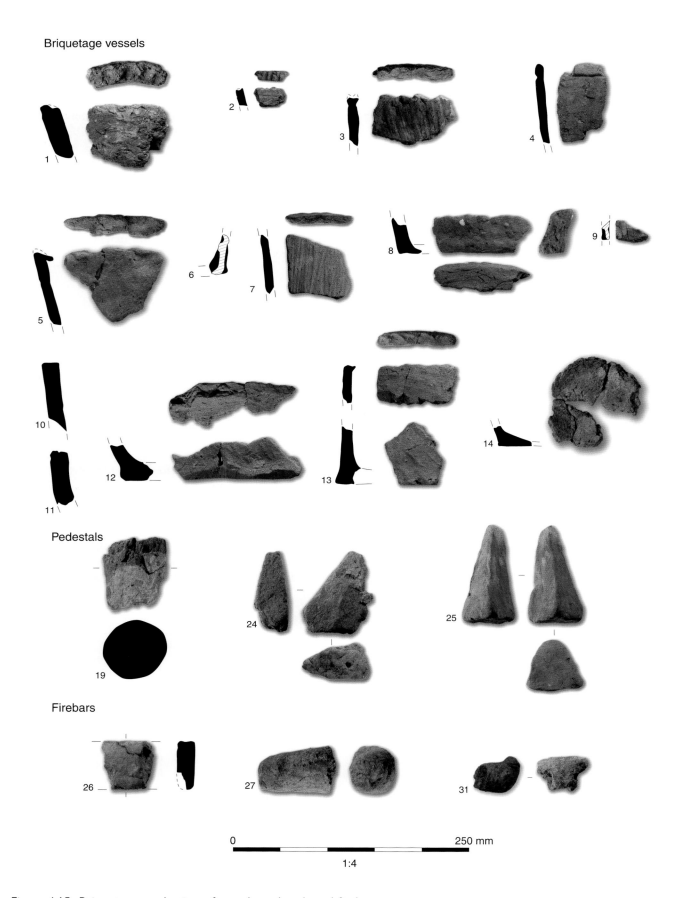

Pedestals

Firebars

0   250 mm

1:4

Figure 4.15 Briquetage, a selection of vessels, pedestals and firebars

Table 4.3: Pottery from the red hills (excluding cut features and redeposited red hill layers)

Fabric	Red hill 6717			Red hill 6718			Red hill 9504			Red hill 9505		
	Sherds	Weight (g)	EVE	Sherds	Weight (g)	EVE	Sherds	Weight (g)	EVE	Sherds	Weight (g)	EVE
BSW Black-surfaced ware (intrusive)							3	35				
FLINT Flint-tempered fabric	9	193	0.03				23	784				
GLAUC Glauconitic-tempered fabric	312	3311	1.32	6	395	0.58	1	6		9	101	
GRF Fine grey ware (intrusive)							7	94	0.13			
GRS Sandy grey ware (intrusive)	21	109		1	5		2	118				
MICW Misc. Iron Age coarse fabric	3	79										
MWSRS Misc. white-slipped red ware (intrusive)				2	5							
NKG North Kent grey ware (intrusive)							3	13				
RED Oxidised ware (intrusive)	9	30					2	20				
SAND Sand-tempered fabric	14	276		24	371	0.07	9	80	0.11	2	37	
SHELL Shell-tempered fabric	1	1										
STOR Storage jar fabric (intrusive)							2	144				
Total	369	3999	1.35	33	776	0.65	52	1294	0.24	11	138	0

the stratigraphy, although given the preponderance of late Iron Age to early Roman red hills along the Essex coast (Kinory 2011, 41), a date later in the middle Iron Age sequence, rather than earlier, seems more likely. This view is supported by the OSL measurement obtained from red hill 9504, which gave a date of 250 BC-AD 150 (2000 ± 200 BP; GL09090). In any case, the extent and depth of the red hills indicates that activity must either have taken place over a considerable period of time, or have been very intensive. The fact that probable ditch 6253 was partially overlain by red hill 6717 also indicates that there was a relatively long term sequence of occupation within the middle Iron Age.

The pottery and scientific dating identifies the Stanford Wharf red hills as being among the earliest examples in Essex. Generally, pottery from other red hill sites falls into a date range of c 50 BC to AD 200 (Jefferies and Barford 1990a, 35), and while early or middle Iron Age sites are known, the chronological distribution of red hill sites from a ceramic perspective shows a concentration between the late 1st century BC/early 1st century AD and c AD 100. Some of the earliest evidence has been found close to Stanford Wharf. Briquetage from the North Ring, Mucking, including pedestal and firebar fragments, provides evidence for Bronze Age salt-evaporation hearths (Barford 1988b, 41), and salt production during the early or middle Iron Age near Gun Hill, West Tilbury is suspected (Drury and Rodwell 1973, 93). Other sites potentially contemporary with Stanford Wharf based on pottery evidence include Peldon, south of Colchester, and Kirby-le-Soken and Walton east of Colchester (Fig. 1.6; Fawn et al. 1990). A middle Iron Age salt production site, comprising the remains of red hills, hearths and a probable settling tank, is also known at Tollesbury Creek, Tollesbury (Germany 2004). At the same time that the red hills were operational at Stanford Wharf, salt was being produced on the opposite side of the Thames near Gravesend (Allen et al. 2012). The few scientific dates that have been obtained preserve the chronological

pattern of the Essex red hills; a hearth from Peldon produced an archaeomagnetic date of 10 BC-AD 40 and a radiocarbon date of 34 cal BC-cal AD 134 (HAR 1832). However, a radiocarbon date of 342-110 cal BC (Q 1173) from a burnt layer in a red hill at Osea Road, Maldon, on the Blackwater estuary (Fawn et al. 1990, table 3), is closer to the chronology of the Stanford Wharf red hills.

Formation of the red hills

The battery of chemical, micromorphological and other scientific analyses (Macphail et al., specialist report 24) undertaken on red hill 6717 (sequence 19) offers tremendous insight into its formation, and though earlier descriptions of the composition of red hills (Rodwell 1979, 133; Fawn et al. 1990, 31; Wilkinson and Murphy 1995, 166) remain broadly correct, the recent analysis has permitted us to reconstruct the sequence of deposition with an unparalleled level of detail. This is a significant achievement of the archaeological investigation, and fulfils a research objective set in the post-excavation scoping report (OA 2009c). The earliest deposits in the sequence, which overlay the natural brickearth, are characterised by fine red hill-type sediments. These contained traces of monocotyledon salt marsh plants and possible dung, which had been used as fuel. Further deposits of red hill sediments, composed of fuel ash derived from salt marsh plants and burnt salt marsh sediment, were subsequently laid down and used as occupation or working surfaces. Such surfaces were recognised because trampling had caused the surviving silica of the plant material, or phytoliths, to fragment. Some of the surfaces may even have been cobbled using large fragments of briquetage and hearth debris. During this formation process, the red hill was affected by tidal inundation, bringing in deposits of alluvial clay. In general terms, the red hill contexts show a sequence of hiatus, dumping, and surface formation.

The microstratigraphy demonstrated that many of the contexts were formed from multiple depositional episodes, some tidal, some of human origin.

This sequence can be detected in the stratigraphy of red hill 6717 and others. Red hill 9504 comprised a sequence of layers which had developed from north to south. The earliest layers were situated on the northern side of the mound, suggesting that material had been pushed northwards from a central location and that the mound was formed by periodically clearing away the salt-making debris – the fuel waste and briquetage fragments – from a working area, possibly at the beginning of each new salt-making season. It is possible that the material was derived from the raking out of hearths at the end of each salt making episode, or prior to the commencement of a new episode. In contrast, the layers making up red hill 9505 were stratified vertically, with each new layer apparently laid down uniformly over the previous one. Red hill 6717 largely appeared to have formed in a similar manner to red hill 9505, although there was some indication of a sequence extending from west to east at the eastern end of the mound.

Examination of the stratigraphy of the red hill at Osea Road, Maldon, reveals a similar sequence of dumping and surface creation. Sections through the feature show tip lines which indicate dumping of red hill material. As at Stanford Wharf, this material appeared to comprise mainly fuel waste; quartz counts undertaken on the material found that the deposits were more typical of hearth material than briquetage (Fawn *et al.* 1990, 31). The tip lines show a progressive sequence of dumping from the centre of the red hill outwards, indicating that the red hill extended in area over time. Settling tanks had been dug into the dumped layers, showing that areas of the red hill had been levelled and used as a working surface (ibid., 32).

The use of Stanford Wharf's red hills as working surfaces is clear enough from the existence of hearths or ovens and pits cut into them. Red hill 9504 incorporated at least six hearths and seven pits, while a hearth and two pits were recorded in red hill 6707. Hearths and pits were also uncovered within red hill 6717. The hearths have been interpreted as such on the basis of charcoal and burnt clay recovered from them. The function of the pits is less certain, though the use of clay linings in pits 5829 and 5833 in red hill 9504 is consistent with storage of water, presumably brine. The larger rectangular pits in red hills 6707 and 6717 (6498 and 6400 respectively) can also be seen as brine-storage pits – and it is worth noting their similarity in terms of shape and size to the so-called settling tank in late Roman saltern 5808 – although their larger surface area and shallow depth may have allowed a greater degree of natural evaporation of the sea water than provided by the smaller round pits. The *ad hoc* positioning of the hearth structures and their relatively insubstantial construction is suggestive of temporary structures built and used on a periodic basis, perhaps in a seasonal manner. The absence of structures for channelling sea water during tidal inundation is also indicative of a moderate level of investment in infrastructure, suggesting temporary or seasonal activity. Other pits and postholes dispersed throughout the red hill sequence may have represented parts of temporary shelters or windbreaks.

Unlike many red hills recorded along the coast of Essex, the red hills at Stanford Wharf had been severely truncated. This much is evident when we consider that a number of mounds in Essex remained visible in the landscape until recent times (hence their description as red hills). Some have since been totally denuded by ploughing, but those in marshland were visible at least until the early 1990s. At the time of the publication of the red hills survey (Fawn *et al.* 1990, 6), a mound at Peldon at Mersea stood to a height of 1.3m above the marshland. Farming on the lower terrace during the 15th and 16th century, and then on former marshland following reclamation in the 17th century, have no doubt been responsible for the destruction of the upper levels of the red hills at Stanford Wharf, but Roman-period activity also took its toll. This is evident from the later Roman disturbance of red hill 9504 suggested by the presence of later Roman pottery within the sequence of deposits. Some of the red hill material may have been quarried to provide working surfaces, for example the extensive area of redeposited red hill material underlying the later Roman enclosure 9506 (see Chapter 6), although to some extent the smaller particles could have been moved through tidal action.

The production process

The conventional understanding of Iron Age salt production in the coastal zone is that seawater was trapped in ponds, naturally-formed channels or ditches cut into the foreshore, and then evaporated over hearths in briquetage troughs or pans to produce the salt. Bradley (1975, 21) makes the assumption that evaporation over hearths in the Iron Age and early Roman periods was preceded by solar evaporation to concentrate the brine. One wonders whether the importance of solar evaporation in British Iron Age salt manufacture has been exaggerated, not least because solar evaporation methods are not particularly reliable in Britain's temperate climate, even during the summer months when most salt making would have taken place (ibid.). Reviewing salt-making processes used in historical and ethnographic examples (see Chapter 1), it is clear that the range of methods available for manufacturing salt using Iron Age technologies is more diverse than is generally realised. Consideration of such methods in the light of the chemical and micromorphological evidence and charred plant remains from the Stanford Wharf's red hills is key to the understanding of the salt-making process at the site. Analysis by Macphail *et al.* (specialist report 24) revealed that Stanford Wharf's red hills predominantly comprised burned salt marsh sediment and the ash of salt marsh plants. The charred plant remains (Hunter, specialist report 19) include cereals, grasses and chaff and suggest that crop waste was used to some extent as a source of fuel at Stanford Wharf, but most of the plant remains assemblage comprised burnt salt marsh plants. By burning the plants (with adhering sediment) for fuel, salters were also producing a salt-rich ash that could be mixed with seawater and filtered to create a brine in a similar way to the methods suggested for La Challonnière and recorded in the Netherlands. The waste from this process was then discarded to form mounds or the red hills.

The idea that salt-impregnated plant matter was burnt for brine is not a new one in relation to Iron Age and Roman red hills and salt making in Essex; the suggestion was mooted in discussion of the data recorded during the Hullbridge survey. However, no supporting evidence was available and the question remained open (Wilkinson and Murphy 1995, 168). The evidence from Stanford Wharf has advanced this discussion by no small measure, and has permitted us to identify a method of salt production that has until now not been recognised in Iron Age (and Roman) Britain. But what advantages would the process have brought to the salters over simply collecting seawater, a ready-made brine? The answer lies in comparative salinity levels. Seawater has an average salinity of 3.5% or 35 parts per thousand (that is, grammes per litre). Brine extracted from springs, such as those exploited at Droitwich and Middlewich, has a higher salt concentration, being about ten times stronger. Consequently, salt yields from brine springs are higher than those from the same amount of seawater; a litre of brine from Droitwich produces 0.29kg of salt, whereas one litre of seawater would produce 0.031kg salt (Woodiwiss 1992, 4). With the open pan method, salters using seawater would have to burn more fuel compared with their counterparts in Worcestershire, or require reliable warm weather to ensure that there was a sufficient amount of natural evaporation and concentration before boiling the brine. The salt marsh would potentially make salt extraction more efficient. Through the process of osmosis, salt marsh plants typically have a higher concentration of salt in their tissues compared with other plants and, crucially, a concentration that is equal to or higher than that of seawater, depending on location (O'Donnell 2009, 41). The location that is characterised by the highest salinity is the high or upper marsh, the relatively elevated area of salt marsh that is inundated infrequently by tidal water (Fig. 2.27). In warm dry summers, the rate of evapotranspiration – the process by which water is removed from the soil – can be considerable, and consequently there is an increased concentration of salt in the soil (Packham and Willis 1997, 69). The plants recorded at Stanford Wharf include rush, sea plantain, sea lavender, sea milkwort and sea arrow grass (Hunter, specialist report 19), which are all characteristic of high marsh. A brine produced by leaching the ash of burnt marsh plants would therefore be more concentrated than seawater, and the process is made more efficient because the ash for leaching reuses the ash created by burning the plants as fuel.

The evidence at Stanford Wharf for a system of ponds and ditches to feed seawater into salt working areas to mix with the ash to create a brine solution ready for filtration and evaporation is somewhat lacking. It is possible that the later Roman activity, particularly the construction of enclosures and structures in that period (see Chapter 6), removed the evidence, but it is possible that ceramic and briquetage vessels were used to collect brine from temporary water traps provided by undulations in the ground surface or emerging natural channels and hollows. The briquetage assemblage from the middle Iron Age red hills (Poole, specialist report 8) included troughs, pedestals, hand squeezed lumps and clips as well as cylindrical and other vessels, and a bellows guard from pit 6361, towards the north-eastern end of red hill 6717. The cylindrical and flared briquetage vessels are among the forms likely to have been used to collect seawater. The ash may have been added to the vessels holding the seawater, and the brine subsequently filtered into pits, or the seawater was poured into the pits before being mixed with ash. The briquetage pedestals were placed in or around the hearth to support the troughs that contained brine, allowing evaporation and crystallisation to occur with the heat produced by the hearth. The fuel was provided largely by more salt marsh plants, and the resulting ash was used to produce more brine. Pottery is also likely to have been used in the production process. A thick deposit of reddish-brown clayey material on the internal surface of a middle Iron Age body sherd (Fig. 4.14) was unfortunately not analysed, but may potentially be identified as the red-hill-like ashy residue of burnt salt marsh sediment and plants. The vessel may have held a solution of ash and seawater, which was allowed to stand for a while to increase the concentration of the brine, or perhaps was used simply as a general scooping or transportation vessel.

While the method of producing and evaporating brine at Stanford Wharf has been recorded to greater or lesser extents at other salt-producing sites in various locations and periods, it might be regarded as curious that red hills, the residue of salt making, appear to be a particularly distinctive feature of Iron Age and Roman salt making in Essex. However, it is not the case that mounds related to salt making are restricted to Essex. For example, the residue produced by the sleeching method used at Wainfleet St Mary was discarded next to areas of salt working to form rows of elongated mounds up to c 50m long; the mounds also covered evidence from earlier phases of salt working and generally caused ground levels to rise (McAvoy 1994, 136-8). Excavation at La Challonnière revealed spreads of superimposed layers, which contained fragmented pottery and briquetage, and traces of fuel – mainly wood charcoal – but predominantly comprised burnt alluvial clay. Some layers consisted exclusively of very fine particles of burnt clay. The report authors concluded that these layers represented mounds generated by discarding alluvial clay, which had been raked, burnt, then leached through with seawater to create the brine (Dartevelle et al. 1998, 45). At Kibiro, the waste from the leaching of salt-impregnated soil was deposited to form low banks around salt gardens. The dried banks were then broken up and spread back onto the ground surface to draw up more salt and repeat the salt-making process (Connah *et al.* 1990, 32). A comparison of the soil from the various types of mounds produced would no doubt return differences in composition and colour, reflecting the variation of processes and resources used, but it is reasonable to suggest that other sites have their equivalent of the Essex red hills. Indeed, it has been suggested that *Rutupiae*, the Roman name of Richborough in Kent, means 'red tops', referring to mounds of red-coloured soil generated through salt production (Durham and Goormachtigh 2012). The absence of late Roman red hills at Stanford Wharf is considered in Chapter 6.

Seasonality

As with the technicalities of the production process itself, the ethnographic literature provides evidence for very divergent means of organisation. A broad summary of the evidence suggests that seasonal working has more often been correlated with induced evaporation, that is, the kind of boiling of brine seen in the British Iron Age and Roman periods. In contrast, traditional inland and coastal salt production in modern Africa is carried out on a more permanent basis, though sometimes part-time by communities also engaged in farming and fishing (cf. Alexander 1975, 81). At Kibiro (Uganda), salt production constituted the main means of year-round social and economic engagement for an entire community; the only other industry was fishing and the community was reliant on the exchange of salt for its means of subsistence, having no animals and growing no crops. In Western Niger nomadic groups gather periodically at Tegidda-n-tesemt to extract salt from saline soil created by the outflow of saline springs, and in this case the labour is undertaken by the entire community (Gouletquer 1975, 47-48). Studies of prehistoric salt production in Britain have largely interpreted salt-making as a seasonal, or periodic, activity, either carried out by parts of communities, or by entire communities for short periods of time. In his study of prehistoric to Roman salt-making on the south coast of England, Bradley (1975) argued that salt making activity was largely seasonal, taking place in the summer months between May and August, when the climate was optimal for salt production through solar evaporation. In addition, salt making was seen as an activity that was integrated into the agricultural cycle, taking place in the interval between the sowing of the spring crop and the harvesting of the winter crop. This seasonal salt making activity may have been partially linked with seasonal farming and fishing in these areas, with herds of animals being brought to the coastal salt marshes for summer grazing concurrently with the salt manufacturing. Pottery and brick making may also have been part of this same pattern of seasonal industrial and agricultural activities (Bradley 1975, 22). Elaine Morris too,

although not arguing explicitly for a seasonal pattern of activity, has suggested that salt working sites in the Lincolnshire fens dating to later prehistory and the early Roman period were not occupied for long periods of time, thus implying the possibility of seasonality (Morris 2007, 442).

The evidence from Stanford Wharf suggests that Iron Age salt making activity at the site involved temporary visits for the purposes of salt manufacture, perhaps incorporating some other parallel activities such as herding and fishing, which would leave little trace in the archaeological record. The archaeological features from the site which date to this period, including red hills and hearths, relate exclusively to salt making, with no evidence of domestic occupation, other than the presence of pottery, which could anyway be related to the salt making process, and a little animal bone. This lack of evidence for settlement activity and normal domestic activities such as cooking and butchery can be taken at face value and used to infer the lack of such activities in the immediate vicinity, given that a large area around the red hills was investigated during the excavation. This suggests that temporary activity is represented. Possibly a small sub-section of a local community, perhaps based on age or sex, visited the site on a temporary, but regular, basis in order to make the salt. Alternatively, the salt makers visited the site on a seasonal basis; this is perhaps more likely, given that the optimal conditions for the process would obtain in the summer months, when rainfall was at its lowest and sunlight at its highest levels, whether or not solar evaporation was used as part of the manufacturing process. It should be noted in this connection that the peak time for salt making at Kibiro is during the dry season (Connah *et al.* 1990, 31) and this is in an environment with higher temperatures and less rainfall than we can assume for temperate Britain in the middle Iron Age. Temporary domestic structures associated with short-term occupation under either of these scenarios would not be expected to leave a significant trace in the record, and in any case need not have been sited immediately adjacent to the red hill locations.

Social aspects of salt making

Several different possible divisions of labour in salt manufacturing are possible, as can be seen from the ethnographic examples cited above. While salt manufacture and trade at Kibiro was exclusively controlled by women, in other ethnographic examples, including the nomadic peoples from Niger described by Gouletquer (1975), both men and women were involved in the process. At Kibiro, the division of labour extends to age. Girls aged 10 to 14 accompany older sisters or adults to the salt gardens to gather the salty soil. Girls aged 15 or over are permitted to leach the soil and boil the brine, though they are supervised by their mothers or grandmothers. All girls and women help with the collection of firewood (Connah *et al.* 1990, 35-6). Elaine Morris' study of prehistoric to Roman salt manufacture in the Lincolnshire fens suggests a possible change in the division of labour over time, with salt making being the responsibility of women during the earlier phase of activity, between the late Bronze Age and early Iron Age, when the manufacturing activity was conducted at a household level and concentrated close to settlement sites on the edge of the fens, but passing into the control of men from the beginning of the late Iron Age when production intensified and moved into the fens and away from settlement sites (Morris 2007, 440-41). Alternatively, however, both men and women may have been involved in production in the later phase (ibid., 442).

The evidence from the middle Iron Age period at Stanford Wharf is equivocal, with little indication from the scale of production, organisation, or material culture of a specifically gender-based division of labour. The only evidence which might be expected to give an indication of the division of labour is the briquetage, which Morris (2012) suggests, in a discussion of salt production in north-east Kent, was likely to have been made by women in the early Iron Age, based on a model of household production for handmade and bonfire-baked pottery. She notes, however, that at times of peak production during the summer months, the entire community, involving girls, boys, men and women, is likely to have been involved (ibid., 245). After all, there was no shortage of tasks – gathering and preparing fuel, digging out clay for briquetage, shaping and firing the vessels, collecting seawater, tending fires, and so on.

There is no evidence from middle Iron Age Stanford Wharf that salt making was a high status activity, or that it was controlled by an absentee elite, such as a warrior or priestly cast (cf. Kinory 2011, 77). The pottery assemblage is largely composed of a standard range of vessel forms, with no indication of high status, and there is little animal bone from the site to give an indication of what the diet of the salt producers may have been. No small finds which might give an indication of social status were found. In addition, no structures associated with the red hills were discovered and it is likely that the salt producers lived away from the salterns, or occupied temporary camps. Given this lack of evidence there is no reason to believe that the salt makers had a particularly high status in society, or that they controlled networks of salt distribution beyond the immediate vicinity of their settlements.

It can be argued that salt forms a central component in ritual and magic in many human cultures, and Morris (2007, 442) suggests that this was no less the case in the British Iron Age and early Roman periods, with the manufacture of salt potentially being seen as a magical process, and the capacity of salt to delay decomposition of organic materials itself being seen as magical (ibid.). Unfortunately none of the evidence from the middle Iron Age phase throws any light on the potential use of ritual or magic in the salt making process at Stanford Wharf.

Distribution of salt

Evidence for the distribution and exchange of salt in Iron Age and Roman Essex is less extensive than that from other regions, and the evidence from Stanford Wharf does not add much information to this picture. The central problem with studying the exchange of salt is that it does not survive in the archaeological record without exceptional conditions of preservation, and so the presence of briquetage on non-salt-producing sites is usually taken as proxy evidence for salt exchange. The role of briquetage containers as transportation vessels has long been a matter of debate. The distribution of cylindrical briquetage vessels around Droitwich, for example, points to their use as containers for salt transportation during the Iron Age and Roman periods (Rees 1986; Woodiwiss 1992, 183), and cylindrical vessels have been recorded at the Iron Age hillfort at Danebury in Hampshire (Poole 1991). For the late Iron Age and earlier Roman period in Essex, however, Janice Kinory (2012) has confirmed the essentially coastal pattern of distribution of briquetage, and builds on Barford's sparse list of inland briquetage finds, which are confined mainly to sites reasonably close to the coast or areas of estuarine salt production, such as Little Oakley, St Osyth, Heybridge and North Shoebury, although sites further inland, notably Great Chesterford and Chelms-ford, are also represented. Even so, most vessel sherds appear to belong to troughs, rather than containers more suited to salt transportation (Barford 1990, 79-80). There are exceptions, however; Nina Crummy (2007, 377) makes the reasonable suggestion that at Stanway, Colchester, briquetage vessels recovered from mortuary enclosures dating to the mid 1st century AD carried salt used for the preparation of the deceased or as part of a funerary ritual. Generally, though, inland finds are rare, and the large number of coastal production sites can be sharply contrasted with a small number of inland occurrences. Of 281 sites in the Essex region at which briquetage was found, only 31 have no evidence for salt production itself (Kinory 2011, 119). Paul Sealey (1995, 68) has argued on the basis of inland finds in Essex that salt was to some extent distributed through trade or by salters returning from the coast to their homes in the hinterland, but this has been rejected by Barford (2000, 276-7), who suggests that the inland finds provide evidence for a secondary market in broken briquetage, which was acquired by farmers and used as salt licks for livestock. Neither explanation convinces Janice Kinory, who sees the presence of inland finds as symbolising and reinforcing social links between coastal and inland settle-ments (Kinory 2012, 52). With relatively little salt production dated to the middle Iron Age, information on the distribution of briquetage during that period is understandably limited, although what few data are known are consistent with a restricted, coastal distribu-tion and argue against containers being used for salt transportation. A pedestal was recorded at Little Waltham, north-west of Chelmsford in central Essex (Drury 1978, 112), and pan or trough fragments were recovered from a ditch at Gun Hill, West Tilbury (Drury and Rodwell 1973, 93).

In general, then, the distribution of briquetage away from the coast and the main salt producing sites of Essex in the later Iron Age appears to be sparse, suggesting that the distance that salt was transported was not much further than the production sites themselves, and certainly never as great as the distribution of salt obtained from inland brine springs in the north-west (Morris 2001, fig. 122). Unlike in north-west Britain, the use of briquetage for salt transportation in Essex seems doubtful. Cynthia Poole (specialist report 8) suggests that the quantity of cylindrical vessels and moulds that had been broken up at Stanford Wharf argues against their use as transportation containers, although the vessels appear to have been used to store salt while it dried, probably on the hearth, and solidified into cakes.

If we can discount briquetage as a container for distribution of salt, whether in trade or other contexts, it may be worth considering pottery vessels as an alternative. Internal residues or white staining were recorded on a number of middle Iron Age vessels at Stanford Wharf, including a globular bowl or jar with everted rim in a glauconitic fabric. It is possible that these vessels contained brine or salt, although it is far from clear whether their use related to salt production or distribution. Nigel Brown notes that the distribution of middle Iron Age pottery decorated with a free-flowing curvilinear pattern and scored motifs is concentrated in the Thames Estuary and encompasses sites in north-west Kent as well as south Essex, including Mucking (Brown 1991, 165). This no doubt reflects cultural links connecting the north and south sides of the Thames Estuary in the middle Iron Age, and raises the possibility that communities gathered to exchange commodities, including pottery, which may have carried salt. Nevertheless, this still implies an essentially local distribution for coastal Essex salt. There are other possibilities for salt containers, such as leather bags, wooden containers or other organic vessels. However,

with no known traces of such material in Essex, their use in the salt industry must remain speculative.

In the absence of evidence for the widespread salting of meat for storage over winter, the arguments for salt being a widely traded staple for prehistoric and Roman farming communities are not convincing. Much of the evidence in support of the use of salted meat derives from butchery marks on pig bones from southern and central late Iron Age sites, such as Mount Batten, Ower, Braughing and Silchester (Maltby 2006, 119-20) and is coupled with evidence suggesting that the mortality profiles of domestic animals peaked during the autumn (Albarella 2007, 394). However, the widespread consumption of pig is largely a phenomenon of the late Iron Age and restricted to high status sites, with sheep, and in Central and Eastern England cattle, being more common on lower status rural sites (ibid.). In Central Southern and Western England and North Wales, where briquetage is fairly widely distributed and is found in some quantity at certain hillfort sites (Kinory 2011, 125), salt may have been in fairly widespread use for the preservation of meat over the autumn and winter. The need for salt in these regions may have been a consequence of the need for large quantities of food among the communities inhabiting the hillforts, both for their ongoing reproduction and during periodic episodes of increased population when the hillforts were undergoing repair and reconstruction (Sharples 2010). In the east of England, where there were fewer hillfort based communities, the widespread use of salt, unlike in central England and the west, was perhaps restricted to the coastal regions and their immediate hinterlands.

The evidence seems therefore to suggest that salt distribution in the Essex region in the middle Iron Age was a relatively localised phenomenon which primarily fulfilled the needs of the coastal communities, while exporting a small amount of salt to the hinterland. This situation perhaps resulted from a lack of need for large-scale food preservation in the hinterland, where, unlike in Wessex and the west, communities were not concentrating large amounts of food resources.

Chapter 5

Early Roman salt production, burial and wooden structures

by Dan Stansbie, Edward Biddulph and Damian Goodburn

INTRODUCTION (Fig. 5.1)

Between the end of the middle Iron Age and the beginning of the early Roman period there appears to have been a hiatus in activity at Stanford Wharf Nature Reserve, and when occupation resumed in the late 1st to early 2nd century AD the character of that occupation appears to have been very different from the industrial activity of the earlier phase. Salt production, identified from a group of pits and channels and dumps of production waste, moved to Area B at the eastern end of the site. The main focus of activity in Area A was defined by a probable timber mooring structure or boathouse and an associated timber group. Other features included a pit in Area A, a wattle-lined channel in Area D, and a human cremation burial in Area C (Fig. 5.1).

EARLY ROMAN FEATURES IN AREA A
(Figs 5.2-5.14)

A mooring/boathouse structure and an associated timber group (Figs 5.2-5.9)

Structure 9500, interpreted as a probable boathouse, or less likely a mooring structure, was represented by an arrangement of 14 oak piles (Figs 5.2-5.3). The piles had been driven through the middle alluvium (unit G5b, see Chapter 2), which represented marine inundation during the Iron Age (Fig. 5.4; see also Fig. 2.5). After the structure was abandoned, and the posts decayed, further inundation caused the structure to be buried by upper alluvium (unit G5c), which dated from the late Roman period onwards. The structure was orientated NW-SE. It was open at its south-eastern end, where it met the edge of the tidally influenced palaeochannel that ran east-west through Areas E to F (see Fig. 2.2) and joined the Thames Estuary. It is unclear whether the southernmost piles, 1520 and 1516, marked the entrance to the structure, or whether erosion of the channel edge through tidal action had removed further timbers. The north-western end of the structure was roughly apsidal in form and defined by two posts, 1474 and 1465 *c* 1.8m apart. Overall, the structure measured *c* 13m in length by *c* 7m in width and the posts of the long walls were spaced approximately 2m apart. The oak piles themselves survived to a length of up to 1.17m, and measured up to 0.18m in diameter (Figs 5.5-5.7). The uprights in the north-west wall, which possibly formed the jambs of a doorway, were much smaller, surviving to a diameter of only 70mm. The wall timbers would originally have been at least 2.2m long (probably more) and required some form of light piling rig to drive in. The level from which the piles were driven is uncertain. Alluviation after abandonment sealed the decayed timbers and removed any evidence of floor or ground surfaces. However, the timbers consistently showed a thinning of the pile at between 1.1m and 1.2m AOD, with the wood above this point being more decayed than the wood below it (Fig. 5.3). In addition, a section across the west side of the structure at pile 1204 (Fig. 5.3, section 1030) shows a thin vertical band of light blue clay (1203) either side of the pile. In section, the clay suggests the profile of a posthole, but no cut was detected, and instead it may represent alluvium washed into a gap created by a loose pile. In any case, the height at the top of this deposit is *c* 1.25m AOD. It is possible that *c* 1.2-1.25m AOD represents the level of the early Roman ground surface around the structure, and that the wood above that level was exposed and subjected to a greater degree of weathering than the portion below it, which retained its tip and edges. Radiocarbon dates were obtained from two oak piles. Pile 1424 on the western side of the structure returned a date of 30 cal. BC-cal. AD 130 (94.5%; 1945 ± 30 BP: SUERC-24881 (GU-19628)). Pile 1119, from the eastern side of the structure, returned a date of cal. AD 50-240 at 94.6% confidence and cal. AD 20-40 at 1.4% confidence (1885±40 BP: SUERC-24584 (GU-19377)). Dating by dendrochronology was attempted on two of the structure's timbers, but the wood was too decayed to date.

Damian Goodburn notes that the five pairs of driven posts of the long walls and the two north wall stakes were all made of small whole oak logs with the branches and some bark removed. Pencil-form points were axe-hewn, leaving nearly complete narrow axe stop marks up to *c* 70mm wide on pile 1477 (Fig. 5.8). The shape of the tips varied considerably, and was such that we might suggest that the work was carried out by several different hands. The timber used was of fast to medium growth and probably came from some form of fairly open managed woodland.

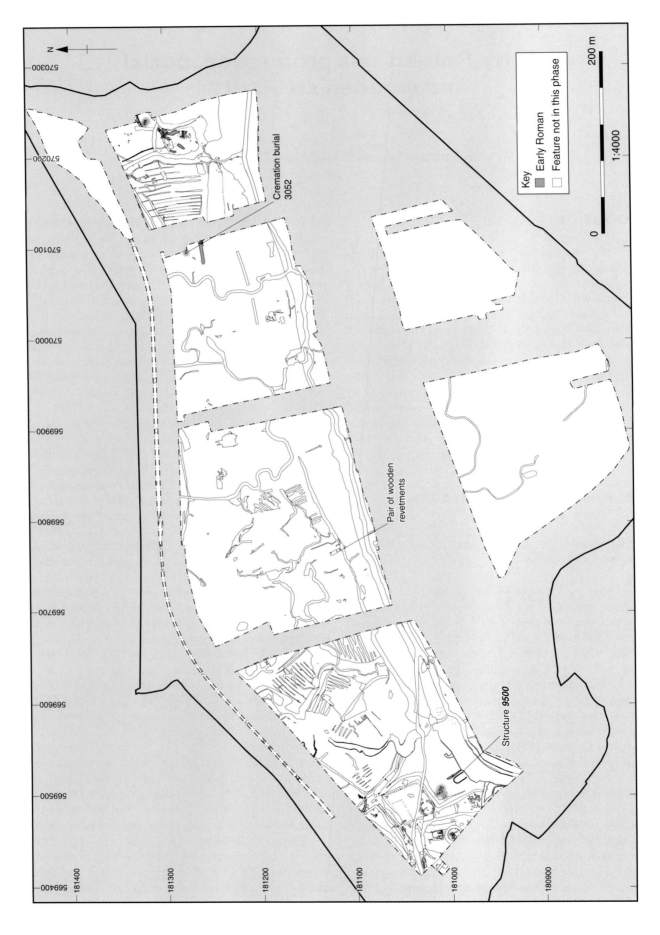

Figure 5.1   Early Roman activity

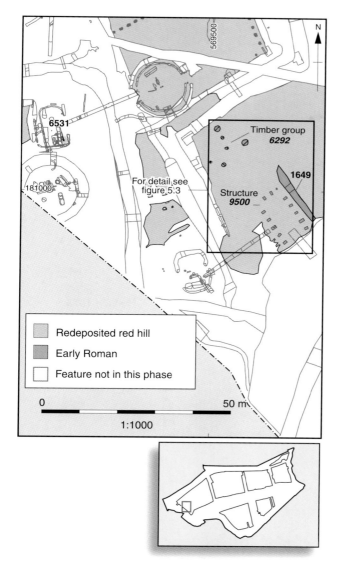

Figure 5.2 Early Roman activity in Area A

surviving up to *c* 1.5m long with rot-truncated tops. Pile 5969 was the heaviest example with a diameter of 170mm and an unusual 'flat' hewn on the lower part of one face; it also had traces of charring on the opposite face, clearly showing that it was reused. The original function is uncertain, and although it had *c* 50 annual rings, no sapwood survived and so it was not selected for tree-ring study. Pile 5778 can be taken as a slightly fresher pile with a little sapwood surviving, but it also had too few annual rings to be viable for tree-ring dating. It was *c* 160mm in diameter and survived to a length of 1.49m. The timbers may have represented part of a windlass structure or device for hauling boats out of the water.

A ditch (1649) lay parallel to the eastern side of structure 9500 (Fig. 5.3). The ditch, cut into the alluvial unit G5, measured *c* 17.65m in length and had a maximum width of *c* 2.4m. It had a shallow profile, being *c* 0.2m deep with concave sides and a flattish base. No dating evidence was recovered, but its position suggests that the ditch was contemporary with the boathouse, and perhaps served as a drainage ditch to take water back into the palaeochannel to the south. A fragment of worked chalk of indeterminate function, identified by Ruth Shaffrey (specialist report 10) from ditch 1649 hints at the possibility that at some point chalk was being shaped on site.

Posthole 6531 (Fig. 5.2)

A posthole recorded within late Roman structure 6090 is likely to have predated that feature. It cut a redeposited red hill-type layer (possibly part of red hill 1018 underneath a late Roman structure or shelter defined by features 6513, 8515 and 8516 – see Chapters 4 and 6), and contained 26 sherds of early Roman pottery and residual middle Iron Age fragments. The pottery was dated to the first quarter of the 2nd century AD on the basis of a white-slipped fabric from the Hadham region in east Hertfordshire, with the date supported by a poppyhead beaker and high-shouldered necked jar, both in fine grey ware (GRF). A jar in black-surfaced ware and a residual jar in glauconitic ware were also recovered from the context.

CHANNEL 2148 AND WATTLEWORK PANELS, AREA D (Figs 5.10-5.14)

A naturally-formed channel (2148), orientated north-south and up to 3.5m wide and 0.8m deep, was recorded in Area D (Figs 5.10 and 5.11). A pair of wattle panels (2027 and 2136), *c* 4m apart, had been inserted across the channel, and effectively blocked it at two points (Fig. 5.10). It is likely that the space between the panels was filled with soil to create a causeway across the channel. Panel 2136 was only partly excavated, but comprised at least five timber posts and three wattles. Panel 2027 was fully exposed, and consisted of vertical

A small amorphous group of six truncated oak stakes, stake holes and small piles (group 6292) was found about 12m north-west of the north end of structure 9500 (Fig. 5.3). Three of the piles (5598, 5780 and 5715) were aligned with the central axis of the structure, while a further three (5643, 5902 and 5970) lay either side of this line. No dating evidence beyond five sherds of broadly-dated Roman pottery was recovered from this group. However, its stratigraphy – the piles had been driven into the same alluvial unit (G5b) into which some of the structure's timbers were set – and its spatial relationship with the boathouse suggest that group 6292 and structure 9500 were contemporaneous and functionally associated. All the lifted examples were of round oak log piles similar to those of structure 9500, with axe-cut tips of varied form, from blunt and four-sided, to elongated and pencil-form piles (timbers 5969 and 5778) (Fig. 5.9). None of the piles looked very freshly made, having what resembled old drying splits or 'shakes' even near the tips, which would have remained pristine if used freshly cut. The diameters of the uprights varied from *c* 100mm to *c* 170mm, with the longest

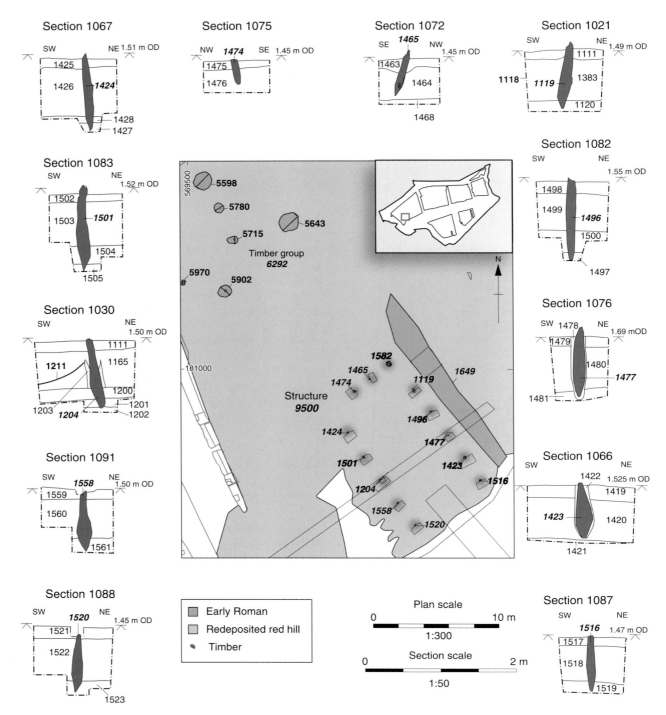

Figure 5.3 Structure 9500 and associated posts

posts and horizontal wattles, which were woven around the posts (Figs 5.11-5.14). Unusually, the uprights were made of comparatively heavy oak poles hewn flat on two faces, mixed with some smaller round oak stakes. Some of the heavy stakes, for example 2139, were over 130mm across, and were among the heaviest wattle stakes seen by Damian Goodburn. After careful cleaning off-site, it was clear that at least two of the stakes had been skilfully hewn from the top of relatively small young oak poles with *c* 30-35 annual rings. The woodsmen were making full use of all possible lengths of wood, even if they were rather crooked. The tips were neatly axe-cut to a variety

of shapes. Stake 2139 had surviving axe stop marks up to 70mm wide. The rods were also quite robust, up to 50mm in diameter, and woven in a plain in-and-out weave. The ends were neatly cut to a chisel or wedge form with a number of blows from a small axe with a rounded blade. This structure, too, has no specifically Roman features but would not be out of place in a rural Roman context. Unfortunately, the revetment is not closely dated – a radiocarbon determination from one of the timbers returned a date of cal. AD 60-250 (95.4%; 1860 ± 40 BP: SUERC-24586 (GU-19379)), and no associated finds were encountered – but it is placed here

Figure 5.4   North-west facing view of structure 9500. The remains of the timber piles lie underneath the white sample buckets

Figure 5.5   North-west facing view of pile 1119. Scale 1m

Figure 5.7   North-west facing view of pile 1477. Scale 1m

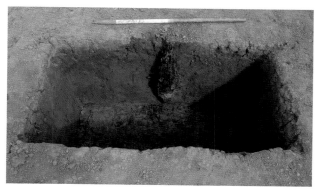

Figure 5.6   North-west facing view of pile 1423. Scale 1m

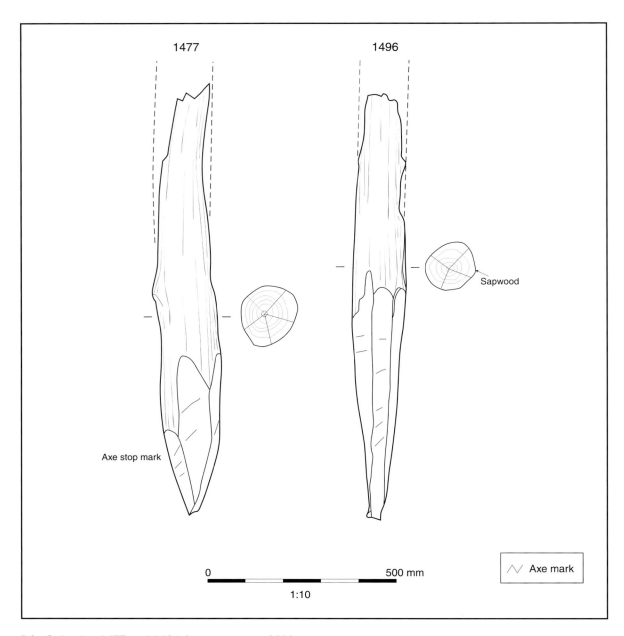

Figure 5.8 Oak piles 1477 and 1496 from structure 9500

on the basis of its rustic character (which allies it more to structure 9500 than, say, to the late Roman timber-lined drain (Chapter 6)) and its earliest possible date provided by the radiocarbon determination.

EARLY ROMAN FEATURES IN AREA C
(Fig. 5.15-5.17)

Cremation burial 3052 (Figs 5.16-17)

An isolated unurned cremation burial lay at the eastern side of Area C, to the west of the scatter of industrial pits and ditches concentrated in Area B. Grave 3052 was sub-circular in plan, with a concave base and moderately sloping sides. It measured 0.85m in width and its maximum depth was 0.13m (Fig. 5.16). The pit contained one fill (3053), a mixed grey-brown and red-brown firm silty clay (Fig. 5.17). The deposit of cremated bone, weighing 148.1g, was predominantly restricted to the lower third of this fill, although the excavator noted some small fragments towards the top of the deposit. Large fragments of charcoal were also noted as present, and were restricted to the south-east side of the pit. There was no evidence for *in situ* burning. A fragmented ceramic vessel (SF 3001) was also present within fill 3053, apparently overlying the cremation deposit, but not containing it. The vessel was a ledge-rimmed jar in a flint-and-sand-tempered fabric dating to *c* AD 1-70.

Helen Webb (specialist report 12) suggests that the cremated bone probably represents a formal cremation burial, although it is clear from the low bone weight that only a small proportion of the deceased individual's remains was deposited here. While poor preservation of trabecular bone may account for some reduction in the

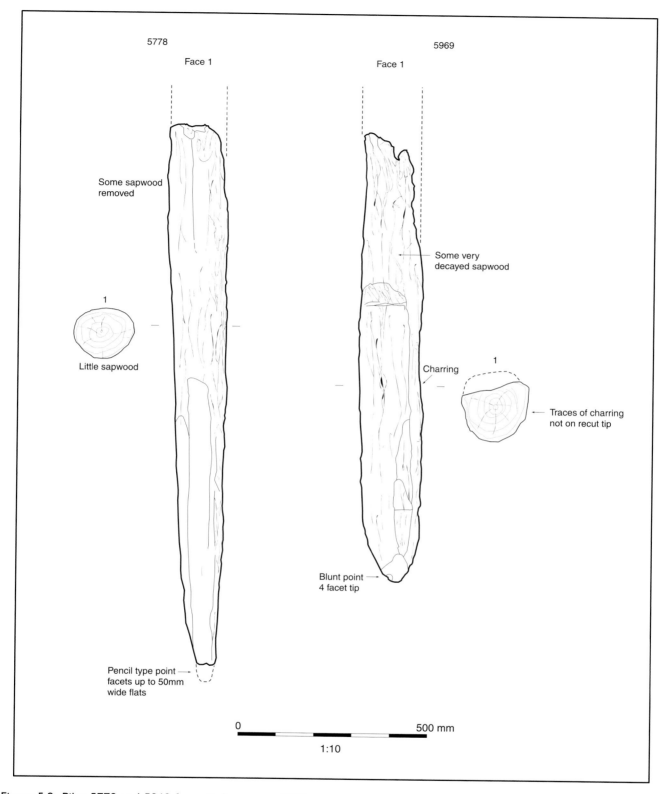

5778

Face 1

Some sapwood
removed

1

Little sapwood

Pencil type point
facets up to 50mm
wide flats

5969

Face 1

Some very
decayed sapwood

Charring

1

Traces of charring
not on recut tip

Blunt point
4 facet tip

0   500 mm

1:10

Figure 5.9 Piles 5778 and 5969 from timber group 6292

final bone weight, the extent of this influence remains in question. The original nature of the deposit is probably the most significant factor. It is possible, given the presence of large charcoal fragments in the fill, that this deposit represents redeposited pyre debris – the material remaining at the end of cremation, including fragments of cremated bone not collected to form part of the formal 'burial'. However, the main component of redeposited pyre debris is fuel ash, possibly with burnt stone and burnt clay (McKinley 2000, 41). These were not noted to be present by the excavator. It is possible therefore, that the deposit is a 'token' burial, with the rest of the bone perhaps having been buried elsewhere, or perhaps scattered, or distributed amongst the funeral attendants

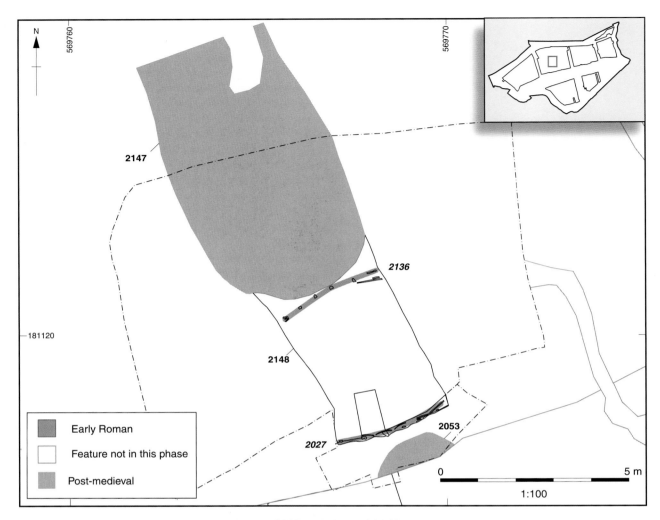

Figure 5.10 Plan showing wattle panels 2136 and 2027 and channel 2148

(McKinley 2000, 42). Even in intact, well-preserved burials, it is rare, if ever, that the skeletal remains of an entire individual are present (McKinley 1997, 137).

The cremated bone deposit was highly fragmented (Table 5.1). The high fragmentation may be due to a range of factors relating both to funerary practices and taphonomy. It is possible that the human remains were deliberately broken up by mourners following cremation, as part of the funerary ritual, possibly to symbolise the end of corporeal existence and to emphasise the separation of the deceased from the world of the embodied living (McKinley 2000, 42-3). Alternatively, fragmentation of the bone may have occurred at any or several of the stages between collec-

Table 5.1: Summary of skeletal elements represented and weights of bone present from grave 3052.
Key: MC = metacarpal; Fem = femur; Tib = tibia; Frag = fragment; Phal = phalanx; prox = proximal

Skeletal region	*> 10mm frags*	*Weight (g)*	*10-4mm frags*	*Weight (g)*	*4-2 mm frags*	*Weight (g)*	*<2mm frags*	*Weight (g)*
Skull	x2 probable occipital frags, x1 temporal frag, other vault frags.	7.1	Vault frags, possible temporal frag, tooth root (broken)	3.3	–	0	–	0
Axial	Rib frag.	0.1	–	0	–	0	–	0
Upper limb	Long bone shaft frags, MC shaft frag.	6.8	Partial radial head, MC/phal shaft frags, x4 prox. or intermed. phal. heads, x5 dist. phals	5.1	–	0	–	0
Lower limb	Fem/tib shaft frags	9.3	Prox phal base/shaft frag, fem/tib shaft frags	3.7	–	0	–	0
Unidentified long bone	–	2.9	–	8.2	–	0	–	0
Unidentified	–	8.1	–	9.3	–	0.5	–	<0.1
Total weight		34.3		113.3		0.5		<0.1

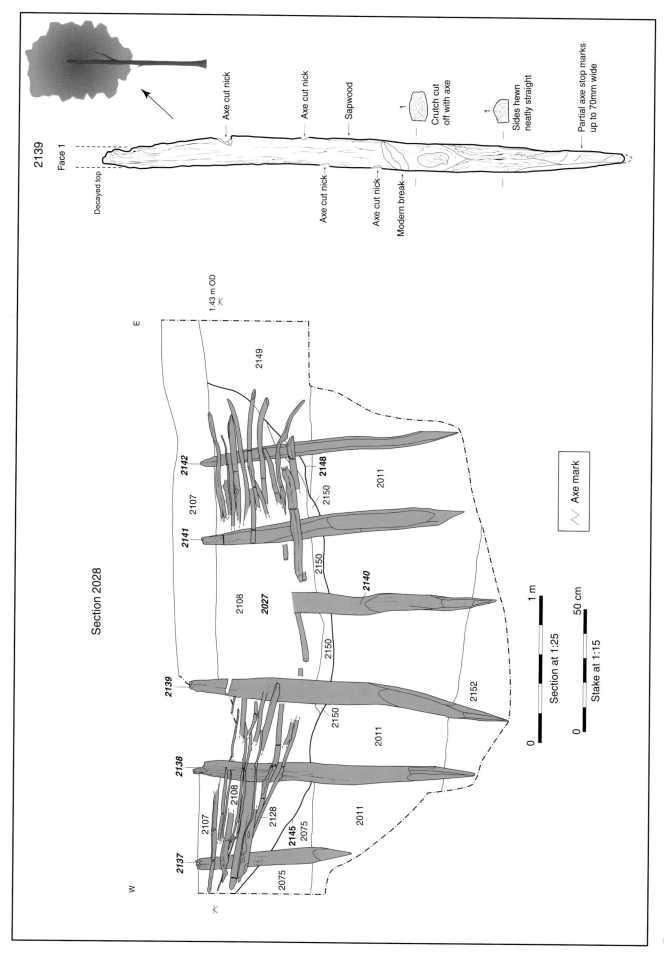

Figure 5.11 Wattlework panel 2027

Figure 5.12 View of panels 2027 and 2136, looking north. Scale 2m

Figure 5.13 Excavating panel 2027

tion from the funerary pyre to archaeological excavation and post-excavation processing. The marked fragmentation of this assemblage made identification of skeletal elements, age and sex problematic. With regard to the overall colour of the bone, it appears that a high efficiency of cremation had been achieved, with the vast majority of bone being a greyish-white colour.

Staining on a number of the bone fragments is likely to have been caused by metal objects coming into contact with the bone; these were probably personal copper alloy items worn by the deceased on the pyre. Only a single fragment of animal bone was identified within the cremated remains; this was a frog. While animals (typically sheep or goat, pig, ox and domestic fowl) were sometimes placed on the funeral pyre as food offerings during the Iron Age and Roman periods (Philpott 1991, 195), it is more likely, in this instance, that the animal was unwittingly burnt in the pyre, possibly having found shelter within the timber structure before the funeral.

Channel or ditch 3034 (Fig. 5.15)

Channel or ditch 3034 lay approximately 14.5m south of cremation burial 3052 (Fig. 5.15). The feature was aligned east-west, and its exposed portion was *c* 25.3m in length and up to *c* 4.6m in width. It was not excavated

Figure 5.14 Panel 2027 exposed after excavation

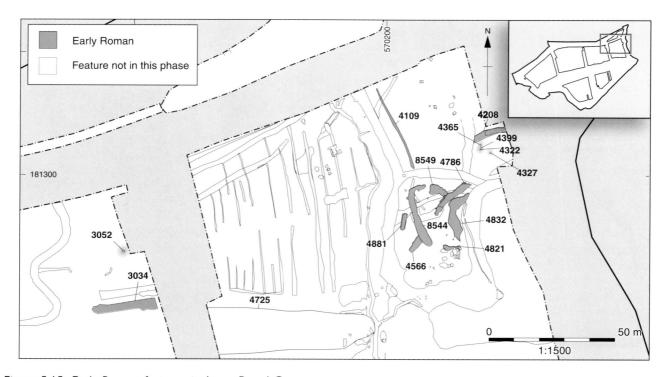

Figure 5.15 Early Roman features in Areas B and C

to its full depth, and so no profile was recorded, but the feature was at least 0.47m deep. While the western terminus was uncovered, no trace of the feature's eastern end was seen. It clearly continued beyond the eastern limit of Area C, though may have extended only for a further 25m, as the feature did not appear in the adjacent Area B. Feature 3034 contained three fills of clay and silty clay, which produced 31 sherds of early Roman pottery, including fragments of ledge-rimmed jars in early shell-tempered fabrics, sandy grey wares, and a ring-necked flagon in a red ware, which together date to the third quarter of the 1st century AD.

EARLY ROMAN SALT PRODUCTION IN AREA B (Figs 5.15 and 5.18)

Early Roman features in Area B (Fig. 5.15) included a concentration of rather amorphous pits and ditches (4208, 4322, 4327, 4365, 4399, 4566, 4786/4844, 4821, 4832 4881, 8544 and 8549) towards the north-east corner of the area. These features did not appear to form a particularly coherent pattern, but are likely to have related to salt making activity on a similar basis to that recorded for the middle Iron Age and later Roman period. The features were located at the edge of a plat-

form, which was formed from a sequence of interleaved alluvial and occupation deposits (Chapter 2). The character of this sequence suggests that the area was subject to frequent tidal inundation. Layers of debris from salt making and general domestic occupation were laid in between the flooding events (Fig. 6.38). An east-west ditch (4208) projected from the eastern side of the excavated area. Its extant section was *c* 13.4m long and 3.7m wide, and on excavation was seen to be *c* 0.96m deep with concave sides and a flat base. Its western terminus appears to have been truncated by late Roman ditch 4242. A small cluster of pits and postholes was recorded immediately south of the ditch. Posthole 4365 was 0.6m in diameter and 0.12m deep, with steep sides and a concave base. A second posthole (4327) was 0.65m across and 0.06m deep. This feature was filled with an ashy deposit, while 4365 was filled with clay and occasional briquetage fragments. Pits 4399 and 4322, next to the postholes, measured up to 1.2m across and 0.25m deep. The clay bases of both features appeared to have been burnt, and they were filled with burnt ash or charcoal and briquetage fragments.

The main concentration of ditches lay just to the south-west, in an area of subsequent intensive activity in the late Roman period (cf Fig. 6.36). The earliest feature was probably an amorphous hollow 8549, which was up to 6.8m long and 3.4m wide and was filled with black ashy deposits. This was cut by ditch 4786/4844, irregular in plan, though broadly orientated NE-SW, approximately 18.3m long, 2.7m wide and 0.6m deep, with irregular edges. It was filled with a sequence of silty

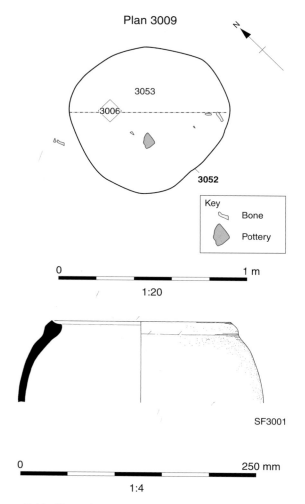

Figure 5.16 Plan of cremation burial 3052

Figure 5.17 Excavation of cremation burial 3052

clay deposits containing black, ashy, pieces and briquetage fragments. Ditch 4832, east of 4786/4844, was another very irregular feature. Curvilinear in plan, it was some 20m long and 4m wide, and had gently-sloping sides and a flat base. The ditch was c 0.7m deep and was filled initially with a silty clay, alluvial, deposit, and then with dumps of red or dark clay deposits mixed with briquetage and fuel debris fragments. A sherd of early Roman shelly ware was recovered from an upper fill. Pit or ditch 4821, south of ditch 4832, was also somewhat irregular in plan but was aligned roughly east-west; it was c 6.2m long, 1.6m wide, and 0.6m deep, and had a U-shaped profile. It was filled with deposits of dark grey or black silty clay, which contained traces of fuel debris and briquetage.

A large pit or short length of ditch, 4566, a little further to the west but on approximately the same alignment as 4786/4844 to the north-east, was sub-rectangular in plan, c 9m long and 2.7m wide. The feature was only 0.3m deep with a concave profile, and was filled with alternating deposits of burnt clay, fuel debris and briquetage fragments and alluvium. Some 50 sherds of pottery were recovered from the feature, including grog-tempered ware, shelly ware, and sandy wares and North Kent grey ware, which point to a date of deposition within the second half of the 1st century AD, possibly in the third quarter. The feature's relationship with ditch 8544, an L-shaped feature to the north of 4566, is unclear; it seems likely that 8544 cut 4566, as shown on Figure 5.15, but the extent of 8544 was not clearly visible until there had been further ground reduction of the area by machine. Ditch 8544 was aligned roughly north-south along the greater part of its length (23m) and then returned to the east for 6m at its northern end. It was between 2.5m and 3.5m in width, with a concave profile and a single dark grey or black silty clay fill, which contained a shelly ware bead-rimmed jar and grog-tempered ware, suggesting deposition in the mid/late 1st century AD. Pit 4881, west of 8544, was a rectangular shaped feature with rounded ends. It measured c 6.8m long, 1.8m wide and 0.55m deep, and had moderately steep, slightly stepped, sides with a flat base. It was filled with clay deposits, some of which contained fragments of briquetage, fuel debris and 20 sherds of pottery, including ledge-rimmed jars in shelly and sandy wares, South Gaulish samian ware, and grog-tempered ware.

One other feature can be placed in this phase. Ditch 4109, situated in the north-east corner of Area B, was aligned NNW-SSE and was c 36.4m long, being cut away at its southern end by late Roman ditch 4063 and ending to the north in a rounded terminal.

Three environmental samples from ditch 4786/4844 were analysed. These contained abundant monocotyledonous leaf/stem fragments with salt marsh seeds, including sea lavender, sea plantain, sea-milkwort and over 100 *Juncus* seeds with sea rush seed capsules. Lady's bedstraw, glasswort and slender hare's ear, which are plants of maritime habitats, were also identified (Hunter, specialist report 19).

Most early Roman pottery groups were recovered from Area B (Table 5.2; Fig. 5.18). In contrast to Area A, all the pottery fits within the second half of the 1st century AD. The dominant fabric is early shell-tempered ware. Forms were confined to lid-seated jars (type G5.1; Fig. 5.18, nos 27-32 and 37-38). Production of shelly ware lid-seated jars is attested at Mucking (Rodwell 1973, 22-24) and Gun Hill, West Tilbury (Drury and Rodwell 1973, 82), both a short distance from Stanford Wharf. Fine grey ware made a significant contribution. A poppyhead beaker, butt-beaker, and jars unidentified to type were recorded (Fig. 5.18, nos 35-36). Black-surfaced ware was another important fabric. It was available, like the shelly ware, as lid-seated jars only, and a local origin is again likely. Rodwell (1973, 24) notes that such jars in sandy fabrics with little or no shell were fired in Mucking kiln VI. More lid-seated jars were seen in sandy grey ware (GRS; Fig. 5.18, no. 33), although other forms were available. These included a jar with bifid rim (type G28; Fig. 5.18, no. 34), a type that was produced at Mucking from the late 2nd century onwards (Rodwell 1973, 26), although production from c AD 125 is known at Dagenham (Biddulph et al. 2010). Its presence at Stanford Wharf suggests that the type has earlier origins still. Another form in sandy grey ware was a platter (Fig. 5.18, no. 23). More lid-seated jars were seen in sandy oxidised wares, which were also used for bead-rimmed jars and high-shouldered necked jars (Fig. 5.18, nos 24 and 25). A large narrow-necked storage jar was another probable local product.

The most important source of pottery from outside the area in terms of quantity was North Kent. Potters there were responsible for a platter and a necked jar. Fine grey ware arrived from Highgate Wood, while sandy white ware was a product of the Verulamium region. Buff ware reached the site from Colchester,

Table 5.2: Early Roman pottery from key ceramic groups (Area B), AD 43-130. Quantification by EVE. * = fabric present, but with no surviving rim.

Fabric	A Platters	C Bowls	G Jars	H Beakers	Total	%
BSW			0.71		0.71	17
BUF		0.14			0.14	3
COLB					*	
ESH			1.17		1.17	27
GRF			0.36	0.57	0.93	22
GROG					*	
GRS	0.05		0.36		0.41	10
HGG					*	
MWSRF					*	
MWSRS					*	
NKG	0.15		0.29		0.44	10
RED			0.23		0.23	5
SGSW					*	
STOR			0.23		0.23	5
UPOT					*	
UWW					*	
VRW					*	
Total	0.20	0.14	3.35	0.57	4.26	-
%	5	3	79	13	-	-

although no form was recognised. A footring in South Gaulish samian ware belonged to a Drag. 18R or 15/17R platter.

Briquetage was found in reasonable quantity (see Table 4.2). Vessels included moulds, troughs and some round vessels. Furniture included pedestals, firebars, wedges, and a variety of hand moulded wedges, props, plaques, hand-squeezed lumps and pedestals (Fig. 5.19). Structural elements comprised luting, lining, probable fuel debris and indeterminate walling or flooring fragments (Poole, specialist report 8).

DISCUSSION (Figs 5.20-22)

The character of early Roman salt working

After a hiatus in the late Iron Age, activity resumed in the early Roman period, although this appears to have been on a smaller scale than that seen in the middle Iron Age. Evidence relating to salt production appears to have been restricted to Area B, while the main activity in Area A seems to have consisted of the construction and use of a boathouse. Other activity included the digging of pits

Figure 5.18 Early Roman pottery

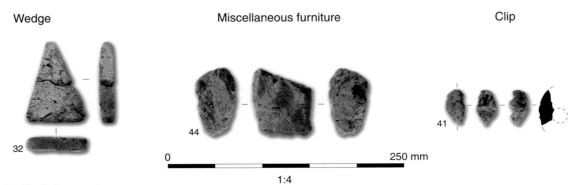

Figure 5.19 Early Roman briquetage

and short amorphous ditches and the interment of a human cremation burial at the eastern side of Area C.

Early Roman activity in Area B – pottery appears to largely confine this to the third quarter of the 1st century AD – comprised a number of irregularly-shaped ditches and pits, postholes and other cut features. The ditches and some of the pits, among them 4786/4844, 4832, 8544 and 4566, contained alluvial deposits alternating with dark, almost, black fills, which consist of a mixture of clay and fuel debris. Charred plant remains from ditch 4786/4844 included abundant ash from salt marsh plants, and identify Area B in the early Roman period as a salt production area (Hunter, specialist report 19). Presumably, as was argued in relation to the middle Iron Age evidence, the plants had been burnt as fuel and to make brine. Small pits 4399 and 4322 possibly represented hearths in which the plants were burnt to provide fuel to allow evaporation of brine. The ditches and elongated pits may have been used to trap seawater, which was mixed with the burnt plants to create the saline solution, or to store brine ready for evaporation. The microfaunal evidence from Area B is consistent with this. The foraminifera and ostracods assemblage included a number of marine foraminifera, which probably washed into the ditches and pits in suspension with the tide (Whittaker, specialist report 22). Over time, the features silted up and were used to dump fuel waste and the residue of brine filtration.

As noted above, the ledge-rimmed jar, usually in shelly ware, but also available in coarse sandy fabrics, was the principal jar form seen in Area B (Fig. 5.18, nos 27-33). The form was made locally (see above), and though it was reasonably widely distributed, reaching central Essex and north-west Kent (Going 1987, 23; Seager Smith *et al.* 2011, 55), it does not appear to have been manufactured outside south Essex. Such factors led Rodwell (1979, 161) to suggest plausibly that the type was used 'for the storage and transportation of crystalline salt'. Indeed, a strong association between the form and salt may have prevented the type from being taken up more generally across Essex and elsewhere and incorporated into local pottery repertoires. If the jar was regarded mainly as a salt storage vessel, then it would rarely have seen domestic use, for instance as a cooking pot, thus reducing the chances of the form being copied by local potters. It may also be significant that the ledge-rimmed jar was one of the few (and perhaps the only) south Essex shelly-ware forms recorded at Springhead (Seager Smith *et al.* 2011, 55-8). Other jars encountered – bead-rimmed jars, storage jars, hooked-rim jars and facetted jars – are well known north Kent types, but do not (or rarely) appear in potters' repertoires in south Essex. This suggests that the jar did not travel with other pottery in the trade of general household wares, but was isolated and traded for its intrinsic qualities or its contents (Biddulph and Stansbie, specialist report 2).

Given the conventional late Iron Age/early Roman dating of red hills and salt-making along the Essex coast, the fact that none of Stanford Wharf's red hills in Area A can be placed with any conviction between *c* 50 BC

and AD 100 is noteworthy. Certainly the reasonably large middle Iron Age pottery assemblage recovered from the red hills and the OSL date taken from a red hill deposit provide very strong grounds for the chronology offered, but the red hills had been truncated through natural, probably tidal, and human agencies, and it is possible that late Iron Age or early Roman deposits have been lost. The extensive spread of redeposited red hill material (1384) recorded south of the middle Iron Age red hills (and underlying the later Roman enclosure 9506 (see Fig. 6.2) and other features) contained middle Iron Age pottery, as did the later Roman ditches cut into it, suggesting that the layer had originally derived from the area of middle Iron Age red hills. Interestingly, though, the layer also contained a sherd of late Iron Age pottery and some 50 sherds of early Roman pottery. It is uncertain whether this pottery had been incorporated into the layer as it was being formed as red hill, or whether it had been deposited as the layer was being reworked as a surface during later activity, but the pottery does at least indicate that there was some late Iron Age and Roman activity in the vicinity of Area A. Much of this may derive from the salt-working in Area B, but parts of Area A, particularly below the late Roman horizons towards the west, remained unexcavated, and may still hold evidence for early Roman red hills and salt working. The small quantity of late Iron Age and early Roman pottery from Area A should not provide any concern, as pottery recovered from red hills along the Essex coast has typically had little bearing on the scale of activity during the late Iron Age and early Roman period. Colin Wallace (1995, table 54) records 37 sherds (35 from a single shelly ware vessel) from two red hills in the Crouch estuary, and an average of two or three 1st-century sherds was recovered from red hills in the Blackwater estuary.

Of more concern, however, is the mass of briquetage from Stanford Wharf, which Cynthia Poole (specialist report 8) suggests saw little typological change from the middle Iron Age to the late Roman period. One would expect a gap of some 300 years between major periods of salt production to result in differences in technology or abandonment of middle Iron Age technology altogether, especially with the development of processes and emergence of new equipment, such as lead pans. Some changes are apparent – the fabric of middle Iron Age briquetage tended to derive from sandy brickearth clay, while the briquetage recovered from late Roman deposits tended to be made with alluvial clay with an organic temper. In addition, Area B in the late Roman period saw the introduction of a type of pedestal which was perhaps used in conjunction with metal pans – but overall there was much similarity between the middle Iron Age and late Roman groups. It is possible that the late Roman assemblage contained a relatively high proportion of residual material, which had belonged to the putative early Roman phase, the focus of which may be found near the site, as well as in unexcavated areas of the site. Conversely, the possibility that briquetage remained in use well into the late Roman period should

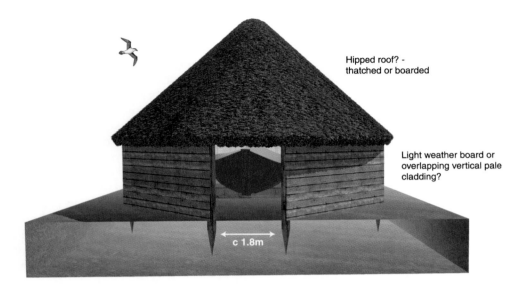

Hipped roof? -
thatched or boarded

Light weather board or
overlapping vertical pale
cladding?

c 1.8m

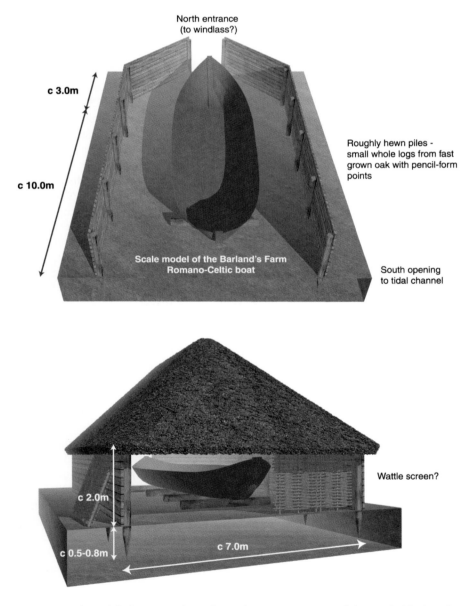

North entrance
(to windlass?)

c 3.0m

c 10.0m

Roughly hewn piles -
small whole logs from fast
grown oak with pencil-form
points

Scale model of the Barland's Farm
Romano-Celtic boat

South opening
to tidal channel

Wattle screen?

c 2.0m

c 0.5-0.8m

c 7.0m

Figure 5.20 3D computer-generated model showing a hypothetical reconstruction of the probable boathouse (model by
Elizabeth Stafford; boat based on a model of the Barland's Farm boat by Selina Ali)

not be dismissed, as the material was recovered from sites that potentially continued in use well into the 2nd century or beyond, among them Goldhanger (RH 176), Leigh Beck (RH 269-71) and Canvey (RH 278) (Fawn et al. 1990, 70-1). Thus, the technology still current in parts of Essex in the later Roman period may then have returned to Stanford Wharf with the migration of salters, maintaining a degree of typological continuity. Much firmer dating of other red hills is, of course, required before we are able to trace the spread and development of briquetage and salt making in Essex, but the material from Stanford Wharf raises challenging questions for the study of red hills, which cannot be fully addressed here.

The probable boathouse structure

Early in the excavation in Area A the truncated remains of a structure built on a NW-SE alignment was uncovered. It survived as a very elongated 'U' shaped arrangement of 12 oak log piles with what may have been an open or lightly built end to the south-east facing a silted estuarine channel. It seems likely that the east-west channel at the south end eroded away any smaller timbers that were associated with the apparently open end. Unfortunately a later phase of erosion and or decay and robbing of the structure removed any clear 'floor-type' layers which could have provided much corroborative evidence of how the structure was used.

The main posts were set on the long walls around 2m apart and could have supported a light weather board or overlapping vertical pale cladding (for a hypothical reconstruction, see Fig. 5.20). Thin, stable, and weather-resistant cleft oak weather board and fence pales are common finds on London and Carlisle Roman sites where they were clearly used for sheathing buildings and making wind-proof fences (Ridgeway 2009; Goodburn 2011a; Zant 2009, 240). Such boards were simply nailed to upright framed or earth-fast posts or driven piles trimmed to varying degrees. The fact that the uprights were set squarely opposite each other probably implies that some form of tie beam was set between them. None of the plan features of the building such as the post spacing nor the remaining woodworking details are specifically Roman, but appear to reflect local rustic workmanship (in contrast with the more distinctly Roman techniques seen on wood belonging to the late Roman phase, for example the wood-lined drain from ditch 8551 (see Chapter 6)).

The very unusual building form and its location end on to a tidal channel are the most diagnostic evidence for its original function as a boathouse. Other interpretations could be considered, such as a mooring structure or a jetty, but it would be very difficult to imagine any other likely function for a structure of such an odd form with one tapering end in such a location. At the tapered north-west end, two smaller uprights were driven about 1.7m apart either side of the structure's central access. Given that the south-east end of the structure opened onto a palaeochannel, these uprights are likely to have

formed a doorway to give access through the north end. Any ropes used to haul a vessel into the boathouse would also have been taken through this opening to a hauling party or some form of windlass (see below).

Until the discovery of modern paints and sealants the planks of wooden planked vessels were prone to damage by being dried out, shrunk and split by fast changes in humidity caused by strong winds and the sun. They were also prone to damage by freshwater-induced rot and absorbing excessive amounts of water if kept permanently afloat. Boathouses are indeed still features of the River Thames today where they are used to protect lightly built, often antique wooden pleasure craft. Historic boathouses with and without roofs are also common features of the coastal areas of northern Scotland and the Isles, as well as western Scandinavia. In the Atlantic island locations the wind was the main limiting factor with the very lightly built boats used there, but further east and south the wind and sun and also damage by fresh water falling as rain or snow are also factors which led to the construction of structures to protect boats (Christensen 1979, 20). Substantial boat or ship houses are a feature of the coastal and riverine scene from the Bronze Age in some parts of Europe, particularly in the classical Mediterranean world (Blackman 2000; Morel 1986, 205). In a Roman context further north, small fortlets for patrol boats were also built along the Rhine (Mason 2003, 20-2; R Bokius, pers. comm.).

Although the variously preserved and excavated remains of three Roman-period planked vessels have been found towards the head of the estuary in London, none can be used to provide a possible model for the vessel likely to have been sheltered in the boathouse at this site (Marsden 1994). Two, the Blackfriars 1 and County Hall ships, were too large and the much shallower and narrower Guy's Hospital vessel was only very partially recorded. Therefore, although it dates to the later Roman period (early 4th century) and was found some distance away in the Severn estuary, the Barland's Farm boat (Nayling and McGrail 2004) provides a plausible model for a boat to be housed in the probable boathouse. This vessel was found largely complete, missing only the very bow end. It had a fairly flat-bottomed hull, pointed at both ends, and the remains of a mast step (Fig. 5.21). Following a detailed analysis it was suggested that it was a small estuary barge, originally about 11.4m long by 3.16m wide and around 0.9m deep. Clearly these proportion are ideal as a fit for the dimensions of the probable boathouse at Stanford Wharf. The vessel was calculated to have carried 2.5 to 6.5 tonnes, depending on the weather conditions, and to have been propelled by the tides, poles, oars and fair winds. Such a size and form of vessel could have multiple functions from bringing in fuel and victuals and taking salt out, to small scale coastal trading or even being used as an estuary fishing boat.

A varied group (6292) of six stakes and piles to the north of the boathouse are directly in line with the northern central doorway opening (Fig. 5.22). Today

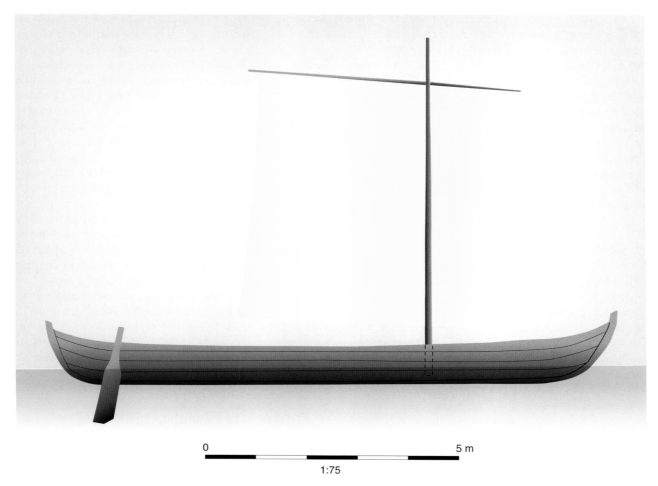

Figure 5.21   The Barland's Farm Romano-Celtic boat, the type of craft likely to have been stored in structure 9500 (after Nayling and McGrail 2004, Fig. 8.20; original drawing by Owain Roberts)

English beach fishermen lay out a line of block and tackle for hauling craft a long way up the shore. Evidence for Roman block and tackle was found on the Blackfriars 1 wreck (Marsden 1994, 37). The landward end of such a tackle or windlass would need strong anchor points, which could have been provided by any of these timbers.

A note must be made of the suspected level of the ground surface around the probable boathouse. The height of *c* 1.2-1.25m AOD is comparable to levels obtained from later 1st century timber quays and revetments in London, among them Billingsgate Buildings, Pudding Lane/Peninsular House, and Miles Lane in the City, which give a range for mean high water of between 1m and 1.5m AOD (Killock 2005, 36, 38; Yule 2005, 16). After the 1st century, water levels appear to have fallen in London by up to 1.5m, a drop not reversed until the Saxon period (Wilkinson *et al.* 2000, 17). How far this affected waterfront structures further down the Thames is unclear, although perhaps the fall in water level was not so keenly felt around Stanford Wharf; a height of between 0.9m and 1m AOD recorded for the truncated tops of the timbers forming the late 2nd/early 3rd century riverside revetment and quay at Northfleet villa (Biddulph 2011b, 222) is not far below the level of the suspected ground surface around the boathouse.

Other early Roman activity

Other evidence for early Roman activity at Stanford Wharf is suggestive of low intensity occupation. A small pit or posthole (6531) near to the north-western limit of occupation may have related to some form of industrial activity, but could just as easily have been related to domestic occupation. Wattle panels found within a channel in the south-western part of Area D appear to relate to management of the area. The orientation of the channel and panels indicate that the panels blocked the channel, rather than being used to revet its sides. In plan, both panels buckle outwards, and it seems likely that earth had been dumped in between them to form a causeway and means for people to cross the channel as they moved their animals from one area of grazing to another, or sought areas of wild-fowling and fishing. The weight of the earth pushing against the wattle revetments caused the panels to bend.

One activity suggesting more permanent domestic occupation in the area was the interment of a human cremation burial near the eastern limit of Area C during to the 1st century AD. The cremation burial was placed within a simple pit and accompanied by a ledge-rimmed pottery jar. The function of the jar is not certain; the grave was too disturbed to identify the

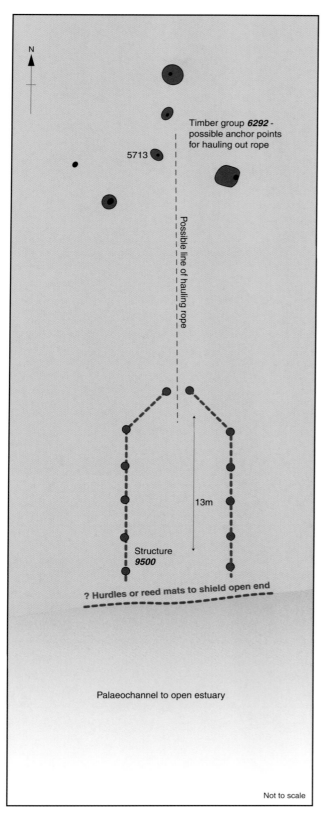

Figure 5.22 Relationship between structure 9500 and timber group 9292

vessel either as an accessory vessel or the funerary urn. Though apparently isolated, the date and location of the burial potentially identify the individual as a salter; as discussed above, the jar itself may have had particular resonance for the individual and the mourners as a storage and transportation vessel for salt (Rodwell 1979, 161; Biddulph and Stansbie, specialist report 2). More generally, the burial is consistent with funerary traditions in the region. At Dagenham, a small cremation cemetery used from the 1st century BC to the late 1st century AD is characterised by simple graves; most were unurned, and grave goods were restricted to a single jar in a two or three graves, or a few pieces of personal metalwork, such as brooches. As at Stanford Wharf, some of the bone had green stains deriving from the burning of metal objects on the pyre (Biddulph *et al.* 2010). One of two unurned cremation graves found on the route of High Speed 1 in West Thurrock and dating to the mid or late 1st century AD contained copper alloy and glass objects that had been burnt on the pyre, while the other burial contained a brooch and a fragment of another metal object; no pottery was recovered (Andrews 2009, 14). The larger late Iron Age cremation cemetery at North Shoebury, near Southend, contained a ceramic assemblage of jars, bowls and pedestalled vessels (Thompson 1995). The Stanford Wharf burial matches the Dagenham and West Thurrock cemeteries in terms of simplicity, but what particularly links the tradition expressed at Stanford Wharf with those recorded at Dagenham and North Shoebury is the selection of jars – kitchen or storage vessels outside the grave – rather than the dining forms (beakers, platters, cups and flagons) seen in cemeteries where Gallo-Roman tradition was followed, such as the 1st century AD cemetery at King Harry Lane, Verulamium (Stead and Rigby 1989) and, closer to Stanford Wharf, Great Wakering, also near Southend (Dale *et al.* 2010, 197; cf. Biddulph 2005). That is not to say that burial tradition in the region was not variable; a loose tradition of late Iron Age and early Roman inhumation burial can be identified in the Essex and Kent Thameside region. In Essex, Iron Age inhumation burials are known at North Stifford, Grays, and Mucking (Wilkinson 1988, 37; Going 1993, 19), and two early Roman inhumation burials were uncovered at the Stratford Market Depot site in West Ham (Hiller and Wilkinson 2005, 18-20). The excavations in West Thurrock also revealed a small cemetery of 14 early Roman inhumation burials (Andrews 2009, 14), and inhumation was the dominant rite during the 1st and early 2nd centuries at Pepper Hill, Southfleet, in north-west Kent (Biddulph 2006), while cremation burials were more regularly recovered from other early Roman sites on the line of High Speed 1 (Booth 2011, 311-312).

Chapter 6

The salt industry expands – the later Roman period

by Edward Biddulph and Dan Stansbie

INTRODUCTION

The site saw limited activity in the 2nd and earlier 3rd centuries. Just two features, both confined to Area A, were dated to the middle Roman period, pointing to a further period of hiatus or abandonment across the site. This situation changed dramatically during the 3rd century and 4th century, which was a time of renewed activity and a significant expansion of the salt industry compared with Iron Age and (particularly) early Roman levels. Salt-production evidence was recorded in both Areas A and B. Two phases of later Roman activity were uncovered in Area A. Features associated with the first comprised a large square enclosure, internal fence-lines, a quarry and a cess-pit, and enclosure ditches and track-ways. A saltern was established on the surface of a middle Iron Age red hill. In the second phase, the land-scape was defined by boundary and enclosure ditches, which created spaces within which structures and buildings used for salt production were built, among them a circular structure, a rectangular building, and an enigmatic building with a square core encircled by a gully and bank.

MIDDLE ROMAN FEATURES (c AD 120-250)
(Fig. 6.1)

Middle Roman features comprised two pits, both in the centre of Area A, in the area of later Roman enclosure 9506 (Fig. 6.1). Pit 6484 had largely been cut away by later features, but was probably originally sub-circular or sub-rectangular in shape. The feature measured at least 4.65m in length by *c* 1.75m in width. It contained six sherds of middle Roman pottery, weighing 54g. The extent of pit 5863 was similarly uncertain, having been truncated by the north-east corner of later Roman enclosure 9506. The pit measured at least 3m in length by 2.25m in width and contained three fills which produced 41 sherds of middle Roman pottery, weighing 459g.

A silty clay layer (5735) 0.12m thick, recorded in the southern part of Area A, was assigned to this phase on the basis of its stratigraphic relationships and ten sherds of pottery recovered from it. The layer contained small iron flakes, an iron nail and ferruginous concretions (total 5g) which may be waste from smithing or represent iron and resultant corrosion products (Keys,

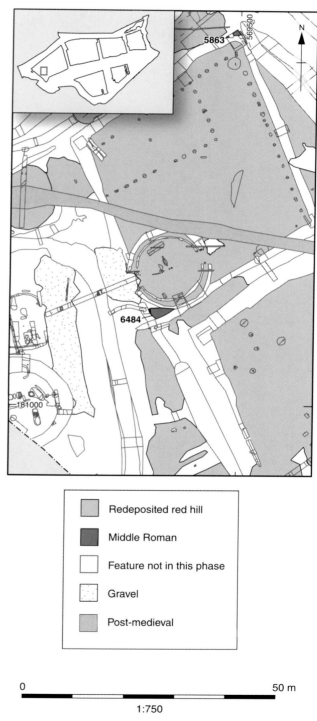

Figure 6.1 Middle Roman activity

Legend:
- Redeposited red hill
- Middle Roman
- Feature not in this phase
- Gravel
- Post-medieval

0   50 m

1:750

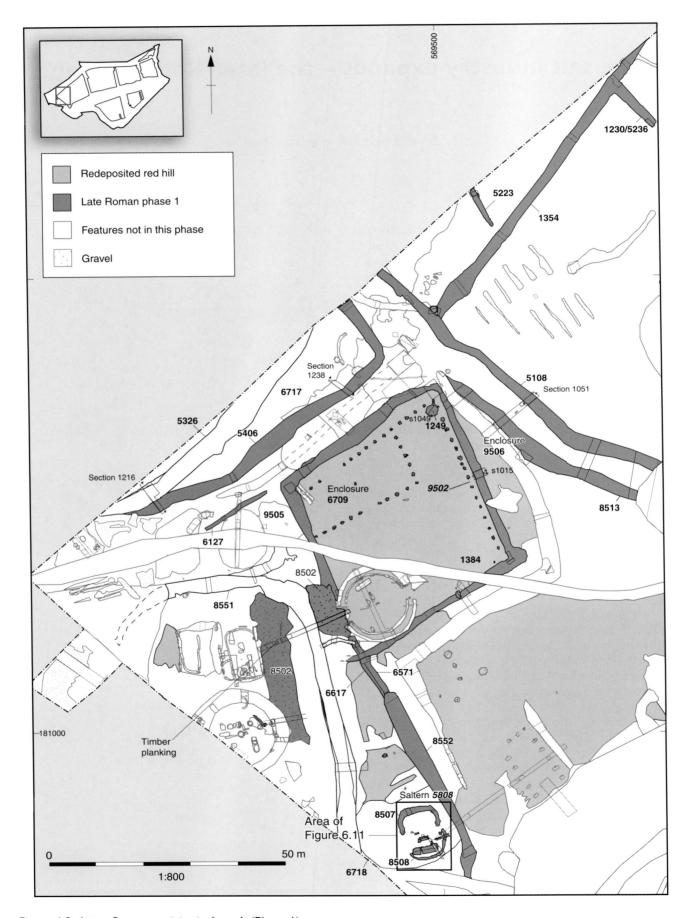

Figure 6.2　Later Roman activity in Area A (Phase 1)

specialist report 6). The deposit overlay a silty clay layer (5732) which in turn covered the surface of the early Roman boathouse 6500 (Fig. 6.2).

LATER ROMAN ACTIVITY, PHASE I (AD 200-410) (Figs 6.2-6.13)

Enclosure 9506 and associated features (Figs 6.2-6.5)

Enclosure 9506 was situated in the north-west corner of Area A (Fig. 6.2). It cut both the *in-situ* middle Iron Age red hill deposits 6717 and 9505 along its north-western boundary, and cut the extensive layer of redeposited red hill soil (1384), which served as the working surface within the enclosure. The enclosure was trapezoidal in plan and defined by a single continuous ditch, with a 7m-wide entrance in the south-west corner. Overall, the enclosure measured *c* 44m NW-SE by *c* 36m NE-SW and encompassed an area of approximately 1585m². The entrance was defined by the end of the southern, NE-SW-aligned, arm of the enclosure, which cut an earlier ditch (6571/6617) that terminated a few metres north of it. The north side of the enclosure entrance was not seen, but it was probably cut by the outer ditch of the later circular structure of saltern 6501 (see Fig. 6.14). The ditch had steep sides and a concave or flat base, and was on average 1.6m wide and 0.7m deep (Fig. 6.3). Dating evidence from the enclosure suggests that its ditches received pottery and other material at least from the early 3rd century onwards, and possibly slightly earlier. Some 50 sherds of pottery from one intervention through the ditch included Nene Valley colour coated ware, Hadham oxidised ware, Central Gaulish samian, a plain-rimmed dish, and wide-mouthed jars or so-called bowl-jars, which together point to a date for deposition after AD 200. Deposition appears to have continued into the later 3rd century. Grey ware dropped-flange dishes or bowls dating to *c* AD 250 onwards, were recovered from two interventions. The redeposited red hill material into which the enclosure ditch was cut also contained a dropped-flange grey ware dish, and an assemblage of some 250 sherds from a silty clay spread (5536) overlying the red hill deposit and probably laid during or shortly

after the use of the surface included Nene Valley colour-coated ware, a small, typically late Roman, storage jar, plain-rimmed dishes and an incipient bead-and-flanged dish which, taken as a whole, belong to the mid to late 3rd century AD. It is possible that the pottery collected from the ditch marks a period of use associated with later features, notably Roman phase 2 saltern 9501 (see below), but it is telling that residual pottery recovered from the ditch and the red hill layer or surface was largely of middle Iron Age date, with no clear earlier Roman indicators. Environmental samples from enclosure ditch 9506 contained exceptionally well preserved cereal remains (Hunter, specialist report 19). These consisted of what appeared to be complete or near complete ears of spelt with straw. There were articulated rachis nodes with glumes still attached, some containing mature and immature grains, and a number of primary rachis nodes with and without sterile spikelets were also present. There were examples of the more typical double-grained spikelets, and also single-grained examples where the second grain either did not exist or failed to develop. The preservation was so good that hairs on the grains survived.

A roughly sub-rectangular area of gravel metalling (8502) measuring approximately 11m north-south by 7m east-west lay immediately outside the enclosure entrance. The metalling was truncated by late Roman phase 2 ditch 8551, but it resumed after a gap of some 5m, where it appeared to turn at right angles to the south, forming a trackway extending approximately 33m. The trackway towards the south was 6.35m in width, similar to the width of the gravel area by the entrance of the enclosure. Three fragments of timber planking or boards were recorded on the surface of the trackway. It is uncertain whether the wood had been used with the trackway, for instance as part of a drain or revetment.

A row of postholes (9502) inside the north-west and north-east sides of the enclosure, marked out a fence or palisade. The fence-line consisted of 30 sub-circular postholes divided into two lines, one orientated NE-SW and *c* 32.7m in length, and the other orientated NW-SE and *c* 34.9m in length. The postholes were cut into the red hill layer 1384. A rectangular sub-enclosure (6709),

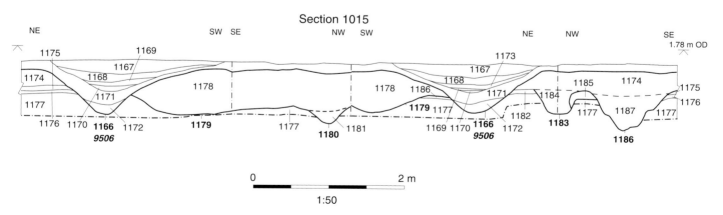

Figure 6.3 Section through enclosure ditch 9506

also defined by posts, occupied the north-west corner of enclosure 9506 and utilised the north-western arm of the fence-line on its north-western side. Enclosure 6709 was orientated NE-SW and had maximum dimensions of *c* 24.5m in length by *c* 12m in width; it comprised 26 sub-circular postholes, ten of which were incorporated from fence-line 9502. There were gaps in the north-west and south-east sides of enclosure 6709, perhaps serving to give access to the north-west ditch. There were no posts on the south-west side of the enclosure, which was presumably formed by the ditch of enclosure 9506.

The very decayed and friable remains of the small post bases were found in some the postholes (Goodburn, specialist report 14). Three pieces of wood (5547, 5858 and 5669) were solid enough to record. Although initially recorded as round they were actually hewn to rectangular cross sections from whole or halved logs (Fig. 6.4). Post 5669 was a neatly hewn, boxed heart post with a sawn base, and is typical of Roman workmanship. It was *c* 0.17m tall and measured *c* 120mm by 110mm. The piece was cut from slow grown oak. Post 5547 was slightly smaller, made from a half log with an axe cut base and measured 0.22m tall by 80mm wide by 50mm thick. The third example (5858) was more distorted but appeared to have an axe felling cut at the base. It measured 0.27m tall by 100m wide by 80mm thick. The acute curve of the grain at the felled end is probably a coppiced heel. It is likely that these posts supported fence rails to which light cleft oak paling was nailed, a system of fencing well known from a range of Roman London sites (Goodburn 2011a). Posthole 1022, part of the fence-line, contained a small

quantity of non-magnetic, silica-rich slag spheres. Enclosure ditch 9506 contained six pieces of undiagnostic slag (Keys, specialist report 6).

Enclosure 9506 was largely devoid of other internal features. However, pit 1249, which was located in the northern corner of the enclosure, was contemporary with its use. The pit was 2.45m in diameter and 1.6m deep (Fig. 6.5). It was dug through the redeposited red hill soil (1384) and into the brickearth below, and it possible that it was dug to extract the brickearth. The pit contained a remarkable series of deposits and finds. The sequence of deposition began with some slumping from the sides. The pit was then filled with a dump of woodworking chips and waste. Sandy material from the sides fell into the pit again, and this was followed by dumps of wet silty clay and cess or human waste (1248). Plant material, including fruit stones, coriander seeds, and cereal bran, preserved in the wet clayey deposit revealed something of the diet of the inhabitants. The foul conditions were perfect for dung beetles and other insects, and such species were recorded in abundance (E Allison, below). The excavator recorded that, even after 1600 years, the pit had retained an aroma characteristic of human waste. Other plant remains, such as weed species and wheat chaff, indicated that other waste material was thrown into the feature, and this also included a semi-articulated calf, a piece from a wooden ladder or litter, a fragment of a leather shoe, and two near complete ceramic vessels (see below; Fig. 6.6). The pottery comprises types current in the region in the 3rd or 4th century, although the kilns at Mucking in which the pottery had been fired ceased operating by *c* AD 250

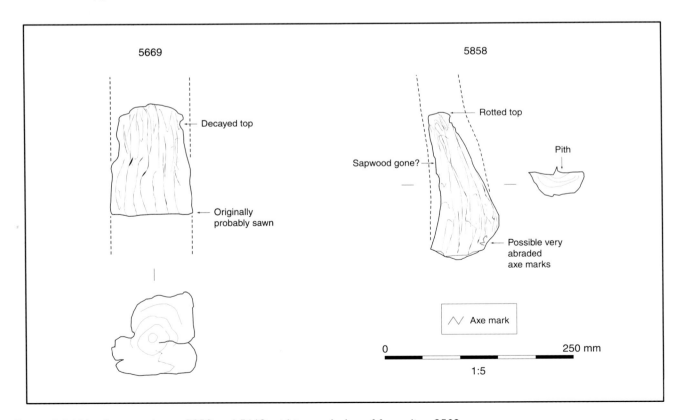

Figure 6.4 Wooden post bases 5858 and 5669 within postholes of fence-line 9502

Section 1049

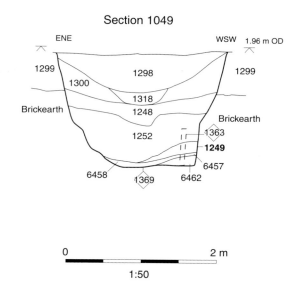

0   2 m

1:50

Figure 6.5 Section through pit 1249. The photograph shows the feature only partly emptied. Scales 1m

(S J Lucy, pers. comm.), which may confine the vessels' deposition to the 3rd century.

The contents of pit 1249 (Figs 6.6-6.9)

Pottery by Edward Biddulph and Dan Stansbie
Two complete or near-complete vessels were recovered from fill 1248. One vessel (SF 1596) was a large, jar-sized globular and funnel-necked beaker (type H41) in a burnished black-surfaced ware that was almost certainly a Mucking product (Rodwell 1973, fig. 10.105). It was found with a smaller version of the same type (SF 1594), although the vessels were not identical (Fig. 6.6). The large beaker contained a remarkable

assemblage of well-preserved plant remains. Such an assemblage naturally invites the suggestion of a structured deposit, perhaps made in a propitiatory act. However, analysis of the surrounding pit fill revealed an almost identical plant assemblage to that recovered from the vessel, the only difference being that the remains in the vessel were relatively well-protected and so were better preserved that those without. Overall, therefore, a special, ritual, deposit is unlikely, but quite why both complete vessels were discarded is uncertain. It is possible that both became contaminated, or were regarded as such, and so deemed inappropriate for continued use. Their deposition may simply have been accidental, but it would be too much to speculate on the

0   250 mm

1:4

Figure 6.6 Two complete beakers from pit 1249

possible events which might have led to the vessels being accidentally dropped into the pit.

Leather by Quita Mould

The broken remains of a leather insole from a shoe of nailed construction of adult size was found in a middle fill (1248) of pit 1249 (Fig. 6.7). The insole was damaged at the forepart and this area was displaced slightly to the left, with the toe and much of the outer edge of the insole broken away. It was broad in shape, tapering slightly toward what remained of the wide seat with no defined waist. A series of very small worn areas running along the surviving right side mark the line of nailing along the inner edge. There was no evidence for constructional thonging visible at the waist and seat. Cherry pips, plum stones and a wood fragment lay directly in contact with the underside of the insole, indicating that the insole was placed on its own in the pit and had not been part of a complete (or near-complete) shoe when it was discarded. The fact that there is no evidence that a complete shoe was deposited in the pit, but only part of a shoe, and a broken part, suggests it to be the result of casual domestic rubbish disposal rather than part of a deliberate act of closure.

Worked wood by Damian Goodburn

A jointed oak pole (6505) from fill 1252 was possibly part of a litter, stand frame or ladder (Fig. 6.8). The timber was *c* 85mm diameter and 1.12m long with neatly chamfered ends, which suggests that it was designed to be carried. One face was hewn flat and been pierced by three rectangular through mortices *c* 40-55mm long which had clearly held cross pieces of some kind. The marks of chisels 18mm wide and spoon augers were found in the mortices. The timber had not been used long as bast was still adhering in places.

Fish and other animal bones by Rebecca Nicholson and Lena Strid

A small quantity of fish remains was recovered from sample 1368, taken from the main lower fill (1252) of

0   100 mm

1:2

Figure 6.7 Leather shoe from pit 1249

pit 1249. Pike (*Esox lucius*) was identified on the basis of a dentary fragment from a small fish and four small/tiny vertebrae. This is the only evidence from the site for fishing in fresh water. Other fish remains from this fill included stained and probably chewed bones from smelt, clupeid(s), eel, stickleback, pogge and flatfish. The condition of these bones is consistent with an origin in faeces. Animal bone from fill 1248 included a semi-articulated calf; most of the skeleton is present, only lacking the phalanges and the metacarpals.

Insects by Enid Allison

Beetle and bug remains were abundant and very well-preserved in the sample recovered from fill 1248 of pit 1249. The assemblage consisted almost entirely of terrestrial forms, nearly half of them decomposers. The composition of much of the assemblage was consistent with the presence of foul organic matter within the pit. Bean or seed weevils were common and are often associated with deposits that appear to have contained cess, where it is presumed they were eaten with infested pulses and subsequently voided in faeces. Taxa tolerant of foul to very foul conditions were common and included several species of scarabaeid dung beetles. The most numerous dung beetles were *Aphodius granarius*

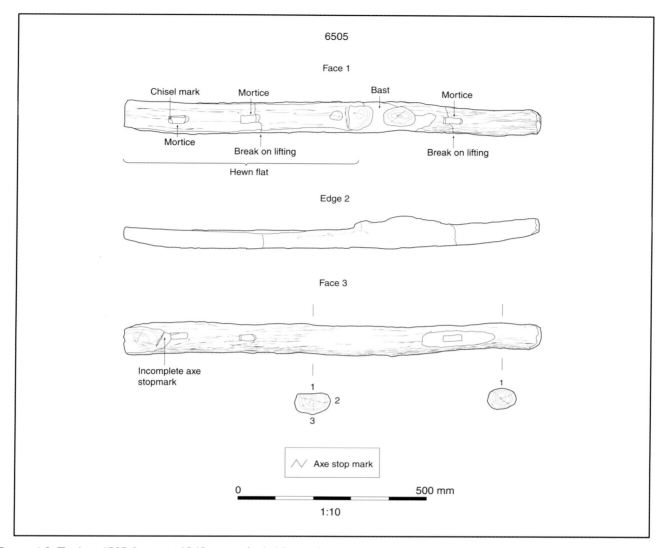

Figure 6.8 Timber 6505 from pit 1249, part of a ladder or litter

and *A prodromus* and/or *sphacelatus*, all commonly associated with foul waste other than herbivore dung and often found in deposits associated with human habitation. Eurytopic decomposer beetles included taxa such as *Corticaria* and *Ptenidium*, and there was a sizable group of oxyteline beetles that would have lived in wet organic-rich mud within, and perhaps around, the pit. Another large and distinctive group of decomposer beetles typical of rather dry, mouldy organic material indicated that material other than faeces was present in the pit. These are typical of a fauna that would have formed within a building, and woodworm beetles (*Anobium punctatum*) and powder-post beetle (*Lyctus linearis*) probably also belong with the same group since they commonly infest structural timber. The occurrence of such a large group of these beetles is highly suggestive of litter from a building of some sort having been introduced into the pit. Single individuals of two grain pests, a saw-toothed grain beetle (*Oryzaephilus surinamensis*) and a small-eyed flour beetle (*Palorus ratzeburgi*), were recorded. The saw-toothed grain beetle is often common in very spoiled grain, and the small-eyed flour beetle is a particular indicator of foul grain and other

rotting residues, and the presence of these species in Roman deposits is often indicative of stable litter. Animals are likely to have been fed poorer quality grain than humans, and any residues building up in stables may have become rather rotten.

A considerable number of insects in the assemblage appeared to have come from habitats outside the pit, suggesting that it had remained open for some time. Insects from definite 'outdoor' habitats (unable to live in decaying organic material or within buildings) included *Calathus mollis* found mainly in coastal dunes (Luff 2007, 122), and *Brachinus crepitans* which occurs on chalky soils in grasslands and waste ground, often in coastal locations, where the larvae are parasitic on pupae of other beetles (Luff 2007, 33). *Bembidion varium* is found on bare and partly vegetated ground near water (ibid., 84), and a number of other ground beetles were indicative of open ground in the vicinity of the pit, with grassland and disturbed or waste ground. *Anchomenus dorsalis*, *Harpalus ?tardus* and *Microlestes maurus* were all suggestive of dry soils. A range of plant-feeding beetles and bugs from grassland and disturbed or waste ground habitats were also common. It is possible that grassland

2 mm

Figure 6.9 Coriander seeds

species in particular could have been introduced with litter from a building, but the number and excellent condition of the remains, combined with the proportion of other 'outdoor' beetles, suggests that most could have come from plants growing close to the pit. Insect remains from the fill of the large and complete ceramic beaker or jar (SF1596) were very well preserved but their concentration was lower than in the sample from the general fill.

Waterlogged plant remains by Kath Hunter

Three samples from pit 1249 contained relatively well-preserved waterlogged plant remains. There are similar species in each sample but the contents of the ceramic vessel SF1596 are significantly better preserved and contain what is possibly cereal bran and a flower. Small amounts of waterlogged and charred wheat chaff were both present. Potential arable/grassland weeds include stinking chamomile, oxeye daisy, swine cress, small nettle, common fumitory, mallow knotweed, and dock. Sea arrow grass and sea-milkwort are plants found on salt splashed grassland, while wild celery is found in brackish conditions. Coriander occurs in all three samples (Fig. 6.9). Various fruit stones including domestic plum, sloe, and wild cherry are present, along with apple, brambles and rose. A single possible fig seed is present in one sample. *Glaucium flavum* (yellow horned poppy) and henbane are indicative of a shingle beach environment.

Section 1051

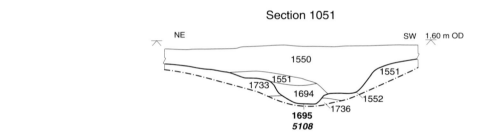

Section 1216

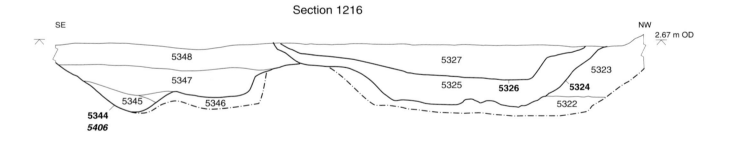

Section 1238

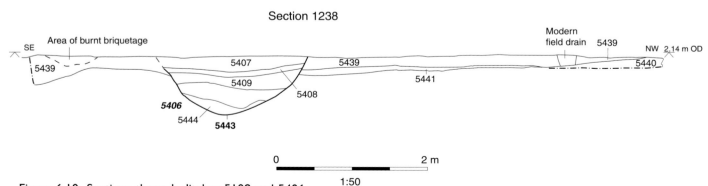

0   2 m

1:50

Figure 6.10 Sections through ditches 5108 and 5406

Soil micromorphology and microchemistry, chemistry and magnetic susceptibility, and FTIR by Richard Macphail, John Crowther and Francesco Berna

Sedimentary sequence 23 through pit 1249 included pyrite at the base of the pit, which testifies to its waterlogged nature. The yellow colour of the fill around bark-covered wood is due to the formation of jarosite (iron potassium sulphate), which forms in marine acid sulphate soils, developing as a reaction product of weathering pyrite and K-bearing deposits. Ash dumping in the pit, as indicated by a large 'white nodule', may have provided this potassium.

Boundary ditches and trackways

A series of three successive ditches extended SSE from the south-western corner of enclosure 9506, on a NNW-SSE alignment (Fig. 6.2). The earliest ditch (6571) had a surviving length of c 14-14.5m and was 0.75-1.6m in width. It was recut along its western side by ditch 6617, and both were then cut by the south-east ditch of enclosure 9506 and, to the south, by ditch 8552. The latter ended in a rounded northern terminal approximately 9m south-east of enclosure 9506. Ditch 8552, which was up to 3.8m wide, extended approximately 43.5m towards the south-east and the palaeochannel running across the southern part of the area. However, no southern terminus was recorded, as the ditch was cut at its southern end by an undated (post-medieval?) east-west linear feature. Pottery from ditch 8552 included an East Gaulish black-slipped fine 'Rhenish' ware beaker and a decorated samian bowl, a bead-rimmed and grooved plain-rimmed dishes in sandy reduced wares, and a small storage jar. Together the pottery offers a date for deposition in the late 2nd or first half of the 3rd century, which is consistent with the dating evidence from pit 1249 and enclosure 9506.

In the north-west part of Area A, the line of the north-western arm of enclosure 9506 was continued to the south-west by ditch 6127, with a gap of c 3m between the two. 6127 was aligned NE-SW, ending in a rounded terminal to the north-east and fading out to the south-west. It measured 15.4m in length by c 0.65-1.5m in width and 0.27m in depth. Parallel to this alignment to the north-west an L-shaped ditch (5406), which cut middle Iron Age red hill 6717, extended beyond the limit of excavation to the north-west and probably represented the south-eastern boundary of an enclosure contemporary with 9506. The ditch was traced for a distance of c 76m (it was cut at its south-western end by late Roman phase 2 ditch, 5326) and was between 2m and 4m wide and 0.8m deep. Ditch 5406 curved slightly westwards in its south-western part and returned to the north-west at its north-eastern end (Figs 6.2 and 6.10). Together with enclosure 9506 and ditch 5127 to its south it defined a NE-SW orientated space approximately 50m long and 6-7m wide, which probably functioned as a trackway. The north-west return of 5406, together with ditches 8513

and 5108, formed part of an adjoining trackway orientated NW-SE. The extent of this trackway to both north-west and south-east is unknown – a length of approximately 76m was recorded; the width ranged from c 3.5-10m (Fig. 6.2). Ditches 8513 and 5108 measured between c 4.3m and 1.8m in width (Fig. 6.10), becoming narrower from south-east to north-west.

A further NE-SW aligned ditch, 1354, formed a right-angle with ditch 5108 and extended approximately 72.5m from it beyond the limit of excavation to the north-east. It ranged from approximately 2-4.2m in width and was up to 0.49m deep. The ditch was cut at its south-west end by 5108, and the two possibly formed the south-eastern and south-western boundaries respectively of a sub-rectangular enclosure to their north, which lay mostly beyond the limit of excavation. A short section of another ditch (1230/5236) extended south-eastwards for c 11m from the south-east side of 1354, while the southern terminus of another ditch (5223) was recorded emanating from the northern edge of excava-

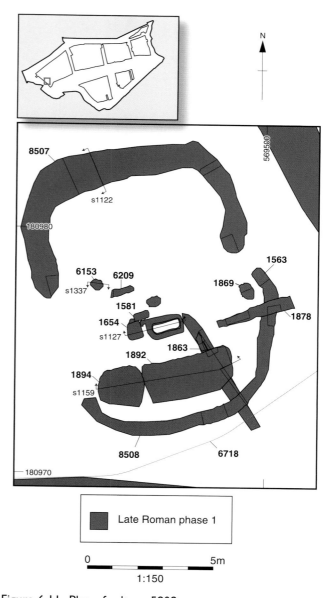

Figure 6.11 Plan of saltern 5808

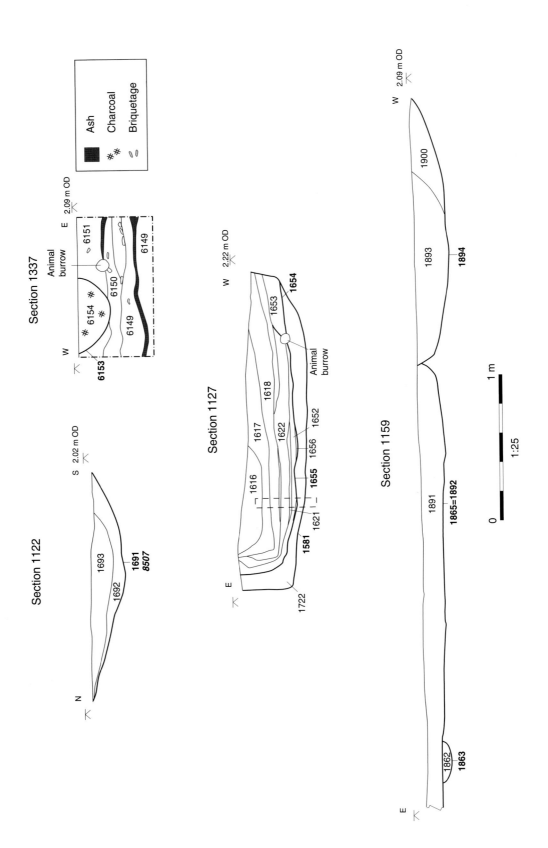

Figure 6.12 Sections through ditch 8507, tanks 1892 and 1894, hearth 1581, pit 6153 and underlying red hill

tion north of 1354; this was at least 9m long and at its widest measured 1.2m.

Dating evidence from the ditches indicated that the features filled during the 3rd century or later. Ditch 8513 contained jars, bowl-jars, a Drag. 32 dish in East Gaulish samian ware, and East Gaulish 'Rhenish' ware, which together suggest a date within the first half of the 3rd century or later. Ditch 1354, which was earlier than ditch 5108 in the stratigraphic sequence, contained late shell-tempered ware, which in Essex typically dates to the late 4th century AD (Wallace and Turner-Walker 1998, 98-101). Black-burnished ware from ditch 5223 dates to the 2nd century or later. A single sherd of undiagnostic Roman-period grey ware was recovered from ditch 1230/5236.

Saltern 5808 (Fig. 6.11)

Saltern 5808 was situated immediately to the west of ditch 8552 near the southern edge of Area A (Fig. 6.11). It was located on a red hill (6718) consisting of multiple layers of brownish red silty clay measuring approximately 19.7m NE-SW by 15.3m NW-SE (Fig. 6.12). These layers were dated by pottery to the middle Iron Age (see Chapter 3). The red hill subsequently served as a working platform at a height of c 2.1m aOD, and had several features cut into the top of it. The earliest Roman feature in this area seems to have been gully 1863, aligned NNW-SSE, parallel to ditch 8552 (see below). This was cut by one of a pair of curvilinear, almost semi-circular, ditches (8507 and 8508) which defined the working area, c 10m north-south. The northernmost ditch (8507) curved to the south and the corresponding ditch (8508) mirrored it and curved to the north. Ditch 8507 measured c 15.2m in length by up to c 1.5m in width and ditch 8508 was approximately 12.5m in length by up to 0.5m in width (Fig. 6.12, section 1122). The ditches surrounded an off-centre pit (1581), sub-rectangular in plan and orientated ENE-WSW, c 2.2m long, more than 0.9m wide and 0.4m deep. This contained a substantial sandy clay lining (1722) for a hearth. Cut 1655, itself 2.05m long, 0.9m wide and 0.35m deep, may have represented a secondary hearth structure (Figs 6.12 and 6.13), and was associated with a smaller sub-rectangular feature (1654) at the western end of the hearth which seems to have served as the stoke-hole. It measured c 0.8m north-south by 0.54m east-west and was 0.2m deep; a single fill of dark greyish-black clay-silt contained frequent inclusions of fuel debris and frequent lumps of burnt clay.

Two sub-rectangular settling tanks (1892 and 1894), both aligned east-west, lay immediately south of hearth 1581. The more easterly, larger settling tank (1892) measured c 3.6m by 1.6m and 0.2m deep (Fig. 6.12). The western settling tank (1894) measured c 1.8m by c 1.5m and was also 0.2m deep (Fig. 6.12). Other features were recorded, although their function within the saltern is unclear. Posthole 6153 and pit 6209 lay in the central part of the saltern. Both contained fuel debris, which perhaps originated in the hearth and was dumped.

Another posthole (1869) lay close to the eastern terminus of ditch 8508. Gully 1863 appeared to extend southwards from the east end of hearth 1581. Its relationship with the hearth is not certain, but it was cut by tank 1892 and ditch 8508 and appears to pre-date the saltern; no southern terminus was seen, and its course beyond the saltern could not be determined. A second gully, 1878, was later than saltern ditch 5808 but was on the same roughly east-west alignment as the hearth and the two settling tanks; neither end was located. The gullies may have served to drain water, but their relationships with the saltern features suggests that their use was not contemporary with those features.

The dating evidence from saltern 5808 is somewhat equivocal. Three sherds of Roman-period pottery, including white-slipped oxidised ware dating from the later 1st to 3rd century AD, were recovered from the red hill deposits. The material was intrusive, but it may have been introduced when the saltern features were in use. (Middle Iron Age pottery recovered from the saltern features was conversely brought up from the layers below and redeposited when the features were dug.) Of the saltern features, tank 1894 contained the latest pottery, including grey ware bead-rimmed and plain-rimmed dishes. The former dates to the 2nd or 3rd century AD, while the latter was of a type that was produced until the end of the Roman period. The pottery is consistent with the dating evidence collected from ditch 9506, and is placed in later Roman phase 1 for that reason. However, the use of the saltern was not necessarily contemporary with that of the enclosure, and an exclusively 2nd century (or indeed early Roman) date remains possible.

Figure 6.13 Hearth 1581 in saltern 5808, looking east. Scale 2m

London Gateway: Iron Age and Roman salt making in the Thames Estuary

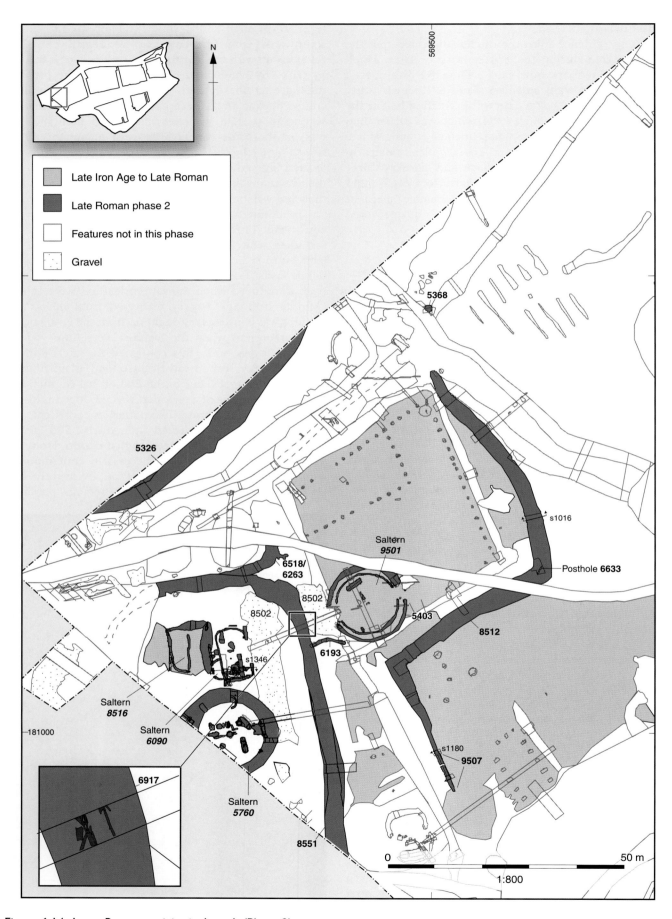

Figure 6.14 Later Roman activity in Area A (Phase 2)

LATER ROMAN ACTIVITY, PHASE 2 (c AD 250-410) (Fig. 6.14)

Introduction (Fig. 6.14)

The second phase of later Roman activity in Area A is marked by the abandonment of saltern 5808 and the trapezoidal enclosure (9506) and associated ditches and trackways. The enclosure is likely to have remained a visible part of the landscape, however, as ditch 8512, dated to phase 2, reflected the line of the north-east and south-east sides of the enclosure, and a circular structure was erected in the southern corner of the enclosure.

Three other salterns, enclosed by a ditch (8551), were built to the west of the circular structure, including a structure defined by four substantial postpads and a surrounding gully (5760). All the salterns assigned to Phase 2 saw salt working to lesser or greater extents, but other economic roles were introduced.

Ditch 8551 (Figs 6.14-6.18)

Areas of activity were defined by substantial enclosure or boundary ditches. Ditch 8551 enclosed three contemporaneous structures: salterns 5760, 6090 and 8516. The

Plan 1440

Figure 6.15 Wooden drain 5973 within ditch 8551. Scale in photograph 0.5m

ditch was an L-shaped feature that defined the eastern and northern sides (at least *c* 60m and 55m long respectively) of a probable rectangular enclosure in the western corner of Area A, extending beyond the limits of excavation to the south and probably to the west, although the western part of the north arm of the ditch was overlain by a layer of alluvium. At this point, ditch 8551 cut an earlier feature (6518/6263) which appeared to mirror 8551 in plan, curving to the north for a short distance. Ditch 8551 had been recut at least once at its southern end and was approximately 3-5m in width, and 0.7m in depth. An intervention in the northern part of the east side of the enclosure (ditch cut 5971) contained a length of timber sided drain (5973). The drain was exposed for a length of 0.84m and was approximately 0.7m in width (Fig. 6.15). There is no suggestion from other interventions that the drain continued further north or south, and it seems likely that it did not extend much beyond the length exposed in cut 5971. The intervention was filled with alluvial clay deposits. Clearly the drain was designed to allow water – presumably seawater – to flow through the ditch at this point, which implies an impediment to water flow around the drain or elsewhere along the ditch. Such an impediment may have been in the form of a causeway, created with clay dumps, which enabled site workers to cross the ditch when, say, moving from saltern 9501 to salterns 5760, 6090 and 8516.

Worked wood by Damian Goodburn

The disturbed remains of the drain resembled those widely used in Roman Carlisle where logs or cleft timbers formed the roughly revetted sides. Such drains had no bottom planking but were originally covered with lid planking that seemed to double as a board walk surface (Zant 2009, 142). The silted up drain was partly filled with woodworking debris. One of the oak kerb timbers (5975) was a reused plank, recut at one end with a saw in the Roman period, with one edge split off while the other was smoothly rounded (Fig. 6.16). It survived to a length of 0.5m and width of 130mm, and was 65mm thick. One clear oval lashing hole *c* 12mm wide and 40mm long was found, and traces of another 150mm away. A totally certain identification of the origin of this plank fragment is not clear but it may have been part of the top plank of a lashed plank boat, or perhaps part of the repaired side of a large dugout boat that had split. We should also note that large dugout vessels resembling dugout boats were used in some salt making processes and called 'salt ships' – four examples, dating to the medieval period, are known at Nantwich (Nantwich Museum, nd) – and this might be another possible origin. Another piece of wood recovered from intervention 5971 was a broken fragment (5864) of radially cleft oak board *c* 0.2m long, 100mm wide and 15mm thick. Around the edge were traces of 19 through holes, which tapered down to *c* 3mm diameter and were *c* 10mm apart (Fig. 6.17). It is clear that this was the base of small very finely woven basket. Fibres in the holes were examined by Dana Challinor, who identified them as a diffuse porous species with small radial files, perhaps Betulaceae (birch or hazel) or Salicaceae (willow). A similar but larger oak basket base was found in Roman Carlisle (Howard-Davis 2009, 810).

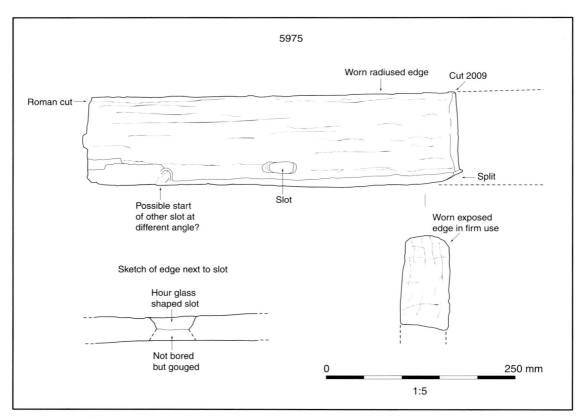

Figure 6.16 Timber 5975, originally part of a boat or a 'salt ship'

Fish remains by Rebecca Nicholson

A sample (1160) from cut 5099 in the southern part of ditch 8551 produced fish remains of outstanding quantity and quality (Table 6.1). A 10 litre sub-sample processed to 0.5mm by bulk flotation almost entirely consisted of tiny fish bones and scales, weighing 920g in total (Fig. 6.18). The majority of these were from either juvenile herrings (*Clupea harengus*) or sprats (*Sprattus sprattus*) and juvenile smelt (*Osmerus eperlanus*), although bones from a range of other small fish were also present, together with an unquantified number of small crustacean carapace fragments. The estimated number of tiny clupeid and smelt vertebra from the sample is around 1000 per gramme of residue. Most of the vertebrae have a hollow centrum and transparent walls, typical of very young fish in which ossification has only just begun. The estimated size of the great majority of the fish is 30-50mm, with only occasional specimens of 50-100mm. Bones from all parts of the skeleton are present, although vertebrae appear somewhat over-represented, probably a consequence of preservation, since the small flat head bones tend to be broken. Salt or gypsum crystals were noticeable within the deposit, encrusting a proportion of the remains even after flotation. The abundance and concentrated nature of the material from sample 1160 suggests that the sample may represent a fortuitously preserved element of what could have been a significant by-product of salt production, at least in the late Roman period, namely the production of a fish sauce, *garum*, *liquamen*, or more likely, a derivative, *allec* (Curtis 1984) (R Nicholson, specialist report 16).

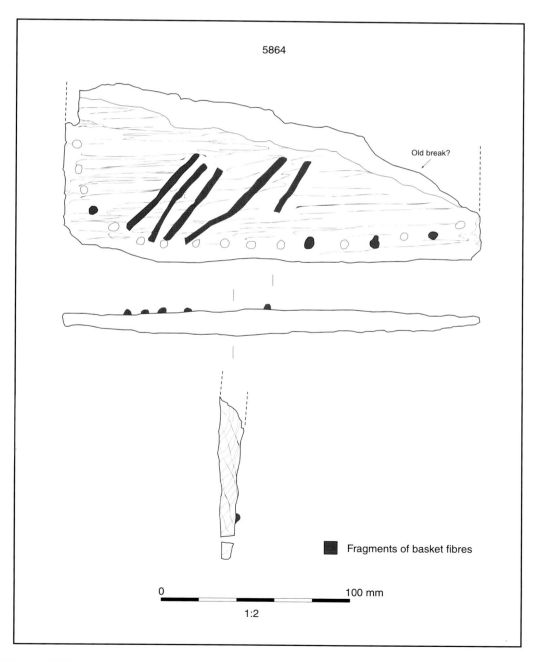

Figure 6.17 Timber 5864, part of a cleft oak basket base

Table 6.1: Fish remains from sample 1160 (5103). Number of identified specimens.

Species	10-4mm (100% of residue)	4-2mm (50% of residue)	2-0.5mm (3mls of residue)
Herring family (Clupeidae)	1	7	1760
Herring (*Clupea harengus* (L.))		2	4
Shads (*Alosa* sp.)		4	
Smelt (*Osmerus eperlanus* (L.))		6	503
Eel (*Anguilla anguilla* (L.))	1	26	8
Pipefish (*Syngnathus* spp.)		2	72
Cod family (Gadidae)	5		
Whiting (*Merlangius merlangus* (L.))	46		
Bass (*Dicentrarchus labrax* (L.))			3
Grey mullet cf. thin-lipped (*Lisa* sp.)		1	
Gobies (Gobidae)		4	263
Sand/common goby (*Pomatoschistus* spp.)			61
Gurnards (Triglidae)			8
Cottids (Cottidae)	1	13	5
Bullrout (*Myoxocephalus scorpius* (L.))			1
Sea scorpion (*Taurulus bubalis* (Euphrasen))	3	1	
Pogge (*Agonus cataphractus* (L.))	1	58	45
Sticklebacks (Gasterostidae)	6	118	61
3-spined stickleback (*Gasterosteus aculeatus* (L.))			12
Flatfishes		3	12
Right-eyed flatfishes (Pleuronectidae)	3	17	
Plaice (*Pleuronectes platessa* (L.))	1	1	
Dab (*Limanda limanda* (L.))		7	
Soles (Solidae)			3
Dover sole (*Solea solea* (L.))		14	
Unidentified		7	176
Grand Total	68	291	2997

1 mm

a

1 mm

b

Figure 6.18 Fish bones from sample 1160, ditch 5099. Images show a) abundant bones and b) salt- or gypsum-encrusted bones

Other finds

Other finds from the ditch included some 106g of undiagnostic iron slag, probably re-deposited (Keys, specialist report 6), a group of seven cattle scapulae or shoulder blades, all but one being perforated (Strid, specialist report 15), and a single cone scale of stone pine (Hunter, specialist report 19). Over 200 sherds were recovered from intervention 5099 through the southern part of ditch 8551. The assemblage included a disc-necked flagon in Hadham oxidised ware, a bowl in Oxford white ware, a funnel-necked globular beaker in Nene Valley colour-coated ware, and dropped-flange grey ware dishes, together pointing to a date after AD 250/60 for deposition (Biddulph and Stansbie, specialist report 2).

Ditches 8512 and 5326 (Fig. 6.19)

Ditch 8512 to the east of enclosure 8551 bordered an irregular area containing saltern 9501. From the north, ditch 8512 had a broadly NW-SE alignment, returning to the south-west at its southern end and then again to the south-east. It measured approximately 118.2m in length by 5m in width at its widest point, tapering to

0.5m at its southern end. The ditch largely respected the outline of the enclosure 9506, reaffirming the area defined by the enclosure. However, it cut both the northern corner of the enclosure ditch and the northern terminus of trackway ditch 8513 (see Fig. 6.2), indicating a later date. Ditch 8512 contained some notable finds, including a complete horse skull and a maxillary fragment of another horse skull (Strid, specialist report 15). A wooden post at least 2m long and 0.22m wide lay at the bottom of the ditch at the point where it curved round the eastern corner of enclosure 9506. A posthole (6633), 0.6m wide by 0.3m deep, had been cut at that corner through the base of the ditch, and it is tempting to view the wood as a fallen post erected there, possibly as part of a fence or revetment. Ditch 8512 incorporated several shallow troughs (9507) at its southern terminus (Fig. 6.19). The earliest, 5098, was also the deepest at 0.6m; the feature was cut by a shallower trough, 5096, which was just 0.2m deep. This was in turn replaced by trough 5052, which was 0.3m deep.

Ditch 5326 was recorded along the northern edge of Area A north of enclosure 8551 and ditch 8512. The ditch curved slightly towards the north, though it had a prevailing NE-SW orientation, and extended beyond

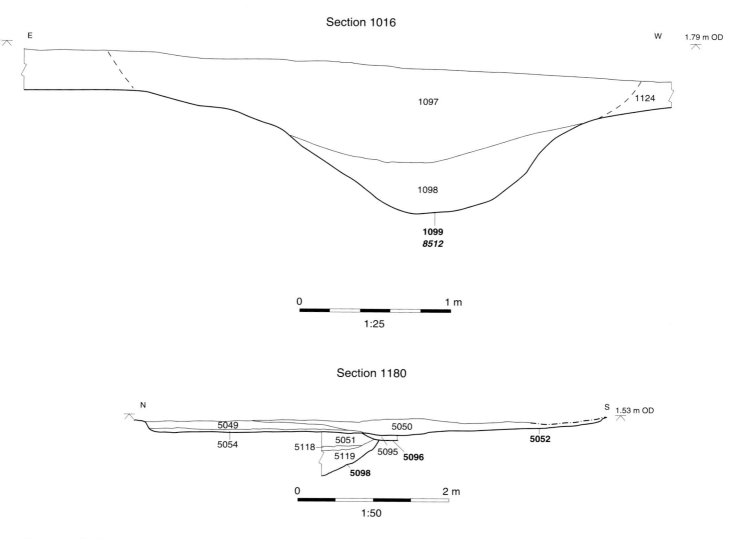

Section 1016

E   W   1.79 m OD

1097

1124

1098

1099
8512

0   1 m

1:25

Section 1180

N   S   1.53 m OD

5049   5050

5054   5118   5051   5052

5119   5095 **5096**

5098

0   2 m

1:50

Figure 6.19   Sections through ditch 8512 and troughs (9507) at the terminus of ditch 8512

the north-western limits of excavation at both ends. It was c 56m long, 4m wide and 0.5m deep, and had been recut on at least one occasion.

Pottery from ditch 8512 included middle Iron Age and early Roman material. However, its stratigraphic relationships place the feature in the 3rd century or later. No pottery was recovered from ditch 5326, but again stratigraphy suggests that the feature was cut in the later Roman period.

Saltern 5760 (Figs 6.20-6.24)

Saltern 5760 was located at the south-western edge of Area A within the area enclosed by ditch 8551. It comprised a circular bank and depression or shallow gully, which surrounded a clay floor, substantial postpads and a complex sequence of other deposits and ancillary features (Fig. 6.20). The gully was difficult to characterise, as it was only recorded in detail in one intervention through its eastern side (Fig. 6.21, section 1044). The section indicated that the feature at this point comprised a shallow depression almost 4m wide

created by the crest or agger-like profile of late Roman phase 1 trackway 8502 and its west-facing slope. The resulting hollow was subsequently filled with an alluvial deposit and a silty clay layer. Other interventions through the circular feature identified a mound of clay, red hill soil, and occasional gravel. A section through the feature at the south-western edge of excavation (Fig. 6.21, section 1000) recorded a bank of redeposited terrace gravel some 0.4m high, and an accumulation of alluvial deposits against its north-west side. This somewhat disparate evidence, however, was seen in an overhead view as a ring approximately 2m to 4.5m in width and 19.75m in external diameter (Fig. 6.22). The northern part of the circular feature overlay a narrow sharply curving gully (5532), which represents an earlier phase of activity in that part of the site. Fired clay and fuel ash slag were recovered from its fill.

The internal features of the saltern included a clay surface, a central hearth (5202), four large rubble postpads, and several other pits and postholes. The floor of the saltern consisted of a trampled or rammed clay layer (1444) up to 0.1m thick and up to c 6m north-south and 5m east-west, and lay at a height of

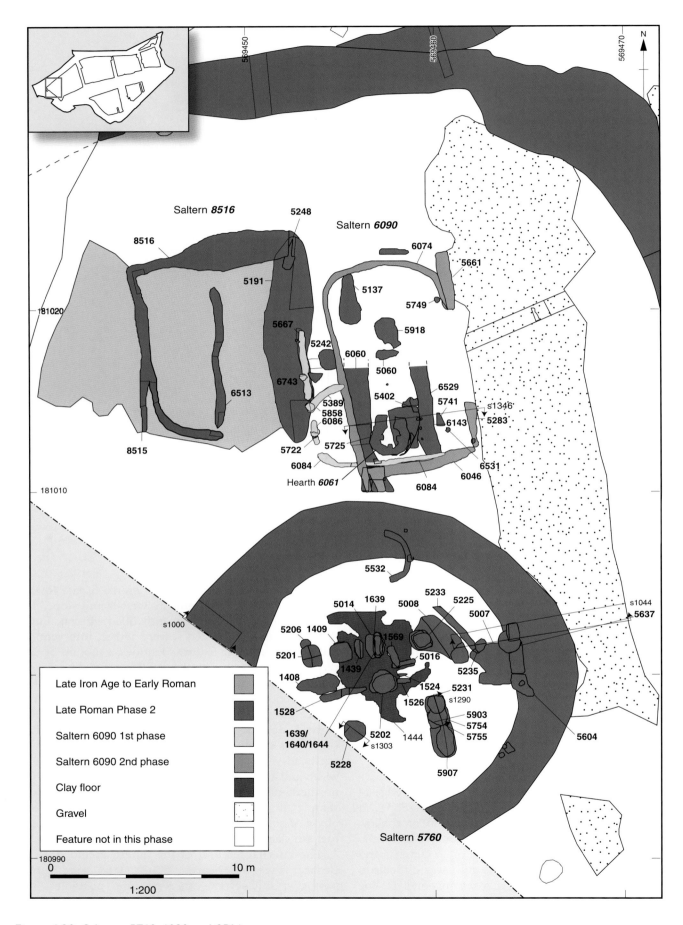

Figure 6.20   Salterns 5760, 6090 and 8516

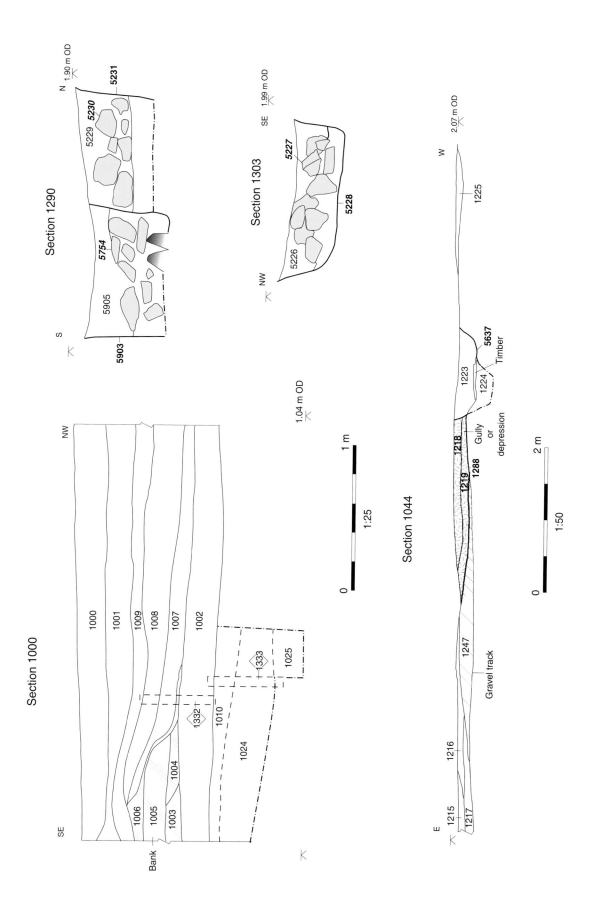

Figure 6.21 Sections through the gully and bank of saltern 5760, and postholes 5903/5231 and 5228

approximately 2m AOD. The floor was largely contained within the space defined by the large postpads, though it extended a little north of them. The floor was cut by the pits for the postpads, indicating that the surface had been laid before the holes were dug. Postpads 1409, 5225, 5903 and 5228 were positioned centrally within the building and formed a *c* 4.5m by 4.5m square (Fig. 6.22). They were all rectangular in plan, with the exception of postpad 5228, which was circular, and were approximately 1m across and varied from *c* 0.2m to 0.45m deep (Fig. 6.21); the cuts had been made from the level of the floor. Each postpad contained closely packed chalk and flint rubble. Base 5754, within cut 5903, sat on an additional layer of timber (5755; Fig. 6.21, section 1290). Damian Goodburn (specialist report 14) notes that the debris is typical of that produced by carpentry operations in which medium sized oak logs were hewn into squared beams (Fig. 6.23). The most intact large wood chips derived from notch and chop hewing to produce beams around 200mm square from logs around 0.35m in diameter. The notches or weakening cuts were cut about 300mm apart to make it easy to

split off the bulk of the waste, which was normally recycled as fuel. The axe marks were very well preserved, particularly on knotty beam end off-cut 5868, where a stop mark 80mm long was identified.

Postpad 5903 was subsequently replaced or reinforced by two more chalk postpads, 5907/1635 and 5231, which were also rectangular in plan and together measured up to 1.9m across and 0.5m deep (Fig. 6.21). Hearth 5202 in the centre of the area defined by the postpads was sub-rectangular in plan and measured 1.24m in length by 1.04m in width and 0.19m in depth. It was sealed by a thin occupation layer, which was then cut by a second hearth (1443), indicating two phases of use and a short hiatus between them (Fig. 6.24).

Saltern 5760 contained several ancillary features, which were generally shallow – no more than 0.22m deep – and of circular or oval form (Fig. 6.20). Four of these features (1406, 1439, 1639, and 5014) had scorched sides and may be interpreted as further hearths. Hearth 1406 had been cut into 5201 and represents a renewing of the feature. Hearth 1639 was one of a number of superimposed hearth bases (along with 1640 and 1644), which suggested several episodes

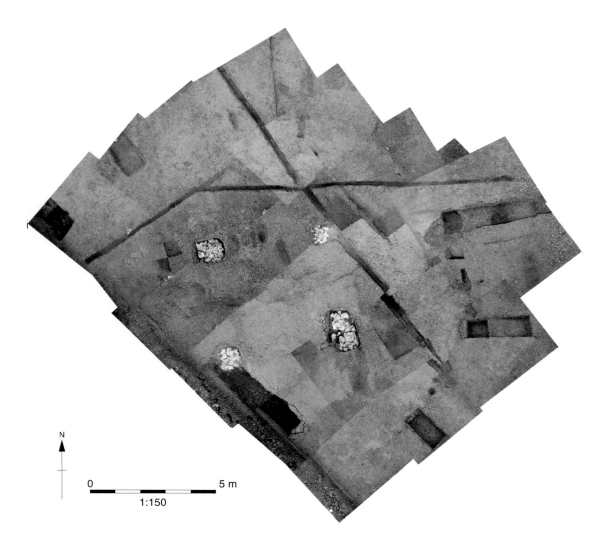

N

0   5 m

1:150

Figure 6.22 Overhead view of saltern 5760

Figure 6.23 Timbers 5757-5759 and 5868, off-cuts found in a post-pad in saltern 5760

Figure 6.24 Hearth 5202/1443, cut into floor surface 1444 within saltern 5760, looking north. Scale 1m

of use and renewal. Features 1524, 1526, 1528, 1569 and 5016, were short narrow slots of uncertain function, and other features included a small cut or hollow 5206. In addition, there was a short gully (5233) and two large amorphous hollows (5007 and 5008). Gully 5233 was orientated NW-SE and measured 3.3m in length by 0.34m in width. Hollows 5007 and 5008 measured 2.3m in length by 2.1m in width and 3.15m in length by 2.15m in width respectively. Features 1439, 1526, 5014, 5016 and 1528 had been cut into the floor surface 1444, indicating that they were were later in date than the floor and the postpads. Two pits, 5637 and 5604, had been cut into the inside edge of the circular gully or mound and were positioned either side of hollow 5007.

Evidence suggests a mid 3rd century or later date for the use of the saltern. Pottery recovered from the earliest alluvial layer that accumulated against the gravel bank included a range of dish forms – incipient bead-and-flanged dishes, bead-rimmed dishes, dishes with grooves below the rim – that together date to the second or third quarter of the 3rd century. The overlying clay layer contained pottery dated after AD 250, including the dropped-flange dish, which typologically succeeded the incipient bead-and-flanged form. Pottery from deposits that accumulated over gravel trackway 8502 was consistent with this dating. Floor 1444 also contained a fragment from a dropped-flange dish. Two fragments of a small leaf-shaped spearhead (Fig. 6.54) with closed and welded socket were recovered from a deposit in

feature 1635 overlying postpad 5903 within the structure. There is no visible nail to secure the socket to the spear shaft, but the socket is not complete (Scott, specialist report 5).

Environmental samples were taken from a number of features within the saltern (Hunter, specialist report 19). Wheat grains and a large number of cultivated pea seeds and numerous large legumes and legume fragments were found in a hearth rake-out deposit overlying hearth 1640. Nutlets of *Galium uliginosum* (fen bedstraw), a plant which prefers rich marshy places, were recovered from hearth 1644. The sample also contained one seed of ribwort plantain (*Plantago lanceolata*), often found in short trampled grassland. A layer of occupation debris trampled into the floor surface contained a mixture of a few cereals (mainly wheat), and a few monocotyledonous fragments, thrift seeds, sea lavender, and sea plantain. More cereal remains were recorded in a sample from feature 1569. It contained a relatively large number of oat pedicel fragments, oat grains, and wheat grains (one of which has a compact rounded shape that might suggest it is a free-threshing type). The majority of the chaff was from wheat, although there were also several barley rachises. A few seeds of plants of arable land and or grassy places, such as field madder (*Sherardia arvensis*), self heal and stinking chamomile, were present, as well as relatively small quantities of grass and rush seeds. Posthole 5235 cutting hollow 5007 contained abundant saltmarsh taxa, including over 1000 rush seeds, over 200 sea plantain seeds, 164 sea lavender seeds, and 155 sea thrift seeds. Occasional monocotyledonous stem/leaf fragments and 68 grass caryopses were also present. A single rose-type spine was noted from an occupation layer cut by slot 1528.

More evidence for fuel was found within the structure, and elsewhere, in the form of abundant white nodules, which are characteristic of ash derived from the combustion of monocotyledonous plant stems and leaves (Macphail *et al.*, specialist report 24). Charcoal was also recorded, having been recovered from hollow 1408, slots or cuts 1644 and 1569, and the surrounding gully. Oak and alder appear to be the most common wood used, although charcoal from hollow 1408 and the basal fill of cut 1644 was dominated by gorse/broom-type (Druce, specialist report 20).

Micromorphological analyses (Macphail *et al.*, specialist report 24) through floors in saltern 5760 found on-site estuarine sediments to be strongly influenced by occupation deposits including latrine waste, and a series of beaten floor deposits formed in the structure under generally moist conditions. The floor deposits also recorded alternating hearth and kitchen waste from internal trampling, and incorporation of alluvial clay from outside. Sequence 22, against the bank seen in section on the west side of 5760, was composed of layered deposits that include sands, brickearth and domestic hearth, kitchen and latrine waste. It can be suggested that these are trampled floor sweepings.

Saltern 8516 (gullies 6513, 8515 and 8516)
(Fig. 6.20)

A group of three gullies (6513, 8515 and 8516) and a wider ditch (5191) immediately north-west of saltern 5760 defined the enclosure or structure of a probable saltern (identified in later discussion as 8516), although no hearths or other internal features were present (Fig. 6.20). A first phase of the saltern was represented by two parallel north-south gullies (6513 and 8515) approximately 3.75m apart. The western gully (8515) had been cut away by a later feature (8516, see below); what survived of it measured *c* 3.4m long, 0.5m wide and 0.1m deep. The eastern gully (6513) was 7.75m long, 0.4m wide and 0.06m deep, and had rounded terminals at both ends. Gully 8515 was replaced by 8516, which defined, or re-defined, the southern, western and northern edges of the enclosure. Its southern terminus met the south end of 6513, and it curved round towards the north for *c* 10m, and then turned sharply eastwards and widened substantially before meeting ditch 5191. Gully 8516 ranged in width from 0.3m to *c* 1.7m and was 0.12m deep. Ditch 5191 defined the eastern side of the enclosure, and consisted of a wide and shallow cut 11.25m long and up to 2.45m wide. A short length of a small north-south gully (5248) was recorded at the north end of ditch 5191. Together, the features defined a sub-rectangular area *c* 11m north-south by 7m east-west. The gap between the south-eastern terminus of

8516 and the south end of 5191 provided the entrance to the enclosure, some 3m wide. Gully 6513 may have served as a partition separating different areas of use. The gullies may have held posts or fences creating a temporary shelter or screens. All features were cut into a red hill deposit 1018, which formed the working surface of the enclosure.

Pottery collected from the fill of gully 8515 included Nene Valley colour-coated ware and a plain-rimmed dish with groove below the rim, which suggests a 3rd century or later date for filling. A dropped-flange dish, dating to the late 3rd century onwards, was recovered from gully 6513. Over 1100 sherds of pottery were recovered from ditch 5191. The assemblage included late Roman dropped-flange dishes among a mass of pottery, such as Nene Valley colour-coated globular beakers with funnel necks, more broadly dated to the 3rd or 4th century.

A sample from a fill of 5191 contained significant numbers of fish bones (Nicholson, specialist report 16). The remains here were very similar to those found in ditch 8551 (see above), but anchovy (*Engraulis encrasicolus*) was also present. A large whale bone, probably a vertebra, recovered from the ditch, was another interesting find (Fig. 6.56). Whale bones are occasionally found on Roman sites (Bendrey 2008, 254; Jones *et al.* 1985, 172; Marvell and Owen-John 1997) and it has been suggested that these probably represent utilisation of stranded individuals rather than off-shore hunting (Jones *et al.* 1985, 172). The bone displayed chop marks from several directions, but it is unclear whether these derive from meat removal or shaping the bone for working (Strid, specialist report 15).

Saltern 6090 (Figs 6.20, 6.25-6.28)

A saltern (6090) was established immediately to the north of saltern 5760. It was defined by gullies of at least two phases, the earlier of which postdated the ditch enclosing saltern 8516 to the west. The first phase was represented by gullies (6084, 6086 and 5667), which formed the southern and western sides of an enclosure or structure. Gully 6084, orientated east-west, was *c* 6m long. It turned at right angle towards the north and continued for *c* 7m as an intermittent gully (6086 and 5667), which cut ditch 5191 from the adjacent enclosure. An additional short curving gully (5389) formed a semi-circular space within the corner of the structure. The gullies along the western side were cut by three postholes (5722, 5858 and 6743). What form the first-phase structure took is uncertain, but it is possible that posts inserted into the gullies belonged to a temporary structure, such as a fence, screen or windbreak.

This first-phase structure was succeeded by a larger sub-rectangular structure, measuring approximately 11.7m by 6.3m. The southern side of the structure was defined by a wide, very slightly curvilinear gully (6046) orientated east-west, 6.15m long, 0.6m wide and 0.25m

Figure 6.25 Hearth 6061 in saltern 6090, looking south

Figure 6.26 Hearth 6061, stoking area and gullies of south and west walls of structure 6090, looking west. Scale 1m

deep. On its western and northern sides the structure was defined by gully 6074, which curved at its northern end, returning for a short distance towards the south. A single posthole (5749), which was *c* 0.3m in diameter and lay immediately to the west of the northernmost of these ditches, may have also been part of the structure. The structure or enclosure was largely open on its eastern side. However, two short stretches of gully (5661 and 5283), respectively *c* 3.1m long and 0.75m wide, and 2.45m long by 0.45m wide, flanked the open side of the structure and may represent a later modification, as gully 5661 cut 6074. Gully 5283 had been cut through a sandy clay deposit (5658) that contained large quantities of finds and may represent a dump of material to build up the surface. As with the first-phase structure, the gullies of the second-phase structure may have held

a fence or posts that formed a screen or temporary shelter.

Saltern 6090 housed a number of features related to salt making. Chief among these was a tile-built hearth (6061) situated in the south-west corner of the structure (Fig. 6.25). The hearth comprised a circular chamber approximately 2m across with an internal diameter of *c* 1m, with a north-south aligned flue *c* 0.6m long. The hearth was partially set within a hollow or construction cut (5725) and consisted of two courses of tile with three internal raised pilasters surviving to three courses in height. White residue on lumps of fired clay recovered from the hearth suggests that the feature was associated with salt evaporation; the pilasters are likely to have supported evaporation pans. Hazel charcoal was fairly well represented within the hearth (Druce, specialist

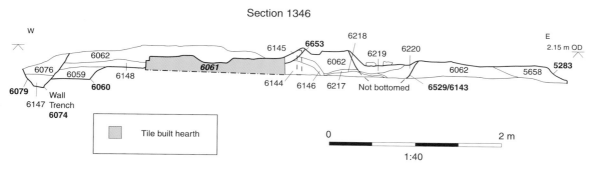

Figure 6.27 Section through saltern 6090

Figure 6.28 Hearth 5918, part of saltern 6090, second phase, looking south

report 20). The stoke-hole or stoking area was clearly indicated by a patch of burnt soil at the opening of the flue (Fig. 6.26). The hearth was flanked by two shallow flat-based and steep sided gullies (6060 and 6529/6143), both orientated north-south and measuring at least *c* 5m long and up to 1m wide. Their northern termini were not detected (Fig. 6.27), and in the case of 6060, as well as features associated with the second phase of saltern 6090, the southern limit is also uncertain, and was perhaps obscured by the gully/hollow surrounding saltern 5760 to the south. Feature 6529/6143 was backfilled with burnt material.

A second hearth (5918), a roughly pear-shaped feature aligned NW-SE, was situated in the north-central part of saltern 6090. The hearth was 1.7m long, 1.1m wide and 0.16m deep, and was filled with a layer of burnt silty clay, along with several layers rich with fuel debris incorporating fragments of tile (Fig. 6.28). Other pits, scoops and gullies (5060, 5137, 5402 and 5741)

were distributed within saltern 6090 and probably related to industrial activity within it, although their function is unclear. The fill of tile-built hearth 6061 contained crushed iron dust, very occasional broken hammerscale flake, tiny iron flakes, and a very small quantity of undiagnostic iron slag. Despite the small quantities recovered, the evidence suggests that saltern 6090 could have been used for a one-off smithing event, perhaps involving shaping or repair of flat iron objects, including, perhaps, iron pans (Keys, specialist report 6). Metal vessels were not restricted to iron. Exceptionally high concentrations of lead, phosphate, calcium and tin were associated with visually apparent 'iron' staining in the floor deposits. This staining records localised water-logging and the use of tin and lead, presumably from vessels used to heat brine. The phosphate and calcium were associated with fuel ash derived from saltmarsh plants and latrine waste weathering (Macphail *et al.*, specialist report 24).

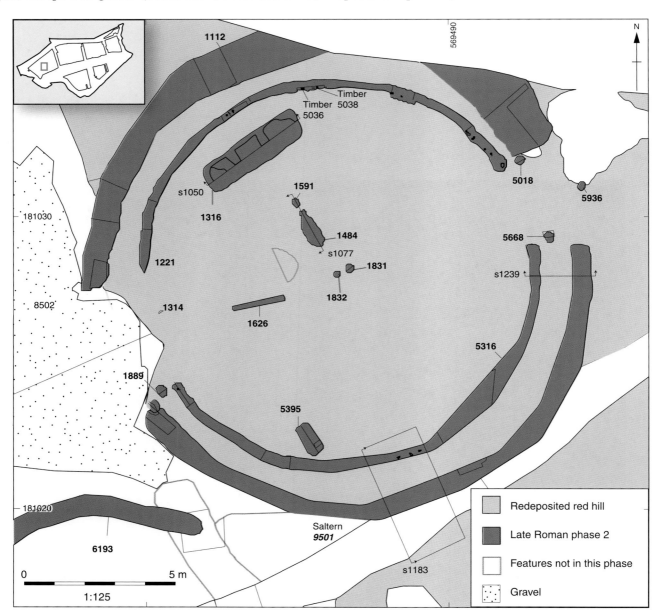

Figure 6.29 Plan of round saltern 9501

It is clear that the 'internal' features were not all contemporaneous, although it is uncertain which phase of structure many of them belong to. North-south gully 6060 was perhaps the primary late Roman feature in this particular area, preceding both phases of the saltern 6090 'structure'. The parallel gully 6529/6143 was also apparently earlier than those structural features, but section 1346 (Fig. 6.27) demonstrates that the two north-south gullies cannot have been contemporary – and indeed suggests that 6529/6143 might have been as late in date as the second phase, although this is not consistent with the evidence of the plan. Either way, the tile-built hearth 6061 lies stratigraphically between the two north-south features, and could even have been contemporary with 6060, again perhaps predating the establishment of either of the structural phases of saltern 6090; it certainly predated the later of these, defined by gully 6074. It is perhaps most likely that hearth 6061 was associated with the first phase structure. Hearth 5918 was largely outside the area covered by the first phase structure, and association with the second phase structure seems more likely. A *terminus post quem* for saltern 6090 is provided by late Roman pottery recovered from ditch 5191, which was cut by the first phase wall trench, and over 200 sherds of pottery, including dropped-flange dishes and a small storage jar characteristic of late Roman deposits, were recovered from a dumped layer 5658 into which ditch 5283 was cut.

Saltern 9501 (Figs 6.29-6.34)

A saltern (9501) was situated west of enclosure 8551. It blocked the entrance to later Roman phase 1 enclosure 9506 and cut the south-eastern arm of the ditch of that enclosure (Figs 6.29 and 6.30). The saltern was defined by two concentric penannular features. The external diameter of the outer ditch (1112) was 17m; the inner gully (5316) had a diameter of 13m. Ditch 1112 was more substantial than the inner gully, especially to the north, where it measured up to 1.73m wide. Gully 5316 was between 0.2m and 0.7m wide (Fig. 6.31, sections 1239 and 1183). The saltern had opposing entrances to the east and west defined by rounded terminals of both the ditch and the gully. The west entrance in the inner gully was *c* 3.8m wide and the east entrance was 3.2m wide. The east entrance was flanked by two postholes (5018 and 5668) up to 0.4m in diameter, which presumably held posts framing a doorway. Another posthole, 5936, was recorded a little way to the east mid way between the two opposing postholes. Posthole 1889, 0.4m across, was seen at the south side of the west entrance. This posthole contained traces of oak charcoal, which is likely to have been deposited after the post had been removed (Druce, specialist report 20). There was no corresponding posthole on the north side of the entrance, though posthole 1314 was recorded in between the termini of the inner gully. The remains of timber oak stakes, the remnants of the superstructure,

Figure 6.30 Elevated view of round saltern 9501 from south-west, showing red earth of redeposited red hill. Scales 2m

survived within the inner gully. Fifteen small oak timbers were found very decayed and desiccated. From the best preserved examples, it could be seen that they were *c* 100-170mm wide cleft half poles set close together as pairs in a trench (Fig. 6.32). The gap between each pair was over 2m and probably originally included light wattlework, which was truncated. The gap between this wooden revetment and the outer ditch was between 0.9m and 1.5m, and may have accommodated a clay mass wall approaching 1m wide at the base, but which need not have been over 1.5m high. This would have been covered by over-sailing thatch and would have been battered (Goodburn, specialist report 14).

Environmental samples collected from the north-west terminus of ditch 1112 contained a few wheat grains with possible oat or brome seeds (Hunter, specialist report 19). One possible free-threshing wheat grain was recorded from the south-east terminal of the outer ditch, and the samples also produced detached cereal embryos and two detached coleoptiles, evidence of the

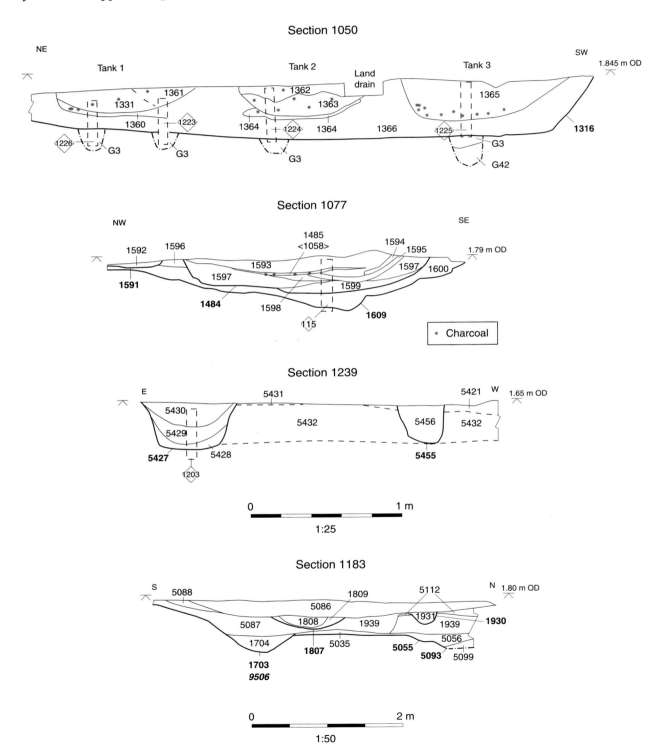

Figure 6.31 Sections through round saltern gullies, hearth 1484 and settling tank 1316

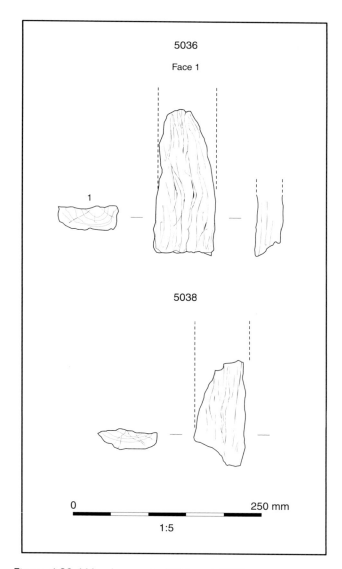

5036

Face 1

1

5038

0   250 mm

1:5

Figure 6.32 Wooden posts 5036 and 5038

early stages of deliberate or accidental germination. Oat grains and possible barley grains were also present. There were relatively large quantities of wheat chaff, including one possible emmer spikelet fork among spelt type chaff. Saltmarsh plant seeds were recorded, among them sea arrow grass, sea thrift, sea lavender and sea plantain. Self heal, stinking chamomile and scentless mayweed, monocotyledonous stem/leaf fragments, and grass caryopses were present in small quantities.

The penannular ditch and gully enclosed a working area containing a roughly central hearth (1484) along with a settling tank (1316), containing three cells, and several other pits, postholes and gullies. Hearth 1484 was oval in plan, with a flat base and steep sides. It was aligned NNW-SSE and c 2.3m long, 0.5m wide and 0.19m deep (Figs 6.31 and 6.33). Clay and sandy clay linings (1599 and 1597) were overlain by an ashy deposit (1598) beneath a possible relining (1595). What may have been the primary fill of this later hearth (1485) comprised a thin layer of fuel debris. Three postholes (1591, 1831 and 1832), measuring 0.33m, 0.29m and 0.24m in diameter respectively, were positioned in

relation to the hearth, one to the north-west and two to the south-east. Settling tank 1316, in the north-west part of the saltern 9501, comprised a single sub-rectangular cut, orientated NE-SW and measuring 3.75m in length by 1.15m in width and 0.4m in depth (Figs 6.31 and 6.34). The cut was lined with clay, into which three sub-rectangular cells approximately 0.9m long were cut. The cells were filled with a mixture of ash and silty clay. Analysis of the charred plant remains from tank 1316 by Kath Hunter identified the majority as saltmarsh plants, comprising abundant monocotyledonous stem/leaf fragments, over 1000 rush seeds with 48 seed capsules, many sea plantain seeds and capsules and a relatively low number of sea lavender seeds. Twenty seeds of lesser sea spurry were also present, while sea milkwort and sea arrow grass were represented by one example each. Other features within the saltern included a slot or short gully (1626), situated to the south-west of hearth 1484, and a sub-rectangular pit (5395) close to the inner penannular gully in the southern part of the saltern. Slot 1626, aligned roughly east-west, was 1.8m long, 0.2m wide and 0.05m deep. It contained a tiny quantity (0.5g) of broken hammerscale flake, tiny iron flakes and burnt clay (Keys, specialist report 6). Pit 5395 was aligned NNW-SSE and was 1.45m long, 0.58m wide and only 0.05m deep.

Micromorphological and chemical analyses by Richard Macphail, John Crowther and Francesco Berna show that the outer ditch, which was cut into marine clay, contained waterlain fills. A basal layer in the ditch included laminated byre waste, indicating animal management, and debris of burned hearth and kitchen origin. Here, and in the inner ditch gully, where natural alluviation predominated, human coprolitic waste indicated domestic occupation. The settling tanks were cut into brickearth and lined with marine alluvial clay. Lower, microlaminated waterlain fills, which also included traces of animal or human excrement, confirm that these tanks held water. The upper fills, however, were dominated by phytolith and fused phytolith-rich monocotyledonous fuel ash waste; burned byre floor waste was also found, suggesting that this material could also have been employed as a slow-burning fuel, as well as confirming the local stabling of stock. The very high phosphate levels in these deposits also results from the presence of latrine waste; such installations often have a secondary 'cess-pit' use. The saltern's hearth was constructed with brickearth, which was laid above a layer of possible sea rush leaves; a cob- or lime-plastered brickearth may have lined the hearth. The loose fill of the hearth was mainly composed of monocotyledonous fuel ash waste (siliceous vesicular white nodules, fused phytoliths, charred monocotyledonous remains) and burned hearth remains (strongly burned brickearth and sands) (Fig. 6.35). Again, notably high phosphate concentrations in part reflect input of human or animal excrement into the hearth. Lastly, very small lead enrichment of the charred sea rush liner may suggest the possibility that lead vessels were used (R Macphail et al., specialist report 24).

Figure 6.33 Hearth 1484 within round saltern 9501, looking east. Scale 1m

Figure 6.34 Settling tank 1316 within round saltern 9501, looking north-west. Scale 2m

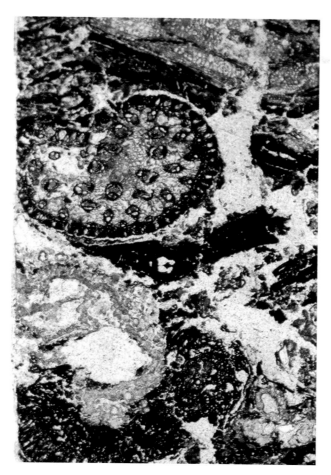

Figure 6.35 Photomicrograph of monocotyledonous fuel ash waste

The saltern cut the southern ditch of late Roman phase 1 enclosure 9506 and is therefore the later feature. Dating evidence from the saltern's ditch and gully included a Nene Valley colour-coated ware globular beaker and East Gaulish 'Rhenish' ware, which dates deposition to the 3rd century or later. A radiocarbon determination of middle to late Iron Age (170 cal. BC-cal. AD 10 (95.4%); 2058 ± 26 BP: OxA-24853) was obtained from spelt grain recovered from the packing fill around a stake in the west terminus of inner gully 5316. Given the stratigraphic associations and Roman-period pottery, the dated material is likely to be residual. The excavator noted that the deposit that contained the grain included 'red earth', and it is possible that this had been redeposited from the underlying red hill material.

Other features

Gully 6193 was situated immediately to the south-west of saltern 9501 (Figs 6.14 and 6.29). The feature cut later Roman phase 1 ditch 6617, though it was in turn cut by later Roman phase 2 enclosure ditch 8551. In its surviving form, the feature was c 7m long, 1m wide and 0.2m deep. It may have served a drainage function at the south side of gravel surface 8502 if, as seems likely, the latter remained in contemporary use with saltern 9501.

North of saltern 9501, pit 5368 was situated close to the north-western limit of excavation of Area A, where it cut later Roman phase 1 ditch 1354 at the point of junction with trackway ditch 5108. The pit was sub-circular in plan, 1.4m across and 0.5m deep (Fig. 6.14).

LATE ROMAN ACTIVITY IN AREA B (Fig. 6.36)

Saltern 6711 (Figs 6.36-6.38)

A naturally-formed channel and a number of ditches enclosed a late Roman saltern, 6711, at the eastern side of Area B (Fig. 6.36). The enclosed space measured approximately 45m north-south and 30m east-west, although the western arm of the channel continued northwards for at least another 40m. The main enclosing channel (8536/8540) was 15m across at its widest point, and interventions through it revealed a profile of steeply sloping or concave sides and, where bottomed, a flat base. In plan the channel formed a loop extending from beyond the north-west edge of Area B, defining the west, south and east sides of the enclosed area and then curving beyond the eastern edges of excavation. It cut through a series of thin tidally-deposited alluvial layers interleaved with occupation and industrial debris, including ash and ceramic fragments, derived from the early Roman salt working (Figs 6.37 and 6.38). These demonstrate frequent inundation, which may have hampered the salters' work during the early Roman period, preventing salt making from becoming well established here. Clearly, though, the late Roman salters overcame this difficulty; the channel, which was filled with alluvium resulting from tidal inundation, protected the working area and trapped large volumes of seawater. Three narrower ditches extended across the loop created by 8536 and 8540. The features (4063, 4347 and 4415) were roughly aligned east-west and ranged from c 1.2m up to c 4m in width. They appeared to link the two sides of the loop, but undoubtedly dated to earlier phases; a section through the intersection of ditch 4063 and 8536/8540 revealed that 4063 had been cut by the larger ditch. Ditch 4063 may in turn have been later than a north-south aligned feature (4242), up to 4m wide and 1.15m deep, which extended c 23m northwards, but the relationship was not certain. Equally, a curvilinear gully (4375), approximately 14m long and 0.85m wide, aligned roughly NNW-SSE and cutting an early Roman feature 8544 (see Fig. 5.15) in the northern part of the enclosure, was earlier than ditch 4347, although a flanged dish in white-slipped Hadham oxidised ware from its fill suggests a date for deposition after AD 100. These features were therefore probably significantly earlier than the later phases of channel loop 8536/8540.

What is more, the depositional histories of the main channel and the east-west cross ditches were different. Ditch 4063 and to a lesser degree 4415 were filled with a series of layers derived from tidal deposits and salt-making debris (similar to the deposits into which the

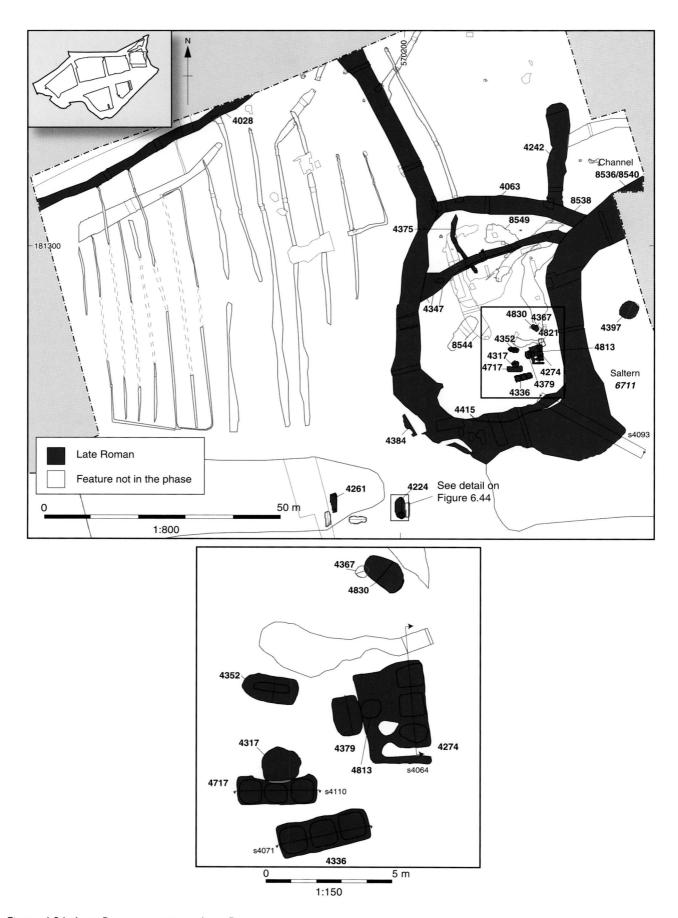

Figure 6.36 Late Roman activity in Area B

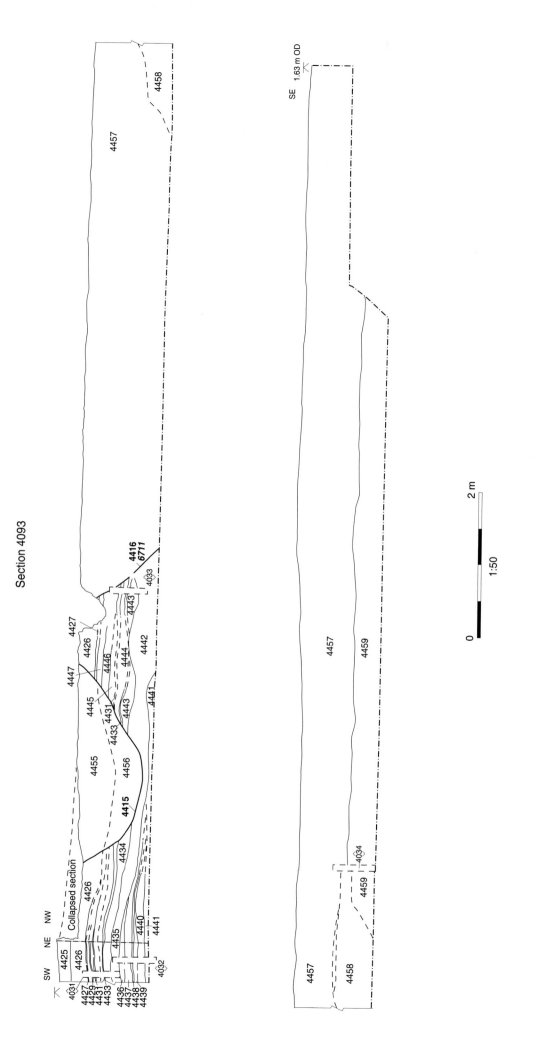

Section 4093

SW
NE
NW

4425
4426
4031
4427
4429
4431
4433
4436
4437
4438
4439
Collapsed section
4426
4455
4435
4440
4441
4032

4447
4445
4433
4431
4443
4456
4415
4434
4427
4426
4446
4444
4442
4441
4443
4033
4416
6711

4457
4458

SE   1.63 m OD

4457

4459

4457
4458
4034
4459

0   1:50   2 m

Figure 6.37 Section through saltern 6711 and ditch 4415

Figure 6.38 North-west facing view of machined slot through channel enclosing saltern 6711 (section 4093). Scale 2m

ditches were cut). But while it is possible that the ditches, particularly 4063, belong to the early Roman phase of activity, pottery recovered from the features included material dated to the later 4th century, such as Hadham oxidised ware, Oxford colour-coated ware, late shell-tempered ware, Alice Holt grey ware and Rettendon-type flint-tempered ware, indicating that the ditches remained open to some extent and available for deposition in the late Roman period. A similar range of pottery was recovered from channel 8536/8540, and pointed to a date after *c* AD 350 for the final episode of filling.

Samples from ditch 4415 at the south of the enclosed area contained wheat, barley and oat grains, along with spelt and barley chaff. Stinking chamomile and scentless mayweed and *Papaver* cf. *dubium* (possible long headed poppy), all arable weeds, were present. Saltmarsh maritime plants – sea lavender, lesser sea spurry, sea plantain, sea arrow grass and *Aster tripolium* (sea aster) – were recorded. The rush seed heads from this sample were particularly well preserved and *Juncus gerardii* (saltmarsh rush) and *Juncus maritimus* (sea rush) were both represented. There were also frequent monocotyledonous leaf/stem fragments (Hunter, specialist report 19).

Briquetage recovered from channel 8536/8540 provided strong support for the combination of saltmarsh plants and briquetage in salt making. Some fragments had a green glaze, which on analysis was

Figure 6.39 North-west facing view of hearth 4352. Scale 1m

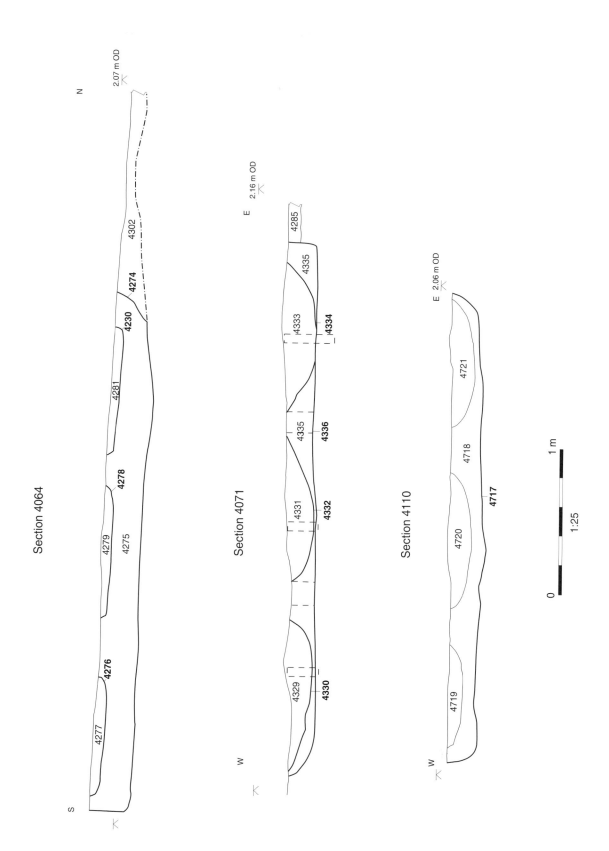

Figure 6.40 Sections through settling tanks 4274, 4336 and 4717

found to be a strongly heated silicate glass containing higher quantities of sodium, phosphorus and iron compared with the briquetage to which it was attached. Evidently, the briquetage had come into contact with the hearth or flame, and as a result, the iron possibly gave the briquetage a green colour, while the potassium derived from concentrated burned fuel (Macphail *et al.*, specialist report 24).

Features within saltern 6711 (Figs 6.36, 6.39-6.43)

Salt making activity appears to have been concentrated within the south-east corner of saltern 6711. This activity was represented by five hearths (4317, 4352, 4379, 4813 and 4830) and three rectangular groups of settling tanks (4274, 4336 and 4717). Hearths 4317 and 4813 were both sub-circular and cut rectangular pits 4717 and 4274 respectively, indicating that not all the salt making activity belonged to a single phase. Hearth 4317 measured 1.6m in diameter and 0.2m in depth and had a flat base with steep sides, while hearth 4813 measured 0.8m in diameter and 0.16m in depth and had a flattish base with concave sides. Both features contained deposits of burnt material. Hearths 4352, 4379 and 4830 were all sub-rectangular in plan with flat bases and concave or vertical sides. Hearth 4352 was 2.2m long and 1m wide (Fig. 6.39). Hearth 4379 was 1.7m long, 1.2m wide and 0.3m deep, and the dimensions of hearth 4830 were similar – *c* 1.7m long, 1.1m wide and 0.22m deep. The sub-rectangular hearths contained multiple fills incorporating burnt material.

All three settling tanks were lined with clay into which three square or sub-circular cells were cut (Fig. 6.40). Settling tank 4274 was orientated north-south and had a row of three cells along its eastern side. The cells measured approximately 1m-1.4m across, varied in depth from *c* 0.06m to 0.2m, and were filled with a mixture of silty clay and ash (Fig. 6.41). It is possible that hearth 4813, which was inserted into the western side of settling tank 4274, in fact represents a fourth cell, or that 4274 initially contained two rows of three cells. Settling tank 4336 was aligned east-west and measured 3.65m long, 1.4m wide and 0.24m deep; its cells were *c* 1m across and approximately 0.2m in depth with concave profiles (Fig. 6.42). Settling tank 4717 was also aligned east-west and measured 3.3m long, 1.2m wide and 0.24m deep. Its cells were approximately 0.8m across and up to 0.17m deep with concave profiles (Fig. 6.43). Pottery from the hearths and settling tanks was broadly dated, but was generally consistent with the late Roman date offered for the filling of the channel and associated ditches.

Environmental samples from tank 4336 mainly contained seeds of saltmarsh types, including sea lavender, sea plantain, sea-milkwort and rush. At least one sea rush seed capsule was present, and there were relatively large numbers of grass seeds as well. One sample contained frequent monocotyledonous leaf/stem fragments with abundant fuel ash slag. The only cereal remains was a single spelt type glume base (Hunter, specialist report 19).

A small pit or posthole (4367), 0.6m in diameter, lay immediately adjacent to hearth 4830. It was undated, but the location suggests an association with the late Roman salt working.

Deposits and features outside saltern 6711
(Figs 6.36, 6.44-6.45)

Late Roman industrial and other activity was not limited to the interior of saltern 6711, but was also spread

Figure 6.41 West facing view of settling tank 4274. Scale 2m

Figure 6.42 North facing view of settling tank 4336. Scale 2m

Figure 6.43 North facing view of settling tank 4717. Scale 2m

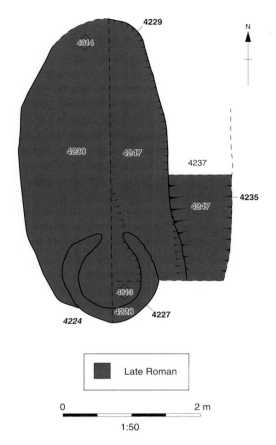

Late Roman

0   2 m

1:50

Figure 6.44 Plan of kiln or oven 4224, and ditch/gully 4235

around the area immediately outside it. Kiln/oven 4224 lay to the south-west, and immediately west and north of this were two industrial spreads or occupation layers (4261 and 4384). Pit 4397 lay immediately to the east of the enclosure (Fig. 6.36).

Kiln or oven 4224 comprised a simple penannular structure (4227), with a north facing entrance and a large sub-circular rake-out hollow (4229). A gully (4235) on the eastern side of the kiln/oven complex was cut by hollow 4229. Structure 4227 measured 1.4m in diameter and consisted of a single course of fired clay bricks measuring 0.2-0.22m in width and 0.1m in height, with an entrance approximately 0.32m across. The rake-out hollow to the north of and partly surrounding the structure was aligned north-south and measured *c* 4m long, 2.2m wide and at most 0.14m deep. In profile, the hollow had a flat base, with gently sloping concave sides (Fig. 6.45). Both kiln and hollow were filled with a mixture of ashy material, burnt plant remains, and fired clay kiln lining material. These included a relatively large number of cereal remains, legume seeds and saltmarsh plant seeds, among them sea plantain seeds and capsules, rush seeds and one sea-milkwort seed. Monocotyledonous leaf/stem fragments were rare (Hunter, specialist report 19). Pottery recovered from the rake-out deposit was broadly dated to *c* AD 120 onwards, suggesting a date for deposition some time within the middle or late Roman period. Gully 4235, extending along the eastern side of the hollow, may have been part

Figure 6.45 View of kiln or oven 4224, looking west. Scale 2m

of the structure. It was at least 3m long, 0.7m wide and 0.35m deep, and had a rounded base with steeply sloping sides. The gully had two fills, both comprising a mixture of clay, fuel debris and kiln lining.

Layers 4261 and 4384 were amorphous in plan (and only partly excavated as shown on Fig. 6.36), but layer 4261 was somewhat the more sub-rectangular of the two. It comprised a 0.08m thick deposit of dark reddish brown silty-clay with frequent inclusions of ceramic building material and fuel debris, measuring approximately 6m in length by 4.5m in width. This layer was sealed by a deposit of ash (4248). Layer 4384, north-east of layer 4261 and just south-west of the channel defining saltern 6711, comprised a dark bluish-brown silty clay, with frequent inclusions of fuel debris and briquetage. It measured approximately 5.6m in length by 2m in width and was 0.19m thick. The deposits appeared to have formed from episodes of dumping of industrial waste which might have resulted in the accumulation of distinct mounds. Both 4261 and 4384 contained Roman pottery dated to the second half of the 4th century. This included Oxford colour-coated ware, Hadham oxidised ware, and dropped-flange dishes in grey wares.

Pit 4397 was sub-circular in plan with a flat base and steeply sloping sides, and was approximately 4m in diameter but only 0.4m deep. The single fill comprised silty clay, with inclusions of flint and fuel debris and produced two sherds of pottery, including a fragment of Nene Valley white ware mortarium probably dating to the later 3rd or 4th century AD.

PARALLEL GULLIES IN AREAS A, B and D
(Fig. 6.46)

Blocks of closely spaced parallel gullies were observed in the north-eastern corner of Area A, in the north-western corner of Area B, and in Area D (Fig. 6.46). Those in Area A comprised seven clusters of gullies spaced approximately 2-4m apart and generally orientated NE-SW or NW-SE. The gullies in Area B had a prevailing north-south orientation. The features in Area B were spaced approximately 2.5-5m apart and were bounded by a ditch (4028) to the north and by medieval ditch 8532 to the east (Figs 6.36 and 7.3). Ditch 4028 was aligned ENE-WSW, running parallel to the north-western limit of Area B and extending beyond the limits of excavation at both ends. The recorded length was approximately 52m and the ditch was up to 2.4m wide and 0.5m deep, and had a flat base with steeply sloping sides. There were also three small clusters of similar gullies recorded in the centre of Area D. The gullies were spaced approximately 2m apart and were orientated NE-SW and NNW-SSE.

Dating evidence was limited to the Area B gullies. A post-medieval date for these features is possible, based on analogy with similar gullies found at a site in Lymington, Hampshire, and dated to the post-medieval period (Powell 2009), but on the whole a Roman date is preferred. Four

sherds of pottery broadly dated to the Roman period were recovered from some of the gullies, and the gullies appear to respect the shape of saltern 6711 better than they do the alignment of post-Roman features. For further discussion of the parallel gullies, see Chapter 7.

THE FINDS

Pottery by Edward Biddulph and Dan Stansbie

Ceramic groups dating between *c* AD 120/30 and 250 and assigned to the middle Roman period amounted to less than 1% of the entire Iron Age and Roman pottery assemblage by EVE. Indeed, the middle Roman assemblage included a high proportion of residual middle Iron Age forms, notably an S-profiled jar in a glauconitic fabric. Nevertheless, the presence of bead-rimmed dishes in black-burnished ware (BB) and sandy grey ware (GRS), as well as a dish with a groove below the rim in sandy grey ware, indicates that pottery reached the site in the middle Roman period, probably largely from Mucking, where production of those dish forms and fabrics is attested (Rodwell 1973, 20).

Pottery recovered from contexts assigned to late Roman phase 1 (LR1) spans the late Roman period, but the emphasis is on the earlier part of the period, *c* AD 250-320, to which 38% of the phase group belongs. Just 17% necessarily dates after AD 350.

The phase group (Table 6.2) is dominated by two fabrics, sandy grey ware (GRS) and black-surfaced ware (BSW). The former took a share within the group of 33% by EVE, and was available as plain-rimmed,

Table 6.2: Late Roman (phase 1) pottery from key ceramic groups, AD 250-400+. Quantification by EVE. * = fabric present, but with no surviving rim.

Fabric	B Dishes	C Bowls	E Bowl-jars	G Jars	H Beakers	Total	%
ABAET						⋆	
BSW	0.38			1.47	0.04	1.89	44
CGRHN						⋆	
CGSW		0.01				0.01	0
EGRHN						⋆	
EGSW						⋆	
FLINT						⋆	
GLAUC				0.03		0.03	1
GRF	0.36		0.13	0.20		0.69	16
GRS	0.52		0.08	0.81		1.41	33
HAR						⋆	
HAX						⋆	
LSH						⋆	
NKG						⋆	
NVC					0.18	0.18	4
OXWM						⋆	
RED	0.05					0.05	1
RET						⋆	
SAND						⋆	
STOR						⋆	
Total	1.31	0.01	0.21	2.51	0.22	4.26	-
%	31	0	5	59	5	-	-

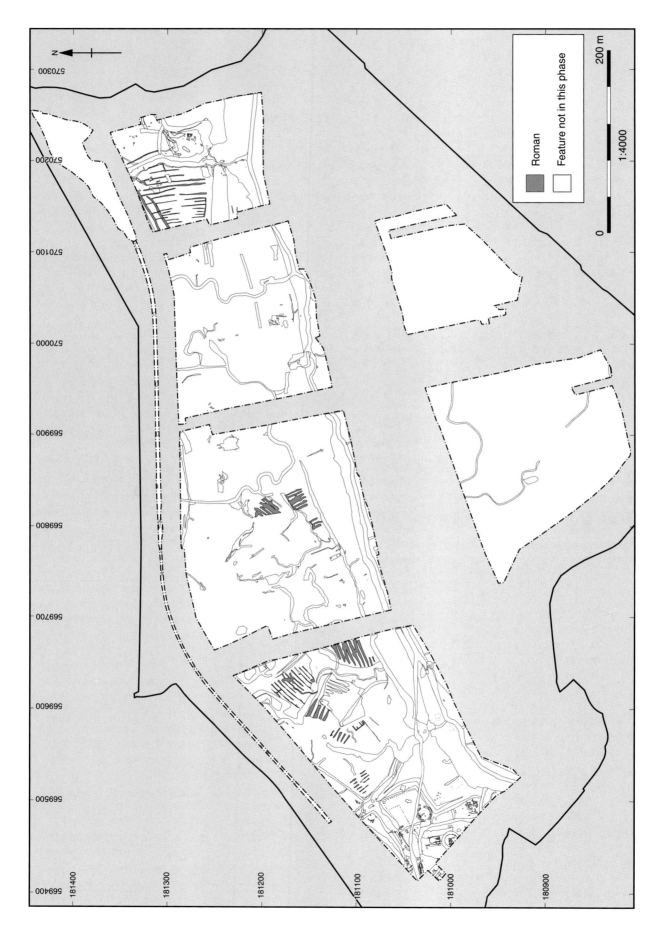

Figure 6.46 Blocks of parallel gullies in areas A, B and D

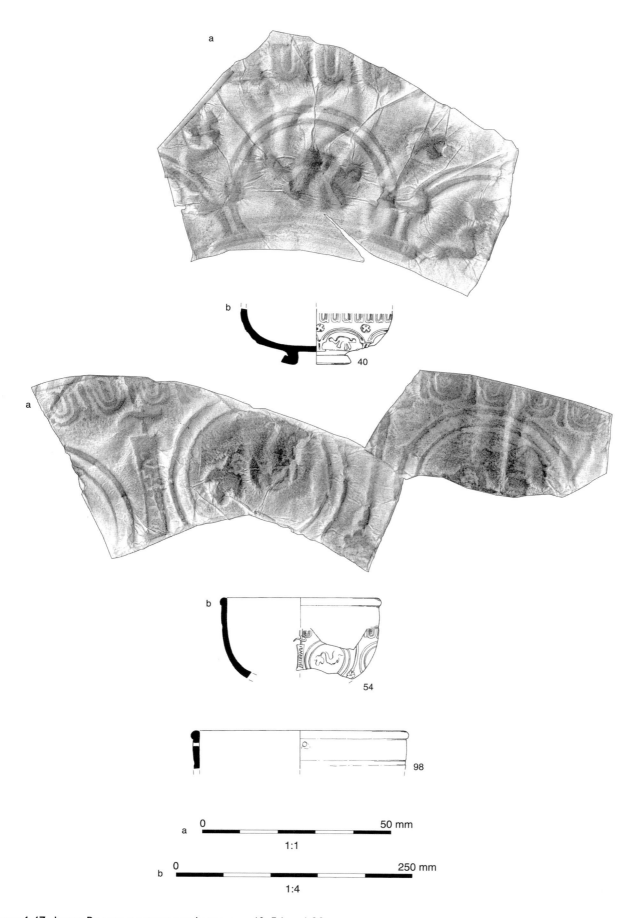

Figure 6.47 Later Roman pottery, catalogue nos 40, 54 and 98

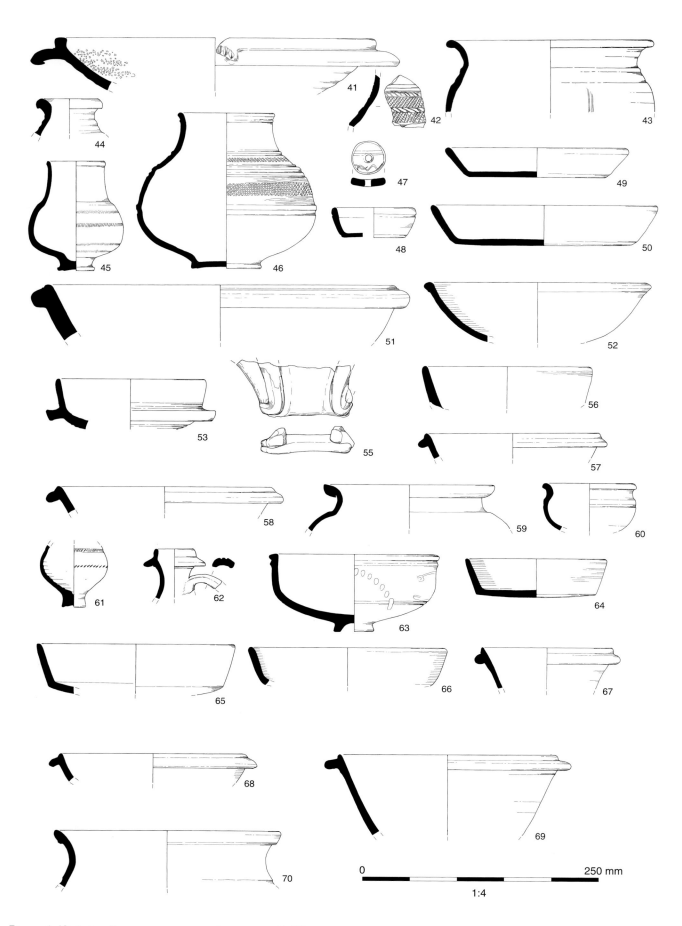

Figure 6.48 Later Roman pottery, catalogue nos 41-70

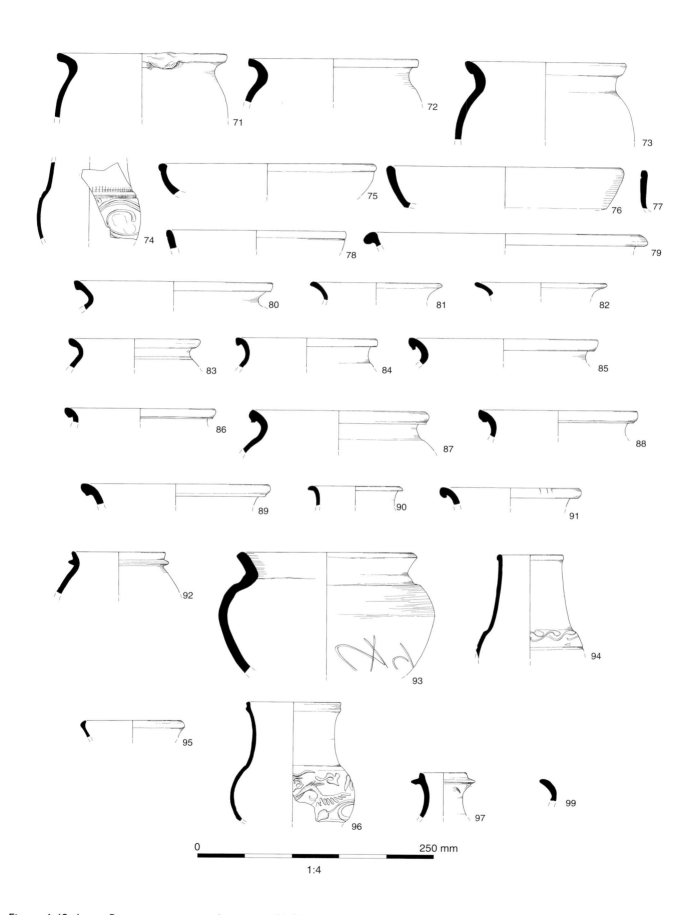

Figure 6.49 Later Roman pottery, catalogue nos 71-99

groove-rimmed, incipient-bead-and-flanged, and dropped flanged dishes (types B1, B3, B5 and B6 respectively), and necked, bifid-rimmed and small storage jars (types G24, G28 and G42 respectively). A wide-mouthed jar or bowl-jar (type E5) was also recorded (Fig. 6.48, no. 43). All these types were manufactured at Mucking. An almost identical range of forms was seen in black-surfaced ware, which contributed 44% by EVE; the same dish and jar forms were represented, but the fabric lacked the bowl-jar. A beaker, though unidentified to type, was also noted. Fine grey ware (GRF) was another important category. Dishes (types B1, B2 and B6) were recorded, along with oval-bodied necked jar type G24 and the ledge-rimmed bowl-jar type E2, another Mucking type (Rodwell 1973, 24). A bead-rimmed dish (type B4) in a sandy oxidised fabric may also have a Mucking origin.

Although contributing small quantities, pottery from a number of regional sources was noted. The Hadham industry was responsible for grey ware (HAR) and fine oxidised ware (HAX), and late shell-tempered ware (LSH) arrived from the Harrold kilns in Bedfordshire or sites in the eastern region. Nene Valley colour-coated ware (NVC) had already been introduced to the site before AD 250, but reached the site in greater quantity after that date. Two beakers were represented: a folded beaker with scale decoration (type H32) and a globular, funnel-necked beaker (type H42). A white ware mortarium arrived from Oxford (Fig. 6.48, no. 41). North Kent grey ware (NKG) is likely to have been residual by this phase. Flint-tempered reduced fabric, Rettendon ware (RET) was recorded in this phase. Kilns producing the fabric are known at sites in east central Essex, including Chelmsford and Rettendon itself (Going 1987, 10).

Pottery with continental origins comprised amphorae from southern Spain and samian were from central and eastern Gaul. The amphora fabric is consistent with that of Dressel 20 olive oil containers (ABAET). The Central Gaulish samian ware (CGSW) included a flanged hemispherical bowl (Drag. 38) and a footring from a deep Drag. 36 flanged dish. The East Gaulish material (EGSW) could not be identified to form. All these continental wares are likely to have been residual at the time of deposition, as importation from their sources ceased during the first half of the 3rd century.

More pottery from context-groups dated on the basis of ceramics to c AD 250-350 was assigned to late Roman phase 2 (LR2). The LR2 pottery was similar to that of LR1 in terms of composition, the two assemblages being broadly contemporaneous. Thus, sandy grey ware (GRS) and black-surfaced ware (BSW) dominated (Table 6.3). The sandy grey wares, which accounted for 40% of the phase group by EVE, were recorded as dishes and jars, and to a lesser extent bowl-jars. The range of dishes encountered in phase LR1 – types B1, B3, B5 and B6 – was seen here, along with bead-rimmed dishes B2 and B4 (Fig. 6.48, no. 50). In terms of jars, the standard G24, G28 and G42 types (Fig. 6.49, nos 73, 83, 86 and 89) were joined by a black-burnished-style cooking-pot (G9) (Fig. 6.49, nos 81-82), narrow-necked jar or flask G40, and storage jar G45. The E5 bowl-jar was also recorded (Fig. 6.49, no. 70). Black-surfaced wares contributed a similar range of types – B1, B3 and B6 dishes (Fig. 6.48, nos 48-49, 56, 67-69), G24 and G28 jars (Fig. 6.48, no. 59; Fig. 6.49, nos 71-72), and E2 bowl-jar – that were recorded in the fabric in the phase LR1 key groups, and these were joined by B2/B4 dishes (Fig. 6.48, no. 52) and the G40 narrow-necked jar or flask. Fine grey ware contributed a

Table 6.3: Late Roman (phase 2) pottery from key ceramic groups, AD 250-350. Quantification by EVE. * = fabric present, but with no surviving rim.

Fabric	B Dishes	C Bowls	D Mortaria	E Bowl-jars	F Cups	G Jars	H Beakers	J Flagons	Total	%
BB	0.35								0.35	3
BSW	1.84			0.13		1.48			3.45	29
CGSW					0.12				0.12	1
COLB								0.65	0.65	5
COLC									★	
EGRHN									★	
EGSW			0.13						0.13	1
GRF	0.67	0.09		0.35		0.10	0.25		1.46	12
GRS	1.56			0.38		2.80			4.74	40
NFWW									★	
NKG									★	
NVC							0.59		0.59	5
OXW									★	
OXWM									★	
PATCH									★	
RED	0.05					0.38	0.06		0.49	4
SGSW									★	
STOR									★	
UWW									★	
Total	4.47	0.09	0.13	0.86	0.12	4.76	0.90	0.65	11.98	-
%	37	1	1	7	1	40	8	5	-	-

smaller, though still significant, proportion (12% by EVE), but a wider range of forms (Fig. 6.48, nos 57-58; Fig. 6.49, nos 77-78). These included B1, B4 and B6 dishes, E5 bowl-jars, and a carinated bowl, C12. Jars and beakers were also represented, but these could not be identified to type. The B2 dish, and G24 and G40 jars were available in sandy oxidised ware (RED; Fig. 6.49, nos 80, 84, 85 and 87). Most, if not all, the pottery in GRS, BSW, GRF and RED fabrics was of local origin, with Mucking probably being the main source.

Pottery from regional sources took a larger share in this phase compared with the early Roman and LR1 phases. Colchester potters supplied buff ware (COLB) and colour-coated ware (COLC). A bead-rimmed flagon (type J4) was recorded in the former. A white-ware vessel from the New Forest (NFWW) – not enough of it survived to identify the type – represents a rare arrival in Essex, although New Forest grey ware was identified at Chelmsford (Going 1987, 9). North Kent grey ware was recorded, but is likely to be residual; the Patch Grove ware from West Kent may be too, although storage jars, to which the recorded sherds belong (Fig. 6.49, no. 93), continued to be produced into the 3rd century (Pollard 1988, 212). Nene Valley colour-coated ware (NVC) was relatively well represented at 5% of the phase assemblage by EVE. Two beaker types, both funnel-necked globular beakers, were recorded (Fig. 6.48, no. 61).

Though residual, samian ware accounted for 2% of the phase assemblage. A closed form, possibly Drag. 67, was seen in South Gaulish samian ware (SGSW). Central Gaulish potters were responsible for a Drag. 33 conical cup and a Drag. 37 decorated bowl (Fig. 6.47, no, 98). A Drag. 43 mortarium and body sherds from Drag. 45 mortarium were recorded in East Gaulish samian ware. East Gaulish factories also provided a Drag. 31 dish (recorded as a footring).

Table 6.4: Late Roman (phase 2) pottery from key ceramic groups, AD 350-400+. Quantification by EVE. * = fabric present, but with no surviving rim.

FABRIC	B Dishes	C Bowls	D Mortaria	E Bowl-jars	G Jars	H Beakers	J Flagons	K Lids	R Misc	Total	%
ABAET										⋆	
BB	0.10									0.10	0
BB1	0.01									0.01	0
BB2										⋆	
BSW	0.68			0.13	0.87	0.03				1.71	4
BUF					0.19					0.19	0
CGSW		0.16								0.16	0
COLB										⋆	
COLBM			0.17							0.17	0
EGRHN						0.06				0.06	0
EGSW	0.07	0.17								0.24	1
ESH					0.08					0.08	0
GLAUC										⋆	
GRF	0.40				0.05	0.07				0.52	1
GRS	7.29	0.07		0.59	22.73	0.64		0.01	0.10	31.43	82
HAB	0.12									0.12	0
HAR	0.13			0.12		0.18				0.43	1
HAX	0.03			0.10			1.00			1.13	3
LSH					0.14					0.14	0
MEK					0.26					0.26	1
MWSGF	0.06									0.06	0
MWSGS		0.19			0.05					0.24	1
NKG										⋆	
NKO										⋆	
NKWO										⋆	
NVC						0.25				0.25	1
NVP										⋆	
OXP										⋆	
OXRC					0.14					0.14	0
OXRCM										⋆	
OXW										⋆	
OXWM										⋆	
PATCH										⋆	
PORD					0.10					0.10	0
RED	0.02				0.53					0.55	1
RET										⋆	
SGSW										⋆	
STOR					0.06					0.06	0
UWW					0.16					0.16	0
Total	8.91	0.59	0.17	0.94	25.36	1.23	1.00	0.01	0.10	38.31	-
%	23	2	0	2	66	3	3	0	0	-	-

A large proportion of the entire assemblage (16% by EVE) was recovered from context groups dated on ceramic grounds to the second half of the 4th century onwards and assigned to late Roman phase 2 (Table 6.4). A much wider range of forms and fabrics was evident in this group compared with earlier key groups. That said, sandy grey ware continued to dominate, and indeed increased its representation to 82% by EVE (although the divisions between black-surfaced wares, fine grey wares and sandy grey wares were not always clear-cut, and in cases of ambiguity, pottery was identified as sandy grey ware by default). Jars took the largest share of forms in sandy grey ware. Many could not be identified to type, having broken at the rim, although it is likely that most are the oval-bodied and necked type, G24, which is the best represented of the jars identified to type. This is followed by the bifid-rimmed jar, G28, and the cooking-pot type, G9. Narrow-necked jars (types G35, G36 and G40) were also present, along with a small storage jar (type G42) and ledge-rimmed jar (type G5). Dishes remained another important category. Plain-rimmed (type B1) and drop-flanged (B6) dishes were the principal forms. Bead-rimmed (type B2/B4), groove-rimmed (type B3) and incipient bead-and-flanged (type B5) dishes were recorded, although occurrences are likely to be residual by this date (cf. Going 1987, 14-5). Bowl-jars E2 and E5 were joined by the small, S-profiled, E3. Beakers were represented by the funnel-necked globular beaker H39/H41, a bag-shaped beaker H19, and a narrow beaker, H4, which appears to imitate black-burnished forms (for example Gillam 1976, fig. 2.19). The dishes B1, B2/B4, B3, B5 and B6 were also recorded in black-surfaced ware, as were jars G24 and G28. Fine grey ware was available in small quantities as B1, B2, B3 and B6 dishes. More G24 and G28 jars were recorded in sandy oxidised ware (RED). As in earlier phases, most, if not all, of this material is of local origin.

A local source, probably Mucking, can be suggested for the wheel-thrown black-burnished ware (BB2), although no forms were identified and indeed the material could well be residual. Handmade Dorset black-burnished ware (BB1), on the other hand, arrived mainly, if not exclusively, after AD 350, albeit in small quantities. A drop-flange B6 dish was identified. Colchester was responsible for buff ware (BUF, BUFM), including a wall-sided mortarium (type D13), although the form was residual at the time of deposition (cf. Hull 1963a, *Cam* 501). The growth of the Hadham industry in the second half of the 4th century (Going 1999, 297) is apparent at Stanford Wharf, as the proportion of Hadham products increased from under 1% in phase LR1 to 4% in the latest part of phase LR2. The burnished reduced fabric (HAB) is represented by a B2 dish (probably residual), while the (often burnished) grey ware is represented by a B6 dish, an E3 bowl-jar and an unspecified beaker. Fine Hadham oxidised ware was available as a B2 dish, an E5 bowl-jar and a disc-necked flagon. Late shell-tempered ware was available solely as a necked jar (type G27). A variety of white-slipped grey wares (MWSGF/S) of uncertain source were noted. A plain-rimmed dish (type B1), a necked jar (G24) and a carinated bowl (type C13) were recorded. North Kent products, including Patch Grove ware, continued to be present as residual occurrences. Like Hadham wares, Nene Valley products were better represented in this latest phase than they had been in earlier phases, although identifiable forms were restricted to funnel-necked globular beakers (type H41). Oxford products also increased their representation. White ware vessels – a mortarium and a bowl (Fig. 6.48, nos 55 and 63, the latter a rare form) – were joined by red colour-coated ware forms, including a mortarium (OXRCM) and a narrow-necked jar (Young 1977, type C16). So-called 'Portchester D' ware, a sandy oxidised fabric made in the vicinity of Overwey in the Hampshire/Surrey region, was available as a jar with everted rim (type G9). Rettendon ware from east central Essex was noted, but no forms identified.

Of the imported wares, samian wares continued to form the largest group, despite being residual at the time of final deposition. A sherd from a decorated vessel was recorded in South Gaulish samian ware (SGSW), while a Drag. 44 bowl was present in Central Gaulish samian ware (CGSW). East Gaulish potters (EGSW) including those from Rheinzabern were responsible for Drag. 31 dishes, Drag. 37 decorated bowls, and a beaker with barbotine decoration (Fig. 6.47, nos 40 and 54; Fig. 6.49, no. 96). East Gaulish potters – specifically those working in the Trier region – were also responsible for a relatively rare black-slipped or 'Rhenish' ware beaker (Fig. 6.49, no. 95; Symonds 1992, fig. 40.771). Lid-seated jars (type G5; Gose 1950, type 546) in coarse Mayen ware (MEK) arrived from the Eifel region of Germany; two examples were recorded.

Briquetage and fired clay *by Cynthia Poole*

A very small quantity (5.2kg) of material was assigned to the middle Roman phase. This predominantly comprised briquetage vessels in sandy fabrics, plus two pedestals, a pinch prop, and a small amount of oven wall and lining.

The late Roman briquetage and fired clay accounted for almost 167kg, or 67% of the fully recorded assemblage. Briquetage vessels accounted for 54%, furniture for about 10% and structural and fuel debris for 21%. Briquetage vessels included troughs (V4; Fig. 6.50, nos 15 and 16), bowls (V3) and moulds (V1 and V2; Fig. 6.50, no. 18). A wide range of rim types was present, though finger impressed rims were frequent (Fig. 6.50, no. 17), together with rounded rims and flat rims. Cut edges indicative of split moulds were also common. Organic tempered fabrics – analysis of the fabrics by Kath Hunter (specialist report 19) suggests that the fabrics were tempered with grasses and cereal chaff – were considerably more common (62kg) than the sandy fabrics (15kg), which derived from sandy clays and brickearth. Furniture included several pieces of trian-

Vessels

Pedestals

Firebars

0   250 mm

1:4

Figure 6.50 Selection of briquetage from late Roman deposits: vessels, pedestals and firebars

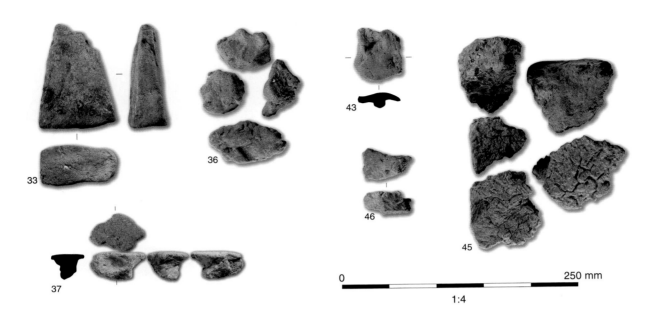

Figure 6.51 Selection of briquetage from late Roman deposits: wedges, miscellaneous furniture and structural briquetage

gular firebar (FB6; Fig. 6.50, nos 28 and 30), a range of pedestals (PD2, PD3, PD4, PD18; Fig. 6.50, nos 20-23), wedges (W1; Fig. 6.51, no. 33), and a wide variety of hand moulded supports and stabilisers, including wedges, pinch props, plaques, plates, clips, rods and hand-squeezed lumps (Fig. 6.51, nos 36, 37 and 43). Structural material was largely indeterminate hearth or oven wall or floor, lining and occasional luting (Fig. 6.51, no. 46).

The introduction in the late Roman period of pedestal type PD18 (Fig. 6.50, no. 22) in Area B suggests that a further development took place, possibly indicating the use of larger vessels or a change of shape in the evaporating vessels. The pedestals could have been used either with rectangular vessels with flared sides or with large rounded vessels with a convex base, or possibly even with metal pans. However, briquetage vessels had not gone out of use in the late Roman phase judging by the increase in quantities of briquetage vessel debris. Although there must have been some element of residual material from the earlier red hills cut through by later features, the degree of abrasion does not indicate considerable reworking of material and much of the softer fired clay fabric would not have survived if not rapidly deposited and buried.

A bellows plate or guard from a late Roman feature (4412) took the form of large blocks of fired clay 45-50mm thick from a flat plate (Fig. 6.51, no. 45). Two corner fragments indicate that it was a square or rectangular object with straight, flat or slightly bevelled sides. One side is extremely heavily vitrified with thick green glaze. The fired clay shows the typical colour gradation commonly seen in furnace lining. The surviving back face has been less intensely fired and it is possible that the original surface remained unfired and has worn away. These characteristics are typical of bellows plates. Similar items are more commonly

found in association with metalworking such as those from Ireland (Scott 1990, 162-8), where it is suggested they were associated with iron smithing and forging, and at the late La Tène enclosure at Trégueux, Côtes d'Armor, France (Poole 2012).

Ceramic building material *by Ruth Shaffrey*

Virtually all the ceramic building material at Stanford Wharf Nature Reserve was recovered from features of late Roman date (91% by weight), of which the bulk (78%) was from later Roman Phase 2 contexts. These include a number of *in situ* structures, including hearth 6061. A total of 277 fragments (60kg, approximately 25% of the assemblage) are definite tegulae with a further 497 fragments (52kg) of flat tile that are also likely to be from tegulae (Table 6.5). Of the definite tegulae, 32 have missing flanges that appear to have been removed deliberately, possibly enabling them to be used more easily. No complete dimensions of tegulae survive except thickness, which ranges from 10mm to 28mm and averages at 19mm. A quarter of the assemblage is brick, although further bricks were recorded on site but not retained. Very few bricks survived sufficiently to be measurable. Two almost complete bricks from structure 6061 are most likely to be *pedales*. Five other examples could only be measured in one dimension (apart from thickness) and these could be either *pedalis* or *lydion* bricks (Brodribb 1987). A total of 162 fragments (22.3kg) of imbrices were recovered, making up 8.9% of the assemblage by weight. Imbrices vary from 10-17mm in thickness but as they generally survived as small pieces no complete widths or lengths are present. Almost 40% of the assemblage was recorded as flat tile because of a lack of distinguishing features, such as a

moulded
cut

Figure 6.52 An unusual tegula flange and selected ceramic building material signatures from late Roman deposits

flange or a thickness in excess of 40mm. Some of these are so thick that they are likely to be brick. Tile with only one surviving flat surface was recorded as flat/indeterminate (6.3kg). The remaining 52.4kg were identified as flat tile and most, if not all of these would have been tegulae. One possible tegula mammata was recovered, but is only a fragment. Flue tile is a rare occurrence in the assemblage, accounting for 1% (11 fragments from five contexts). The combing is generally coarse and the one surviving vent hole is circular (34mm diameter).

A variety of signature marks were present, although many could not be easily assigned to existing types. The 26 identifiable signatures are virtually all of curved forms but include a number of variants in shape or have been combined with crossing or adjacent straight lines (Fig. 6.52). Evidence from Beauport Park indicated that signatures can be associated with individual tile makers (Warry 2006, 90), and thus the generally similar nature of the signatures at Stanford Wharf could mean that the tiles have the same point of origin. The subtle variations within the scheme might be seen as representing different tile makers or groups of tile makers.

The high mean fragment weight and generally low degree of wear suggest that the tile was new. However, few fragments could be reassembled, which might indicate that broken tiles were being brought onto site. Because of this, in addition to the occasional presence of tile of different types, such as flue and imbrex, it seems most likely that the tile represents reuse of material from

Table 6.5: Quantification of ceramic building material types by weight

Type	Weight (g)	%
Tegula	60,412	24
Flat	52,425	20.8
Brick	59,655	23.7
Brick/flat	44,899	17.9
Imbrex	22,317	8.9
Flat/indeterminate	6,264	2.5
Box/flue	2,829	1.1
Indeterminate	2,202	0.9
Tegula mammata	489	0.2
Grand Total	251,492	100

elsewhere. Comparison of material from Stanford Wharf and Mucking shows that the range of fabrics and forms was similar, although this does not prove that the tile from one was being taken and used at the other, but rather that both shared a source, with the inhabitants at both Stanford Wharf and Mucking perhaps collecting tiles from nearby villa sites. These sites could have been on either side of the Thames as cross-river links have been demonstrated by the distribution of other materials such as querns and pottery (Shaffrey, specialist report 10; Biddulph and Stansbie, specialist report 2), and it is plausible that tile was also moved across the river perhaps as ballast.

The late Roman date of the tile at Stanford Wharf is clear evidence of a change in the way that at least some hearths and kilns were being constructed during the latest phase of activity; it is clear that tile and bricks were brought onto site for the construction of some hearths. Analysis of the tiles and bricks recovered from *in situ* contexts reveal careful selection of tile. Some features of selection are consistent across the structures, for example, the rare use of imbrices, no doubt a practical preference for flatter tile, or the removal of flanges from tegulae when the positioning of the tile required it. These features reflect practical considerations, as might the emphasis on brick in hearths 5725 and 6061. However, the high number of flue tiles from hearth 1407 in saltern 5760 does not have a functional explanation, nor can the high number of 'signed' pieces from hearth 5288 be explained by fragment size alone. These must be considered a reflection of the tile available rather than a deliberate choice. Thus the implication of the evidence is that tile was collected and utilised on a hearth by hearth basis, with the tile being used reflecting what was available at that time.

Coins *by Paul Booth*

Six Roman coins range in date from the later 2nd century to at least the mid 4th century, but all were in poor condition, most being encrusted and several incomplete, and cleaning by a conservator resulted in only minimal refinement of provisional identifications. No fully referenced identifications were possible. A small *as* of the later 2nd century was recovered as a residual occurrence in late Roman posthole 1634. The coin showed a bearded obverse bust, most probably of Marcus Aurelius or Commodus. One of two fragmentary *antoniniani* was probably an irregular issue, while the status of the other is uncertain. A SOLI INVICTO

SF1004

SF1505

0   20 mm

2:1

Figure 6.53 Selection of glass beads

0   50 mm

1:1

Figure 6.54 Spearhead (SF1004) and plate brooch (SF1505)

COMITI issue of London (c AD 313-317), unfortunately incomplete, is the only coin whose original condition can be assessed; as so often with these coins it was only slightly worn when lost. Nevertheless, encrustation of the surviving obverse legend still precludes close identification. A completely encrusted AE3 is perhaps most likely to date to the second quarter of the 4th century, and the latest closely datable piece is an issue of Magnentius or Decentius, apparently from Trier, but again with other legends completely lost or obscured.

Glass by Ian Scott

There are 21 glass sherds from Area A, including four beads (five fragments) and 16 sherds of vessel glass. The beads all date to the late Roman period and comprise two small annular beads, a small ovoid bead and a 3rd- to 4th-century segmented bead. In Area B, a single piece of glass is a dark blue cylindrical bead from a late Roman context (Fig. 6.53).

Metal objects by Ian Scott

The Roman finds are dominated by nails, which come mainly from middle and late Roman contexts. What is notable about the nails is the predominance of stem fragments and scarcity of complete nails or nail heads. This suggests that the contexts with nails may well have been disturbed or the finds re-deposited. There is a single incomplete small spearhead of Roman form (Fig. 6.54, SF1004) from posthole 1635 within saltern 5760, a fragmentary symmetrical plate brooch of 2nd- or early 3rd-century date (Fig. 6.54, SF1505), an eroded and fragmentary hair pin, a hair pin stem and an unidentified cast copper alloy fragment with an iron insert. There are only three household items, comprising two lead rivets for repairing ceramic vessels and a fragment of a knife blade, unfortunately not identifiable to form. Structural items other than nails comprise a piece of melted lead used to secure an iron fitting to stone, two lead washers, and a possible fragment of a small iron clamp. There are just 18 metal fragments from Area B, most of them from undated contexts, including two pieces of structural lead, and five pieces of melted lead waste. Area B produced only a single fragment of nail stem.

Stone by Ruth Shaffrey

The assemblage of worked stone includes an estimated 11 rotary querns or millstones of Lava and Millstone Grit and two whetstones. All the dated worked stone objects were retrieved from late Roman contexts. Stone was also used structurally, although with little evidence of deliberate modification. Eight of the querns are made of Millstone Grit, and although some could be from mechanically operated millstones, the fragments are too small to be diagnostic. One is of a slightly different form to others and has poorly incised harped grooving on the grinding surface, which is not typically associated with the form (Fig. 6.55, SF1566). The grooving may be in imitation of lava querns. The remaining three querns are of lava and are of flat disc type. None has the wide kerb typical of lava querns, but one, the most complete quern, has a clear line demarcating a kerb (Fig. 6.55, SF1503). This is not typical of lava querns and does not fit into the existing lava quern typology (Crawford and Röder 1955), although it has been observed on a quern from a 3rd century deposit in Carlisle (Shaffrey 2009, 877) and on two querns from the Tees valley (Gwilt and Heslop 1995, 43).

Table 6.6: Identified animal species/phase for all phases from Area A. MNI within parentheses. *: includes articulated calf skeleton (65 fragments)

Species	IA	MIA	ER	MR	MR-LR	Phase LR1	LR2	LR	R	IA-LR
Cattle	1 (1)	5 (1)	9 (1)	5 (2)	1 (1)	168* (5)	209 (8)	57 (2)	4 (1)	3 (1)
Sheep/goat		5 (1)	4 (1)			8 (1)	53 (3)	4 (1)	1 (1)	3 (1)
Pig			2 (1)			4 (1)	22 (1)	3 (1)	1 (1)	1 (1)
Horse		2 (1)				7 (1)	15 (2)	1 (1)		
Deer sp.							18 (1)			
Red deer							1 (1)			
Roe deer				1 (1)						
Dog							1 (1)			
Cetacean						1 (1)				
Indet. bird						2				
Small mammal							1			
Medium mammal		4	1	1		11	47	7		
Large mammal		8	35	4	1	66	297	16	10	
Indeterminate		29	73	5		357	1231	216	11	218
Total fragment count	1	53	124	16	2	624	1895	304	27	225
Total weight (g)	9	195	1114	524	94	10137	22011	2245	259	278

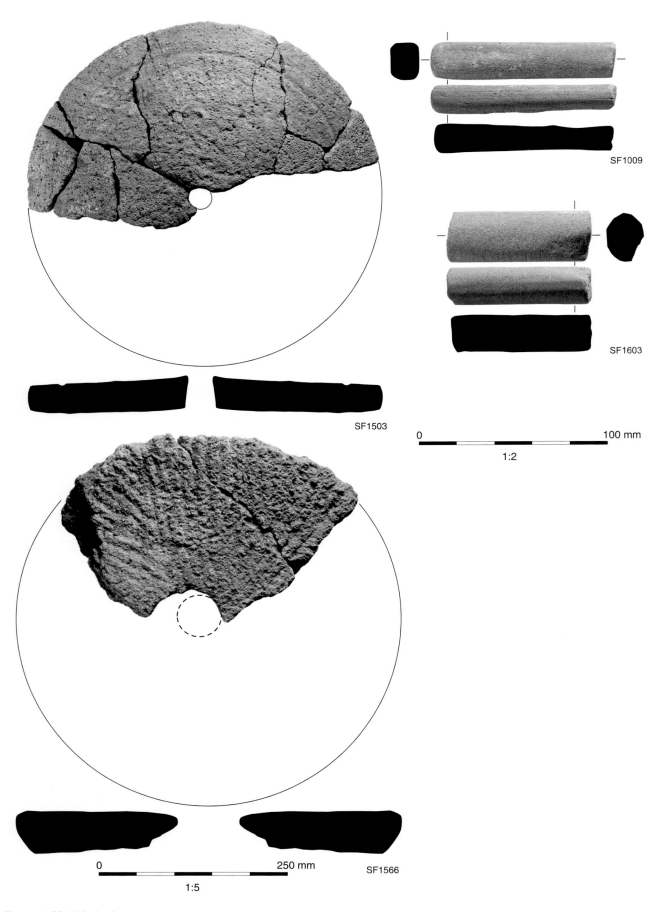

Figure 6.55 Worked stone

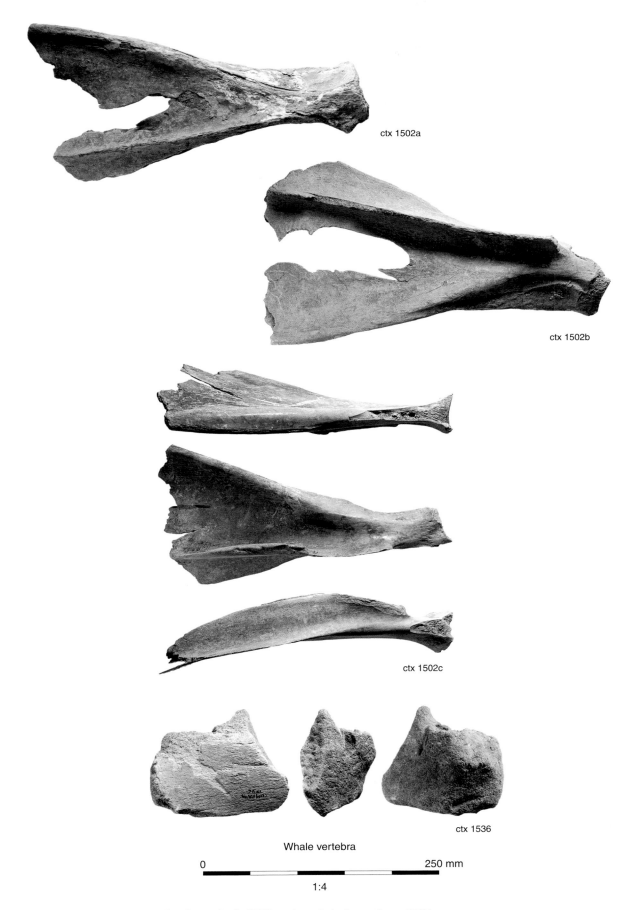

ctx 1502a

ctx 1502b

ctx 1502c

ctx 1536

Whale vertebra

0   250 mm

1:4

Figure 6.56 Pierced cattle scapulae from ditch 8551 and a whale bone from 5191

Stone used structurally included some Greensand blocks (not *in situ*) as well as roughly hewn chalk blocks used in groups to form substantial post-bases associated with saltern 5760. One fragment of worked chalk hints at the working of it on site or nearby. Other worked stone includes two whetstone fragments of micaceous sandstone, possibly Reigate stone (Fig. 6.55, SF1009 and SF1603). These were probably associated with metal working, for which other evidence was also found on the site, although one was recovered from a dumped layer (1111) and the other was a surface find (1416), both in Area A.

Animal bone *by Lena Strid*

Four fragments of animal bone, including fragments from the long bone of a large mammal, probably cattle, were recovered from middle Roman pit 6484. A total of 3403 fragments of animal bone were recovered from late Roman contexts. Of these, 2823 fragments were identified to species. In terms of minimum number of individuals, cattle were best represented at 15 individuals. Sheep/goat accounted for five individuals. A minimum of three pigs, four horses, two deer and one dog were recorded. In addition, there was one bone fragment from a whale (Fig. 6.56).

The skeletal element distribution shows an over-representation of cattle scapulae and metatarsals, each representing a minimum of seven individuals (Table 6.6). The high number of mandible fragments (a minimum of four individuals) is mostly due to fragmentation rather than over-representation. The case is less clear for metacarpals, which despite a high element count only amounted to a minimum of four individuals present. The metacarpals were not more fragmented than the metatarsals and the discrepancy may be due to chance in connection to siding. Similar element distribution has been observed at the Roman baths at Caerleon (O'Connor 1986, 230) and in Roman York (O'Connor 1988, 82-84). Over-representation and/or dumps of cattle scapulae are usually interpreted as waste from specialised preparation of smoked or salted shoulder of beef for consumers. The scapulae from Stanford Wharf Nature Reserve and York had been roughly filleted with cleavers. Several of them have a perforation through the scapula blade, probably from hanging them on hooks during smoking or storing (Fig. 6.56). The reason for the over-representation of metapodials is less clear. As metapodials are not covered in flesh they are therefore not connected to food processing, but rather to slaughter and tannery waste or bone working. There is little evidence for bone working at the site, and the comparative scarcity of phalanxes and skull fragments would seem to exclude cattle slaughter or hide tanning. Perhaps cattle hides were used during the industrial processes at the site and the metapodials were merely an accidental inclusion, possibly used as handles.

DISCUSSION (Figs 6.57-6.63)

A middle Roman pause and late Roman resumption

The two pits dated to the middle Roman period were poorly defined, having been cut by later features. Little can be said of them, but as they had been dug into silty clay, it is possible that the features were intended as quarry pits. The near-absence of features dated to the middle Roman period strongly points to a break in activity at the site during the 2nd century. Ceramic evidence had offered some grounds for suspecting a more significant middle Roman element, but stratigraphic analysis indicated that most of that pottery was residual, having been deposited after *c* AD 250. It can also be argued that some forms that conventionally ceased to be made by *c* AD 250 (Going 1987, 14-5) in fact had longer periods of use. This may have been the case with grey ware or black-burnished bead-rimmed dishes, a common form made at neighbouring Mucking which was recorded in most of the 60 or so groups of pottery collected from across the site and dated on ceramic terms to the later Roman period. Exotic fine ware imports such as samian and 'Rhenish' wares, which are another important middle Roman indicator, also have the potential for an extended life, being carefully looked after and likely to survive longer than, say, a cooking pot.

Cynthia Poole (specialist report 8) notes that the briquetage shows considerable uniformity in form and fabric from the middle Iron Age to the late Roman period, and suggests that breaks in activity apparent at Stanford Wharf, which might be expected to disrupt the use of established types and allow variation of those types or new equipment and materials to be introduced with the resumption of activity, were not absolute. Rather, the focus of salt making activity may have moved a short distance away from Stanford Wharf during the late Iron Age, early Roman and middle Roman period, effectively resulting in a continuous sequence of activity from the middle Iron Age to late Roman period in the vicinity of the site, but not on it. Nearby activity may also have contributed to the presence of residual middle Roman pottery at Stanford Wharf.

The 3rd century saw a resumption of activity at Stanford Wharf. In Area A, enclosure 9506 was established within a system of trackways and field ditches. A saltern (5808) was set up at the southern edge of the area. Ceramic evidence offers a date within the first half of the 3rd century AD for the start of this phase (late Roman phase 1). The enclosure ditch was abandoned after *c* AD 250 (late Roman phase 2), although the survival of a trace of the ditch, perhaps in the form of a low bank or a difference in the height of vegetation growing over the ditch compared with growth either side of it, is possible, as a new ditch (8512) followed the outline of the southern and eastern sides of the enclosure. The western part of Area A was used for salt production. A saltern (8516) was set out within an enclosure. It was replaced later by saltern 6090, and a structure (5760), defined by four substantial postpads and surrounded by a bank or shallow gully, was also used for salt production. Salt production resumed in Area B, too. The saltern there was characterised by an enclosure and gullies which surrounded hearths, tanks and other features related to salt-production. A kiln was built outside the enclosure.

The latest coins recovered from Stanford Wharf indicate that the site was occupied into the second half of the 4th century (Booth, specialist report 4). The chronology is supported by pottery, which points to deposition at Stanford Wharf after *c* AD 350 (Biddulph and Stansbie, specialist report 2). This is indicated by Oxford red colour-coated and white-slipped red wares, late shell-tempered ware, Alice Holt grey ware, Mayen ware, Portchester D ware, and Céramique à l'éponge, as well as increased proportions of Hadham products in stratified groups. To this list we can add late Roman grog-tempered ware (LGROG), a fabric rare in Essex, but prolific after the second or third quarter of the 4th century in west Kent where production is likely (Pollard 1988, 149). Of the Oxford products, it is notable too that these include a carinated bowl form with rosette-stamped decoration (Young 1977, type C84). The form was one of the latest products of the industry, with production dating to *c* AD 350-400+ (Young 1977, 170). A white ware mortarium (Young 1977, type M23) recovered from Stanford Wharf also has a date after 350. There is, however, nothing to indicate with certainty deposition after AD 400.

The scale of late Roman activity at Stanford Wharf sets the site apart from other salt-working and red hill sites along the Essex coast, which have tended to record low quantities of late Roman material, or no material of this date whatever. No doubt the strategic location of Stanford Wharf helped to isolate it from other red hill sites and transform it into a significant production centre, although the extent of late Roman activity at red hill sites has perhaps been underestimated. Colin Wallace (1995, table 54) notes later 2nd and 3rd century pottery, admittedly in small quantities, from two sites in the Blackwater estuary and one at Leigh Beck on Canvey Island, and 4th century pottery from one site in the Crouch estuary and three sites in the Blackwater estuary. P M Barford suggests that red hill sites, which provided dry raised mounds and good working surfaces in areas of alluvium, continued to be attractive for occupation in the later Roman period after they were abandoned as sites of salt production (Barford 2000, 248; Wallace 1995, 173). Nevertheless, the nature of the later Roman activity at such sites is unclear (though possibly relating to farming) and Stanford Wharf must still be viewed as exceptional.

Salt from the sea: extracting salt in the late Roman period

The tidal waters of the Thames drew salt workers to Stanford Wharf in the late Roman period, just as they had during the middle Iron Age and early Roman period. Saltern 5808, in Area A, was established on the

remains of an earlier red hill, which provided a slightly elevated surface and protected the workers and features from inundation. The saltern was partially enclosed by two horseshoe-shaped ditches, and the space created by the ditches was taken up with hearths and tanks. The saltern bears a remarkable similarity to the first phase late Roman saltern at Middleton, Norfolk (Crowson 2001, fig. 47). The salterns are roughly the same size in plan and both take the form of a pair of semi-circular ditches or, as described by Crowson (ibid., 167), an interrupted sub-rectangular ditch, which enclose a rectangular settling tank and evaporation hearth (Fig. 6.57). There is a difference in the means by which the ditches, which trapped seawater, were fed. The ditches at Middleton were connected to feeder ditches which carried flood water (ibid., 239); the seawater was subsequently transferred to the settling tank, presumably manually, and, after a period of settling and natural evaporation, scooped out into pans placed over hearths and evaporated further to crystallise the salt. At Stanford Wharf, the ditches were flooded by the rising tide. By analogy a similar process of producing salt to that suggested at Middleton is plausible. Salters filled the settling tanks of saltern 5808 using buckets, brique-tage containers or ceramic vessels with the seawater collected in the saltern's ditches. The tanks allowed the silt particles in the water to settle on the floor of the features, and, on warm days, permitted water to evaporate to some degree naturally through solar evaporation, increasing the salinity of the solution or brine held in the tank. It is possible that one tank contained brine ready for boiling, while the other contained brine at an earlier stage of settling. This ensured that there was a continuous flow of salt production stages. The brine was transferred to hearth 1581 for heating and evaporation. Fragments of briquetage vessels found with the remains of the hearth's clay wall lining and fuel debris included flat body pieces that probably derived from troughs. These wide, shallow, vessels made ideal containers for the brine, and were placed above the hearth and supported by pedestals. Pottery may also have been used; cream-white deposits recorded inside necked jars may be the encrusted traces of salt which formed during boiling. The heat from the hearth, provided by the adjacent stoke-pit (1654), concentrated the brine further, resulting in the final product, salt crystals. Inevitably, however, this conventional *chaîne opératoire* can be questioned in light of the use of saltmarsh plants in the middle Iron Age and other late Roman salterns. Unfortunately, no analysis was undertaken on environmental samples taken from this saltern's ditches and tanks, but the plant remains from the hearth pointed to a mixed fuel of wheat chaff and arable weeds and a range of saltmarsh plants. Potentially, then, the ash created by burning saltmarsh plants on the hearth was mixed with seawater from the ditches to create a brine solution that was filtered into the tanks (Fig. 6.58), but the evidence is unclear on the matter. More certain evidence for the continued use of saltmarsh plants is found in other salterns.

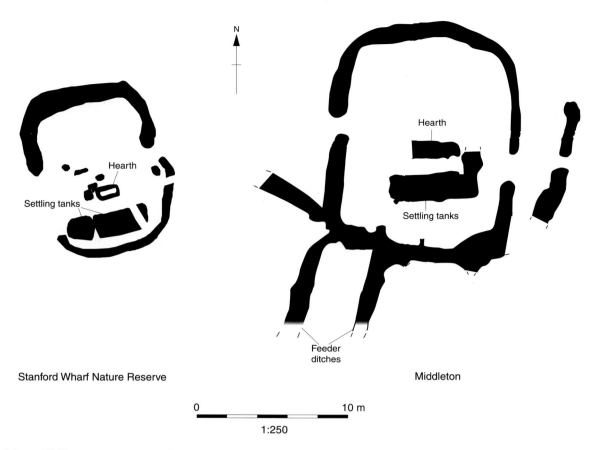

Figure 6.57 Saltern 5808 in comparison with a late Roman saltern from Middleton, Norfolk (after Crowson 2001, Figure 47)

Saltern 6711 in Area B shared aspects of form with saltern 5808. The channel (8536/8540), which enclosed the salt-working features, filled during periods of tidal inundation. Sections through the ditch show thick deposits of alluvial mud which were laid as seawater flooded the ditch, then receded. Stratigraphy and dating evidence provide no clue as to whether the saltern's three settling tanks (4274, 4336 and 4717) were in contemporaneous use, or whether they formed a sequence of use and replacement, but they were largely identical in form and, presumably, in function, although the rectangular clay-lined cut of tank 4274 was double the width of those of 4336 and 4717 and the tank may have been intended to serve at double capacity. Three-celled tanks are well attested in Essex (Fig. 6.59). Two three-celled tanks have been uncovered at Goldhanger, near Maldon (Fawn *et al.* 1990, 8), while at Osea Road, also near Maldon, three three-celled tanks, one four-celled tank, and one two-celled tank have been found (Rodwell 1979, 136). A three-celled tank was recorded at Peldon, West Mersea, and Leigh Beck, on Canvey Island, has produced a further two (Fawn *et al.* 1990, 8). There is another close parallel at the Iron Age site of Landrellec on the Brittany coast (Fig. 6.59). A salt-working building uncovered there housed a hearth and two batteries of tanks. One tank was divided into five cells, the other had four cells. Both tanks had been cut into the naturally laid alluvial silt, and the cells, divided by stone slabs, cut into a clay lining. The tanks were

interpreted as storage tanks (Daire and Langouet 1994, 35; Daire *et al.* 1994, 98-9). The method of salt-extraction at that site was a form of sleeching, and the sand-filtering stage seems to have been carried out outside the building, probably on the beach. It is notable that the second phase of activity at Middleton included two three-celled settling tanks (Crowson 2001, fig. 175), and though a single ditch, which fed seawater into a pond, replaced the first phase ditch, the basic method of extraction – the open pan method – did not change (Fig. 6.59). Crowson (ibid., 244) considered that the provision of three cells within a rectangular cut permitted a continuous cycle of filling, settling and cleaning, and in that respect the tanks can be regarded as a refinement of the two rectangular settling tanks in Area A saltern 5808. It is, however, worth drawing attention to an explanation offered in *De Re Metallica*, the 16th century treatise on mining and metallurgy by Georgius Agricola, for a method of salt-production apparently used in medieval Germany, which incorporated a system of rows of tanks, each with three basins. Seawater is let into the first basin and allowed to stand, settle and, after a certain point, flow into the second basin. As it does so, the first basin refills. The water in the second basin stands there for a time, and then is moved into the third basin. Through the sequence, the water becomes progressively more concentrated (Hoover and Hoover 1950, 546-7). There was, however, no direct means of communication between the cells in

1. Bundles of dried saltmarsh plants are ready to be used as fuel
2. The fuel is burnt below troughs of brine prepared earlier
3. The ash from the hearth is mixed with seawater
4. The solution is filtered to create a concentrated brine
5. The brine is transferred to a settling tank
6. The brine is evaporated in briquetage troughs. It is possible that as the water evaporated, the brine was moved to progressively hotter troughs, thus maintaining constant temperatures within individual vessels.
7. The resulting salt crystals are skimmed off and allowed to dry further and harden into cakes
8. The salt, transferred to pottery vessels or baskets, is ready for transportation

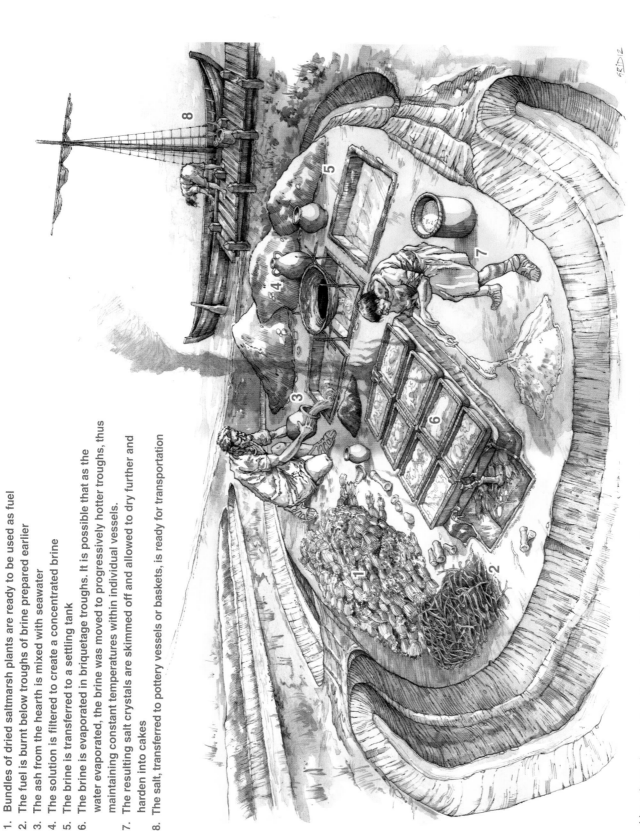

Figure 6.58 Hypothetical reconstruction of salt making in the late Roman period at Stanford Wharf Nature Reserve, showing a composite of elements from different salterns (drawing by Mark Gridley)

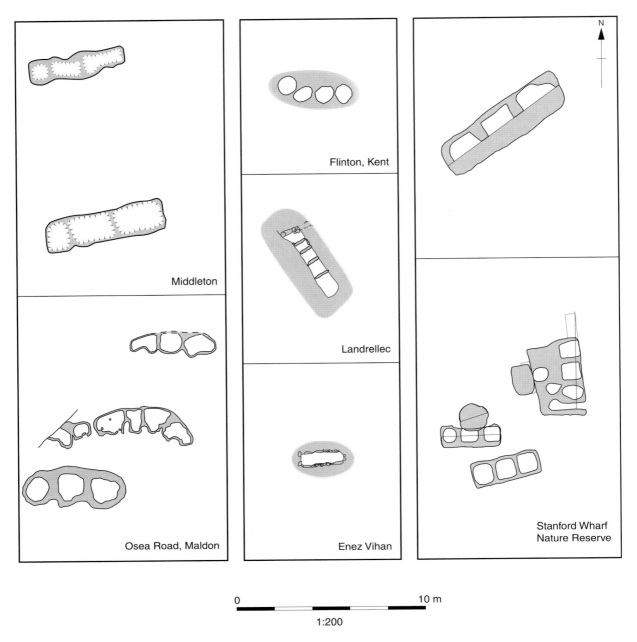

Figure 6.59 Comparative plans of settling tanks

the Stanford Wharf tanks, and transfer of water from one to another, if carried out, must have involved the use of hand-held containers.

It is a reasonable assumption that the seawater from the ditch of saltern 6711 was simply transferred to the settling tanks before being evaporated over hearths, but crucially tank 4336 contained burnt saltmarsh plants, including sea lavender, sea plantain, sea-milkwort and rush. The plants had been gathered for fuel, but, as seen in the middle Iron Age, the ash created by burning the plants had potentially been mixed with seawater and filtered to produce a more concentrated brine ready to be evaporated. The features within saltern 6711 are not inconsistent with this. Once the ash had been mixed with seawater, the three-celled tanks were used to capture the brine leaching through filters resting above. The tanks may also have stored seawater ready for

pouring onto the ash. Perforated briquetage or ceramic pots may have been used as filtration vessels, although none is recorded at Stanford Wharf. This absence is not necessarily conclusive, given the fragmentary character of the ceramic assemblages, but in any case items such as baskets or nets provide alternative filters.

However the tanks in saltern 6711 were used, the brine was scooped out and heated above hearths. None of the five hearths contemporary with the tanks was connected to stoke-holes, and it is likely that fires were lit in the hearths' bases. Trough fragments account for a large proportion of the briquetage assemblage (almost 35% by fragment count) from late Roman deposits in Area B. These contained the brine and were placed above the hearths on top of rectangular pedestals, of which fragments were also recovered. The pedestals were designed to be set vertically in rows to support the evaporating troughs. The presence of briquetage in saltern 6711, as well as Area A saltern 5808, indicates that the material continued to be used well into the late Roman period, considerably later than its conventional Iron Age and early Roman dating (Fawn *et al.* 1990). It is possible that vessels were fired in kiln 4224, although it seems more likely that this structure served as a hearth or closed oven for salt evaporation. Cynthia Poole (specialist report 8) notes that the distinctive pedestals recovered from Area B were not found in Area A, or, indeed, at any other site along the Essex coast. While the salt making processes in areas A and B were broadly identical, the introduction of the new pedestal type suggests that salters were to some extent culturally separate from their neighbours in Area A, allowing them to develop their salt making practices independently. Conversely, lead evaporation vessels were introduced in Area A, but not apparently in Area B (although Cynthia Poole suggests that the Area B pedestals were able to support lead vessels; micromorphological analysis, which might have detected traces of lead, was not undertaken in the Area B saltern). It is possible that there was less chronological overlap between the two areas than has been proposed, but we can also suggest that the two areas were worked by groups that were not related by kinship or social ties, resulting in a degree of cultural isolation and development of practices along separate trajectories.

Salt was extracted in saltern 9501. Unlike in salterns 5808 and 6711, the activity here was under cover. The saltern's inner gully was structural – wooden stakes found within it suggest a wattle and oak timber wall – but the outer ditch was open. According to the micromorphological, charred plant, pollen and diatom evidence, the ditch contained water-lain deposits of increasingly high salinity, showing periods of inundation, but the basal fills of the ditch also contained cereal, saltmarsh plant, hearth and animal waste. The evidence suggests that the structure saw a range of activities – domestic and animal occupation, cereal processing and salt-making – and that the ditch was available for dumping rubbish when the saltern was occupied. If this dumping prevented salters from usefully trapping seawater in the outer ditch, then water was probably carried to the settling tank within the saltern from shallow troughs (9507) at the southern end of ditch 8512. Microfaunal evidence from the ditch indicates that tidal seawater washed into the feature. The three-celled settling tank (1316) was identical in form to those from saltern 6711, although its cells were slightly deeper. After being held in the tanks, the brine was removed and heated above hearth 1484. Micromorphological analysis offers a very clear view of how the hearth was built. The base and sides of the feature were cut into the underlying brickearth, lined first with a mixed layer of brickearth and sea rush leaves, and then with a layer of cob- or lime-plastered brickearth. Briquetage vessel fragments were recovered from the saltern's ditches and internal features, and it is possible that containers such as this were used for evaporation.

Intriguingly, traces of lead on the charred sea rush lining of the hearth raise the possibility that the brine was evaporated in lead pans. The lead signature was weak, however, and it is likely that lead was used only occasionally or in combination with briquetage vessels.

The fuel used in the hearth was mixed. The charred plant remains from the settling tank and the hearth suggest that saltmarsh vegetation was selected for fuel, but traces of animal or human excrement were also found in the hearth, which may indicate (most likely) the use of dung as a slow burning fuel. Again, the evidence points strongly to the notion that the plants were the residue of filtering a solution of hearth ash waste and seawater to create brine, with the settling tank being used as a filtration unit. The palaeoenvironmental remains are critical here. The secondary fill of one of the settling tank cells was dominated by ash waste. Micromorphological analysis (Macphail *et al.*, specialist report 24) makes clear that this waste was the result of combustion of saltmarsh vegetation, as well as straw, sand and gravel-sized pieces of alluvial clay or saltmarsh sediment. The upper fill was equally rich in ash.

The workers within saltern 5760 used a mixed fuel strategy, or one where one type of fuel replaced an earlier type. The characteristic white nodules of fuel ash derived from the burning of saltmarsh plants were recovered from deposits within the structure (Macphail *et al.*, specialist report 24), but wood charcoal was also recovered, indicating that wood was selected as fuel (Druce, specialist report 20). This represents a significant change, as wood charcoal is scarce in earlier periods and other structures and wood appears to have been largely ignored in preference to cereal remains and saltmarsh plants. The switch to wood appears to have coincided with the introduction of lead tanks, but is likely to reflect increased demand for fuel. It is possible that wood was converted to charcoal before being used in the hearths, but the evidence for this is unclear. Some of the hearths uncovered in the building had been cut by replacement hearths, suggesting a relatively prolonged period of occupation. As with saltern 9501, there appears to have been no direct supply of water to the structure, but instead brine may have been transferred from nearby naturally-formed channels. If the method akin to selnering was employed, then the lead tanks may have been used both as filtering vessels, with water again drawn from nearby channels, as well as evaporation vessels. No larger fragments of tanks were recovered, and none can be reconstructed, but two inscribed lead tanks from Henhull, near Nantwich, are likely to provide a close match. The vessels, described by the excavators as brine tanks, are shallow rectangular pans measuring up to 1m long by 1m wide by 0.13m deep. Both tanks were perforated through the side for drawing off liquid (RIB II 1994a, 2416.2-3). While the interpretation that lead vessels were used in the open pan or selnering-like methods may be correct, the use of the building as a saltern remains problematic, not least because of the post-bases that supported massive posts, which implies a substantial building very different from saltern 9501 and other buildings in Area A that served as salterns. This is discussed further below, but it is worth noting that, apart from the traces of lead vessels and the presence of hearths, micromorphological analysis also indicates that the floor deposits accumulated under moist conditions. This is likely to be the result of industrial activity and strongly points to salt making. At Kibiro in Uganda, thermometer readings taken at intervals in covered salt-boiling buildings over 2½ hours in the morning gave a constant air temperature of 34°C, 5° above the outside air temperature (Connah et al. 1990, 34).

The tile-built hearth or oven belonging to the first phase of saltern 6090 was a more permanent feature, compared with the hearths of other salterns. Small amounts of briquetage were recovered from the saltern, and it is probable that lead pans were used here too. The pilasters of the tile-built hearth would have been well suited to support a lead pan, presumably of circular form. Saltern 6090 was not exclusively used for salt evaporation; small quantities of iron dust, flakes, slag and hammerscale recovered from the hearth suggest that smithing was carried out here. Lynne Keys views this as relating to a one-off event, perhaps for the shaping or repair of iron pans. As with saltern 5760, there is no clear evidence in saltern 6090 for settling tanks or filtration units, although it is possible that gullies either side of the hearth served this function. In its second phase, the focus of activity moved to the north end of the structure and around hearth 5918. Compared with the lead traces from saltern 5901, a much stronger lead signature was associated with saltern 6090. Its floor surfaces were found to have a very high level of lead enrichment, which Richard Macphail judges to indicate the use of lead vessels. Such vessels were appropriate for salt making, and in the open pan method, they would have contained brine and been placed above hearths, allowing the brine to evaporate.

While the late Roman salters, like the middle Iron Age salters before them, produced brine using burnt saltmarsh plants, the absence of late Roman red hills indicates that the processes used in those periods were not identical. The middle Iron Age salters gathered saltmarsh plants, but they also took saltmarsh sediment (the predominant component of red hills), which adhered to the plants, and burnt both. In contrast, the late Roman salters appear to have taken greater care to harvest the plants only, possibly as part of a management strategy to ensure that plants survived through the growing season and into the following year. Kath Hunter (specialist report 19) notes that the relatively low numbers of rhizome and root fragments among the plant ash recovered from saltern 9501 and Area B tanks suggest that live plants were being cut above ground level. Consequently relatively little sediment was burnt and available for dumping. The blocks of closely spaced parallel gullies in the north-eastern corner of Area A, the north-western corner of Area B, and the central part of Area D may have been part of this managed landscape, the gullies being cut to improve the irrigation of the

saltmarsh with seawater (D Cranstone, pers. comm.) and increase salinity levels. Another factor contributing to the absence of red hills may have been the increase in the use of wood, perhaps as charcoal, as fuel within salterns 6090 and 5760, which together with the introduction of lead vessels and tile hearth structures, signals a more fundamental change in the technology of late Roman salt production. The various traces of lead waste and fragments recovered in small quantities across the site (Scott, specialist report 5) may be related to the repair, if not production, of lead vessels, and reflect the intensity and longevity of lead vessel use. It is notable, too, that Area B lacks red hills or spreads of red hill material. The reason might be largely chronological – there was no middle Iron Age salt making there, and no red hills were generated. But no red hills were generated in the late Roman period either, because saltmarsh sediment was not burnt in that period, whether in the course of brine evaporation, or more probably during the preparation of brine. The occupation layers interleaved with alluvial deposits – a sequence into which the main channel of saltern 6711 was cut – were characterised by dark brown, almost black clay silt, which had hinted at the use of a different fuel, such as peat or dung (Carey, specialist report 25). Unfortunately, no micromorphological analysis was carried out on the sequence to confirm the composition of the soils, but the microfauna evidence from the sequence included relatively few occurrences of the burnt and recrystallized foraminifer Trochammina inflata, which characterised red hill deposits in Area A. The contrast indicated that the salt-related occupation layers of Area B had not been formed from burnt salt-marsh sediment (Whittaker, specialist report 22), despite the fact that plant remains recovered from Area B were dominated by the ash of saltmarsh plants, just as they were in Area A, suggesting a similar process of early and later Roman salt production.

Another difference between middle Iron Age and late Roman practices was seen in the types of briquetage fabrics used. In the middle Iron Age, sandy, brickearth-derived fabrics were dominant, whereas the briquetage of the late Roman period was largely made with alluvial clay and tempered with grass and cereal chaff (Poole, specialist report 8; Hunter, specialist report 19). The distribution of the two fabrics shows the chronological difference clearly (Figs 6.60 and 6.61). The brickearth derived fabrics were concentrated in the northern part of Area A, where the red hills were located and the redeposited red hill spread was investigated. There was also a concentration around the red hill below late Roman saltern 5808. Area B was largely devoid of the fabric. In contrast, Area B contained a large proportion of briquetage made with the alluvial clay and tempered with chaff. In Area A, this fabric was concentrated in later Roman features, including saltern 9501, and salterns 5760, 5808 and 6090. The difference in the choice of fabrics is less likely to represent a deliberate rejection of brickearth-derived fabrics in the late Roman period than the effect of chance and cultural drift. By

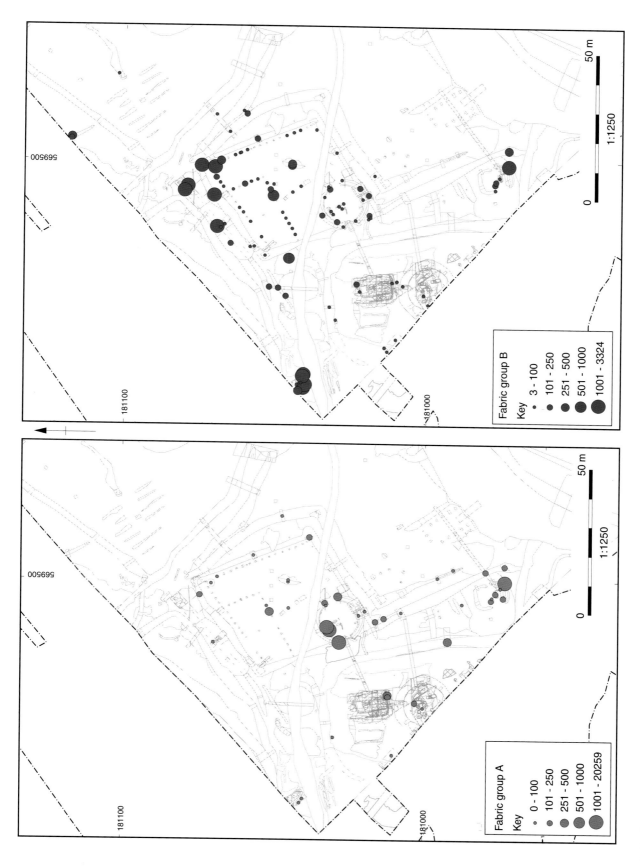

Figure 6.60 Distribution of the alluvial/organic briquetage fabric (fabric group A) and brickearth-derived fabric (fabric group B) in Area A

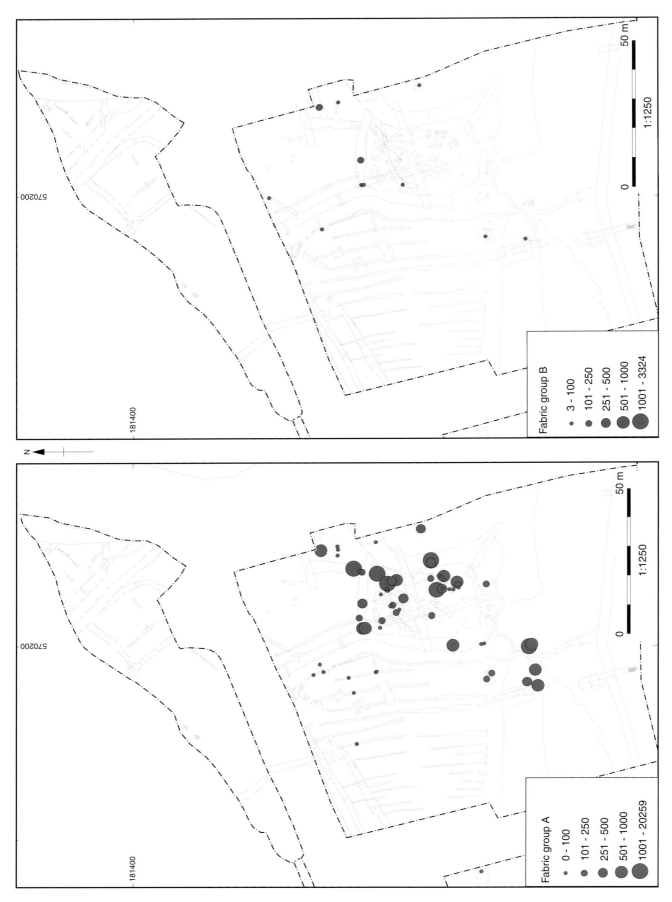

Figure 6.61 Distribution of the alluvial/organic briquetage fabric (fabric group A) and brickearth-derived fabric (fabric group B) in Area B

the late Roman period, the brickearth that had been quarried for briquetage fabrics during the middle Iron Age had been deeply buried under successive deposits of alluvium, making it more difficult to access. In contrast, alluvial clays were easier to exploit, but their composition meant that an additional temper, in this case grass and cereal chaff, was required.

Brine was boiled in briquetage and lead pans over hearths until white salt crystals formed. Observation at Kibiro records that crystals appeared in 1½ to 2 hours, although we can expect variation in the rate of crystallisation depending on the site of the evaporation vessels, the concentration of the brine, the temperature of the fire, and so on. At Kibiro, once the water has evaporated, the still wet, porridge-like, mass of salt crystals is ladled out of the pan and dumped onto the building floor, where the salt rapidly hardens and solidifies into cakes or cones ready for transportation. It is possible that the salt prepared at Stanford Wharf was dumped on the floor of the saltern. There were no spreads of encrusted salt on the floors of the buildings, although traces of deposits were noted in saltern 5760. Instead the salt may have been ladled into pottery vessels. The function of the early Roman shelly ware ledge-rimmed jar as a salt transportation container has been discussed in Chapter 5. Other pottery forms are likely to have have taken the place of this jar when it ceased to be produced after the end of the 1st century AD. The necked, oval-bodied jar (Going 1987, type G24), which is a very common type at Stanford Wharf, is an obvious replacement as a salt container, but necked jars with a bifid rim (ibid., type G28) would have served equally well, and both types provided examples of vessels with internal salt residues or bleaching. Larger storage jars, which displayed similar deposits, may have been used too.

One aspect of salt production still to consider is the removal of insoluble salts and impurities during crystallisation and the accumulation of scale on evaporation vessels. Filtration and settling of the brine would no doubt remove most of the impurities, and any that remained were removed during boiling. In medieval Cumbria, these were removed by adding the whites of eggs to the brine as it heated. A black scum formed, which was simply skimmed off (Walsh 1991, 38). Similar tricks may have been known to the Iron Age and Roman salters. A waste product of the evaporation process is bittern, which is the concentrated solution of magnesium chloride and other chemicals present in the brine. If salt crystals were removed from the evaporation vessel as they appeared, or if the vessel was allowed to fill completely with crystals, then the salt was largely unaffected by bittern (Fawn et al. 1990, 19-20). However, the number of times that the evaporation vessel could be reused is likely to have been limited, as repeated use of a vessel would result in an accumulation of dried bittern deposits, which would taint the salt produced in the vessel. It is notable that the majority of late Roman briquetage vessels on which internal white deposits were recorded were identified as flat pieces belonging to troughs, the standard briquetage evapora-

tion vessel. It is reasonable to suggest that the vessels had undergone repeated use before being discarded and replaced by fresh vessels.

Structures associated with salterns

Two certain late Roman structures, and two other possible structures, were uncovered at Stanford Wharf. Saltern 9501 took the form of a circular structure defined by two concentric rings. The decayed traces of oak stakes in the inner gully identify this as part of the structure's wall. Damian Goodburn (specialist report 14) suggests that the gaps between the upright timbers were filled with wattlework, and that the space between the inner gully and the outer ditch held a clay mass wall. If so, then this is rare and significant evidence for the use of the construction technique in south-eastern Roman Britain, a region in which well-defined evidence for the structures of roundhouses is scarce. The stakes within the gully would have revetted the internal face of the wall. Postholes at each end of the hearth within the saltern may have held posts that helped support the roof structure, though they seem more likely to relate to a superstructure over the hearth. In his discussion of the later Iron Age and Roman circular structures at nearby Orsett, Carter (1998, 120, fig. 76) notes that the loading weight of the roof increases disproportionately to the diameter of the structure, and calculates that a structure with a diameter of 13m – the diameter of the inner gully – requires a roof with a surface area of c 200m². Building S9 at Orsett 'Cock' faces the same interpretative difficulty as saltern 9501. The structure was large, measuring some 16m in diameter. It was defined by an outer ring ditch, which is viewed as a drainage ditch, rather than a wall trench. Internally there is a single ring of postholes 12m in diameter, and inside that ring a few miscellaneous postholes (Carter 1998, fig. 78). With no thick outer wall, the posts alone might seem too weak to support the roof, but Carter (1998, 123) suggests as a solution that a ground plate was provided, giving the structure another timber-framed wall. Naturally walls that simply rested on the floor tend to leave no trace in the archaeological record. However, if such a wall had existed in saltern 9501, then given the location of the internal postholes, it would have to have passed in between the settling tank and the hearth, approximately 2.8m inside the inner ring gully, resulting in a ring c 7.2m in diameter. Instead, a roof made of poles set onto the wall heads in the manner of crude crucks – the putative outer clay mass wall need not have been more than 1.5m tall – may have been provided (Goodburn, specialist report 14). The roof is likely to have been thatched, probably with local reeds.

'Saltern' 8516 was probably associated with salt working, although no internal features were detected. In its first phase, the saltern comprised two parallel gullies into which posts or stakes of a fence, shelter or crude wall were set. In its second phase, a gully that replaced the first phase gully continued along the north and south ends of the saltern, potentially allowing a greater degree of shelter. Saltern 6090 is unlikely to have been much different to 8516. In its first phase, two gullies held posts or stakes that created an L-shaped shelter, open to the north and east. Part of the gully curved round, probably to provide additional shelter, although this was essentially an internal gully and may simply have separated activities, rather than providing protection from the elements. The second-phase saltern was rectangular and open along its eastern side. The posts or stakes may have been placed into the north, west and south gullies. The saltern was similar in size to the salt-working building at Landrellec, Brittany, though that structure was fully enclosed and had an entrance through one end wall (Daire *et al.* 1994, fig. 63).

Saltern 5760 appeared to take the form of another circular structure. The ring created by the external shallow gully, mound and bank defined a circular outline with an internal diameter of *c* 14m. Chalk and rubble bases set in large square pits held massive posts that supported a roof structure. The postpads mark out an area *c* 4.5m square, but the timber structure they supported is likely to have been open, as features and the floor surface extended beyond the postpads. It is possible, then, that an outer wall was erected. No wall trench or outer postholes were observed, but as with saltern 9501, a clay mass wall may have been erected. The bank seen in section, and the mound seen in other parts of the circular outline, may indeed provide the traces of the wall. The entrance was probably east facing. A hollow (5007), notably aligned with the orientation of the post-pits, may have been created by the action of people repeatedly stepping over the threshold to enter the building; gravel filling the hollow may have been laid in order to level the surface here and repair the floor. We can also view pits cut either side of the hollow and into the inside edge of the 'gully' as postholes marking an entrance. The internal post bases no doubt indicate a substantial structure, and from their size (1m wide and up to 0.45m deep) would not be out of place in an aisled or other post-built structure of the sort recorded commonly in Roman Britain. Aisled building 368 at Great Holts Farm, Boreham, near Chelmsford, for example, was characterised by round postholes between 1m and 2m wide and between 0.4m and 0.7m deep (Germany 2003, 41; figs 34-5). Square postholes defining a rectangular post-built structure near Chignall Roman villa, also close to Chelmsford, measured up to 1.16m in length and 0.64m in depth (Clarke 1998, 29). More pertinent parallels to building 5760 can be found outside Essex. At Shakenoak Farm, Oxfordshire, for example, a circular building some 10m in diameter was provided with four stone-slab post bases, which formed a central 3m-wide square; a construction date around AD 200 was suggested (Brodribb *et al.* 2005, 423-4, 427). A similar structure is known at Winterton, Lincolnshire. It was 15m in diameter and had stone post bases *c* 1.2m across forming a central square 4m wide (Stead 1976, fig. 34). Returning to Stanford Wharf, saltern 5760 plausibly took the form of a circular

structure with a thick outer wall and, perhaps, a thatched roof supported by the internal posts. If we assume that the outer wall, such as a clay mass wall, was not earth-fast, then substantial internal posts may have been necessary in order to bear most of the weight of the roof. Like saltern 9501, the structure had an industrial function, with the features, deposits and palaeoenvironmental evidence from the floor of the structure indicating salt production.

However, it remains possible that the postholes of 5760 were not internal and that there was no outer wall. In this case, the arrangement of postholes is a somewhat substantial version of four-post structures found on rural sites in Iron Age and Roman Britain – for example at White Horse Stone, near Aylesford in Kent (Champion 2011, 202) – and typically interpreted as raised granaries (cf. Bersu 1940, 97-8). By analogy, we could regard the structure as a salt store, with the result being a raised structure of perhaps two levels and open on the ground level. Access to the wooden platforms of the upper level may have been provided by ladders propped up against the edge of a trapdoor. Such an interpretation, however, is difficult to reconcile with the apparent entrance across the gully/bank feature surrounding the posts, as well as the surface, hearths and other evidence for activity on the floor of the structure, which suggest a more open working area. How salt might be stored in such a structure is also subject to speculation. If the salt was stored loose, then presumably walls were required on the raised level to contain the salt, although the caking of the salt might be a problem for subsequent transportation. Alternatively, the salt was stored in ceramic jars, which were stacked in the four-post structure. The store need not have held salt exclusively, and other foodstuffs may have been kept in the structure.

Activity on the floor of the structure also argues against the square timber-framed structure being interpreted as a possible signal tower to be used in times of attack or as a beacon or 'sea mark' for sailors trying to locate the mouth of Mucking Creek, although neither interpretation is without its attractions. The location of the putative beacon lies immediately north-east of a coastguard station named 'the Vigilant' recorded on an 1863 Ordnance Survey map. As for the suggested signal tower, superficially the plan of saltern 5760 resembles towers erected at intervals along the Gask Ridge from Camelon to Strageath in Perthshire and dating to the late 1st century AD (Woolliscroft and Hoffmann 2006, 73-114). The tower at Westerton, for example, has a ditch 14m in diameter (measured from the internal edge), which enclosed four postholes that defined a rectangular tower measuring *c* 4.5m by 2.5m in plan (Fig. 6.62). An entrance through the ditch is aligned with the short axis of the tower (ibid., 106-7). Viewed in the light of the Gask Ridge towers, the four-poster element of saltern 5760 may represent a square tower, its height being two or three times its base width, judging by the depiction of signal towers on Trajan's Column (ibid., 28-9), resulting in the provision of three storeys. The gravel bank

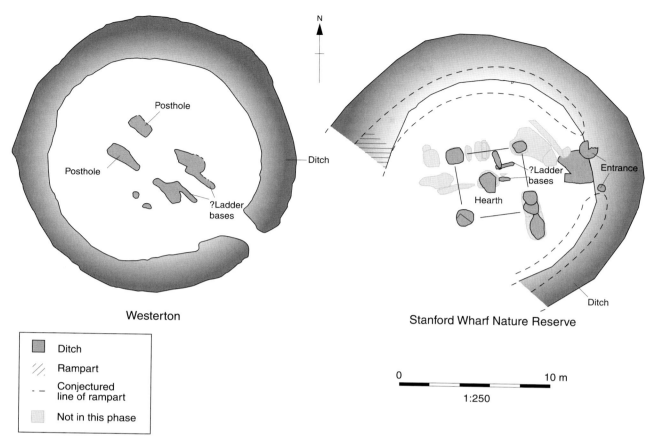

Figure 6.62 Comparative plans of the Westerton signal tower on the Gask Ridge (after Hanson and Friell 1995) and the putative Stanford Wharf tower

recorded on the west side of 5760 can be interpreted as the remains of a rampart. The excavators regarded two narrow slots recorded on the floor of the Westerton tower as marking an entrance or the base for a ladder (ibid., 108), and similarly slots 1526, 1569 and 1526 in 5760 can be suggested as bases for ladders of the sort recovered from pit 1249 (Fig. 6.62).

Despite the attraction of placing a tower in the Thames estuary either to guide craft as they sail along the Thames or enter Mucking Creek, or, perhaps less plausibly, to form part of chain of signal towers relating to the Carausian revolt of c AD 286/7 to 296 (Pearson 2002, 44-6; Bird 2008, 98-9, fig. 2.6.2), there are difficulties with both interpretations. The industrial activity, including the firing of hearths, under and around the structure is especially problematic, and at the very least would have implications for the appearance of the signal tower, which, suggesting an open, scaffold-like structure, would diverge considerably from depictions on Trajan's Column. And though the structure is ideally placed in relation to Mucking Creek, its location on relatively low-lying ground may not have afforded it the height required to function as an effective signal tower. Mucking may have been a better location – interestingly, David Bird (2008, 98-99, fig. 2.6.2) places a signal tower at Mucking in a postulated lines of beacons running along the north Kent coast from Richborough to London – and indeed the relatively elevated position of Mucking allows one to see as far

west as Northfleet and as far east as the Isle of Sheppey (Hamerow 1993, 4). Overall, then, while we cannot be certain of the appearance and function of saltern 5760, a circular structure with an external clay mass wall and substantial internal roof-supporting posts, which was used for salt making and other industrial activity, seems the most likely interpretation.

One-stop shop – using salt at Stanford Wharf

The production of salt allowed other economic activities, of which salt was a vital part, to be established. Most remarkably, the abundant remains in ditches 5099 and 5191 of tiny bones and scales from small and juvenile fish, including herrings, sprats and smelt, strongly point to the production of fish sauce, a product integral to Roman cooking and dining as an essential 'store-cupboard' ingredient in the kitchen and a table condiment (Nicholson, specialist report 16). There were, in fact, several types of fish sauce, and much confusion, even in the Roman world, about what they were called and how they were made. What does seem to be certain, however, is that sauces made with fish blood and intestines were regarded as separate to those made with the whole fish. According to Pliny the Elder, writing in the mid 1st century AD, *garum* was made with fish intestines mixed with salt. This is supported by Martial, who also in the 1st century described a sauce made with the blood of mackerel (Grocock and Grainger 2006, 373). There is more confusion over the term *liquamen*. It appears to refer to a sauce made in much the same way as *garum*, but with the whole fish. *Liquamen* is specified in the collection of recipes begun by Apicius in the 1st century AD and expanded by others subsequently. The bony fish paste that formed at the base of the barrel, pot or trough in which fish were pressed to create the *liquamen* was known as *allec* (ibid., 381; Curtis 1984). *Allec* also describes a bone-free paste that appears to have been generated in transit, for example inside the spikes of amphorae that carried fish sauce. As *tituli picti* on amphorae demonstrate, *allec* was itself an economic product and traded, probably as a relish or table condiment (S Grainger, pers. comm.). Then there is *muria*, which Gargilius Martialis, writing in the late 3rd century, describes as the brine of salted fish; that is, a watery, pale, liquid drawn from fish salted for the market (Grocock and Grainger 2006, 374); *muria* is also the term for ordinary brine (the sort processed by the salters at Stanford Wharf).

The recipes of Apicius (Grocock and Grainger 2006) show how versatile fish sauce (whether *garum* or *liquamen*) was in Roman cooking. *Liquamen* was used in sauces, among them cumin sauce and a sauce for truffles, added to forcemeat or sausage mixtures, used to flavour vegetables, such as cabbage, cucumber and gourds, incorporated into omelette-like dishes known as *patinae*, sprinkled into soups, used with lentils, peas and other pulses, poured over chicken, pork, lamb and other meats and roasted, and used in sauces to add to fish and other seafood.

The recovery of a mass of fish bones from a single deposit at Stanford Wharf, so far unparalleled in Roman Britain in terms of sheer quantity, potentially identifies the product as a form of *liquamen* or *allec*, rather than *garum*. If following the instructions given by Gargilius Martialis, the fish, which was caught locally in the Thames Estuary, would have been layered in a barrel or ceramic vessel with salt (the 10th century manual, the *Geoponica*, gives a ratio of 8:1 by volume of fish to salt), and left for 30 days, although more time – three months or more – was required if a clear liquid was to form. The liquid (*liquamen*) forming above the fish was drawn off, leaving a thick paste full of bones (*allec*) (Grocock and Grainger 2006, 376). As the paste could be traded, the fish bones were presumably removed before being dumped.

Tituli picti, painted inscriptions recording the contents of amphorae, reveal that fish sauce or paste reached various parts of Roman Britain, usually from Spain. These demonstrate that *garum*, *liquamen*, *muria* and *allec* were recognised as economic products, and that the distribution was heavily weighted towards military forts and urban centres. *Allec* is recorded on a Spanish amphora found at Newstead (RIB II 1994b, 2492.6). Inscriptions on Spanish Dressel 2-4 amphorae from London record *muria* (RIB II 1994b, 2492.29) and *liquamen* (RIB II 1994b, 2492.24). *Muria* is also identified in a list of provisions on a wooden writing tablet

preserved at Vindolanda, Northumberland (Bowman 1994, 116-7). Cool (2006, 59) estimates that the quantity given, 1.5 *sextarii* or *c* 0.8 litres, would cater for between 25 and 50 people. Other fish products carried in amphorae are attested at Alcester, Chester and York (RIB II 1994b, 2492.10-12). The date ranges of Spanish amphorae of the sort that carried fish products are largely confined to the 1st and 2nd/early 3rd centuries (Peacock and Williams 1986), and the distribution of Spanish amphorae across the western provinces through time reveals a decline in importation into Britain in the 3rd century (Martin-Kilcher 2003, 81-2). The trade did not cease altogether – the 4th-century amphora Almagro 50, which contained fish sauce, is recorded in Britain, including at Northfleet villa in north-west Kent (Biddulph 2011a, fig. 63.71) – but overall, Britain was receiving fewer imported goods in the 3rd and 4th centuries compared with the 1st and 2nd centuries.

The resulting shortage of fish products is likely to have prompted inhabitants of Britain to manufacture their own versions. Production, for example, is suggested to have taken place on the waterfront of Roman London, where a silty deposit above a drain dated to the early/mid 3rd century yielded a mass of juvenile herring and sprat bones (Bateman and Locker 1982). By contrast, the Stanford Wharf assemblage was more diverse, and while dominated by clupeids also contained other species such as pogge and pipefish as well as crustaceans. This variety suggests a different quality of product from one based entirely upon clupeid species. However that may be, Stanford Wharf was ideally placed for fish sauce production. The fish was caught locally, and the site produced the salt necessary for the production process. How, and how far, the resulting *liquamen* and *allec* was exported is uncertain. Old amphorae may have been reused, although the amphora recorded from the site is limited to fragments from round-bodied Dressel 20 olive oil containers, which appear to have been less suitable for the fish products (although the Alcester inscription was found on a Dressel 20 container). Otherwise, smaller ceramic jars may have been employed. Given that fish sauce is likely to have been produced in London, the reach of the fish products made at Stanford Wharf may well have been fairly local, with distribution limited to the villas and towns of south and central Essex and north Kent.

Salt was invaluable for preserving food, not least to ensure that food was available during the winter months. However, evidence for food preservation is rare, being limited to a higher than usual number of cattle scapulae, which had been perforated. The perforation is a butchery mark usually interpreted as a suspension hole for a hook. This allowed the carcass to be hung before it was processed further or after it had been jointed and cured. The joints were dry-salted, or, perhaps more likely, given the large quantities of salt required for dry-salting, wet-cured by being steeped in a brine solution (the stronger the better to reduce the amount of time subsequently required in the smoker) in a brining tub or wood-lined pit (Erlandson 2003, 18). Pierced scapulae are known at various sites in Roman Britain, among them Springhead town and Northfleet villa in north-west Kent (Worley 2011a, 34; 2011b, 45). The context in which the bones were discovered, ditch 8551, reveals little about how and where the preservation took place, but the ditch encloses salterns 5760, 8516 and 6090, and potentially one of these was used for curing beef (the tile-built hearth in saltern 6090 may have been particularly suitable for smoking). Mutton, goat meat and fish may have been salted and cured at the site, too, although the fish bones provide no real evidence for this. The sheep or goat assemblage is dominated by metapodials, skull fragments, mandibles and loose teeth, whereas the meat rich body parts are scarce. This pattern suggests that the animals were slaughtered on site and the meat joints were exported, probably after salting, for consumption away from the site (Strid, specialist report 15).

The animal bone assemblage also hinted at the possibility that cattle hides were cured or prepared for tanning. The proportion of cattle metapodials – the foot bones – is higher than might be expected, and their presence is likely to be connected with slaughter, tannery waste or bone working. Inevitably, given the nature of the site, the bones might reasonably be viewed as evidence for curing, by either covering the hide with dry salt or soaking the hide in brine for some hours before completing the curing process by smoking. However, as with the sheep or goat metapodials, the cattle metapodials might simply represent slaughter waste. Alternatively, skins may have been brought to the site already preserved with metapodials attached (Strid, specialist report 15).

The few late Roman coins recovered from the site, apart from supporting the pottery evidence to suggest that activity continued as far as the mid 4th century or beyond, perhaps suggest that the site did not see commercial trade, or that the activity represented at the site did not otherwise require the use of coins. The assemblage contrasts sharply with the 184 coins from Northfleet, another production site, whose pattern of loss pointed to a proportion that was significantly lower than the national mean for villas in c AD 330-348 (Reece period 17 and a period generally of plentiful coin loss) and significantly higher than the mean in c AD 364-378, or Reece period 19 (Cooke 2011, 186). However, while the comparison is interesting, the assemblage from Stanford Wharf is not large enough to allow meaningful conclusions to be drawn from it.

Seasonality and settlement

The seasonal nature of salt production is attested by medieval documents, which indicate that coastal salt working in England was carried out between the warmest months of the year, between June and September (Keen 1988a, 142-3; Fawn et al. 1990, 18). Richard Bradley (1975) suggests that the optimum time for salt production on the Hampshire/Sussex border-

lands is from May to September. That salt production at Stanford Wharf was seasonal and carried out throughout the summer and early autumn is demonstrated by the plant remains. The recovery from the site of seed heads of rush, plantain and thrift at various stages of maturity suggests that saltmarsh plants were harvested to provide fuel – and possibly to create brine – throughout the growing season (Hunter, specialist report 19). More indications of seasonality derive from the fish remains. The majority of fish bones from sample 1160 (ditch 8551) were identified as juvenile herrings or sprats and immature smelt. Though present in the Thames estuary all year round, smelt spawn in February-March. Juvenile herrings typically enter the estuary in July, but are most common between November and March. Juvenile sprat appear in September and peak in abundance in January. This suggests that the fish recorded at Stanford Wharf were caught in the autumn months, with fishing possibly continuing into winter (Nicholson, specialist report 16). Potentially, then, fishing patterns extend the period during which the site was occupied beyond the May/June to September season assumed for salt production. On this basis, the salt-production and fishing seasons overlapped briefly in September, suggesting that the fish was processed when salt production had largely ceased for the year. The work may have been carried out using surplus salt. Alternatively, salt production continued for as long as practical into late autumn or later.

Outside intensive periods of activity, we might expect that the salters and other workers returned to their homes and families. The Roman-period settlement at Mucking – comprising among other features enclosures, buildings, cemeteries, pottery kilns, corn-dryers and a rich artefactual assemblage – lies just 2km south-east of Stanford Wharf. With the few structures at Stanford Wharf being given over to salt production or other industrial activity, apparently making little room for domestic occupation, it seems reasonable to suggest that the salters employed at Stanford Wharf lived elsewhere for the rest of the year or intermittently during the salt-making season. Mucking, the nearest known settlement, potentially accommodated the salters on this basis. Indeed, the relationship between Mucking and Stanford Wharf may have continued through the salt-making season, with Mucking serving as a parent settlement in terms of supply of goods (certainly including pottery), and possibly, given the presence of briquetage vessels and furniture from the site, as a place engaged in the secondary processing of salt, such as drying and distri-bution (Kinory 2012, 128). However, there is relatively little evidence for late Roman settlement at the site, with activity, including pottery manufacture, largely ceasing by c AD 250 (S J Lucy, pers. comm). The existence of other settlements in the vicinity must be presumed. The settlement at Orsett, some 5km north-west of Stanford Wharf, may have accommodated salters, at least in the mid 3rd century, a period in which pottery kilns and structures are attested at the site, though again 4th-century activity appears to be sparse (Carter 1998). The pottery from Stanford Wharf, however, suggests that the salters' homes were situated closer to the site.

The pottery assemblages associated with salt production phases during the Roman period at Middlewich in Cheshire (Leary 2008) and Middleton, Norfolk (Darling 2001), were dominated by jars or had proportions of jars that were higher than those recorded for phases in which no salt production was carried out. This presumably reflects the industrial bias of the sites, as jars were required as storage vessels, scoops, buckets and containers for transportation (cf. Leary 2008, 92). The late Roman pottery from Area B was closest to the profile offered by Middlewich and Middleton. Its assemblage had a more 'industrial' profile than that from Area A in terms of forms represented, comprising higher proportions of jars and bowls and lower proportions of dishes and beakers (Biddulph and Stansbie, specialist report 2). However, the assemblage from Area A had a different profile, one characterised by proportions of jars, tablewares and drinking vessels that were similar to assemblages recorded at a farmstead at Strood Hall, near Great Dunmow in central Essex, and the villa sites of Great Holts Farm, Boreham, and Northfleet in north-west Kent. In other words, Area A presented a domestic assemblage of low to middling rank, rather than a specialist assemblage related to salt production. It is unlikely that the pottery arrived from Mucking as broken pieces within waste or soils, and it must point to the presence of domestic occupation near by, perhaps on the higher ground on the gravel terrace north of the salterns. In contrast, activity in Area B seems to have been more intermittent and focused more strongly on salt production, largely eschewing other roles, such as food preservation, and seeing relatively little domestic activity. Occupation in Area B was, perhaps, shaped to a larger extent by seasonal constraints. The emergence of slightly divergent processes in Area B, as represented by the introduction of a briquetage pedestal type not seen in Area A, potentially points to separate groups of people working in areas A and B; the salters in Area B perhaps worked largely without much interaction with those in Area A.

In addition to the general character of the pottery that matched the assemblages from the villas of Great Holts Farm and, to a lesser extent, Northfleet, the samian ware, a type of relatively high-status imported pottery which provides a useful index for site ranking (Willis 1998), also placed Stanford Wharf close to Great Holts Farm and Northfleet, though below the urban centre of Colchester (Biddulph and Stansbie, specialist report 2). The ceramic building material provides a correlation. The assemblage, comprising roof and other structural tile reused in hearth structures or recovered from dumped deposits, had an almost identical composition to that from Mucking. That is not to say that the Stanford Wharf tile had been taken from buildings at Mucking – and on observation the material from Mucking was worn and highly fragmentary and suggestive of reuse – but simply that the two locations shared the same source for its material. This source could have included a local villa (Shaffrey, specialist report 9).

If some of the pottery and ceramic building material recovered from Stanford Wharf derived from a nearby villa or a satellite settlement (and it is worth mentioning glass from an early Roman jug or jar which, given its early date, is suggestive of occupation of some pretension in the vicinity of the site (Scott, specialist report 7)), then this raises the possibility that the site was located within a villa estate, and indeed that the salt production was controlled by the estate as one of its economic concerns. There is some support for this at Little Oakley in north-east Essex. The villa there sits close to the coastline on the edge of marshland, which is occupied by red hills. At least seven red hills are known, and these are situated just 1.5km south-east of the villa (Barford 2002a, fig. 122); at least two (red hills 7 and 10) were operational during phases of the villa's use (ibid., 190). Barford (ibid., 177) speculates that red hills to the north-east of Little Oakley in the parish of Dovercourt may represent a cluster of red hills within the estate of a villa at Dovercourt which has been lost to coastal erosion. Unfortunately, apart from the pottery and ceramic building material, there appears to be little evidence for a villa near Stanford Wharf. The finds assemblage from Roman graves uncovered at Hassenbrook Hall, Stanford-le-Hope, included an amphora containing a glass bottle, an iron knife with a carved bone handle, and a grey ware beaker (Hull 1963b, 181). These are high-status items likely to be associated with a settlement whose influence could have reached Stanford Wharf, but otherwise no traces of substantial buildings consistent with a villa are known.

Personal and daily life

The artefactual and environmental evidence offers an insight into the lives of Stanford Wharf's salters beyond their industrial work. Their diet included beef, mutton and pork, although they may not have eaten the meat very often, as most of it was preserved for export. These meats were very occasionally supplemented by venison, and a whale vertebra, complete with chop marks, suggests that whale meat was consumed too (or that the bones were utilised), the inhabitants evidently taking advantage of a chance beaching (Strid, specialist report 15). The composition of cereal remains recovered from the late Roman features and structures argues against cereal processing taking place on site, and instead suggests that processing waste was brought in to be used as fuel and for stabling. The condition of some of the cereal remains was exceptional; ears of spelt recovered from enclosure ditch 9506 were preserved to the extent that hairs on the grains survived (Fig. 6.63; Hunter, specialist report 19). The quern stones present suggest that processed grain was brought in too, and was ground to make flour to provide bread and porridge-like food for the salt workers; that cereal foods were consumed on site is clearly shown by the presence of cereal bran in pit

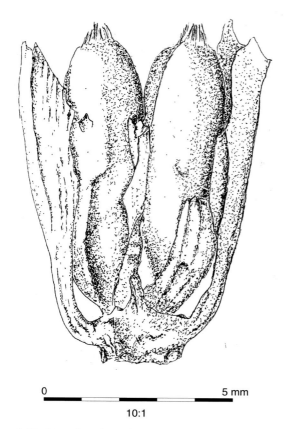

0   5 mm
                10:1

Figure 6.63 Ear of spelt with surviving hairs (drawing by Kath Hunter)

1249, which, as the undigested part of the cereal, was deposited in the pit as human waste. In addition, there was evidence for peas and legumes, and pit 1249 preserved a range of exotic and wild foods, including plums, sloe, apples, cherry, coriander and a possible fig seed, while a stone pine cone scale was recovered from ditch 5099 (Hunter, specialist report 19). No doubt some of these were gathered locally from hedgerows and trees, but others, such as the fig and stone pine remains, will have arrived from further afield.

Food was cooked in pottery jars and dishes over hearths, and mortaria and flanged bowls, including samian versions, were used for grinding and mixing ingredients. The food need not have been bland, of course. The cooks obviously had salt at their disposal to flavour it, and may even have used some of the fish sauce that was produced. The presence of Dressel 20 amphorae from Spain suggests that olive oil reached the site. The cooking techniques and range of ingredients available suggests that recipes of the sort presented in the Roman cookbook, Apicius (Grocock and Grainger 2006) were to some extent feasible. The food was eaten from ceramic dishes and bowls, and was accompanied by wine or ale served in beakers, flagons and glass jugs. We know less about what the inhabitants of Stanford Wharf wore, but the evidence of glass beads from necklaces, a plate brooch, and hair pins shows that some of the inhabitants took care over their appearance, and attests to the presence of women within the community.

While the inhabitants were making salt, preparing and eating food, and generally living, they were sharing their space with livestock. Age measurements and pathology show that cattle were used for traction, presumably to pull wagons and carts carrying salt and fuel. Horses were present and probably provided transport as well as traction, and dogs wandered about the site. Traces of human and animal waste and high phosphate levels demonstrate that saltern 9501 at least, apart from being used to make salt, accommodated salters and served as a byre for livestock (Macphail et al., specialist report 24). The rectangular area defined by postholes in the corner of enclosure 9506 may also have been used as a stockade or byre.

Corridor of life and industry: a Thames Estuary economic and cultural zone

The Thames river from the estuary to the Roman city of London was a corridor of economic and social opportunity. To the inhabitants of Stanford Wharf, it was far from a barrier and gave access to goods and social contacts on the opposite side of the river in Kent. This is evident from the artefactual evidence. The supply of pottery from north and west Kent that had begun in the later 1st century AD with Patch Grove grog-tempered ware and North Kent reduced and oxidised wares continued into the 4th century with late Roman grog-tempered ware. Vessels in this fabric are extremely rare in Essex, but their distribution, confined to south Essex, is expanding and includes Chigborough Farm, near Maldon (Horsley and Wallace 1998, 153), and Ivy Chimneys, Witham (Turner-Walker and Wallace 1999, 130). The trade was not all one way; in the early Roman period, shelly ware ledge-rimmed jars, which were manufactured at Mucking and West Tilbury, were exported to north-west Kent, and have been found in some numbers at Springhead (Seager Smith et al. 2011, 55-8). The form was numerous at Stanford Wharf, and this raises the possibility that the jars were packed with salt and exported across the region, including into north Kent, although this is somewhat akin to 'taking coals to Newcastle', as the north Kent marshes were well established in the early Roman period as areas of salt production (Detsicas 1983, 170-1). There are other examples of cross-river trade; the ceramic building material included pieces from Eccles (Shaffrey, specialist report 9), a villa and tile-manufacturing centre in the Medway valley (Detsicas 1983, 168), and puddingstone quern stones, otherwise rare in south-east Britain (and absent at Stanford Wharf) were present at Mucking and Northfleet villa in relatively high numbers, suggesting a connection between the two sites in terms of supply patterns (Shaffrey, specialist report 10).

The salt making and salting industry of Stanford Wharf was just one concern in the wider economic zone of the Greater Thames region. A boat sailing into the Thames Estuary would have passed oyster beds along the north Kent coast around Whitstable, which supplied oysters to sites along the Thames, including Northfleet villa and Springhead (Wyles 2011, 121), and oyster beds were also exploited along the Essex coast (Barford 2002b, 174-5). As the boat continued up the Thames towards London, it passed areas of salt production on Canvey Island and, on the opposite side of the river, the Upchurch marshes and the Hoo Peninsula (Fawn *et al.* 1990, map 1; Andrews 2004, 20), although whether all or any of the salterns there were operational in the late Roman period is uncertain. Where there was salt production, there was often pottery production. Pottery production at Upchurch and on the Hoo Pensinula declined after the early 3rd century (Monaghan 1987), although later 3rd (and possibly 4th) century production is known at Mucking and Orsett (Jones and Rodwell 1973; Carter 1998). The boat, sailing by the mouth of the Ebbsfleet stream beside which Northfleet villa and Springhead were built, would have passed an area dedicated to malting and brewing (Andrews *et al.* 2011), and dotted along the Thameside region of Kent and Essex were farmsteads and fields for crops and livestock. In addition, evidence for coppiced wood was recorded at Stanford Wharf. Relatively few of the oak charcoal fragments recorded on site possessed tyloses, which suggests that much of it consisted of immature wood (tyloses develop in wood once the tree reaches roughly 50 years in age). This, coupled with the fact that many of the rays exhibited a definite curve, suggests that much of the oak came from small roundwood. Much of the alder/hazel and broom/gorse type wood also consisted of small 'twiggy bits' or 'rods' less than *c* 10mm in diameter. Slightly larger oak, alder and hazel roundwood, with up to six or seven growth rings, dominated the assemblage from hearth 6061. Given that there is a long tradition of harvesting rods on a seven-year cycle (Rackham 2003), it is quite feasible that this material represents coppice wood (Druce, specialist report 20). Evidence for coppicing was also recorded at Springhead and Northfleet (Barnett 2011, 118), pointing to the existence of areas of managed woodland, which provided fuel and construction material. Our boat would not have been alone in the Thames, and would have negotiated its way around trading vessels and barges (and probably a military patrol boat) approaching the channels and creeks to take them inland, and wharfs, such as that recorded at Northfleet, to collect goods for export, or offload goods from distant lands.

With its salterns and buildings and areas of activity, salt production at Stanford Wharf was at a level of output not seen since the middle Iron Age. This intensity could be viewed as an element of the reorganisation of the countryside attested in south-eastern Britain in the late Roman period. We can see evidence for this across Essex and in north-west Kent. The large villa at Chignall St James, near Chelmsford, comprising three ranges of rooms surrounding a courtyard, is likely to have been built in the mid-late 3rd century (though it may have replaced an earlier, more modest structure) and this was accompanied by a remodelling of outlying enclosures

and structures. There was further elaboration of the enclosures, designed to improve the stock-breeding regime, in the late 3rd-late 4th century (Clarke 1998, 137-8). Great Holts Farm was occupied in the early 2nd century as a farming settlement, but was expanded in the early/mid 3rd century and, by the late 3rd/early 4th century comprised a villa, a bathhouse, a granary and a possible workshop or storehouse (Germany 2003). In central Essex, the farmstead at Strood Hall saw in the 3rd and 4th centuries increased food production and the construction of a 'Romanised' house to replace the earlier Roman roundhouses (Biddulph 2007, 141). In north-west Kent, settlements of the earlier Roman period ceased to be occupied or were adapted to serve different functions by the later period. At Northumberland Bottom, near Gravesend, the later 1st to mid 3rd century evidence included structures, enclosures and roads. After 260, activity was focussed around a corn-drier, ovens or kilns and boundary ditches, and the limited evidence for crop-processing evidence in the early Roman period contrasts with rich samples of charred grain from 4th-century features (Askew 2006). Northfleet villa saw increased crop-processing in the 4th century, and its malting oven signals a period of innovation and consequent efficiency-gains relating to brewing. Close to the Medway valley, Thurnham villa produced crops on a large scale, and in the mid 4th century a malting oven or corn-drier was built, although the villa had ceased to be used as such after the mid 3rd century (Lawrence 2006).

The changes seen at these sites suggest significant re-organisation of the landscape. The evidence from Kent, for example, suggests an emptying of parts of the landscape in the later Roman period, with major changes in settlement pattern occurring between the late 2nd and mid 3rd century AD (Booth 2011, 338). The cause is no doubt complex and multifaceted. We could cite the reduction in the level of imported goods in the late Roman period, requiring the inhabitants of south-eastern Britain to become more self-sufficient. However, to what extent this would have affected settlement patterns is uncertain, and in any case a shortage of imported goods would not have affected meat, grain and salt, which would not have been imported from the continent in significant volume (if at all) before the 3rd century; grain and cattle were among the products on Strabo's famous list of exports from Britain. We might consider instead the role of the provincial government and a period of increased centralisation and changes in the mechanism of state and military provision. Evidence from Northfleet villa, including a seal-box, theatre mask, the scale of production, and a well-constructed road leading to the villa, suggests that, while the malting and brewing was organised by the villa owners, who appear to have been high ranking officials at Springhead and members of the local elite, the army or provincial government at least had a significant interest in the operation (Biddulph 2011b, 228-9). In other parts of Roman Britain, the early church, a growing institution in the 4th century, appears to have had a hand in the organisation of salt production, just as, in the medieval period, salt production was carried out in Somerset, Dorset and elsewhere under the aegis of the church (Keen 1988b, 26). A Roman lead brine pan from Shavington, Cheshire, was inscribed VIVENTI [ ]COPI, possibly meaning 'Of Viventius, the overseer (or bishop)'. Another pan was inscribed CLER, possibly 'clericus' (Penney and Shotter 1996, 360-3). A similar relationship between salt production and the state might be seen at Stanford Wharf; as suggested with regard to the brewing at Northfleet, the salt production may have been carried out on a villa estate for the provincial government. But we cannot ignore the requirements of the military, particularly under Carausius and Allectus, which demanded considerable quantities of food and other supplies. This returns us to the tower at Stanford Wharf, and its suggested use as a signal tower. The evidence is hardly conclusive, but a spearhead recovered from the base of a replacement posthole which held one of the tower's corner posts hints at a low-level military presence at the site. After all, the army had its supply of salt and fish sauce to protect.

Chapter 7

Transformation of the post-Roman marshland

by Edward Biddulph, Dan Stansbie and Damian Goodburn

ANGLO-SAXON ACTIVITY (Figs 7.1 and 7.2)

Two oak piles (2058 and 2059), dating to the middle Saxon period, were found in the south-west corner of Area D, overlying a sandy layer (2062) and underlying alluvial clay (2061; G5), immediately to the north of the large – and silted up – palaeochannel (Fig. 7.1). The piles were lying flat, orientated approximately north-south. One pile survived to a length of 1.4m, the other to 1.78m, and they measured 0.12m and 0.13m in diameter respectively. The piles were carefully made and on the tips had well-preserved axe marks, which were too wide and straight to be typical of the Roman period (Fig. 7.2). On pile 2059 the nearly straight stop marks were up to 150mm wide and on pile 2058 up to 170mm wide without being complete, suggesting the use of some form of broad axe with a blade at least 200mm wide. Roman axe marks of this size have only been recorded twice on large oak beams in London but are commonly found on late Saxon timbers (Goodburn 1992). Detailed work on the Northfleet Saxon watermill timbers revealed very broad axe marks tree-ring dated as early as AD 692, but no trace of the use of broad axes on the Roman woodwork (Goodburn 2011b, 337). The piles also seemed a little fresher and less degraded than the piles discussed above. On these grounds it was suggested that the piles might well be of Saxon date. This dating has been confirmed by a radiocarbon date from pile 2059 of cal. AD 660-780 (94.5%; 1287 ± 25 BP: OxA-24582). No other features or deposits of Anglo-Saxon date were identified.

MEDIEVAL ACTIVITY (Figs 7.3-7.5)

There is very limited artefactual or other evidence for medieval activity within Stanford Wharf, although a concentration of generally late medieval–early post-medieval features was found in the extreme north-east corner of Area B (Fig. 7.3). Groups of ditches appeared to form at least two small enclosures. The more south-westerly of these, consisting of ditches 8564, 7039 and 7050, was roughly D-shaped in plan. Ditch 7039 was orientated NE-SW and met 8564 at right angles, although it must be the earlier feature, as it was cut by 8564. Ditch 7039 may relate to ditch 7050, which curved round towards 7039 from the south. Between these ditches were three features: gullies 7005 and 7007 and pit 7009. Gully 7007 was orientated NW-SE, and its identified part measured approximately 17m long, 0.7m wide and 0.09m deep. It was cut by pit 7009, which was 1m across and 0.12m deep. Gully 7005 was orientated NE-SW and was 4.6m long, 1m wide and 0.1m deep. Three ditches to the north-east (7026, 7049 and 8546) may have formed part of a sub-rectangular enclosure, but it was not possible to be certain given the area exposed and the extent of post-medieval truncation. Ditch 7026 was aligned NW-SE; its extant section 6.8m long, 2.8m wide and 0.45m deep. Ditch 7049, which curved almost in mirror image of 7050, was approximately 8m in length, 2m in width and 0.5m in depth. It was cut by 8546, aligned NW-SE, of which a 40m length was exposed. Ditch 8546 continued on a rather irregular alignment beyond the junction with ditch 7049. As with the D-shaped enclosure to the south-west, the area apparently enclosed by ditches 7026, 7049 and 8546 contained three gullies (7034, 7020 and 7036) and a pit (7032). The

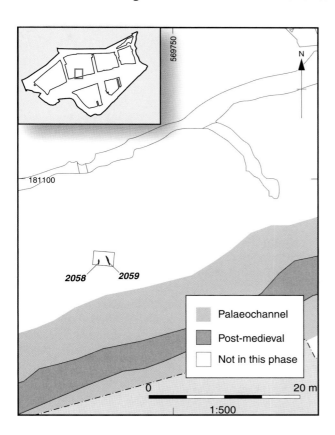

Figure 7.1 Plan of middle Saxon timbers in Area D

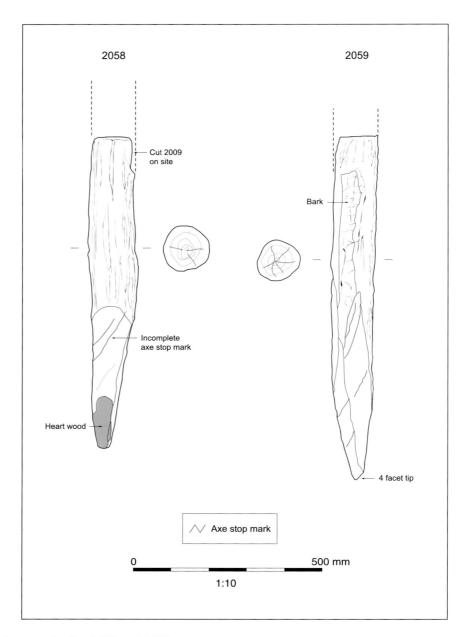

2058   2059

Cut 2009
on site

Bark

Incomplete
axe stop mark

Heart wood

4 facet tip

/\/\ Axe stop mark

0   500 mm

1:10

Figure 7.2 Middle Saxon oak piles 2058 and 2059

gullies were between *c* 5m and 11m in length and 0.3-0.7m in width; 7034 and 7020 were aligned NE-SW, while 7020 was aligned NW-SE. Gully 7036 had been cut away by ditch 7049 at its south-eastern end, indicating that it was the earlier feature. Pit 7032 was sub-circular in plan and measured 0.8m across and 0.4m deep.

To the south of these enclosures, channel 8532, sinuous in plan, with a recorded length of approximately 138m and up to 3m in width, crossed the length of Area B on a roughly north-south alignment. It followed the course of the western arm of late Roman saltern 6711 (cf Fig. 6.36), but is a later feature, as a small subsidiary channel cut the upper fills of the Roman ditch close to timber post structure 9517. The latter, located just south of the centre of Area B, comprised a group of ten small driven piles and stakes of mixed species. Most fell into

two roughly straight parallel lines, aligned approximately north-south (Fig. 7.3). These alignments were approximately 3m apart and crossed the southern side of the silted up late Roman channel of saltern 6711. The group was dated to the medieval period by a single radiocarbon determination on elm pile 4608. This returned dates of cal. AD 1305-1365 (56.2%) and cal. AD 1385-1420 (39.2%) (569 ± 24 BP: OxA-24851). The use of elm is unknown in Roman and Saxon London, but was common in later medieval times, while the solidity of the timber and the presence of a neat, long rectangular mortice of later medieval form are also consistent with this date. As the stakes varied greatly in size, it is unlikely that they once supported any type of bridge. The two alignments would appear to be the truncated remains of revetments to either side of a short

Figure 7.3 (facing page) Plan of medieval, post-medieval and modern features in Area B

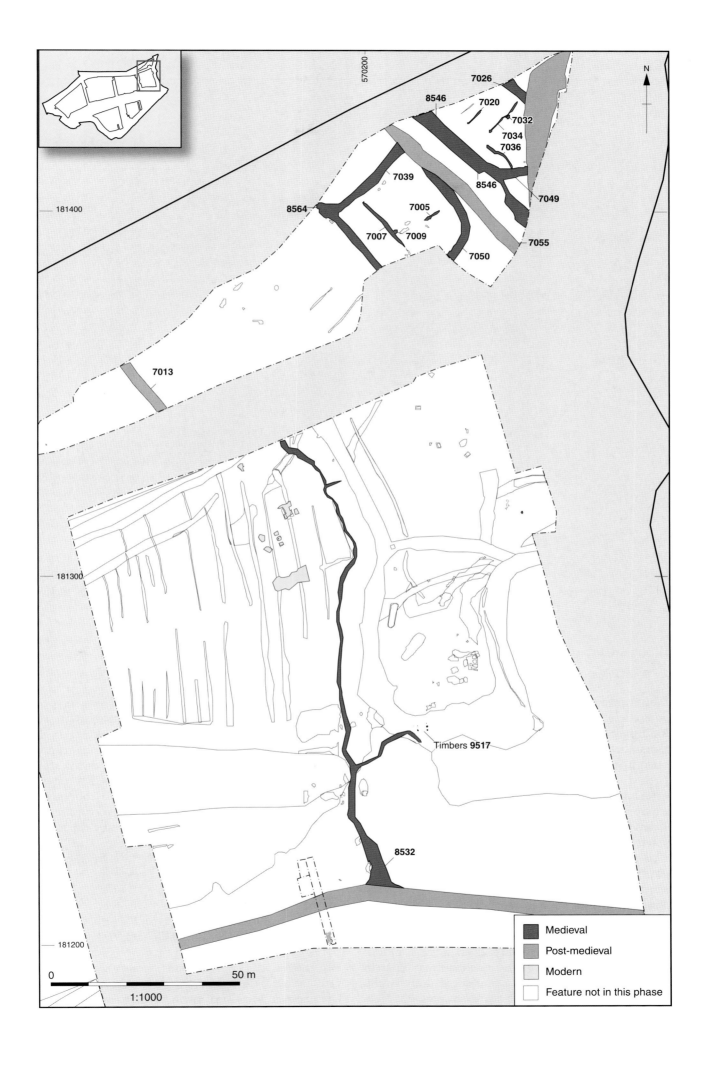

7026

8546

7020

7032

7034
7036

7039

8546

7049

8564

7005

7007 7009

7055

7050

7013

Timbers **9517**

8532

570200

181400

181300

181200

0   50 m

1:1000

N

	Medieval
	Post-medieval
	Modern
	Feature not in this phase

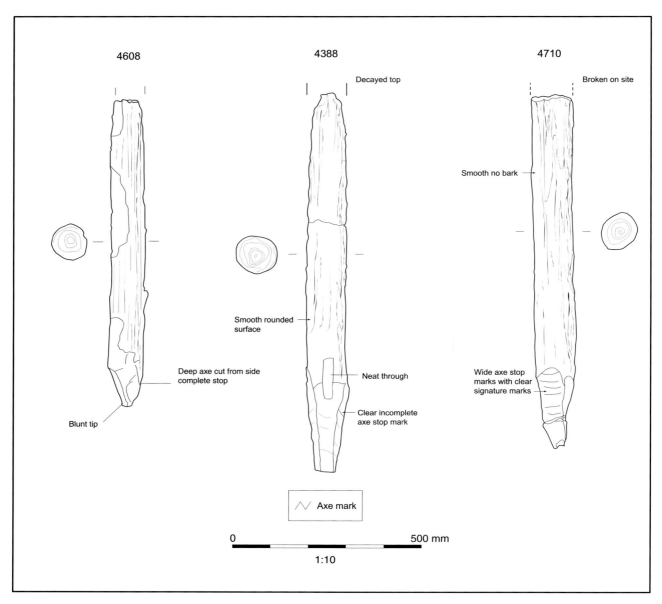

Figure 7.4 Timber piles from structure 9517

earthen causeway, with the sheathing having rotted away. Some of the piles were hewn from small elm logs, including some that had already been used previously, as demonstrated by relict peg holes and a rectangular mortice in piles 4389 and 4388 respectively (Figs 7.4 and 7.5).

Artefacts recovered from medieval deposits were largely restricted to pottery (Cotter, specialist report 3). The earlier part of the pottery assemblage includes some very soft and fragmentary examples of jars/cooking pots in 12th-13th century shelly wares, probably from south Essex. Other grey sandy medieval coarsewares are present, including jars/cooking pots and a few jugs. Most of these are probably Essex products, but a few wheel-turned jar rims may be in South Hertfordshire Greyware. One or two coarsely flint-tempered sherds may be a flintier variant of the latter. White-slipped jugs in London-type ware (mainly *c* 1150-1350) are also fairly common in the earlier assemblage. Three or four sherds in off-white sandy ware may be medieval Surrey whitewares, but these

are plain and unglazed and difficult to assign to specific sources, although finer sherds are probably from 15th-century Cheam whiteware jugs. A few sherds of Mill Green ware jugs were noted from medieval contexts and residual in later contexts. This ware was produced around Ingatestone, near Chelmsford, and has a date range in London of *c* 1270-1350, but may have continued in production as late as *c* 1400 with a more restricted distribution. Mill Green fineware jugs can occur, as here, with an all-over white slip under a clear or green glaze, or with white slip-painted decoration under a clear glaze or no glaze at all. A few Mill Green coarseware jars/cooking pots also occur.

POST-MEDIEVAL ACTIVITY (Figs 7.3, 7.6 and 7.7)

Two ditches (7013 and 7055), both aligned NW-SE, were cut across the northern part of Area B (Fig. 7.3). The exposed section of ditch 7013 measured approxi-

Figure 7.5 Photograph of piles from structure 9517, pile 4388 at left. Scale 2m

mately 16m long, 3m wide and 0.9m deep and extended beyond the limit of excavation at both ends, although it was not seen in the main part of Area B to the south and is likely to have terminated in between. Ditch 7055, some 93-95m further north-east, was at least 39m long, 4m wide and 0.8m deep and also extended beyond the limits of excavation at both ends. Two fills of ditch 7055 contained large quantities of transitional late medieval/early post-medieval redwares, including jugs, jars and plain large bowls, dated to the 15th or early 16th century (Cotter, specialist report 3). In central and southern Essex there may have been a number of late medieval production sites producing fine red earthenwares in the Mill Green tradition and these seem to have evolved in the late 15th century into the first 'post-medieval' red earthenwares – heavier thicker-walled vessels with thin white slip decoration and little or no glaze (Cunningham and Drury 1985). One of the contexts produced sherds from two thumbed jug bases in an unusual pink-buff fabric, which may be late medieval Hertfordshire glazed ware dating to *c* 1350-1450. Another deposit from ditch 7055 produced a small collection of early post-medieval redwares and also the base of a Beauvais sgraffito ware dish with traces of incised and polychrome decoration (Fig. 7.6). This relatively costly tableware is the only continental import in the entire assemblage.

In Area A a timber structure was recorded near the south-eastern edge of the excavation area (Fig. 7.7). It comprised four rows of posts or fences, which defined a rectangular area *c* 5m by 7.5m. The structure, or fenced enclosure, appeared to be open along its northern edge. A calibrated radiocarbon determination (185 ± 40 BP: SUERC-24585/GU-19378) obtained from oak post

0   50 mm

1:1

Figure 7.6 Fragment from a Beauvais sgraffito ware dish

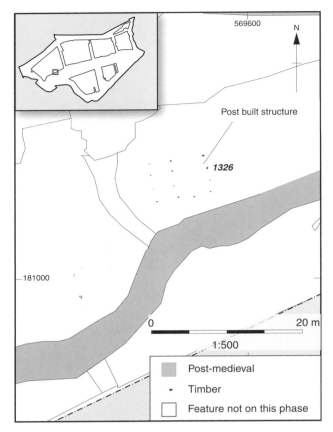

Figure 7.7 Plan of post-medieval features in Area A

Figure 7.8 Timbers from a sea barrier pre-dating the modern sea wall

Figure 7.9 Concrete structure found during the sea wall breach

1326 gave a spread of dates – cal. AD 1640-1710 (21.4%), cal. AD 1720-1820 (48%), cal. AD 1830-1890 (8.2%) and cal. AD1910-1960 (17.8%) – though all placed the timber in the 17th century or later, and the structure is marked as a sheepfold on an Ordnance Survey map of 1863.

Sinuous and meandering channels were recorded across the entire area of excavation. These were not investigated, but were located on late 19th century Ordnance Survey mapping, and probably served as drainage ditches.

MODERN FEATURES (Figs 7.8-7.11)

No certain evidence for earlier sea defences was observed during the breach of the modern sea wall, although a number of half-round wooden stakes approximately 1.6m long and 0.15m wide extending on the same alignment as the line of the original sea wall were recorded (Fig. 7.8). The date of these, however, is unknown.

Several areas of sand with patches of modern brick and plastic tubing were recorded in Areas I and J (8001). These were the remains of engineering testing work during the 1970s for the Thames tidal defences project (S Corbet, pers. comm.), which assessed the stability of earthen sea defences. Their locations correspond to a plan of the facility provided by a member of the project. During the breach of the sea wall, a large concrete platform with steel reinforcing rods measuring approximately 21 m in length and 7 m wide was discovered within the existing sea wall (Fig. 7.9). The platform was edged with steel corrugated sheet piling and was situated within an area of brick rubble on the estuary side. The structure also appears to have been associated with the flood prevention testing as identical plastic pressure tubing and other deposits were visible beneath it. It is likely that this structure was observed in a site visit in 1999 and documented in the county historic environment record.

During the Second World War, the southern part of Stanford Wharf Nature Reserve was the site of Stanford-le-Hope Oil QF (diversionary fire) bomb decoy. A concrete blockhouse comprising a night shelter, control room and oil storage bays was located on the sea wall at the southern edge of Stanford Wharf Nature Reserve. These seem to have been demolished in the late 1940s (Essex Historic Environment Record no. 20303). No remains had clearly been identified prior to breach of the sea wall. However, a series of concrete and brick remains found in Area B (group 9512) are likely to be the remains of some of the oil fire installations (Fig. 7.10).

A wattle structure (9518) was situated close the southern limit of excavation of Area B (Figs 7.3 and

Figure 7.10 Second World War bomb decoy structures

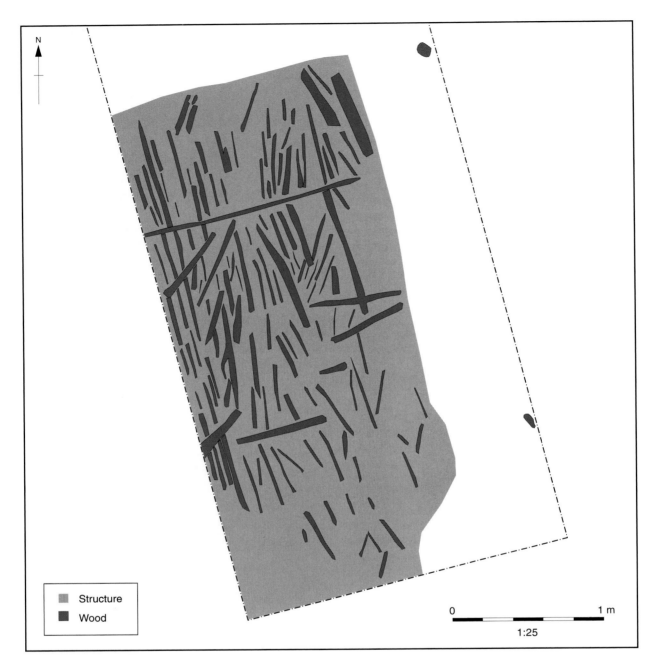

Figure 7.11 Wattle structure 9518

7.11). An area 3.6m long and 1.5m wide was excavated within an archaeological trench, but clearly the structure was more extensive, as it continued to the south and west of the trench. The structure comprised approximately 140 individual wattles, most of which were orientated north-south, with a few east-west orientated wattles holding the whole structure together. It was lying flat and is thought to be a modern collapsed wattle fence.

DISCUSSION (Figs 7.12-7.15)

Despite the wealth of Anglo-Saxon settlement and burial evidence at nearby Mucking (Hamerow 1993), Saxon evidence at Stanford Wharf was restricted to two isolated pieces of wood in Area D. The function of these piles is very hard to ascertain; part of a small jetty or fishing platform might be plausible, although this is very speculative, as the piles were clearly not *in situ*. The wood was radiocarbon dated to the late 7th or 8th century AD. During this time, Mucking saw continued, though diminished, occupation, with settlement of over 50 sunken-featured buildings and 20 posthole buildings becoming dispersed and moving away from the edge of the gravel terrace, which had been densely occupied from the 5th century (Hamerow 1993, 21).

The economic significance of the marshes and terrace around Stanford-le-Hope is clearer after the late 11th century. The coastal marshes of Essex became increasingly important for sheep pasture and other economic activities during the early Norman period. Darby (1971, fig. 64) has plotted the location of Domesday manors in

Essex which possessed pasture for sheep, and found that all the villages with such pasture lie in a belt parallel with the coast, abutting the marshland. We may be able to include the parish of Stanford-le-Hope in this general pattern. There is no direct reference to Stanford-le-Hope in Domesday, but the church of St Margaret of Antioch in Stanford-le-Hope, though mainly 14th century, has 12th century remains, indicating that there was a settlement here by at least this date. In any case, the evidence from Stanford Wharf provides support for farming and coastal activities during the medieval period. The distribution of ditches and gullies, concentrated in the northernmost area of Area B, suggests that farming was restricted to the higher ground of the terrace. The features are likely to be related to sheep farming, and may mark the site of a small 'wick' or sheep dairy, with surrounding fields being available for grazing (S Rippon, pers. comm.). Exploitation of the marsh to the south appears to have been more limited. Timber group 9517 suggests that the marshland was accessed via causeways, which allowed local settlers to reach important resources, such as wild fowl, fish and shellfish, although causeways may also have been used to move flocks of sheep around the marsh to reach fresh grazing (Wilkinson and Murphy 1995, 208). Mucking Creek is also likely to have been navigable from its mouth to at least the edge of the gravel terrace. Further

access through the marsh may also have been gained by using low rises over former areas of Roman salt making, such as Area B saltern 6711, as 'stepping stones' for walking to channels where boats were moored. The rises would also have been useful in connection with wild fowling. That channel 8532 followed the shape of the enclosing channel of saltern 6711 suggests that the ditch, and possibly the saltern it enclosed, remained visible to some extent as an earthwork and low rise. Archaeological investigations at Canvey Island, *c* 5km to the east, produced evidence of a large number of oyster storage pits and numerous fish-traps and duck decoy ponds, which probably date from the medieval period onwards (Wilkinson and Murphy 1995, 207-210). These give a little insight into the range of features that may have existed in the marshland and intertidal zone of Stanford Wharf during the medieval period.

In the 15th and 16th centuries, the Stanford marshlands belonged to Cabborns Manor, later known as Manor Farm (Fig. 7.12). The manor house was located at the point where the Hassenbrook stream empties into Mucking Creek, about 500m north of the excavation site. In a reference in the Calender of Close Rolls dated May 1465, William Hengsey, resident and grocer of London, acquired the manor from Richard Walssh and Richard Pigge. William Hengsey evidently became wealthy from his trade and well able to afford some of the luxuries of

MANOR FARM, STANFORD-LE-HOPE.

Figure 7.12 Cabborns Manor, as sketched by Donald Maxwell in 1925

the time, among them the relatively costly sgraffito ware dish from Beauvais recovered from a ditch in Area B. Dating to 1500-1575, this is likely to have belonged to Hengsey or his descendants.

There remains much uncertainty about the dating and interpretation of the block-like pattern of ditches and gullies in areas A, B and D. The features are placed in the Roman period (see Chapter 6) based on ceramic dating and the preferred interpretation of their function, but the gullies in Area B showed a remarkable similarity with blocks of ditches recorded at Lymington, Hampshire (Fig. 7.13; Powell 2009, fig. 5). Powell (ibid., 35) suggested that the Lymington gullies were related to salt making, possibly being used to feed seawater into the salterns they enclosed. Their 17th-century dating was tentative, however, and based on not entirely satisfactory parallels and historical records of salt making in the region. Dating of the Area B features, and those in areas A and D, to the 17th century onwards is in turn undermined by the absence of post-medieval pottery, as well as the absence of contemporaneous hearths and working surfaces, and any other evidence for salt making at Stanford Wharf during this time. For an alternative explanation, we could point to systems of shallow drainage channels, known as 'ridge-and-vurrow' or 'gripes', employed in the Gwent Levels (Rippon 1996). These drained water from the surfaces of fields into field ditches, which in turn drained the water into 'reens' or larger channels. The form of the blocks of ditches and gullies in areas A, B and D appears to argue against this interpretation, however, as the blocks were not connected to larger ditches that would have taken the water away from those areas. We might also consider the possibility that the channels are the remains of turf cutting, although quite why they would take the form as

revealed by excavation is puzzling, and it is worth highlighting the evidence from the medieval fishing settlement of Walraversijde, near Ostend in Belgium. Here, the resulting pattern from peat cutting (used for salt-making by selnering) was a grid of large square pits separated by baulks of remaining peat (Tys 2006, 27). A more likely explanation, already presented in connection with the late Roman salt-production (Chapter 6), is that the channels were used to irrigate the salt marsh to increase salt content in the marsh plants, which were then burned in order to produce a brine that was more concentrated than seawater. The explanation retains the suggestion given by Powell (2009, 35) that the channels admitted seawater, but takes the Roman pottery recovered from them at face value and places the groups of features in the Roman period, rather than later.

The timber structure in Area A, dated by radiocarbon to the mid 17th century or later, is located at a point marked as 'sheepfold' on the Ordnance Survey map of 1863. A function related to farming is certain, though Damian Goodburn wonders whether it was a stock yard, rather than a sheepfold. Nevertheless, the structure indicates that the marsh, which had seen limited activity in the medieval period, was being opened up for sheep pasture in the post-medieval period. This was made possible with the construction of a sea wall along the Stanford marshes. It is uncertain exactly when the sea defences were constructed. There are documentary references to the granting of commissions for the review and repair of marsh defences in the Essex as early as the 13th century, and by the 14th century a rise in sea level led to the construction of sea walls along sections of the coastal marshes of the county (VCH Essex vii, 185), but Stanford Wharf need not have been included in these earlier phases of work. However, documents in the Essex

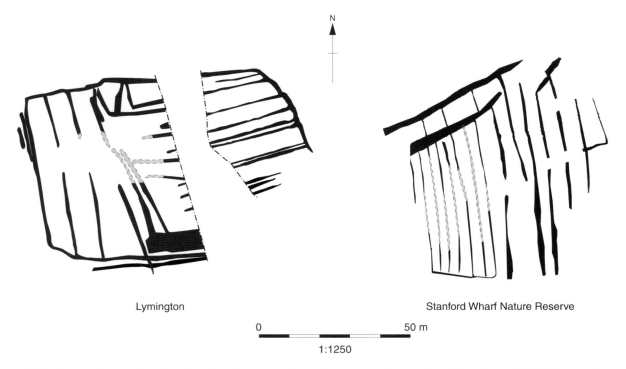

Lymington   Stanford Wharf Nature Reserve

0 ————————————— 50 m

1:1250

Figure 7.13 Comparison of blocks of gullies from Area B and Lymington, Hampshire (after Powell 2009, Figure 5)

Public Records office suggest that Fobbing and Stanford Marshes were reclaimed by the early 1620s; late 19th century legal documents quote two royal commissions under Charles I (1633-4 and 1637-8), which were charged to 'find out what lots had been taken in and concealed from the king'. The commission jury stated that 1500 acres, comprising 'Fobbing Level Marshes', had been 'inned' ten years previously. Chapman and André's 1777 map of the coastline shows a linear feature dividing the intertidal mudflats and the marshland, identified on the map as Stanford Marsh (Fig. 7.14). The mapmakers depict the barrier with a row of short lines or strokes, rather than a solid line, and it is possible that these represent wooden posts. If so, then timber piles revealed during the breaching of the modern sea wall could be the remains of the barrier shown on the map. Successive mapping indicates further consolidation of the sea wall and reclamation of marsh behind it.

Chapman and André's 1777 map is also significant for providing the earliest reference to Stanford Wharf, which marks an area inside the mouth of Mucking Creek on the edge of Stanford Marsh. This was where small boats and craft moored before continuing up the Mucking Creek towards Stanford-le-Hope, or entering the Thames. By 1863, the date of the 1st edition Ordnance Survey 6" map, a coastguard station, named 'The Vigilant', had been constructed up from the wharf immediately beyond the western edge of the area of archaeological investigation (Fig. 7.15). The 1863 and later mapping shows, too, a network of natural, sinuous, channels and straighter ditches of human design extending across the excavation area. These ditches were

revealed in excavation and are testament to the success of reclamation permitted by sea defences. That is not to say that the marsh fields were spared from subsequent flooding. The writer and artist Donald Maxwell noted while exploring the coastline around Stanford-le-Hope and Mucking in the early 1920s that at spring tides the fields around Cabborns Manor (by then known as Manor Farm) were often flooded, and the farm appeared to be on the edge of a broad river. In drier times, Mucking Creek diminished to a stream by the house, and flowed through the adjacent pasture (Maxwell 1925, 18).

The changes in the landscape resulting from reclamation are evident in pollen and diatom analysis of post-Roman alluvial deposits in Area A. The proportion of salt marsh species was lower, compared with Roman-period samples, suggesting that the marsh had retreated. Conversely, the proportions of tree and shrub and grassland taxa had increased, hinting at tree regrowth and expanding pasture (Peglar, specialist report 23). There was occasional flooding, however, as the diatom data showed (Cameron, specialist report 21), and as Donald Maxwell observed.

The London Gateway Development area includes the former Thames Haven oil refinery and storage depot, which was identified as a key defence site during the Second World War. Stanford Wharf, away from inhabited properties, was the site of Stanford-le-Hope Oil QF (diversionary fire) bomb decoy. Concrete and brick remains found in Area B may be the remains of some of the oil fire installations. Bomb decoys were designed to simulate bomb damaged oil tanks to trick German

Figure 7.14 Detail from Chapman and André's map of the county of Essex, 1777

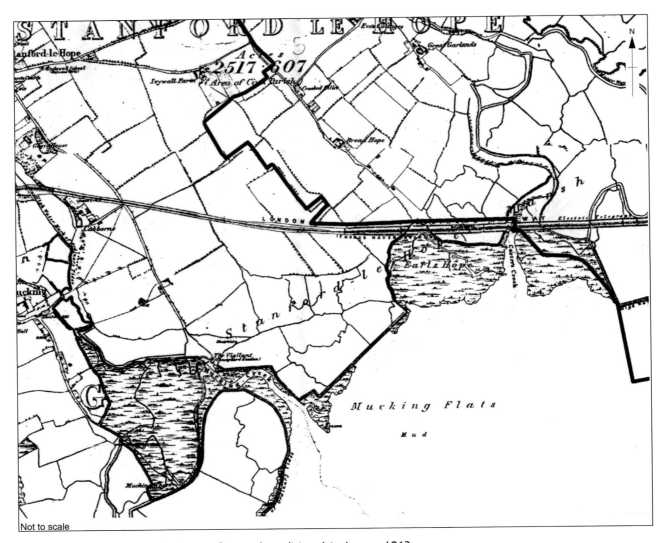

Figure 7.15 Detail from the Ordnance Survey 1st edition 6 inch map, 1863

bomber aircraft into dropping their payload onto the empty marshland. It is unknown whether they succeeded; bomb craters have been recorded at Corringham Marsh, immediately east of Stanford Wharf, but these are currently undated (Strachan 1998, 87). The decoys were part of a wider system of coastal defences. A pillbox at Thurrock is one of many that were built around the coast and incorporated into the 'outer crust' of defences designed in conjunction with natural sandbanks and mudflats to halt or delay a German invasion force (Gilman and Nash 1995, 16), and at Corringham Marsh, cross-shaped ditches were machine-dug to prevent light aircraft from landing on the flat ground (Strachan 1998, 87). The bomb decoys at Stanford Wharf are modest compared with other oil-related devices. In 1944, a fake oil terminal, complete with pipelines, storage tanks and jetties, was built at Folkestone as part of a complex scheme of deception to divert German intelligence from discovering the true launching point for D-Day (Rankin 2008, 571).

Chapter 8

Worth its salt – concluding comments

by Edward Biddulph and Stuart Foreman

AN EXCEPTIONAL SITE

The investigation at Stanford Wharf Nature Reserve recorded a sedimentary sequence commencing in the late Glacial period, a time when sea-levels in the region were much reduced and the Thames was a freshwater river. In the Mesolithic and earlier Neolithic periods, inhabitants took advantage of the dry, sandy, land to manufacture tools, exploit the local resources, and process meat and vegetation for food and clothing (Fig. 8.1; see Chapter 3). In the later Neolithic period, a rise in sea-level resulted in the inundation of the land surface, and a tidal palaeochannel, which was to influence the extent and range of features encountered throughout the prehistoric and Roman periods, was incised across the site. The channel was surrounded by extensive tidal mudflats backed by salt marsh and tidal creeks, and this estuarine environment prevailed until the 17th century AD, when the land was reclaimed (Chapter 2).

The first significant period of activity at Stanford Wharf dated to the middle Iron Age (c 400-100 BC). The evidence was concentrated in the north-western corner of the site and was dominated by red hills, a characteristic feature of long-term salt production on the Essex coast. Other evidence relating to salt production included pits, hearths and briquetage, a coarse ceramic used for making salt-processing equipment, such as cylindrical moulds, troughs, pedestals and firebars (Chapter 4). There was a hiatus in activity during the late Iron Age, but the early Roman period (c AD 43-120) saw a resumption in salt making, which had been transferred to the eastern end of the site. Shallow ponds, narrow gullies and hearths were recorded, as well as the detritus of salt production, such as fuel waste and briquetage fragments (Chapter 5, *Early Roman salt production in Area B*). Activity recorded in the western part of the site was restricted to a curious timber post structure, which had been erected on the edge of the palaeochannel. Its interpretation is not certain, but a boathouse is most likely (Chapter 5, *Early Roman features in Area A*). Between those two areas, a cremation burial, which perhaps contained the remains of a member of the salt-working community (Chapter 5, *Early Roman features in Area C*), and wattle panels, which represent the remains of a causeway across a creek, were recorded (Chapter 5, *Channel 2148 and wattlework panels, Area D*).

There was another gap in activity during the 2nd century AD, although a small amount of pottery belonging to that period was recorded, and it is possible that this derived from nearby occupation beyond the area of excavation. The gap in activity was temporary, and by the first half of the 3rd century a trapezoidal

0 ⟨scale⟩ 50 mm

1:1

Figure 8.1 A flint scraper and retouched blades

enclosure had been established at the western end of the site (Chapter 6, *Enclosure 9506 and associated features*). The enclosure is likely to have served as an area of salt production, but the most notable feature within the enclosure was a former quarry pit, which was reused as a cess-pit and within which a range of plant remains, fruits and other organic material was preserved. A saltern, defined by a hearth, settling tanks, and two horseshoe-shaped ditches, was established south of the enclosure (Chapter 6, *Saltern 5808*). By *c* AD 250, the western part of the site had been reorganised, as new ditches were laid out and four salterns established (Chapter 6, *Later Roman activity, phase 2*). One saltern, erected in the corner of the now abandoned trapezoidal enclosure, contained a hearth, a three-celled tank, and dumps of salt-processing waste. Three more salterns were set up within an adjacent enclosure. One of the salterns was equipped with a tile-built hearth (Fig. 8.2), while another, dating to the late 3rd century AD, featured four substantial chalk rubble post-bases, which formed a 4.5m wide square. The eastern end of the site also saw salt production in the late Roman period. The saltern there was defined by a natural channel and a range of salt-related features (Chapter 6, *Late Roman activity in Area B*). Together, this evidence appears to represent a significant intensification of salt production (discussed below).

The latest coins and pottery recovered from Stanford Wharf Nature Reserve indicate that the site was occupied into the second half of the 4th century. Following the Roman period the site must have reverted to open saltmarsh. Two isolated oak piles of middle Saxon date (*c* AD 650-850) were recorded, but no other features of this period were identified. In the medieval period, ditches in the northernmost area of the eastern end of the site on the higher ground of the gravel terrace are likely to mark out areas of grazing for livestock, or possibly a small dairy. In the southern part of the site, a timber group marked a causeway through the marshland. Reclamation of the marsh began in the 17th century; a sheepfold, identified as such on a 19th-century may and which indicates use of the marsh for pasture, was uncovered. More recent concrete and brick remains found in the eastern end of the site are likely to be the remains of oil fire installations that functioned as Second World War bomb decoys (Chapter 7).

To have determined the sequence of occupation and deposition at the site with reasonable confidence is achievement enough, but this is enhanced in no inconsiderable measure by some notable findings, which have emerged from the post-excavation work. One of the key aims of the project was to investigate the character and formation of the red hills, and this has been addressed definitively through chemical, micromorphological and environmental analyses. The analyses revealed that the mounds consisted of fuel ash derived from burnt salt marsh plants and sediment. The plants (with adhering marsh sediment) had been burnt to fuel hearths, above which brine was evaporated to crystallise salt. A by-product of the fuel burning was a salt-rich ash, which when mixed with seawater, was turned into a highly saline solution. This was filtered, and the resulting

Figure 8.2 Uncovering a tile-built hearth (photograph courtesy of Nick Strugnell)

brine was then also evaporated above salt marsh plant-fuelled hearths. It was the residue from hearths and filtering that was dumped to create low mounds or red hills, which were subsequently used as occupation or working surfaces (Fig. 8.3). The discovery of a method akin to medieval sleeching is of enormous importance for Iron Age studies in Britain, and it revolutionises conventional understanding of salt production and red hill composition. The red hills held one more surprise. Scientific and ceramic dating indicated that they were of middle Iron Age date, and not late Iron Age or early Roman, the periods to which most other Essex red hills have been assigned. This identifies the red hills from Stanford Wharf as among the earliest known in Essex.

Analysis of the plant remains has also enabled us to address questions of continuity and seasonality. The identification of seed heads of rush, plantain and thrift at various stages of maturity suggests that salt marsh plants were harvested from the beginning to the end of the May/June to September growing season, with the implication that salt was produced at the site throughout that period. The recovery of fuel ash dominated by salt marsh plants in Roman-period salterns indicates that the method of brine and salt production, established in the Iron Age, continued to be employed as late as the late 3rd and 4th centuries. There was, however, a significant difference between Iron Age and Roman practices: there were no Roman-period red hills, suggesting that the salt marsh sediment, which gave the red hills its colour, was not itself routinely collected and burnt, pointing to more careful harvesting – and sustainable

management – of the marsh plants in the Roman period. In the late Roman salterns, the hearth and brine residue was dumped in pits and ditches, but in the early Roman saltern in the eastern end of the site (Area B), the residue was dumped in layers to form a platform, or 'black hill', that was used later as a working surface. Elucidation of the plant-based method of salt extraction gives a new understanding of features typically associated with salterns. Pits and multi-celled clay-lined tanks have conventionally been interpreted as settling tanks, and while they no doubt fulfilled this role, it seems likely that they also served to collect brine being filtered through meshes or organic filters suspended above.

As noted, the site reveals continuity from the middle Iron Age to the late Roman period in the use of salt marsh plants, and there is also continuity in the use of briquetage vessels and equipment, although changes in briquetage manufacture and types were apparent. The demonstration of the late Roman use of briquetage was another unexpected outcome of the analysis, as it has been difficult to show in earlier studies of red hill and salt-working sites in Essex that the date of the material extended beyond the 2nd century AD. Indeed, few coastal sites in Essex have offered evidence for late Roman salt working, although pottery and occasional features cutting into red hills have suggested a limited amount of late Roman activity at some sites. The evidence for continuity at Stanford Wharf has also been accompanied by evidence for a fundamental change in the scale and methods of salt production during the late Roman period. Traces of lead recorded in two salterns

Figure 8.3 Excavating one of Area A's red hills (photograph courtesy of Nick Strugnell)

has pointed to the adoption of lead evaporating pans at the site for use alongside, or to replace, briquetage troughs. The use of lead pans is well known in the salt industries of the West Midlands and North-West England, but in Essex had remained a matter of conjecture only, and both factors serve to highlight the significance of the evidence from Stanford Wharf. At the time that lead vessels were being used for evaporation, wood (or possibly charcoal in some cases) was being burnt in the hearths below. This may have been a result of the pressure to obtain large quantities of fuel as salt production intensified and expanded.

Another difference between the middle Iron Age and the late Roman period lies in the use of structures. The middle Iron Age environment (and Area B in the early and late Roman periods) was an open landscape. No buildings were constructed, and salt was produced under the summer sky. In the late Roman period, while there were some open-air salterns, two buildings, both circular structures, were also used for salt-making. The activity had thus been placed under cover. One of the structures, saltern 9501, offered evidence for a clay mass wall and an associated wooden revetment, which would have been placed against the wall's inner face. Inevitably, evidence for the largely non-earth-fast wall construction technique is rare in Roman Britain, and so its apparent use at Stanford Wharf is of some importance to the study of buildings in Roman Britain. A circular clay mass wall is also suspected for another saltern, 5760, although the building's centrally-placed arrangement of large, chalk postpads presents other possibilities for its interpretation, including a raised four-post salt or food store, or a beacon or signal tower. A structure encountered in Area A in the western part of the site and dating to the early Roman period was equally rare. Its arrangement of timber posts, an apsidal end, and the fact that its south end opened onto a tidal palaeochannel, identified the structure as a probable boathouse. Such structures, until now unknown in Roman Britain, have been recorded at sites along the Rhine and in the Mediterranean, and this restricted distribution undoubtedly gives the structure at Stanford Wharf international significance.

The thick layers of alluvium that were encountered at Stanford Wharf Nature Reserve sealed waterlogged deposits in which were preserved an extraordinary range of organic objects and structures. Apart from the timber elements of two buildings, the remains of a wooden drain, wattle panels from causeways built across natural channels, dumps of woodworking debris, and odd wooden objects, including a possible ladder, a basket and a boat fragment, were recorded. The fruits and seeds preserved in the cess pit within the 3rd century trapezoidal enclosure included coriander, plum, sloe, wild cherry, walnut and a possible fig, and cereal bran and a leather shoe were also recovered. The animal bone assemblage has shed much light on the use of animals and the range of economic activities at the site. In the medieval period, the economy of coastal Essex was dominated by sheep farming, and some evidence of that

– the medieval field system, the later sheepfold, and possible livestock refuges – can be seen at Stanford Wharf. In the Roman period, the principal animal represented in the site's bone assemblage was cattle. Scapulae from some individuals had been pierced, probably in the course of preserving meat with salt or brine, and together these findings may reflect the hand of the Roman army in the organisation of the late Roman salt-works. The demands of the army, and possibly the urban population of London, are likely to have been responsible for the intensification of salt production at the site in the late Roman period, but also the production of fish sauce, probably *liquamen* or *allec*, which resulted in the dumping of a mass of tiny fish bones in a ditch. Stanford Wharf is not the first site in Britain to have produced evidence for the manufacture of fish sauce, but never before has the evidence been so abundant and in such a clear association with salt-works.

COASTAL WETLANDS: APPLYING A MODEL OF UTILISATION

The pattern recorded at Stanford Wharf Nature Reserve of exploitation of the salt marsh, hiatus in occupation, intensification of activity, further hiatus, dedication to livestock farming, and finally reclamation finds accords well with Stephen Rippon's model for the utilisation of coastal wetlands. Rippon (2000, 52, fig. 19) proposed a general pattern for utilisation of wetlands across north-west Europe in the later prehistoric, Roman and medieval periods that began with the prehistoric exploitation of the landscape, as the inhabitants of inland or seasonal coastal settlements gathered the natural resources offered by the wetlands. The Roman and earlier medieval periods saw the advent of a second strategy for utilisation, that of modification, as drainage ditches were cut across marshland to bring it into cultivation or to increase generally the range and level of economic activities permitted by the landscape. Finally, the wetlands were transformed during the later medieval or early post-medieval periods with the construction of sea walls to remove tidal influence and impose a systematic use of the reclaimed land through drainage and enclosure.

In Essex, the earliest evidence for coastal exploitation has been recovered from the Crouch estuary, specifically in the form of a wooden paddle (Wilkinson and Murphy 1995, 157-64), and from Mucking (Barford 1988b, 41) in the form of salt making debris (although it is uncertain if this represents production at that relatively elevated location), and dates to the later Bronze Age, although it was not until the late Iron Age and early Roman period (c 50 BC to AD 200) that the Essex coast was more widely exploited, with red hills being the most obvious product of that occupation. The evidence of red hills at Stanford Wharf helps to fill a chronological gap, substantially increasing our knowledge of coastal occupation in the middle Iron Age, and joining contemporaneous salt production sites at Tollesbury in the Blackwater estuary (Germany 2004) and, possibly, Peldon, also on the Blackwater, Kirby-le-Soken and Walton in north-east Essex (Fawn *et al.* 1990), and a site close to West Tilbury in the Thames Estuary (Drury and Rodwell 1973, 93). The absence of salt-production and other activity in the late Iron Age at Stanford Wharf may seem puzzling, given the site's extensive middle Iron Age evidence, but the hiatus fits with the distribution of salt production sites, which places most of the late Iron Age salterns in the north-eastern part of Essex. Production spread into the Thameside region during the second half of the 1st century AD (Rippon 2000, 62; Rodwell 1979), and the re-emergence of the industry at Stanford Wharf in Area B during the early Roman period fits that general pattern. Further insight into the character of coastal exploitation is provided by the probable boathouse in Area A, which hints at coastal fishing or possibly trade of salt and other resources. Rippon (2000, 63) notes some association between salt production sites and cremation cemeteries, suggesting that communities were resident on the marshes for at least part of the year, an idea with which the early Roman cremation burial in Area C is consistent.

Transformation of the coastal wetlands during the later Roman period was restricted to the Somerset Levels, which saw comprehensive change through the imposition of drainage systems to reclaim the marshland. Elsewhere, for example, in the Fenland, the Humber estuary, south-east Dorset and north Kent, there was more modest and localised modification –

Rippon's second strategy of coastal wetland utilisation (ibid., 263) – characterised by expanded salt production, fish and shellfish consumption, and livestock grazing. In Essex, evidence for 3rd and 4th century coastal occupation, limited largely to small pottery scatters and occasional features cut into former red hills, has pointed to a virtual abandonment of salt production areas, while hinting at the use of the marshlands for sheep farming (Barford 2000). This view has changed significantly with the results from Stanford Wharf, which are more in keeping with the type and level of activity seen in the Fenland, Dorset and elsewhere. The site offers, among other critical factors, evidence for the intensification of salt production, modification of the marshland through the cutting of drainage ditches and provision of causeways, and seasonal occupation of the site, to which workers returned year after year, as indicated by permanent structures, the volume of pottery, and the evidence of human and stabling waste. While a review of late Roman evidence from what were in many cases antiquarian or pioneering excavations is to be encouraged, the difference between Stanford Wharf and other parts of the Essex coast is stark, and it is telling that dry land settlements close to Stanford Wharf, notably Orsett 'Cock' and Mucking (Carter 1998; S Lucy, pers. comm.), had largely been abandoned by the late 3rd century. Stephen Rippon (2000, 113) attributes the expansion of coastal activity during the later Roman period outside Essex to imperial control and the presence of a large military force in Britain, and views salt as a mineral resource subject to

Figure 8.4 Selection of pottery from the site

0 _____ 50 mm

1:1

Figure 8.5 A two-piece Colchester brooch from Area A

the same controls as other minerals and metals, such as lead and to some extent pottery and tile. Potential imperial interest in Stanford Wharf with regard to the provision of salt, preserved foodstuffs and fish sauce has been alluded to above, and we can assume that the site's location on the Thames Estuary gave it an advantage over other potential salt production sites on the Essex coast. In any case, the site appears to have been part of a wider late Roman economic zone in the Thames Estuary; the villa at Northfleet, more or less opposite Stanford Wharf on the north Kent side of the Thames, saw large-scale malting and brewing, and there is tentative evidence to suggest that its products were destined for consumption by the army or the government (Biddulph 2011b, 228). Though possibly a provincial state supplier, Northfleet, as a villa estate, was run by local, presumably British, elites (ibid.), and a connection between villa estates and the economic concerns of the reclaimed marshland on the Severn Levels has also been suggested (Rippon 2000, 124-7). We cannot identify a villa close to Stanford Wharf with certainty, but the possibility that such an establishment existed must remain a consideration, and the site offers tantalising support for this from the composition of the tile assemblage, the relatively high-status pottery assemblage, metalwork, and provision of exotic fruits (Figs 8.4 and 8.5).

As also noted above, late Roman Stanford Wharf is remarkable for its under-cover salterns, contrasting with the open-air salterns of the middle Iron Age, early Roman period and early/mid 3rd century, and evidence for the adoption of lead evaporating vessels and wood-

based fuel. These changes can be attributed to a lesser or greater extent to the intensification of salt production, but it is worth highlighting parallel developments at Northfleet, which include the raising in the 4th century of the height of a quay built within a backwater of the Ebbsfleet, which is consistent with a rise in sea level (Biddulph 2011b, 222). Such a rise would undoubtedly have affected the occupation at Stanford Wharf, and we can potentially see the evidence in the deposits of late Roman alluvium that covered the remains of the early Roman boathouse and filled the outer ditch of saltern 9501. A landscape subject to more frequent inundation may have demanded enclosed, covered salterns and a shift from plant-based to wood-based fuel. Nevertheless, while changing environmental conditions may have contributed to some of the developments seen in the late Roman industry, intensification of production remains most likely to account for specific technological changes.

The abandonment of the coastal wetlands during the early medieval period has been attributed to further rises in sea level, which, in Stephen Rippon's words, 'can only have made the coastal wetlands inhospitable' (Rippon 2000, 262). It is tempting to put this forward as an explanation for why Stanford Wharf offers no evidence from the Anglo-Saxon period, with the exception of two pieces of wood, despite the presence of extensive Saxon settlement at Mucking and generally within the Thames Estuary (Hamerow 1993). Environmental evidence from the Saxon tidal mill at Northfleet, built in AD 691-2, appears to suggest that there was a reduction of the tidal range and increased freshwater input in the Ebbsfleet after this date (Stafford 2011, 66), and potentially this coincides with the use of the Saxon timbers from Stanford Wharf, which were radiocarbon dated to cal. AD 660-780 (94.5%; 1287 ± 25 BP: OxA-24582).

Essex appears to have been one of the last major coastal regions in north-west Europe to be subject to large-scale transformation through measures such as embanking, the cutting of drainage systems and the parcelling of farmland. The North Kent marshes show evidence for embanking and ditch cutting from the 8th century onwards, and drainage on Romney Marsh dates to at least the 9th century. There is larger scale reclamation in the Fenland and the Netherlands in the 10th century, while the Gwent Levels, the Pevensey Levels and the Belgian coast were reclaimed in the late 11th/12th centuries. The Essex coast joins the Norfolk broads in apparently seeing few changes throughout the medieval period (Rippon 2000, 266), although Foulness Island had gained sea walls by the late 13th century, and crops were being grown in areas, or former areas, of marsh along parts of the Thames Estuary (ibid., 201). The picture from Stanford Wharf Nature Reserve does not contradict this pattern, though it certainly adds detail. Documentary evidence suggests that the Stanford marshes gained sea defences in the early 17th century. Before then, a marsh environment prevailed in the southern part of Stanford Wharf, and a wooden causeway, radiocarbon dated to the 14th or early 15th century and presumably one of several constructed, was provided to allow movement across it. Medieval-period field or drainage ditches in the north-eastern part of the site suggest that agriculture was possible there. The type of farming practised is unclear, although pasturing of sheep is a strong possibility. The later sea wall opened up the southern part of the site to farming, and the discovery of a structure identified on a mid 19th century map as a sheepfold, suggests that agricultural exploitation of the former marshland was well established by that date.

THE SCOPE OF THE INVESTIGATION

It is important to emphasise the strengths and limitations of the archaeological dataset. No archaeological project is ever conducted in ideal archaeological circumstances or with unlimited resources. As with any archaeological investigation, a balance has to be struck between the pursuit of archaeological objectives on the one hand, and available time and funding on the other. In a developer-funded context, the scope of investigation is to a very large extent determined by the extent of construction impacts. This can be frustrating for archaeologists who naturally wish to pursue the archaeological objectives beyond these bounds. In the case of Stanford Wharf the very extensive but shallow nature of the construction impact effectively shaped the archaeological strategy. The creation of the new mudflat involved reducing the ground level by no more than 1m, and

indeed the salterns in Areas A and B were located within the footprint of the new sea wall, where the impact was even shallower. The principal benefit from the relatively limited construction impact was that significant archaeolgical deposits were preserved *in situ*.

The large-scale open area excavation resulted in a very extensive plan view of the Roman and later phases of activity at the site, and within the 16ha area of investigation, it was possible to compare and contrast two spatially and chronologically distinct salt-producing sites. On the other hand, prehistoric levels remained largely unexcavated, albeit preserved *in situ* beneath varying thicknesses of alluvium, except where revealed by localised investigations and where the alluvial sequence was relatively shallow, notably in the extreme north-west corner of the site. In the most complex archaeological sequence, against the western edge of Area A beside Mucking Creek, a key decision had to be made about the point at which excavation ceased. The 0.5m ground reduction required to create the new mudflat and build a new earthen sea wall was just sufficient to expose the late Roman and later landscape in the north-western corner of the Stanford Wharf site. In the event, extensive late Roman occupation deposits here were largely left *in situ*, obscuring but also protecting from disturbance any early Roman and prehistoric evidence that may have been present underneath. The scale and character of such evidence remains largely unknown. The position of part of the new sea wall in this area was relocated to protect the

Figure 8.6 Site director Katrina Anker discusses the results of the excavation with the environmental manager of DP World London Gateway, Marcus Pearson (photograph courtesy of Nick Strugnell)

Figure 8.7 A view of the Thames from Stanford Wharf Nature Reserve (photograph courtesy of Nick Strugnell)

most complex and significant archaeological deposits *in situ*, as the original design would have left these deposits in an exposed position in front of the sea wall and subject to tidal erosion.

Throughout the fieldwork, decisions had to be made about where to focus the effort of excavation (Fig. 8.6). Stanford Wharf Nature Reserve was relatively unusual in that it combined a development impact over a very wide area with a deeply stratified sediment sequence. Fortunately, the most complex archaeological sequences were concentrated overwhelmingly in two relatively small areas of the site (Areas A and B), of which Area A contained by far the most complex, informative and diverse sequence. Both areas coincided with elevated areas in the underlying terrace gravels, effectively spurs of slightly drier ground projecting into the former marshland. The rest of the site was characterised by natural alluvial sediments in which occasional artefacts were found, such as the Roman wattle panels revetting a causeway across a former creek in Area D, or a patch of redeposited red hill material dumped in the marsh in Area J in the post-medieval period, perhaps to create a livestock refuge.

A LASTING LEGACY

Today, Stanford Wharf Nature Reserve is a thriving habitat for wildlife (Fig. 8.7). Wading birds, such as avocets, black-tailed godwits, and ringed plovers, feed on the marine invertebrates which rapidly colonised the reserve after the sea wall was breached. The reserve is also home for thousands of reptiles, which were relocated

from DP World London Gateway port development, and a diverse range of fish, including common goby, thin-lipped grey mullet, bass, flounder, smelt, eel, and whiting. In addition the reserve provides a natural refuge and place of relaxation and enjoyment for the local community and visitors from further afield. There are echoes of the past in the modern site. The area was a thriving salt-marsh habitat for plants and animals in the Iron Age and Roman periods, attracting visitors who utilised the plants to make salt and fished the waters of the estuary for some of the same species of fish that are found in the reserve today. Further echoes can be heard in the port and logistics park adjacent to the reserve. The container port, built on the site of a former oil refinery, will offer a deep-sea port facility for international commercial shipping, and a hub for the storage and distribution of goods. In Roman times, Stanford Wharf Nature Reserve similarly served a significant economic role. Every summer during the late Roman period, workers produced tons of salt, the site's most important commodity, preserved meat, and made luxury fish sauce. These products were distributed by river, sea and across land to towns and forts in the region, or perhaps even beyond.

The modern nature reserve is a lasting legacy of the redevelopment of the oil refinery. Another is the archaeological and historical archive generated through three years of fieldwork, sorting, cataloguing, research and analysis, resulting in a monograph that presents the story of 6,000 or more years of occupation at the site; this is the legacy of the dedication of the field team, the post-excavation staff and the specialists, and the commitment and support of DP World London Gateway.

Bibliography

Albarella, U, 2007 The end of the sheep age: people and animals in the late Iron Age, in Haselgrove and Moore 2007, 389-402

Alexander, J A, 1975 The salt industries of Africa: their significance for European prehistory, in de Brisay and Evans 1975, 81-3

Allen, T, Donnelly, M, Hardy, A, Hayden, C and Powell, K, 2012 *A Road through the Past: Archaeological discoveries on the A2 Pepperhill to Cobham road-scheme in Kent*, Oxford Archaeology Monograph **16**, Oxford

Andersen, S Th, 1979 Identification of wild grasses and cereal pollen, *Danmarks Geologiske Undersøgelse 1978*, 69-92

Anderson-Whymark, H, forthcoming The struck flint, in *The Archaeology of the Eton Rowing Lake and the Maidenhead to Windsor flood alleviation scheme: Volume 1: Neolithic to early Bronze Age archaeology* (T G Allen, A Barclay and A Cromarty), Oxford Archaeology Thames Valley Landscapes Monograph, Oxford

Andrews, C, 2004 Roman Kent, in *An historical atlas of Kent* (eds T Lawson and D Killingray), Phillimore, Chichester, 20-24

Andrews, P, 2009 West Thurrock: late prehistoric settlement, Roman burials and the medieval manor house, Channel Tunnel Rail Link excavations 2002, *Essex Archaeology and History* **40**, 1-77

Andrews, P, Biddulph, E, Hardy, A and Brown, R, 2011 *Settling the Ebbsfleet Valley. High Speed 1 excavations at Springhead and Northfleet, Kent: the late Iron Age, Roman, Saxon and medieval landscape. Volume 1: the sites*, Oxford Wessex Archaeology, Oxford and Salisbury

Askew, P, 2006 *The prehistoric, Roman and medieval landscape at Northumberland Bottom, Gravesend, Kent*, CTRL Integrated Site Report Series, Archaeological Data Service, http://archaeologydataservice.ac.uk/catalogue/adsdata/arch-335-1/dissemination/pdf/PT1_Int_Site_Reps/04_Northumberland_Bottom/WNB_ISR_Text/WNB_ISR_Text.pdf

Barford, P M, 1988a Briquetage, in Wilkinson 1988, 97-8

Barford, P M, 1988b Salt production equipment (briquetage), in Bond 1988, 39-41

Barford, P M, 1990 Briquetage finds from inland sites, in Fawn *et al*. 1990, 79-80

Barford, P M, 2000 Marshland-inland relationship in Roman Essex: sheep, salt-licks and seasonal salters – a reply to Sealey, *Essex Archaeology and History* **31**, 276-9

Barford, P M, 2002a *Excavations at Little Oakley, Essex, 1951-78: Roman villa and Saxon settlement*, East Anglian Archaeology **98**, Chelmsford

Barford, P M, 2002b Shellfish and other marine resources, in Barford 2002a, 174-5

Barnett, C, 2011 Wood charcoal, in Barnett *et al*. 2011, 113-9

Barnett, C, McKinley, J I, Stafford, E, Grimm, J M and Stevens, C J, 2011 *Settling the Ebbsfleet Valley. High Speed 1 excavations at Springhead and Northfleet, Kent: the late Iron Age, Roman, Saxon and medieval landscape. Volume 3: late Iron Age to Roman human remains and environmental reports*, Oxford Wessex Archaeology, Oxford and Salisbury

Barrett, J C and Bond, D, 1988 The pottery, in Bond 1988, 25-37

Batchelor, C R, 2009 Middle Holocene environmental changes and the history of yew (*Taxus baccata L*) woodland in the Lower Thames Valley, unpublished PhD thesis, Royal Holloway, University of London

Bateman, N and Locker, A, 1982 The sauce of the Thames, *The London Archaeologist* **4.8**, 204-7

Bates, M R, 1998 Locating and evaluating archaeology below the alluvium: the role of sub-surface stratigraphical modelling, *Lithics* **19**, 4-18

Bates, M R, 1999 A geoarchaeological evaluation of the Thames/Medway alluvial corridor of the Channel Tunnel Rail Link, CTRL Union Railways Ltd, unpublished client report

Bates, M R and Barham A J, 1995 Holocene alluvial stratigraphic architecture and archaeology of the Lower Thames area, in Bridgland *et al*. 1995, 35-49

Bates, M R and Stafford, E C, forthcoming *The Thames Holocene: a geoarchaeological approach to the investigation of the river floodplain for High Speed 1*, Oxford Wessex Archaeology, Oxford and Salisbury

Bates, M R and Whittaker, K, 2004 Landscape evolution in the Lower Thames valley: implications for the archaeology of the earlier Holocene period, in Cotton and Field 2004, 50-65

Bates, M R, Walker, M J C, Cameron, N, Druce, D and Whittaker, J E, 2003 London Gateway Logistics and Commercial Centre Outline Planning

Application. Cultural heritage assessment refinement in respect of the proposed development of London Gateway Logistics and Commercial Centre. Technical Report Volume 2. Appendix O, prepared by Oxford Archaeology for P&O

Bates, M R, Bates, C R, Cameron, N, Huckerby, E, Nicholson, R and Whittaker, J E, 2012 A multi-disciplinary investigation of the sediments at the London Gateway site, Essex: Geophysics, palaeo-environment and dating. Final deposit model update, unpublished report by Oxford Archaeology for DP World

Behre, K E, 2007 Evidence for Mesolithic agriculture in and around Central Europe? *Vegetation History and Archaeobotany* **16**, 203-19

Bendrey, R, 2008 The animal bone, in *At the Great Crossroads: Prehistoric, Roman and medieval discoveries on the Isle of Thanet, 1994-1995* (P Bennett, P Clark, A Hicks, J Rady and I Riddler), Canterbury Archaeological Trust Occasional Paper **4**, Canterbury, 233-262

Bersu, G, 1940 Excavations at Little Woodbury, Wiltshire. Part I: The settlement as revealed by excavation, *Proceedings of the Prehistoric Society* **6**, 30-111

Biddulph, E, 2005 Last orders: choosing pottery for funerals in Roman Essex, *Oxford Journal of Archaeology* **24 (1)**, 23–45

Biddulph, E, 2006 *The Roman cemetery at Pepper Hill, Southfleet, Kent*, CTRL Integrated Site Report Series, Archaeological Data Service, http://archaeologydataservice.ac.uk/catalogue/adsdata/arch-335-1/dissemination/pdf/PT1_Int_Site_Reps/02_Pepper_Hill/PHL_ISR_Text/PHL_ISR_Text.pdf

Biddulph, E, 2007 Conquest and change? The Roman period, in *A slice of rural Essex: archaeological discoveries from the A120 between Stansted Airport and Braintree* (J Timby, R Brown, E Biddulph, A Hardy and A Powell), Oxford Wessex Archaeology, Oxford and Salisbury, 81-147

Biddulph, E (ed.), 2010 Stanford Wharf Nature Reserve, London Gateway, Stanford-le-Hope, Essex. Vol. 2: Artefactual, geoarchaeological and palaeoenvironmental appendices, Oxford Archaeology, unpublished

Biddulph, E, 2011a The pottery from Northfleet, in Biddulph *et al.* 2011, 134-57

Biddulph, E, 2011b The development of Northfleet Villa, in Andrews *et al.* 2011, 213-30

Biddulph, E, Brady, K, Ford, B M and Murray, P, 2010 Roman settlement, pottery production, and a cemetery in the Beam valley, Dagenham, *Transactions of the Essex Society for Archaeology and History* **1**, 109-65

Biddulph, E, Seager Smith, R and Schuster, J, 2011 *Settling the Ebbsfleet Valley. High Speed 1 excavations at Springhead and Northfleet, Kent: the late Iron Age, Roman, Saxon and medieval landscape. Volume 2: late Iron Age to Roman finds reports*, Oxford Wessex Archaeology, Oxford and Salisbury

Biddulph, E, Simmonds, A, Leader, P, King, L, Wenban-Smith, F and Lawrence, S, 2012 M25 DBFO Widening Section 4: Post-excavation assessment and project design, Oxford Archaeology, unpublished

Bird, D, 2008 'The rest to some faint meaning make pretence, but Shadwell never deviates into sense' (further speculation about the Shadwell 'tower'), in *Londinium and beyond: essays on Roman London and its hinterland for Harvey Sheldon* (eds J Clark, J Cotton, J Hall, R Sherris and H Swain), CBA Research Report **156**, York, 96-101

Blackman, D, 2000 Progress in the study of ancient ship sheds: a review, in *Boats, ships and shipyards: Proceedings of the 9th International Symposium on boat and ship archaeology, Venice 2000* (ed. C Beltrame), Oxbow Books, Oxford, 81-90

Bond, D, 1988 *Excavation at the North Ring, Mucking, Essex: A late Bronze Age enclosure*, East Anglian Archaeology **43**, Chelmsford

Booth, P, 2011 The late Iron Age and Roman periods, in Booth *et al.* 2011, 243-340

Booth, P, Champion, T, Foreman, S, Garwood, P, Glass, H, Munby, J and Reynolds, A, 2011 *On Track: the archaeology of High Speed 1 Section 1 in Kent*, Oxford Wessex Archaeology Monograph **4**, Oxford and Salisbury

Bowman, A K, 1994 *Life and letters on the Roman frontier: Vindolanda and its people*, Alan Sutton, Stroud

Bradley, R, 1975 Salt and settlement in the Hampshire-Sussex borderland, in de Brisay and Evans 1975, 20-5

Bridgland, D R, 1994 *Quaternary history of the Thames*, Geological Conservation Review Series, Chapman and Hall, London

Bridgland, D R, Allen, P and Haggart, B A, 1995 *The Quaternary of the lower reaches of the Thames: field guide*, Quaternary Research Association, Durham

Brodribb, A C C, Hands, A R and Walker, D R, 2005 *The Roman villa at Shakenoak Farm, Oxfordshire. Excavations 1960-1976*, BAR British Series **395**, Oxford

Brodribb, G, 1987 *Roman brick and tile*, Alan Sutton, Gloucester

Bronk Ramsey, C, 1995 Radiocarbon calibration and analysis of stratigraphy, *Radiocarbon* **36**, 425–30

Bronk Ramsey, C, 1998 Probability and dating, *Radiocarbon* **40**, 461–74

Bronk Ramsey, C, 2001 Development of the radiocarbon calibration program, *Radiocarbon* **43**, 355-63

Brown, D, 2007 *Archaeological archives: a guide to best practice in creation, compilation, transfer and curation*, Archaeological Archives Forum

Brown, N, 1991 Middle Iron Age decorated pottery around the Thames Estuary, *Essex Archaeology and History* **22**, 165-6

Brown, N and Glazebrook, J (eds), 2000 *Research and archaeology: A framework for the eastern Counties. Vol. 2:*

Research agenda and strategy, East Anglian Archaeology Occasional Paper **8**, Norwich

Carey, C and Dean, R, 2009 London Gateway: Compensation Site A. Geoarchaeological assessment of cultural and palaeoenvironmental resources, unpublished report by Oxford Archaeology for DP World

Carey, C, Nicholson, R and Stafford, E, 2009 London Gateway, Stanford-le-Hope, Essex, Compensation Site A archaeological investigation: Preliminary post-excavation assessment of geoarchaeological and palaeoenvironmental samples (microfossils, soils and sediments), unpublished report by Oxford Archaeology for DP World

Carrott, J and Kenward, H, 2001 Species associations among insect remains from urban archaeological deposits and their significance in reconstructing the past human environment, *Journal of Archaeological Science* **28**, 887-905

Carter, G A, 1998 *Excavations at Orsett 'Cock' Enclosure, Essex, 1976*, East Anglian Archaeology **86**, Chelmsford

Champion, T, 2011 Later prehistory, in Booth *et al.* 2011, 151-241

Champness, C and Donnelly, M, 2012 Dagenham and Washlands, Public Realms Enhancement, Dagenham, Greater London, NGR TQ 5033 8369. Archaeological Watching Brief Report and Updated Project Design, Oxford Archaeology, unpublished

Christensen, A E (ed.), 1979 *Inshore craft of Norway*, Conway Maritime Press, London

Clark, A, 1993 *Excavations at Mucking volume 1: the site atlas*, English Heritage Archaeol Report **20**, London

Clarke, C P, 1998 *Excavations south of Chignall Roman villa, Essex, 1977-81*, East Anglian Archaeology **83**, Chelmsford

Cleal, R M J and Chowne, P, 2001 Phase 2: late Bronze Age-Early Iron Age, in *Excavations at Billingborough, Lincolnshire, 1975-8: a Bronze-Iron Age settlement and salt-working site* (P Chowne, R M J Cleal and A P Fitzpatrick, with P Andrews), East Anglian Archaeology **94**, Salisbury, 14-6

Connah, G, Kamuhangire, E and Piper, A, 1990 Salt-production at Kibiro, *Azania: Archaeological Research in Africa* **25:1**, 27-39

Cooke, N, 2011 Coins from Northfleet, in Biddulph *et al.* 2011, 184-7

Cool, H E M, 2006 *Eating and drinking in Roman Britain*, Cambridge University Press, Cambridge

Costello, M P, 1997 Prehistoric and Roman material from Rainham: observation at the Rainham Football Ground, 1995, *Essex Archaeology and History* **28**, 93–102

Cotton, J and Field, D (eds), 2004 *Towards a new Stone Age: aspects of the Neolithic in south-east England*, CBA Research Report **137**, York

Crawford, O G S and Röder, J, 1955 The quern quarries of Mayen in the Eifel, *Antiquity* **29**, 68-77

Crowson, A, 2001 Excavation of a late Roman saltern at Blackborough End, Middleton, Norfolk, in Lane and Morris 2001, 162-249

Crummy, N, 2007 The salt briquetage, in *Stanway: an elite burial site at Camulodunum* (P Crummy, S Benfield, N Crummy, V Rigby and D Shimmin), Britannia Monograph **24**, London, 375-7

Cunningham, C M and Drury, P J, 1985 *Post-medieval sites and their pottery: Moulsham Street, Chelmsford*, CBA Research Report **54**, London

Curtis, R, 1984 'Negotiatores Allecarii' and the herring, *Phoenix* **38**, 147-58

Daire, M-Y (ed.), 1994 *Le sel Gaulois: Bouilleurs de sel et ateliers de briquetages armoricains à l'Age du Fer*, Les Dossiers du Centre Régional d'Archéologie d'Alet Supplément Q, Saint-Malo

Daire, M-Y and Langouet, L, 1994 Des ateliers de bouilleur de sel, in Daire 1994, 15-57

Daire, M-Y, Gouletquer, P, Bizien-Jaglin, C and Langouet, L, 1994 La production gauloise de sel en Armorique, in Daire (ed.) 1994, 59-103

Dale, R, Maynard, D, Tyler S and Vaughan, T, 2010 Carved in stone: a late Iron Age and Roman cemetery and evidence for a Saxon minster, excavations near St Nicholas' church, Great Wakering, 1998 and 2000, *Transactions of the Essex Society for Archaeology and History* **1**, 194-231

Dalrymple, R W, Zaitlin, B A and Boyd, R, 1992 Estuarine facies models; conceptual basis and stratigraphic implications, *Journal of Sedimentary Research* **62**, 1130-46

Darby, H C, 1971 *The Domesday geography of eastern England*, Cambridge University Press, Cambridge

Darling, M J, 2001 Roman pottery, in Lane and Morris 2001, 202-17

Dartevelle, H, Laporte, L, Petitot, H, Tastet, J-P and Toledo i Mur, A, 1998 *L'estuaire de la Charente de la protohistoire au Moyen Âge: La Challonière et Mortantambe* (Charente-Maritime) (ed. L Laporte), Editions de la Maison des sciences de l'homme, Paris

de Brisay, K W and Evans, K A (eds), 1975 *Salt: the study of an ancient industry*, Colchester Archaeological Group, Colchester

Detsicas, A, 1983 *The Cantiaci*, Alan Sutton, Gloucester

Devoy, R J N, 1977 Flandrian sea-level changes in the Thames Estuary and the implications for land subsidence in England and Wales, *Nature* **220**, 712-5

Devoy, R J N, 1979 Flandrian sea level changes and vegetation history of the lower Thames Estuary, *Philosophical Transactions of the Royal Society of London* **B285**, 355-407

Devoy, R J N, 1980 Post-glacial environmental change and man in the Thames estuary; a synopsis, in *Archaeology and coastal change* (ed. F H Thompson), Society of Antiquaries Occasional Paper, new series **1**, London, 134-48

Devoy, R J N, 1982 Analysis of the geological evidence for Holocene sea-level movements in south-east

England, *Proceedings of the Geologists' Association* **93**, 65–90

Dickson J H and Dickson, C, 1996 Ancient and modern occurrence of common fig (Ficus carica L.) in the British Isles, *Quaternary Science Review* **15(5–6)**, 623-33

Drury, P J, 1978 *Excavations at Little Waltham, 1970-71*, CBA Research Report **26**, Chelmsford

Drury, P J and Rodwell, W J, 1973 Excavations at Gun Hill, West Tilbury, *Essex Archaeology and History* **5**, 48–113

Durham, A and Goormachtigh, M, 2012 Rutupiae and red hills, *Archaeologia Cantiana* **132**, 327-33

Erlandson, K, 2003 *Home smoking and curing: how to smoke-cure meat, fish and game*, Ebury Press, St Helens

Evans, C and Lucy, S, 2008 Mucking Excavations, Essex: archive and publication project – Prehistoric and Roman – overview and assessment, Cambridge Archaeological Unit, Archaeological Data Service, http://archaeologydataservice.ac.uk/catalogue/adsdata/arch-879-1/dissemination/pdf/Mucking_Assess_Rep.pdf

Fawn, A J, Evans, K A, McMaster, I and Davies, G M R, 1990 *The Red Hills of Essex: salt-making in antiquity*, Colchester Archaeological Group, Colchester

Foreman, S and Maynard, D, 2002 A late Iron Age and Romano-British farmstead at Ship Lane, Aveley: Excavation on the line of the A13 Wennington to Mar Dyke road improvement, 1994-5, *Essex Archaeology and History* **33**, 123–56

Garwood, P, 2011 Early prehistory, in Booth *et al.* 2011, 37-150

Germany, M, 2003 *Excavations at Great Holts Farm, Boreham, Essex, 1992-94*, East Anglian Archaeology **105**, Chelmsford

Germany, M, 2004 A middle Iron Age red hill at Tollesbury Creek, Tollesbury, *Essex Archaeology and History* **35**, 192-6

Gibbard, P L, 1994 *Pleistocene history of the lower Thames valley*, Cambridge University Press, Cambridge

Gibbard, P L, 1999 Thames Valley, in *A revised correlation of the Quaternary deposits in the British Isles* (ed. D Q Bowen), Geological Society Special Report **23**, 58

Gillam, J P, 1976 Coarse fumed ware in north Britain and beyond, *Glasgow Archaeological Journal* **4**, 57-80

Gilman, P and Nash, F, 1995 *Fortress Essex*, Essex County Council, Chelmsford

Glazebrook, J (ed.), 1997 *Research and archaeology: A framework for the eastern Counties. Vol. 1: resource assessment*, East Anglian Archaeology Occasional Paper **3**, Norwich

Going, C J, 1987 *The mansio and other sites in the south-eastern sector of Caesaromagus: the Roman pottery*, CBA Research Report **62**, London

Going, C J, 1993 The Iron Age, in Clark 1993, 19–20

Going, C J, 1999 Oxidised Hadham wares, in *Roman pottery from excavations in Colchester, 1971-86* (R P Symonds and S Wade), Colchester Archaeological Report **10**, Colchester, 297-304

Goodburn, D, 1992 Wood and woodland: carpenters and carpentry, in *Timber building techniques London c 900-1400* (G Milne), London and Middlesex Archaeological Society Special Paper **15**, London, 106-30

Goodburn, D, 2011a Domestic buildings and other structures of timber, in *Roman London and the Walbrook stream crossing: excavations at 1 Poultry and vicinity 1985-96* (J Hill and P Rowsome), Museum of London Archaeology Monograph **37**, London, 414-37

Goodburn, D, 2011b Characteristics of the woodwork in the mill, in Andrews *et al.* 2011, 336-42

Gose, E, 1950 *Gefässtypen der römischen Keramik im Rheinland*, Butzon and Bercker, Kevelaer

Gouletquer, P L, 1975 Niger, country of salt, in de Brisay and Evans 1975, 47-51

Grocock, C and Grainger, S, 2006 *Apicius: a critical edition with an introduction and an English translation of the Latin recipe text 'Apicius'*, Prospect Books, Totnes

Gwilt, A and Heslop, D, 1995 Iron Age and Roman querns from the Tees Valley, in *Moorland Monuments: studies in the archaeology of north-east Yorkshire in honour of Raymond Hayes and Don Spratt* (ed. B Vyner), CBA Research Report **101**, 38-45

Haggart B A, 1995 A re-examination of some data relating to Holocene sea-level changes in the Thames Estuary, in Bridgland *et al.* 1995, 329-38

Hall, A R and Kenward, H K, 1990 *Environmental evidence from the colonia: General Accident and Rougier Street*, Archaeology of York **14**, London, 289-434

Hamerow, H, 1993 *Excavations at Mucking. Volume 2: the Anglo-Saxon settlement*, English Heritage Archaeological Report **21**, London

Hanson, W S and Friell, J G P, 1995 Westerton: a Roman watchtower on the Gask frontier, *Proceedings of the Society of Antiquaries of Scotland* **125**, 499-519

Haselgrove, C and Moore, T (eds), 2007 *The later Iron Age in Britain and beyond*, Oxbow, Oxford

Hedges, J and Buckley, D, 1978 Excavations at a Neolithic causewayed enclosure, Orsett, Essex, 1975, *Proceedings of the Prehistoric Society* **44**, 219-308

Hiller, J and Wilkinson, D R P, 2005 *Archaeology of the Jubilee Line Extension: Prehistoric and Roman activity at Stratford Market Depot, West Ham, London, 1991-1993*, Museum of London Archaeology Service, London

Hirst, S and Clark, D, 2009 *Excavations at Mucking: Volume 3, The Anglo-Saxon cemeteries*, Museum of London Archaeology Monograph, London

Hoover, H C and Hoover, L H, 1950 *Georgius Agricola:*

De Re Metallica, translated from the first Latin edition of 1556, Dover Publications, New York

Horsley, K and Wallace, C R, 1998 The late Iron Age and Roman pottery, in *Archaeology and the landscape in the lower Blackwater valley* (S Wallis and M Waughman), East Anglian Archaeology **82**, Chelmsford, 142-57

Howard, A J, Gearey, B R, Hill, T, Fletcher, W and Marshall, P, 2009 Fluvial sediments, correlations and palaeoenvironmental reconstruction: The development of robust radiocarbon chronologies, *Journal of Archaeological Science* **36**, 2680-8

Howard-Davis, C, 2009 The wooden artefacts, in Howard-Davis (ed.) 2009, 805-16

Howard-Davis, C (ed.), 2009 *The Carlisle Millennium Project: Excavations in Carlisle, 1998-2001. Volume 2: Finds*, Lancaster Imprints **15**, Lancaster

Hull, M R, 1963a *The Roman potters' kilns of Colchester*, Report of the Research Committee of the Society of Antiquaries of London **21**, London

Hull, M R, 1963b Roman gazetteer, in *The Victoria History of the counties of England. A history of Essex, volume III* (ed. W R Powell), Oxford University Press, Oxford, 35-203

Hurcombe, L, 2007 Plant processing for cordage and textiles using serrated flint edges: new chaînes operatoires suggested by ethnographic, archaeological and experimental evidence for bast fibre processing, in *Plant processing from a prehistoric and ethnographic perspective/Préhistoire et ethnographie du travail des plantes: proceedings of a workshop at Ghent University (Belgium) November 28, 2006* (eds V Beugnier and P Crombé), BAR International Series **1718**, Oxford, 41-66

IfA, nd *Standard and guidance for the creation, compilation, transfer and deposition of archaeological archives*, Institute for Archaeologists, Reading

Jefferies, R S and Barford, P M, 1990a The pottery of the Red Hills, in Fawn *et al.* 1990, 35-6

Jefferies, R S and Barford, P M, 1990b Gazetteer 3: Pottery from Essex Red Hills, in Fawn *et al.* 1990, 73-8

Johansen, J R, 1999 Diatoms of aerial habits, in *The diatoms: applications for the environmental and earth sciences* (eds E F Stoermer and J P Smol), Cambridge University Press, Cambridge, 264-73

Jones, M, 1977 Prehistoric salt equipment from a pit at Mucking, Essex, *The Antiquaries Journal* **57**, 317-9

Jones, M U and Rodwell, W J, 1973 The Romano-British kilns at Mucking, with an interim on two kiln groups, *Essex Archaeology and History* **5**, 13-47

Jones, R, Langley, P and Wall, S, 1985 The animal bones from the 1977 excavations, in *Excavations at Brancaster 1974 and 1977* (J Hinchliffe and C Sparey Green), East Anglian Archaeology **23**, Dereham, 132-74

Juel Jensen, H, 1994 *Flint tools and plant working: hidden traces of Stone Age technology – a use wear study of some Danish Mesolithic and TRB implements*, Aarhus University Press, Aarhus

Keen, L, 1998a Coastal salt-production in Norman England, in *Anglo-Norman Studies* **11** (ed. R Allen Brown), Boydell Press, Woodbridge, 133-79

Keen, L, 1998b Medieval salt-working in Dorset, *Proceedings of the Dorset Natural History and Archaeological Society* **109**, 25-8

Kenward, H K and Hall, A R, 1995 *Biological evidence from 16-22 Coppergate*, Archaeology of York **14/7**, York, 435-797

Killock, D, 2005 Roman river bank use and changing water levels at 51-53 Southwark Street, Southwark, London, *Transactions of the London and Middlesex Archaeological Society* **56**, 27-44

Kinory, J L, 2011 Salt production, distribution and use in the British Iron Age, DPhil thesis, University of Oxford, unpublished

Kinory, J, 2012 *Salt production, distribution and use in the British Iron Age*, BAR British Series **559**, Oxford

Kondo, Y, 1975 The salt industry in ancient Japan, in de Brisay and Evans 1975, 61-5

Lane, T and Morris, E L (eds), 2001 *A millennium of saltmaking: prehistoric and Romano-British salt production in the Fenland*, Lincolnshire Archaeology and Heritage Reports Series **4**, Sleaford

Lavender, N J, 1998 Prehistoric and Romano-British activity at Stifford Clays Road, Grays: excavations at the Williams Edwards School 1997, *Essex Archaeology and History* **29**, 19–32

Lawrence, S, 2006 *The Iron Age settlement and Roman villa at Thurnham, Kent*, CTRL Integrated Site Report Series, Archaeological Data Service, http://archaeologydataservice.ac.uk/catalogue/adsdata/arch-335-1/dissemination/pdf/PT1_Int_Site_Reps/12_Thurnham_Villa/THM_ISR_Text/THM_ISR_text.pdf

Leary, R, 2008 Coarse pottery, in Williams and Reid 2008, 65-116

Long, A J, Scaife, R G and Edwards, R J, 2000 Stratigraphic architecture, relative sea-level, and models of estuary development in southern England: new data from Southampton Water, in *Coastal and estuarine environments: sedimentology, geomorphology and geoarchaeology* (eds K Pye and J R L Allen), Geological Society Special Publication **175**, London, 253-79

Luff, M L, 1998 *Provisional atlas of the ground beetles (Coleoptera, Carabidae) of Britain*, Abbots Ripton

Luff, M L, 2007 *The Carabidae (ground beetles) of Britain and Ireland*, Handbooks for the identification of British insects **4(2)**, 2nd edn, London

Lund, J W G, 1945 Observations on soil algae. I. The ecology, size and taxonomy oof British soil diatoms, part 1, *New Phytologist* **44 (2)**, 196-219

Lund, J W G, 1946 Observations on soil algae. I. The ecology, size and taxonomy oof British soil diatoms, part 2, *New Phytologist* **45 (1)**, 56-110

Macphail, R, I, 1994 Soil micromorphological investigations in archaeology, with special reference to drowned coastal sites in Essex, in H F Cook and D T Favis-Mortlock (eds), *SEESOIL*, Volume 10: Wye, South East Soils Discussion Group, 13-28

Macphail, R I, 2009 Marine inundation and archaeological sites: first results from the partial flooding of Wallasea Island, Essex, UK, Volume 2009, *Antiquity Project Gallery*; http://antiquity.ac.uk/projgall/macphail/.

Macphail, R I, Allen, M J, Crowther, J, Cruise, G M and Whittaker, J E, 2008 *British Academy Small Research Grant SG-49361. Pilot project to assess effects and develop experimental research protocols related to marine inundation of archaeological soils and sites, employing Wallasea Island, Essex ahead of flooding by the RSPB in 2010*, UCL, London

Macphail, R I, Allen, M J, Crowther, J, Cruise, G M and Whittaker, J E, 2010 Marine inundation: effects on archaeological features, materials, sediments and soils, *Quaternary International*, **214**, 44-55

Maldon Salt Company, nd *The magic of Maldon sea salt*, http://www.maldonsalt.co.uk/img/Useful%20Information/Article%20archives/Articles/Magic%20of%20Salt.pdf

Maltby, M, 2006 Salt and animal products: linking production and use in Iron Age Britain, in *Integrating Zooarchaeology* (ed. M Maltby), Oxbow Books, Oxford, 117-22

Marsden, P, 1994 *Ships of the port of London, first to the eleventh centuries AD*, English Heritage Archaeological Report **3**, London

Marsland, A, 1986 The floodplain deposits of the Lower Thames, *Quarterly Journal of Engineering Geology* **19**, 223-47

Martin-Kilcher, S, 2003 Fish-sauce amphorae from the Iberian peninsula: the forms and observations on trade with the north-west provinces, *Journal of Roman Pottery Studies* **10**, 69-84

Marvell, A G and Owen-John, H S, 1997 *Leucarum: Excavations at the Roman auxiliary fort at Loughor, West Glamorgan, 1982-84 and 1987-88*, Britannia Monograph **12**, London

Mason, D J P, 2003 *Roman Britain and the Roman navy*, Tempus, Stroud

Maxwell, D, 1925 *Unknown Essex*, The Bodley Head, London

Mbogoro, D K and Mwakipesile, A, 2010 Economical and ecological research of Bahi Swamp, University of Dodoma, unpublished

McAvoy, F, 1994 Marine salt extraction: the excavation of salterns at Wainfleet St Mary, Lincolnshire, *Medieval Archaeology* **38**, 134-63

McKinley, J I, 1997 Bronze Age 'barrows' and funerary rites and rituals of cremation, *Proceedings of the Prehistoric Society* **63**, 129-45

McKinley, J I, 2000 Phoenix rising: aspects of cremation in Roman Britain, in *Burial, society and context in the Roman World* (eds J Pearce, M Millett and M Struck), Oxbow Books, Oxford, 38-44

Monaghan, J, 1987 *Upchurch and Thameside Roman pottery*, BAR British Series **173**, Oxford

Mook, W G, 1986 Business meeting: Recommendations/Resolutions adopted by the Twelfth International Radiocarbon Conference, *Radiocarbon* **28**, 799

Moore, P D and Webb, J A, 1978 *An illustrated guide to pollen analysis*, Hodder and Stoughton, London

Morel, J-M A W, 1986 The early Roman defended harbours at Velsen, North Holland, in *Studien zu den Militärgrenzen Roms III* (ed. C Unz), Vorträge des 13 Internationalen Limeskongresses, Aalen, 200-12

Morigi, A, Schreve, D, White, M, Hey, G, Garwood, P, Robinson, M R, Barclay A and Bradley, P, 2011 *The Thames through Time. The archaeology of the gravel terraces of the Upper and Middle Thames: Early Prehistory to 1500 BC*, Oxford Archaeology Thames Valley Landscapes Monograph No. 32, Oxford

Morris, E L, 2001 Briquetage, in Lane and Morris 2001, 33-63

Morris, E L, 2007 Making magic: later prehistoric and early Roman salt production in the Lincolnshire fenland, in Haselgrove and Moore 2007, 430-43

Morris, E L, 2012 Briquetage, in Allen *et al.* 2012, 228-45

Morris, M G, 1990 *Orthocerous weevils, Coleoptera Curculionoidea*, Handbooks for the identification of British insects **5(16)**, London

Murray, J W, 2006 *Ecology and applications of benthic foraminifera*, Cambridge University Press, Cambridge

Nantwich Museum, nd The salt ship, http://freespace.virgin.net/nantwich.museum/saltship.htm. Accessed June 2012

Nayling, N and McGrail, S, 2004 *The Barland's Farm Romano-Celtic boat*, CBA Research Report **138**, York

OA, 2008 London Gateway: Northern Triangle East habitat creation and enhancements. Archaeological investigation report, unpublished report by Oxford Archaeology for DP World

OA, 2009a London Gateway Compensation Site A: Archaeological trenching investigation report, unpublished report by Oxford Archaeology for DP World

OA, 2009b London Gateway Compensation Site A: Project design for archaeological mitigation, unpublished report by Oxford Archaeology for DP World

OA, 2009c London Gateway, Stanford-le-Hope, Essex. Compensation Site A: archaeological investigation. Post-excavation assessment scoping report, unpublished report by Oxford Archaeology for DP World

O'Connor, T, 1986 The animal bones, in *The legionary fortress baths at Caerleon. Volume 2: The finds* (J D Zienkiewicz), National Museum of Wales/Welsh Historic Monuments, Cardiff, 225-248

O'Connor, T, 1988 *Bones from the General Accident site, Tanner Row*, Archaeology of York **15/2**, York Archaeological Trust/Council for British Archaeology, London

O'Donnell, D, 2009 *Neighbourhood nature*, The Open University, Milton Keynes

Packham, J R and Willis, A J, 1997, *Ecology of dunes, salt marsh and shingle*, Chapman and Hall, London

Peacock, D P S and Williams, D F, 1978 Petrological examination, in Drury 1978, 58-9

Peacock, D P S and Williams, D F, 1986 *Amphorae and the Roman economy: an introductory guide*, Longman, London

Pearson, A, 2002 *The Roman shore forts: coastal defences of southern Britain*, Tempus, Stroud

Peglar, S M, 1993 The mid-Holocene Ulmus decline at Diss Mere, Norfolk, UK: a year-by-year pollen stratigraphy from annual laminations, *The Holocene* **3**, 1-13

Peglar, S, 2008 Appendix 2 Pollen, in *The Archaeology of the A303 Stonehenge improvement* (M Leivers and C Moore), Wessex Archaeology, Salisbury

Penney, S and Shotter, D C A, 1996 An inscribed Roman salt-pan from Shavington, Cheshire, *Britannia* **27**, 360-5

Philpott, R, 1991 *Burial practices in Roman Britain: A survey of grave treatment and furnishing AD 43-410*, BAR British Series **219**, Oxford

Pollard, R J, 1988 *The Roman pottery of Kent*, Kent Archaeological Society Monograph **5**, Maidstone

Poole, C, 1984 Objects of baked clay, in *Danebury: an Iron Age hillfort in Hampshire. Volume 2, the excavations 1969-78: the finds* (B Cunliffe), CBA Research Report **52**, London, 398-407

Poole, C, 1991 Briquetage containers, in *Danebury: an Iron Age hillfort in Hampshire. Volume 5, the excavations 1979-88: the finds* (B Cunliffe and C Poole), CBA Research Report **73**, London, 404-7

Poole, C, 2011 Ceramic building material and fired clay, in Biddulph *et al.* 2011, 313-50

Poole, C, 2012 La terre cuite structurale et le petit mobilier d'argile, in *Enclos défensif, bâtiment public et habitat nucléé de la Tène 2, et leurs développments à la période gallo-romaine et à l'époque médiévale. Fouilles archéologiques préventives, volume 3, section 2* (T Allen, E Biddulph, M Dodd, M Donnelly, B Gourlin and C Poole), unpublished report by Oxford Archaeology

Powell, A B, 2009 Two thousand years of salt-making at Lymington, Hampshire, *Proceedings of the Hampshire Field Club and Archaeological Society* **64**, 9–40

Priddy, D and Buckley, D G, 1987 An assessment of excavated enclosures in Essex together with a selection of cropmark sites, *East Anglian Archaeology* **33**, 48–77

Rackham, O, 2003 *Ancient woodland: its history, vegetation and uses in England*, Castlepoint Press, Dalbeattie

Rankin, N, 2008 *Churchill's wizards: The British genius for deception, 1914-1945*, Faber and Faber, London

Rees, H, 1986 Ceramic salt working debris from Droitwich, *Transactions of the Worcestershire Archaeological Society* **10** (3rd series), 47-54

Rees, H, 1992 Pottery, in Woodiwiss 1992, 35-58

Reid, M L and Williams, M, 2008 The excavation, in Williams and Reid 2008, 5-37

Reimer, P J, Baillie, M G L, Bard, E, Bayliss, A, Beck, J W, Blackwell, P G, Buck, C E, Burr, G S, Cutler, K B, Damon, P E, Edwards, R L, Fairbanks, R G, Friedrich, M, Guilderson, T P, Herring, C, Hughen, K A, Kromer, B, McCormac, F G, Manning, S W, Ramsey, C B, Reimer, P J, Reimer, R W, Remmele, S, Southon, J R, Stuiver, M, Talamo, S, Taylor, F W, van der Plicht, J, and Weyhenmeyer, C E, 2004 IntCal04 Terrestrial radiocarbon age calibration, 0-26 cal kyr BP *Radiocarbon* **46,3**, 1029-58

RIB II, 1994a *The Roman inscriptions of Britain. II, Instrumentum domesticum (personal belongings and the like). Fascicule 2: Weights, gold vessel, silver vessels, lead vessels, pewter vessels, shale vessels, glass vessels, spoons (RIB 2412-2420)* (eds S S Frere and R S O Tomlin), Alan Sutton, Stroud

RIB II, 1994b *The Roman inscriptions of Britain. II, Instrumentum domesticum (personal belongings and the like). Fascicule 6: Dipinti and graffiti on amphorae and mortaria, inscriptions in white barbotine, dipinti on coarse pottery, samian barbotine or moulded inscriptions (RIB 2492-2500)* (eds S S Frere and R S O Tomlin), Alan Sutton, Stroud

Ridgeway, V (ed.), 2009 *Secrets of the Gardens: Archaeologists unearth the lives of Roman Londoners*, Preconstruct Archaeology, London

Rippon, S, 1996 *The Gwent Levels: the evolution of a wetland landscape*, CBA Research Report **105**, York

Rippon, S, 2000 *The transformation of coastal wetlands: exploitation and management of marshland landscapes in North West Europe during the Roman and medieval periods*, Oxford University Press, Oxford

Rippon, S, 2012 Historic Landscape Character and Sense of Place, *Landscape Research*, DOI:10.1080/01426397.2012.672642

Robinson, M, 2011 The Thames and its changing environment in our era, in Morigi *et al.* 2011, 173-91

Rodwell, K A, 1983 The excavation of a Romano-British pottery kiln at Palmers School, Grays, Essex, *Essex Archaeology and History* **15**, 11-35

Rodwell, W J, 1973 The products of kilns II and III, in The Romano-British kilns at Mucking, with an interim on two kiln groups (M U Jones and W J Rodwell), *Essex Archaeology and History* **5**, 19-46

Rodwell, W, 1979 Iron Age and Roman salt-winning on the Essex coast, in *Invasion and response: the case of Roman Britain* (eds B C Burnham and H B Johnson), BAR British Series **73**, Oxford, 133-75

Scott, B G, 1990 *Early Irish ironworking*, Ulster Museum, Belfast

Seager Smith, R, Brown, K M, and Mills, J M, 2011 The pottery from Springhead, in Biddulph *et al.* 2011, 1-134

Sealey, P R, 1995 New light on the salt industry and Red Hills of prehistoric and Roman Essex, *Essex Archaeology and History* **26**, 65-81

Shaffrey, R, 2009 The other worked stone, in Howard-Davis (ed.) 2009, 873-87

Sharples, N, 2010 *Social relations in later prehistory: Wessex in the first millennium BC*, Oxford University Press, Oxford

Sidell, J and Wilkinson, K, 2004 The Central London Thames: Neolithic river development and floodplain archaeology, in Cotton and Field 2004, 38-48

Sidell, J, Wilkinson, K N, Scaife, R G and Cameron, N, 2000 *The Holocene evolution of the London Thames: archaeological investigations (1991-1998) in advance of the London Underground Limited Jubilee Line Extension*, MoLAS Monograph 5, London

Sidell, J, Cotton, J, Rayner, L and Wheeler, L, 2002 *The prehistory and topography of Southwark and Lambeth*, MoLAS Monograph **14**, London

Simmonds, A, Wenban-Smith, Bates, M, Powell, K, Sykes, D, Devaney, R, Stansbie, D and Score, D, 2011 *Excavations in north-west Kent, 2005-2007: One hundred thousand years of human activity in and around the Darent Valley*, Oxford Archaeology Monograph **11**, Oxford

Southwood, T R E and Leston, D, 1959 *Land and water bugs of the British Isles*, F Warne, London

Stafford, E, 2011 Northfleet sediments and soils, in Andrews *et al.* 2011, 61-6

Stafford, E, with Goodburn, D and Bates, M, 2012 *Landscape and prehistory of the East London wetlands: Investigations along the A13 DBFO Roadscheme, Tower Hamlets, Newham, Barking and Dagenham, 2000-2003*, Oxford Archaeology Monograph **17**, Oxford

Stead, I M, 1976 *Excavations at Winterton Roman villa and other Roman sites in North Lincolnshire*, Department of Environment Archaeological Report 9, London

Stead, I M and Rigby, V, 1989 *Verulamium: the King Harry Lane site*, English Heritage Report **12**, London

Stevens, C J, 2011 Charred plant remains from Springhead, in Barnett *et al.* 2011, 95-105

Strachan, D, 1998 *Essex from the air: archaeology and history from aerial photographs*, Essex County Council, Chelmsford

Stuiver, M and Kra, R S, 1986 Editorial comment, *Radiocarbon* **28(2B)**, ii

Stuiver, M and Polach, H A, 1977 Reporting of 14C data, *Radiocarbon* **19**, 355–63

Sumbler M G, 1996 *London and the Thames Valley*, British Regional Geology, British Geological Survey, Keyworth

Sutton, J E G and Roberts, A D, 1968 Uvinza and its salt industry, *Azania: Archaeological Research in Africa* **3**, 45-86

Symonds, R P, 1992 *Rhenish wares: fine dark coloured pottery from Gaul and Germany*, Oxford University Committee for Archaeology Monograph No. 23, Oxford

Thompson, I, 1995 Belgic, in Wymer and Brown 1995, 88-91

Turner-Walker, C and Wallace, C, 1999 The Iron Age and Roman pottery, in *Excavations of an Iron Age settlement and Roman religious complex at Ivy Chimneys, Witham, Essex, 1978-83* (R Turner), East Anglian Archaeology **88**, Chelmsford, 123-79

Tys, D, 2006 Walraversijde, another kettle of fish? Dynamics and identity of a late medieval coastal settlement in a proto-capitalistic landscape, in *Fishery, trade and piracy: fishermen and fishermen's settlements in and around the North Sea area in the middle Ages and later* (eds M Pieters, F Verhaeghe and G Gevaert), Archeologie in Vlaaderen Monografie 6, Brussels, 19-40

Van Geel, B and Borger, G J, 2005 Evidence for medieval salt-making by burning eel-grass (*Zostera marina L*) in the Netherlands, *Netherlands Journal of Geosciences* **84:1**, 43-9

Walker, K, 1990 *Guidelines for the preservation of excavation archives for long-term storage*, UKIC Archaeology Section, London

Wallace, C R, 1995 Pottery from Blackwater site 11 and other red hills, in Wilkinson and Murphy 1995, 171-3

Wallace, C R and Turner-Walker, C, 1998 The Roman pottery, in Clarke 1998, 98-112

Waller, M and Grant, M, 2012 Holocene pollen assemblages from coastal wetlands: differentiating natural and anthropogenic causes of change in the Thames estuary, UK, *Journal of Quaternary Science* **27**, 461-74

Walsh, D, 1991 Salt-making on the Cumbrian coast, *Archaeology North* **1**, 37-40

Warry, P, 2006 *Tegulae: manufacture, typology and use in Roman Britain*, BAR British Series **417**, Oxford

Whittaker, J E, 2010 Microfauna (foraminifera and ostracoda), in Biddulph (ed.) 2010, Appendix B.6

Wickenden, N P, 1992 *The temple and other sites in the north-eastern sector of Caesaromagus*, CBA Research Report 75, London

Wilkinson, K, Scaife, R, Sidell, J and Cameron, N, 2000 The palaeoenvironmental context of the JLE project, in *The Holocene evolution of the London Thames: archaeological excavations (1991-1998) for the London Underground Limited Jubilee Line Extension Project* (J Sidell, K Wilkinson, R Scaife and N Cameron), MoLAS Monograph 5, London, 11-9

Wilkinson, T J, 1988 *Archaeology and environment in south Essex: rescue archaeology along the Grays By-pass, 1979/80*, East Anglian Archaeology **42**, Chelmsford

Wilkinson, T J and Murphy, P L, 1995 *The archaeology of the Essex coast, volume 1: The Hullbridge Survey*, East Anglian Archaeology **71**, Chelmsford

Wilkinson, T J, Murphy, P L, Brown, N and Heppell, E, 2012 *The Archaeology of the Essex Coast Volume II. Excavations at the Prehistoric Site of The Stumble*, East Anglian Archaeology **142**, Chelmsford

Williams, J and Brown, N, 1999 *An archaeological research framework for the Greater Thames Estuary*, Essex County Council, Kent County Council and English Heritage, Chelmsford

Williams, M and Reid, M L, 2008 *Salt: life and industry. Excavation at King Street, Middlewich, Cheshire, 2001-2002*, BAR British Series **456**, Oxford

Willis, S H, 1998 Samian pottery in Britain: exploring its distribution and archaeological potential, *The Archaeological Journal* **155**, 82-133

Woodiwiss, S (ed.), 1992 *Iron Age and Roman salt production and the medieval town of Droitwich: Excavations at the Old Bowling Green and Friar Street*, CBA Research Report **81**, London

Woolliscroft, D J and Hoffmann, B, 2006 *Rome's first frontier: the Flavian occupation of northern Scotland*, Tempus, Stroud

Worley, F, 2011a Springhead roadside settlement (ARC SHN02), in Barnett *et al.* 2011, 31-42

Worley, F, 2011b Northfleet Roman villa, in Barnett *et al.* 2011, 42-52

Wyles, S F, 2011 Marine shell, in Barnett *et al.* 2011, 119-22

Wymer, J J and Brown, N R, 1995 *Excavations at North Shoebury: settlement and economy in south-east Essex 1500BC-AD1500*, East Anglian Archaeology **75**, Chelmsford

Young, C J, 1977 *The Roman pottery industry of the Oxford region*, BAR British Series **43**, Oxford

Yule, B, 2005 *A prestigious Roman building complex on the Southwark waterfront: excavation at Winchester Palace, London*, Museum of London Archaeology Service Monograph **23**, London

Zant, J, 2009 *The Carlisle Millennium Project: Excavations in Carlisle, 1998-2001. Volume 1: The stratigraphy*, Lancaster Imprints **14**, Lancaster

Index